Grammar Sense 2

SECOND EDITION

SERIES DIRECTOR
Susan Kesner Bland

AUTHOR
Cheryl Pavlik

OXFORD
UNIVERSITY PRESS

OXFORD
UNIVERSITY PRESS

198 Madison Avenue
New York, NY 10016 USA

Great Clarendon Street, Oxford, OX2 6DP, United Kingdom

Oxford University Press is a department of the University of Oxford. It furthers the University's objective of excellence in research, scholarship, and education by publishing worldwide. Oxford is a registered trade mark of Oxford University Press in the UK and in certain other countries

First published in 2012
2018 2017
16 15 14 13 12 11 10

General Manager, American ELT: Laura Pearson
Publisher: Stephanie Karras
Associate Publishing Manager: Sharon Sargent
Managing Editor: Alex Ragan
Director, ADP: Susan Sanguily
Executive Design Manager: Maj-Britt Hagsted
Electronic Production Manager: Julie Armstrong
Senior Designer: Yin Ling Wong
Image Manager: Trisha Masterson

Publishing and Editorial Management: hyphen S.A.

ISBN: 978 0 19 448913 3 Student Book 2 with Online Practice pack
ISBN: 978 0 19 448903 4 Student Book 2 as pack component
ISBN: 978 0 19 448928 7 Online Practice as pack component

Printed in China

This book is printed on paper from certified and well-managed sources

ACKNOWLEDGEMENTS

Although every effort has been made to trace and contact copyright holders before publication, this has not been possible in some cases. We apologize for any apparent infringement of copyright and if notified, the publisher will be pleased to rectify any errors or omissions at the earliest opportunity.

The authors and publisher are grateful to those who have given permission to reproduce the following extracts and adaptations of copyright material:

pp. 4–5. "Mysterious Island." This article first appeared in The Christian Science Monitor on June 16, 1998, and is reproduced with permission. © 1998 The Christian Science Publishing Society. All rights reserved; p. 263. "Mood Foods." Courtesy of Seventeen magazine / Karen Robinovitz, www.seventeen.com; p. 283. From Carnivorous Plants by Cynthia Overbeck. Text copyright © 1982 by Lerner Publications, a division of Lerner Publishing Group. Adapted from a book first published in Japan by Akane Shobo Publishers (Tokyo) entitled Insectivorous Plants by Kiyoshi Shimizu. Used by permission. All rights reserved; p. 303. From the Hammacher Schlemmer catalog; pp. 318–319. From The Personality Compass by Diane Turner. Reprinted with permission by HarperCollins Publishers Ltd; pp. 382–383. "10 Easy Ways to Start Saving Money" by Franny Van Nevel; p. 413. Adapted from "Learn2Fry An Egg" with permission by Learn2.com, Inc. All rights reserved.

Illustrations by: Thanos Tsilis (hyphen): 4, 39, 41, 121, 149, 192, 217, 303, 318,360, 371, 391,413; Alexandros Tzimeros / SmartMagna (hyphen): 56, 74, 95, 103, 118, 129, 138, 195, 207, 213, 230, 252, 269, 338, 420.

We would also like to thank the following for permission to reproduce the following photographs: Devation - Edwin Verbruggen / www.shutterstock.com, Andreas Gradin / shutterstock.com, homydesign / www.shutterstock.com, marekuliasz / www.shutterstock.com, Travel Ink / Getty Images, Cover l to r and interior; Marcin Krygier / iStockphoto, Front matter and back cover (laptop); Pingebat / istockphoto, pg 4 (map); Akos Major / Getty Images, pg 4; G Fletcher / Getty Images, pg. 5; Joe McDonald / Corbis, pg. 8; Wally McNamee / Corbis, pg. 14; Juniors Bildarchiv / Alamy, pg. 18; Layne Kennedy / Corbis, pg. 19; Photodisc / OUPpicturebank, pg. 31; Henry Diltz / Corbis, pg. 48; M&N / Alamy, pg. 49; Bettmann / Corbis, pg. 52; Jim Sugar / Corbis, pg. 54; Digital Vision / OUPpicturebank, pg. 59 (tl); Reda / Shutterstock, pg. 59 (cl); Blend Images / OUPpicturebank, pg. 59 (bl); Jim Craigmyle / Corbis, pg. 59 (tr); Somos Images / Alamy, pg. 59 (cr); Cultura / Corbis, pg. 59 (br); Courtesy of the Rosenberg Library Galveston, Texas, pg. 70; Corbis / Corbis, pg. 71; Jim Reed / Jim Reed Photography - Severe & / Corbis, pg. 82; Parque / Corbis, pg. 90; Pingebat / istockphoto, pg. 90 (map); Michele Burgess / Corbis, pg. 107; Moodboard / OUPpicturebank, pg. 112 (l); C.Devan / Corbis, pg. 112 (r); Comstock / OUPpicturebank, pg. 113 (l); Tanya Constantine / Blend Images / Corbis, pg. 113 (r); Photodisc / OUPpicturebank, pg. 135; Klaus Tiedge / Corbis, pg. 145; CHIP EAST / Reuters / Corbis, pg. 156; Photodisc / OUPpicturebank, pg. 157; Denkou Images / Alamy, pg. 166; Tim Kiusalaas / Corbis, pg. 171; Stephen Frink / Monsoon / Photolibrary / Corbis, pg. 175; Digital Vision / OUPpicturebank, pg. 178; Blue Jean Images / OUPpicturebank, pg. 201; Corbis / Corbis, pg. 225 (l); Corbis / Corbis, pg. 225 (r); James Green / Robert Harding World Imagery / Corbis, pg. 240; David Loftus Limited / the food passionates / Corbis, pg. 268; Corbis / Digital Stock / OUPpicturebank, pg. 282 (pitcher plant); David Frazier / Corbis, pg. 282 (cobralily); Patrick Endres / Visuals Unlimited / Corbis, pg. 282 (sundew); Visuals Unlimited / Corbis, pg. 283; Photodisc / OUPpicturebank, pg. 295 (cactus); Wave / OUPpicturebank, pg. 295 (butterfly); Christopher Talbot Frank / Photex / Corbis, pg. 295 (maple tree); Clive Nichols / Corbis, pg. 295 (rose); Jones, Huw / the food passionates / Corbis, pg. 295 (green pepper); Tobias Bernhard / Corbis, pg. 295 (shark); Corbis / Digital Stock / OUPpicturebank, pg. 296; Photodisc / OUPpicturebank, pg. 313 (sweater); Comstock / OUPpicturebank, pg. 313 (sofa); OUP / OUPpicturebank, pg. 313 (box); OUP / OUPpicturebank, pg. 313 (purse); OUP / OUPpicturebank, pg. 313 (toy airplane); olaf.kowalzik / OUPpicturebank, pg. 313 (hat); Ian Shaw / OUPpicturebank, pg. 346; Image Source / OUPpicturebank, pg. 363; Sarah Rice / Star Ledger / Corbis, pg. 366; Nation Wong / Corbis, pg. 382; Bettmann / Corbis, pg. 396; Martin Sundberg / Corbis, pg. 408; Andrzej Tokarski / Alamy, pg. 413

Reviewers

We would like to acknowledge the following individuals for their input during the development of the series:

Marcia Adato, Delaware Technical and Community College, DE
Donette Artenie, Georgetown University, DC
Alexander Astor, Hostos Community College/CUNY, Bronx, NY
Nathalie Bailey, Lehman College, CUNY, NY
Jamie Beaton, Boston University, MA
Michael Berman, Montgomery College, MD
Linda Best, Kean University, NJ
Marcel Bolintiam, Kings Colleges, Los Angeles, CA
Houda Bouslama, Virtual University Tunis, Tunis, Tunisia
Nancy Boyer, Golden West College, Huntington Beach, CA
Glenda Bro, Mount San Antonio Community College, CA
Shannonine Caruana, Kean University, NJ
Sharon Cavusgil, Georgia State University, GA
Robin Rosen Chang, Kean University, NJ
Jorge Cordon, Colegio Internacional Montessori, Guatemala
Magali Duignan, Augusta State University, GA
Anne Ediger, Hunter College, CUNY, NY
Begoña Escourdio, Colegio Miraflores, Naucalpan, Mexico
Marcella Farina, University of Central Florida, FL
Carol Fox, Oakton Community College, Niles, IL
Glenn S. Gardner, Glendale Community College, Glendale, CA
Ruth Griffith, Kean University, NJ
Evalyn Hansen, Rogue Community College, Medford, OR
Liz Hardy, Rogue Community College, Medford, OR
Habiba Hassina, Virtual University Tunis, Tunis, Tunisia
Virginia Heringer, Pasadena City College, CA
Rocia Hernandez, Mexico City, Mexico
Kieran Hilu, Virginia Tech, VA
Rosemary Hiruma, California State University, Long Beach, CA
Linda Holden, College of Lake County, Grayslake, IL
Elke Holtz, Escuela Sierra Nevada Interlomas, Mexico City, Mexico
Kate de Jong, University of California, San Diego, CA
Gail Kellersberger, University of Houston-Downtown, ELI, Houston, TX
Pamela Kennedy, Holyoke Community College, MA
Elis Lee, Glendale Community College, Glendale, CA
Patricia Lowy, State University of New York-New Paltz, NY
Jean McConochie, Pace University, NY
Karen McRobie, Golden Gate University, CA
Hafid Mekaoui, Al Akhawayn University, Ifrane, Morocco
Elizabeth Neblett, Union County College, NJ
Patricia Palermo, Kean University, NJ
Maria E. Palma, Colegio Lationamericano Bilingue, Chihuahua, Mexico
Mary Peacock, Richland College, Dallas, TX
Dian Perkins, Wheeling High School, IL
Nancy Herzfeld-Pipkin, Grossmont College, El Cajon, CA
Kent Richmond, California State University, Long Beach, CA
Ellen Rosen, Fullerton College, CA
Jessica Saigh, University of Missouri-St. Louis, St. Louis, MO
Boutheina Lassadi-Sayadi, The Faculty of Humanities and Social Sciences of Tunis, Tunis, Tunisia
Anne-Marie Schlender, Austin Community College-Rio Grande, Austin, TX
Shira Seaman, Global English Academy, NY
Katharine Sherak, San Francisco State University, CA
Maxine Steinhaus, New York University, NY
Andrea Stewart, Houston Community College-Gulfton, Houston, TX
Nancy Storer, University of Denver, CO
Veronica Struck, Sussex Community College, Newton, NJ
Frank Tang, New York University, NY
Claude Taylor, Baruch College, NY
Marshall Thomas, California State University, Long Beach, CA
Christine Tierney, Houston Community College, Houston, TX
Anthea Tillyer, Hunter College, CUNY, NY
Julie Un, Massasoit Community College, MA
Marvaette Washington, Houston Community College, Houston, TX
Cheryl Wecksler, California State University, San Marcos, CA
Teresa Wise, Associated Colleges of the South, GA

Contents

Introduction x
Tour of a Chapter xi
Grammar Sense Online Practice xvii

PART 1: The Present

CHAPTER 1: The Simple Present 3
A. **GRAMMAR IN DISCOURSE:** Mysterious Island 4
B. **FORM:** The Simple Present 6
C. **MEANING AND USE:** The Simple Present 11
WRITING: Write a Factual Paragraph 15

CHAPTER 2: Imperatives 17
A. **GRAMMAR IN DISCOURSE:** Dos and Dont's with Bears 18
B. **FORM:** Imperatives 20
C. **MEANING AND USE:** Imperatives 22
WRITING: Write a Recipe 27

CHAPTER 3: The Present Continuous 29
A. **GRAMMAR IN DISCOURSE:** Long-Distance Voyager 30
B. **FORM:** The Present Continuous 32
C. **MEANING AND USE:** The Present Continuous 36
WRITING: Write a Description of Your Current Activities 43
Part 1 Test 45

PART 2: The Past

CHAPTER 4: The Simple Past 47
A. **GRAMMAR IN DISCOURSE:** The Decade That Made a Difference 48
B. **FORM 1:** The Simple Past 50
C. **MEANING AND USE 1:** The Simple Past 57
D. **FORM 2:** *Used To* 62
E. **MEANING AND USE 2:** The Habitual Past with *Used To* 65
WRITING: Write a Post For a History Class Blog 67

CHAPTER 5: The Past Continuous and Past Time Clauses 69
A. GRAMMAR IN DISCOURSE: Galveston's Killer Hurricane 70
B. FORM 1: The Past Continuous 72
C. MEANING AND USE 1: The Past Continuous 76
D. FORM 2: Past Time Clauses 80
E. MEANING AND USE 2: Past Time Clauses 83
WRITING: Write About a Natural Disaster 86

CHAPTER 6: The Present Perfect 89
A. GRAMMAR IN DISCOURSE: The World's Most-Traveled Man 90
B. FORM: The Present Perfect 92
C. MEANING AND USE 1: Continuing Time Up to Now 97
D. MEANING AND USE 2: Indefinite Past Time 100
WRITING: Write About Someone You Admire 106
Part 2 Test 109

PART 3: The Future

CHAPTER 7: Future Time: *Be Going To, Will,* and the Present Continuous 111
A. GRAMMAR IN DISCOURSE: The Election 112
B. FORM 1: The Future with *Be Going To* and the Present Continuous 114
C. MEANING AND USE 1: *Be Going To* and the Present Continuous as Future 119
D. FORM 2: The Future with *Will* 125
E. MEANING AND USE 2: *Will* vs. *Be Going To* 130
WRITING: Write an Email to Post to Your School's Website 134

CHAPTER 8: Future Time Clauses and If Clauses 137
A. GRAMMAR IN DISCOURSE: What Will Happen in the Future? 138
B. FORM: Future Time Clauses and *If* Clauses 140
C. MEANING AND USE 1: Using Future Time Clauses for Events in Sequence 144
D. MEANING AND USE 2: Expressing Future Possibility with *If* Clauses . 146
WRITING: Write a Campaign Flyer 150
Part 3 Test 153

PART 4: Modals

CHAPTER 9: Modals of Ability and Possibility 155

A. **GRAMMAR IN DISCOURSE:** Two Amazing People 156

B. **FORM 1: Modals of Ability:** *Can* and *Could*; *Be Able To* 158

C. **MEANING AND USE 1:** Past, Present, and Future Ability 162

D. **FORM 2:** Modals of Future Possibility 167

E. **MEANING AND USE 2:** Future Possibility 170

WRITING: Write an Email About Your Future After College 174

CHAPTER 10: Modals and Phrases of Request, Permission, Desire, and Preference 177

A. **GRAMMAR IN DISCOURSE:** How *Not* to Ask for a Raise 178

B. **FORM:** Modals of Request; Modals of Permission; *Would Like*, *Would Prefer*, and *Would Rather* 180

C. **MEANING AND USE 1:** Modals of Request 186

D. **MEANING AND USE 2:** Modals of Permission 190

E. **MEANING AND USE 3:** *Would Like*, *Would Prefer*, and *Would Rather* 193

WRITING: Write a Conversation Involving a Request 197

CHAPTER 11: Modals and Phrasal Modals of Advice, Necessity, and Prohibition 199

A. **GRAMMAR IN DISCOURSE:** Tips on Being a Good Dinner Guest 200

B. **FORM:** Modals and Phrasal Modals of Advice, Necessity, and Prohibition 202

C. **MEANING AND USE 1:** Modals and Phrasal Modals of Advice 208

D. **MEANING AND USE 2:** Modals of Necessity and Prohibition 214

WRITING: Write a Memo on Office Rules 218

Part 4 Test 221

PART 5: Tag Questions and Other Additions

CHAPTER 12: Tag Questions 223

A. **GRAMMAR IN DISCOURSE:** Women's Language and Men's Language 224

B. **FORM:** Tag Questions 226

C. **MEANING AND USE:** Tag Questions 231

WRITING: Write a Conversation With Tag Questions 237

CHAPTER 13: Additions with Conjunctions 239
A. **GRAMMAR IN DISCOURSE:** Josh's Travel Blog...................... 240
B. **FORM 1:** Additions with *And . . . Too*, *And . . . Either*, and *But*...... 242
C. **FORM 2:** Additions with *And So* and *And Neither*.................. 247
D. **MEANING AND USE:** Expressing Similarities and Differences 250
WRITING: Write a Paragraph Describing Two People or Things 256
Part 5 Test 259

PART 6: Nouns, Quantity Expressions, and Articles

CHAPTER 14: Nouns and Quantity Expressions 261
A. **GRAMMAR IN DISCOURSE:** Mood Foods 262
B. **FORM:** Nouns and Quantity Expressions.......................... 264
C. **MEANING AND USE 1:** General Quantity Expressions............... 270
D. **MEANING AND USE 2:** Specific Quantity Expressions.............. 276
WRITING: Write a Request for Advice 279

CHAPTER 15: Indefinite and Definite Articles 281
A. **GRAMMAR IN DISCOURSE:** Meat-Eating Plants...................... 282
B. **FORM:** Indefinite and Definite Articles.......................... 284
C. **MEANING AND USE 1:** Indefinite and Definite Articles............. 287
D. **MEANING AND USE 2:** Nouns in General Statements............... 293
WRITING: Write a Summary of a Story.............................. 297
Part 6 Test 299

PART 7: Adjectives and Adverbs

CHAPTER 16: Adjectives.. 301
A. **GRAMMAR IN DISCOURSE:** Unusual Gifts for Unusual People 302
B. **FORM:** Adjectives 304
C. **MEANING AND USE:** Describing with Adjectives 309
WRITING: Write an Advertisement 314

CHAPTER 17: Adverbs 317
A. **GRAMMAR IN DISCOURSE:** The Personality Compass............... 318
B. **FORM 1:** Adverbs of Manner, Possibility, Time, and Opinion 320

C. **MEANING AND USE 1:** Adverbs of Manner, Possibility, Time, and Opinion 325
D. **FORM 2:** Adverbs of Degree 328
E. **MEANING AND USE 2:** Adverbs of Degree 331
F. **FORM 3:** *Too* and *Enough* 335
G. **MEANING AND USE 3:** Contrasting *Too* and *Enough* 337
WRITING: Write About a Sporting Event 340
Part 7 Test 343

PART 8: Comparatives and Superlatives

CHAPTER 18: Comparatives 345
A. **GRAMMAR IN DISCOURSE:** Early to Rise Makes Teens ... Less Attentive? 346
B. **FORM 1:** Comparatives 348
C. **MEANING AND USE 1:** Making Comparisons 352
D. **FORM 2:** *As ... As* with Adjectives, Adverbs, and Nouns 356
E. **MEANING AND USE 2:** *As ... As* with Adjectives, Adverbs, and Nouns 358
WRITING: Write a Paragraph Comparing Teenagers in Two Countries 362

CHAPTER 19: Superlatives 365
A. **GRAMMAR IN DISCOURSE:** Strange but True 366
B. **FORM:** Superlatives 368
C. **MEANING AND USE:** Superlatives 372
WRITING: Write a Thank-you Email 377
Part 8 Test 379

PART 9: Gerunds, Infinitives, and Phrasal Verbs

CHAPTER 20: Gerunds 381
A. **GRAMMAR IN DISCOURSE:** 10 Easy Ways to Start Saving Money 382
B. **FORM 1:** Gerunds as Subjects and Objects 384
C. **FORM 2:** Gerunds After Prepositions 387
D. **MEANING AND USE:** Gerunds 389
WRITING: Write an Application Essay About Your Plans 393

CHAPTER 21: Infinitives 395
A. **GRAMMAR IN DISCOURSE:** The *Twenty-One* Quiz Show Scandal ... 396
B. **FORM:** Infinitives 398
C. **MEANING AND USE 1:** Infinitives 402
D. **MEANING AND USE 2:** Contrasting Gerunds and Infinitives 405
WRITING: Write Your Online Profile 409

CHAPTER 22: Phrasal Verbs 411
A. **GRAMMAR IN DISCOURSE:** "Eggstraordinary" Breakfasts Are Easy! 412
B. **FORM:** Phrasal Verbs 414
C. **MEANING AND USE:** Phrasal Verbs 418
WRITING: Write Instructions on How to Do Something 421
Part 9 Test 423

Appendices A–1

Glossary of Grammar Terms G–1

Index I–1

Welcome to Grammar Sense

A Sensible Solution to Learning Grammar

Grammar Sense Second Edition gives learners a true understanding of how grammar is used in authentic contexts.

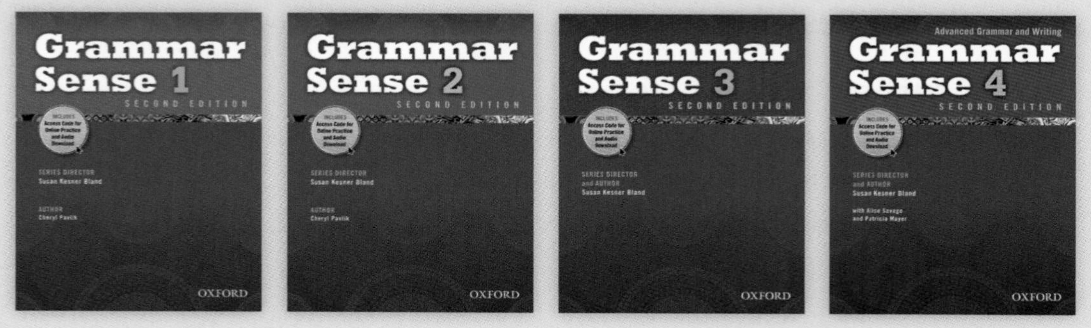

With Grammar Sense Online Practice

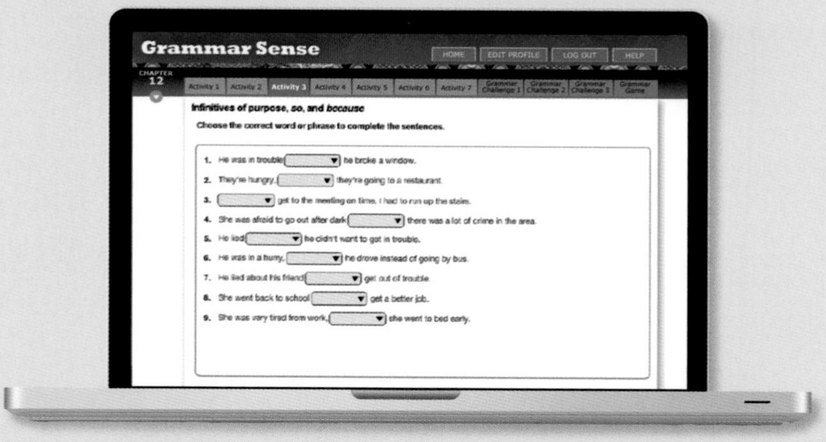

- **Student Solutions:** a **focus on Critical Thinking** for improved application of grammatical knowledge.
- **Writing Solutions:** a **Writing section in every chapter** encourages students to see the relevance of grammar in their writing.
- **Technology Solutions:** ***Grammar Sense Online Practice*** provides additional practice in an easy-to-use **online workbook**.
- **Assessment Solutions:** the Part Tests at the end of every section and the Grammar Sense Test Generators allow **ongoing assessment**.

Each chapter in ***Grammar Sense Second Edition*** **follows** this format.

The Grammar in Discourse section introduces the target grammar in its natural context via high-interest readings.

Pre- and post-reading tasks help students understand the text.

A GRAMMAR IN DISCOURSE

Long-Distance Voyager

A1 Before You Read

Discuss these questions.

Do you think exploring space is important? Why or why not? What do you think we can learn by exploring space?

A2 Read

CD1 T9 **Read the magazine article on the following page to find out about a famous spacecraft.**

A3 After You Read

Write *T* for true or *F* for false for each statement.

_T_ **1.** *Voyager* is a spacecraft.

____ **2.** *Voyager* is traveling through space.

____ **3.** *Voyager* is coming back to Earth soon.

____ **4.** *Voyage*

____ **5.** We are

____ **6.** *Voyage*

Exposure to **authentic readings** encourages awareness of the grammar in daily life: in textbooks, magazines, newspapers, websites, and so on.

Voyager

LONG-DISTANCE

Voyager

Voyager 1 is a spacecraft that left Earth in 1977. Its purpose was to explore our solar system. Scientists expected to receive information about Jupiter and Saturn from *Voyager* for ten to fifteen years. They were wrong. They are still receiving messages from *Voyager* today. *Voyager* is currently moving away from Earth at a speed of over 38,000 miles per hour (over 61,000 kilometers per hour). Now it is so far away that its messages take over fifteen hours to travel to Earth.

How far away is *Voyager 1* now and what is it exploring? *Voyager* is many billions of miles from us. It is farther from Earth than any other human-made object. It is traveling in a part of our solar system beyond all the planets. In fact, it is approaching the outer boundaries of our solar system. These days, *Voyager's* messages are giving us information about this most distant part of our solar system. Large antennas on Earth are receiving its signals.

Soon *Voyager* will leave our solar system. Then it will send us information about interstellar space—the space between our Sun and other stars. *Voyager* will continue into interstellar space, and we will continue to learn from *Voyager*. Finally, sometime between about 2020 and 2025, *Voyager* will stop sending information and will travel silently through space.

The Form section(s) provides clear presentation of the target grammar, detailed notes, and thorough practice exercises.

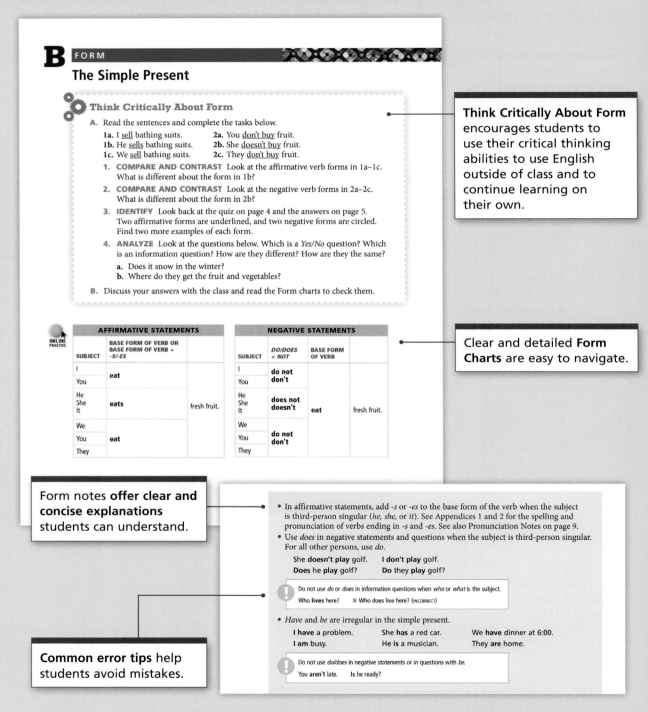

B FORM

The Simple Present

Think Critically About Form

A. Read the sentences and complete the tasks below.

1a. I sell bathing suits. **2a.** You don't buy fruit.
1b. He sells bathing suits. **2b.** She doesn't buy fruit.
1c. We sell bathing suits. **2c.** They don't buy fruit.

1. **COMPARE AND CONTRAST** Look at the affirmative verb forms in 1a–1c. What is different about the form in 1b?
2. **COMPARE AND CONTRAST** Look at the negative verb forms in 2a–2c. What is different about the form in 2b?
3. **IDENTIFY** Look back at the quiz on page 4 and the answers on page 5. Two affirmative forms are underlined, and two negative forms are circled. Find two more examples of each form.
4. **ANALYZE** Look at the questions below. Which is a *Yes/No* question? Which is an information question? How are they different? How are they the same?
   a. Does it snow in the winter?
   b. Where do they get the fruit and vegetables?

B. Discuss your answers with the class and read the Form charts to check them.

Think Critically About Form encourages students to use their critical thinking abilities to use English outside of class and to continue learning on their own.

ONLINE PRACTICE

AFFIRMATIVE STATEMENTS		
SUBJECT	BASE FORM OF VERB OR BASE FORM OF VERB + *-S/-ES*	
I You	**eat**	fresh fruit.
He She It	**eats**	
We You They	**eat**	

NEGATIVE STATEMENTS			
SUBJECT	*DO/DOES* + *NOT*	BASE FORM OF VERB	
I You	**do not** **don't**	**eat**	fresh fruit.
He She It	**does not** **doesn't**		
We You They	**do not** **don't**		

Clear and detailed **Form Charts** are easy to navigate.

Form notes **offer clear and concise explanations** students can understand.

- In affirmative statements, add *-s* or *-es* to the base form of the verb when the subject is third-person singular (*he, she,* or *it*). See Appendices 1 and 2 for the spelling and pronunciation of verbs ending in *-s* and *-es*. See also Pronunciation Notes on page 9.
- Use *does* in negative statements and questions when the subject is third-person singular. For all other persons, use *do*.

  She **doesn't play** golf. **I don't play** golf.
  Does he **play** golf? **Do** they **play** golf?

> Do not use *do* or *does* in information questions when *who* or *what* is the subject.
> Who **lives** here? ✗ Who does live here? (INCORRECT)

- *Have* and *be* are irregular in the simple present.

  I have a problem. She **has** a red car. We **have** dinner at 6:00.
  I am busy. He **is** a musician. They **are** home.

> Do not use *do/does* in negative statements or in questions with *be*.
> You **aren't** late. **Is** he ready?

Common error tips help students avoid mistakes.

The Meaning and Use section(s) offers clear and comprehensive explanations of how the target structure is used, and exercises to practice using it appropriately.

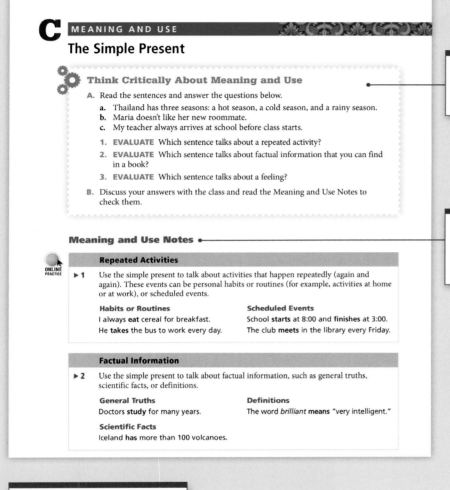

C MEANING AND USE

The Simple Present

Think Critically About Meaning and Use

A. Read the sentences and answer the questions below.

a. Thailand has three seasons: a hot season, a cold season, and a rainy season.
b. Maria doesn't like her new roommate.
c. My teacher always arrives at school before class starts.

1. EVALUATE Which sentence talks about a repeated activity?
2. EVALUATE Which sentence talks about factual information that you can find in a book?
3. EVALUATE Which sentence talks about a feeling?

B. Discuss your answers with the class and read the Meaning and Use Notes to check them.

Think Critically About Meaning and Use helps students analyze real world grammar usage.

Meaning and Use Notes

Explanations with authentic examples illustrate the various meanings and uses of the structure.

ONLINE PRACTICE

Repeated Activities

▶ 1 Use the simple present to talk about activities that happen repeatedly (again and again). These events can be personal habits or routines (for example, activities at home or at work), or scheduled events.

Habits or Routines
I always **eat** cereal for breakfast.
He **takes** the bus to work every day.

Scheduled Events
School **starts** at 8:00 and **finishes** at 3:00.
The club **meets** in the library every Friday.

Factual Information

▶ 2 Use the simple present to talk about factual information, such as general truths, scientific facts, or definitions.

General Truths
Doctors **study** for many years.

Scientific Facts
Iceland **has** more than 100 volcanoes.

Definitions
The word *brilliant* **means** "very intelligent."

Practice exercises enable students to **use the grammar structure appropriately and fluently**.

C1 Listening for Meaning and Use

▶ Notes 1, 2

CD1 T5 Listen to each statement. Is the speaker describing a personal routine or a general truth? Check (✓) the correct column.

	PERSONAL ROUTINE	GENERAL TRUTH
1.		✓
2.		
3.		
4.		
5.		
6.		

Special sections appear throughout the chapters with clear explanations, authentic examples, and follow-up exercises.

Beyond the Sentence demonstrates how structures function differently in extended discourses.

Beyond the Sentence

Combining Ideas

When you compare people or things, it is important to combine your ideas by using additions with *and . . . too, and . . . either, and so, and neither,* and *but.* If you do not combine ideas, your writing will be very repetitive. Compare these two paragraphs. Notice how combining ideas makes the second paragraph sound less repetitive.

Repetitive

My best friend and I have many similarities. I have a sister. Carol has a sister. I like vanilla ice cream. Carol likes vanilla ice cream. I'm not good at math. Carol isn't good at math. There is one big difference. Carol lives in the United States. I don't live in the United States. I live in Costa Rica.

Not Repetitive

My best friend and I have many similarities. I have a sister, **and so does** Carol. I like vanilla ice cream, **and** Carol **does, too.** I'm not good at math, **and neither** is Carol. There is one big difference. Carol lives in the United States, **but** I **don't.** I live in Costa Rica.

D6 Avoiding Repetition

Read this paragraph. Underline the parts that are repetitive. Then rewrite the paragraph combining sentences where possible.

The United States and the United Kingdom have many similarities and differences. One of the similarities is language. People in the United States speak English. People in the United Kingdom speak English. Some people say that Americans don't speak very clearly. Some people say that the British speak very clearly. American and British food is also similar in some ways. Americans like to eat meat and potatoes. The British like to eat meat and potatoes. The two countries also both have strong traditions of volunteer work. Many Americans give some of their time to help others. Many Britons also give some time to help others. One big difference is the political system. The United Kingdom has a queen. The United States doesn't have a king or a queen. In the United States, voters elect a president. In the United Kingdom, voters don't elect a

Pronunciation Notes

Pronunciation of Verbs Ending in *-s* or *-es*

The letters *-s* or *-es* at the end of third-person singular verbs are pronounced in three different ways, depending on the final sound of the base form of the verb.

1. The *-s* or *-es* is pronounced /s/ if the base form of the verb ends with the sound /p/, /t/, /k/, or /f/.

   stop — stops /stɑps/ like — likes /laɪks/ laugh — laughs /læfs/

2. The *-s* or *-es* is pronounced /z/ if the base form of the verb ends with the sound /b/, /d/, /g/, /v/, /ð/, /m/, /n/, /ŋ/, /l/, /r/, or a vowel sound.

   leave — leaves /livz/ run — runs /rʌnz/ go — goes /goʊz/

3. The *-es* is pronounced /ɪz/ if the base form of the verb ends with the sound /s/, /z/, /ʃ/, /ʒ/, /tʃ/, /dʒ/, or /ks/. This adds an extra syllable to the word.

   notice — notices /ˈnoʊt̬əsɪz/ buzz — buzzes /ˈbʌzɪz/ watch — watches /ˈwɑtʃɪz/

B3 Pronouncing Verbs Ending in *-s* or *-es*

CD1 T4 **A. Listen to the pronunciation of each verb. What ending do you hear? Check (✓) the correct column.**

		/s/	/z/	/ɪz/
1.	lives		✓	
2.	practices			
3.	works			
4.	closes			
5.	arranges			
6.	tells			

B. Work with a partner. Take turns reading these sentences aloud. Be sure to pronounce the verb endings correctly.

1. Pablo lives in San Diego.
2. The team practices every day.
3. The computer works just fine.
4. My mother closes the window at night.
5. Tony arranges all the meetings.
6. Sheryl tells everyone's secrets.

CHAPTER 1 | 9

Pronunciation Notes show students how to pronounce forms of the target language.

Informally Speaking clarifies the differences between written and spoken language.

Informally Speaking

Reduced Form of *Going To*

CD1 T34 Look at the cartoon and listen to the conversation. How are the underlined forms in the cartoon different from what you hear?

Are you going to see Mary tonight?
No, I'm going to study. I have a lot of homework.

In informal speech, *going to* is often pronounced /gənə/.

Standard Form	What You Might Hear
They are **going to** call.	"They're /gənə/ call."
He is **going to** buy a new phone.	"He's /gənə/ buy a new phone."
I am **going to** stay home.	"I'm /gənə/ stay home."

B5 Understanding Informal Speech

CD1 T35 **Listen and write the standard form of the words you hear.**

1. We ___*are going to make*___ dinner soon.
2. I ____________ to the beach.
3. We ____________ him in Seattle.
4. Our class ____________ next Wednesday.
5. The store ____________ in five minutes.
6. Mark ____________ at Lincoln University.
7. The children ____________ happy about this.
8. They ____________ the test tomorrow.

Vocabulary Notes

Adverbs and Time Expressions with the Present Continuous

***Still* and the Present Continuous** *Still* is an adverb that is often used with the present continuous. *Still* emphasizes that the activity or state is in progress. It often suggests surprise that the activity or state has not ended. Place *still* after *be* in affirmative statements, before *be* in negative statements, and after the subject in questions.

Affirmative Statement	Negative Statement
He is **still** living with his parents.	He **still** isn't living on his own.
***Yes/No* Question**	**Information Question**
Is he **still** living with his parents?	Why is he **still** living with his parents?

Time Expressions with the Present Continuous Time expressions are also commonly used with the present continuous. Some time expressions refer to an exact moment in the present. These include *now, right now,* and *at the moment.*

Others refer to a longer time period that includes the present moment. These include *this morning, this afternoon, this evening, this week, this month, this semester, this year, these days,* and *nowadays.*

Time expressions can occur at the beginning or end of a sentence.

Exact Moment	Longer Time Period
Now I'm making dinner.	She's working hard **this morning.**
He's sleeping **right now.**	**This week** I'm doing research at the library.
He's taking a shower **at the moment.**	She's feeling much better **these days.**

C4 Using Adverbs and Time Expressions with the Present Continuous

In your notebook, write sentences about yourself and people you know. Use the present continuous and these subjects and time expressions.

1. I/right now
   I am studying English right now.
2. My best friend/these days
3. Some of my friends/still
5. My family/nowadays
6. I/still
7. I/this year

40

Vocabulary Notes highlight the connection between the key vocabulary and grammatical structures.

The Writing section guides students through the process of applying grammatical knowledge to compositions.

WRITING Write a Description of Your Current Activities

Think Critically About Meaning and Use

A. Complete each conversation.

1. A: Stop her! She ____ !
   B: What's the matter?
   a. leaves
   (b.) is leaving
   c. leave

2. A: Why ____ he ____ German?
   B: He's not studying enough.
   a. does/fail
   b. is/failing
   c. does/failing

3. A: How ____ the soup ____?
   B: It's delicious.
   a. is/tasting
   b. is/taste
   c. does/taste

4. A: What ____?
   B: My parents. I'm worried about them.
   a. do you think
   b. do you think about
   c. are you thinking about

B. Discuss these questions in small groups.

1. **EVALUATE** Which conversation uses a stative verb as an action verb? What is the verb?
2. **ANALYZE** Which two conversations use the present continuous for an activity in progress at the exact moment the speaker is talking? Which conversation uses the present continuous for an activity in progress that is not happening at the exact moment the speaker is talking?

Edit

Find the errors in this email and correct them.

Hi Donna,

I love Sunrise Inn. It is ~~having~~ has a very restful at

tree in the garden. I don't worrying about any

blows, and birds singing. I have a wonderful v

Write and tell me your news.
Myles

Editing exercises focus students on **identifying and correcting problems** in sentence structure and usage.

Integrating grammar into the writing process helps students **see the relevance of grammar to their own writing.**

Write

Imagine that you are updating your profile on a social-networking site. Follow the steps below to write a description of your current activities. Use the present continuous.

1. **Brainstorm** Make a list of things that you are doing these days. Include some details about each of these activities. Use these categories to help you.
   - classes and other school activities
   - work activities
   - activities with friends
   - activities with family members
   - other free-time activities
   - unexpected situations

2. **Write a First Draft** Before you write your draft, read the checklist below. Write your draft using the present continuous.

3. **Edit** Read your work and check it against the checklist below. Circle grammar, spelling, and punctuation errors.

DO I ...	YES
tell about various activities?	
use the present continuous?	
include at least one time expression?	
use the simple present for stative verbs?	

4. **Peer Review** Work with a partner to help you decide how to fix your errors and improve the content.

5. **Rewrite Your Draft** Using the comments from your partner, write a final draft.

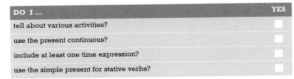

Home Profile Account

Current activities

Collaborating with classmates in **peer review** helps students improve their own grammar skills.

Assessment

PART 1 TEST | The Present

Choose the correct word or words to complete each sentence.

1. ______________ write in the margins of your test booklet, class.
   a. Doesn't   c. Not
   b. Don't   d. No
2. Please ______________ the bottom of this form, sir.
   a. sign   c. signing
   b. signs   d. to sign
3. Many economists believe the world economy ______________ right now.
   a. am shrinking   c. are shrinking
   b. is shrinking   d. shrinking
4. Naomi and Emily ______________ two brothers.
   a. are having   c. has
   b. having   d. have

Part Tests allow ongoing assessment and evaluate the students' mastery of the grammar.

Teacher's Resources

Teacher's Book

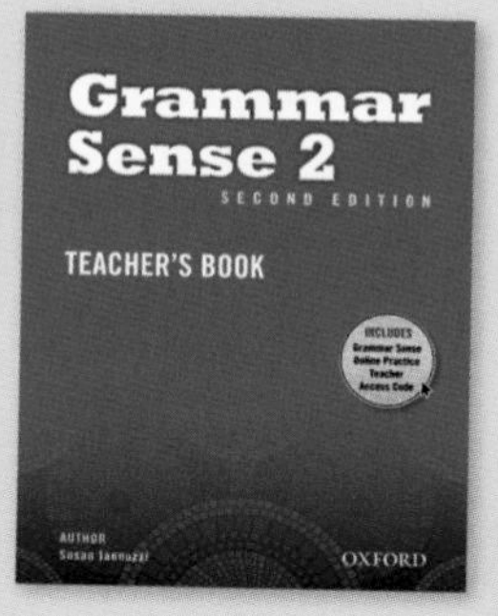

- Creative techniques for presenting the grammar, along with troubleshooting tips, and suggestions for additional activities
- Answer key and audio scripts
- Includes a ***Grammar Sense Online Practice*** Teacher Access Code

Test Generator CD-ROM

- Over 3,000 items available!
- Test-generating software allows you to customize tests for all levels of Grammar Sense
- Includes a bank of ready-made tests

Class Audio

- Audio CDs feature exercises for discriminating form, understanding meaning and use, and interpreting non-standard forms

Oxford Teachers' Club

Grammar Sense Teachers' Club site contains additional teaching resources at www.oup.com/elt/teacher/grammarsense

Grammar Sense Online Practice is an online program with all new content. It correlates with the *Grammar Sense* student books and provides additional practice.

FOR THE STUDENT

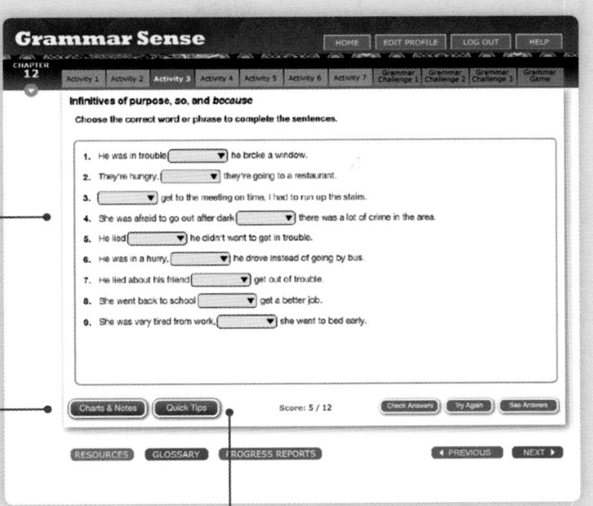

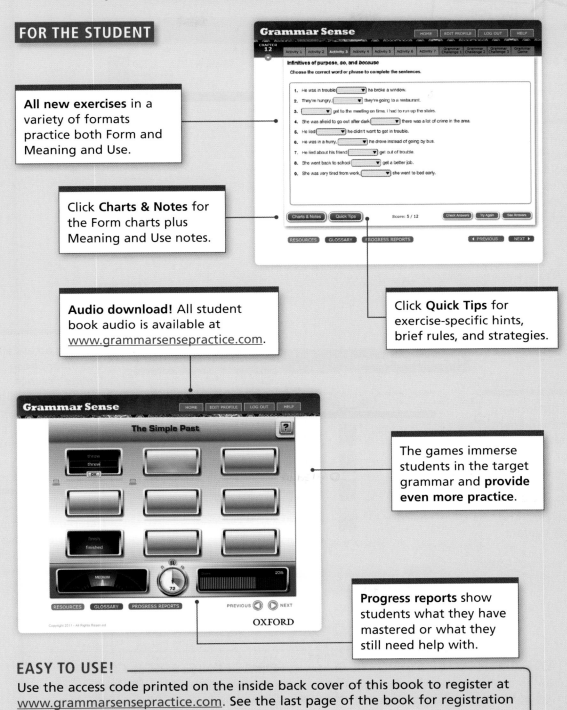

All new exercises in a variety of formats practice both Form and Meaning and Use.

Click **Charts & Notes** for the Form charts plus Meaning and Use notes.

Click **Quick Tips** for exercise-specific hints, brief rules, and strategies.

Audio download! All student book audio is available at www.grammarsensepractice.com.

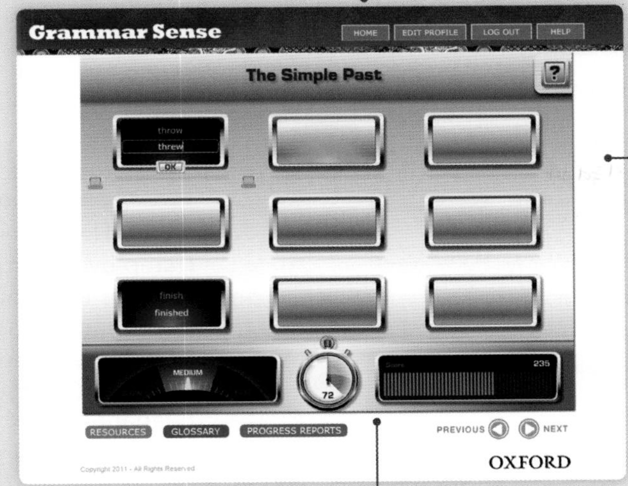

The games immerse students in the target grammar and **provide even more practice**.

Progress reports show students what they have mastered or what they still need help with.

EASY TO USE!

Use the access code printed on the inside back cover of this book to register at www.grammarsensepractice.com. See the last page of the book for registration instructions.

FOR THE TEACHER AND THE ADMINISTRATOR

Flexible enough for use in the classroom or easily assigned as homework.

***Grammar Sense Online Practice* automatically grades** student exercises and tracks progress.

The easy-to-use online management system allows you to **review, print, or export** the reports you need.

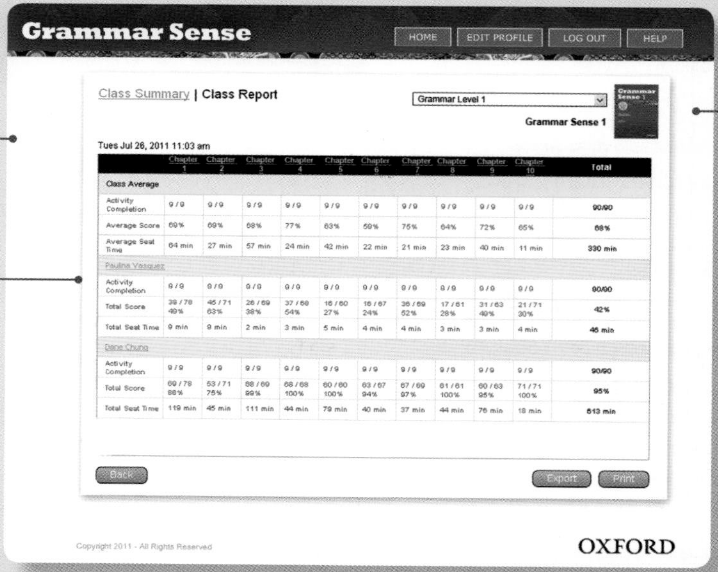

You can **access all *Grammar Sense Online Practice* activities**, download the student book audio, and utilize the additional student resources.

The **straightforward online management system** allows you to add or delete classes, manage your classes, plus view, print, or export all class and individual student reports.

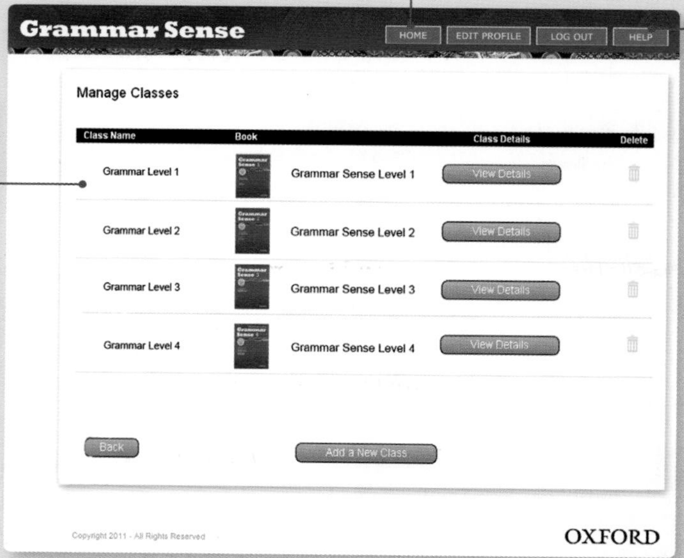

Click Help for simple, step-by-step support that is **available in six languages**: English, Spanish, Korean, Arabic, Chinese, and Japanese.

FOR ADDITIONAL SUPPORT

Email our customer support team at grammarsensesupport@oup.com and you will receive a response within 24 hours.

FOR ADMINISTRATOR CODES

Please contact your sales representative for an Administrator Access Code. A Teacher Access Code comes with every Teacher's Book.

PART

1

The Present

CHAPTER

1

The Simple Present

A. **GRAMMAR IN DISCOURSE: Mysterious Island** 4

B. **FORM: The Simple Present** 6

He **eats** fresh fruit.

Pronunciation Notes: Pronunciation of Verbs Ending in *-s* or *-es*

C. **MEANING AND USE: The Simple Present** 11

Repeated Activities

Factual Information

States or Conditions

Adverbs of Frequency with the Simple Present

WRITING: Write a Factual Paragraph 15

A GRAMMAR IN DISCOURSE

Mysterious Island

A1 Before You Read

Discuss these questions.

What do you think about when you imagine an island? Do you imagine warm weather or cold weather? Can you name any islands that are countries?

A2 Read

CD1 T2 **Read this geography quiz to find out more about Iceland.**

QUIZ

ICELAND IS A TRULY UNIQUE ISLAND—in fact, it's like nowhere else on Earth. The interior of this island nation contains incredible contrasts. It has tundras, huge glaciers, volcanoes, and waterfalls.

Read these amazing facts about Iceland. Then guess the answers to the questions. Check your guesses on page 5.

1 Swimsuit maker Speedo® sells a very large number of bathing suits in Iceland. Is it warm here all year?

2 The island's climate is cool, but most people don't pay much money for heat. Energy is very cheap and it doesn't cause pollution. What kind of energy do Icelanders use?

3 Icelanders eat fresh fruit and vegetables all year, but they rarely buy them from other countries. Where do they get them?

4 Icelanders like to play golf all night during the summer. How do they see the ball?

A geyser in Iceland

ANSWERS

1 No. Winters are cold in Iceland, but the people of Iceland swim all year in heated swimming pools.

2 They use geothermal heat from under the ground. Icelanders use water from volcanoes, hot springs, and geysers. Pipes carry the heated water throughout the country. The water heats buildings.

3 They get them from greenhouses. Icelanders use geothermal energy to grow fruit and vegetables in greenhouses, even in the winter. This means they don't need to import produce.

4 Iceland is very close to the Arctic Circle. In the summer the sun doesn't go down, so people can play sports all night.

Adapted from *The Christian Science Monitor*

climate: the typical weather conditions of a place
geyser: a hot spring that shoots water into the air
glacier: a large body of ice that moves slowly over land
greenhouse: a glass building used for growing plants
produce: foods such as fruit and vegetables
tundra: a large, flat area of frozen land without trees
volcano: a mountain from which hot melted rock, gas, smoke, and ash can escape from a hole in its top

A3 After You Read

Write *T* for true or *F* for false for each statement.

____ **1.** Iceland is warm in the winter.

____ **2.** Icelanders use geothermal energy.

____ **3.** Geothermal energy comes from the sun.

____ **4.** Icelanders heat their houses with oil.

____ **5.** Icelanders don't grow fresh fruit.

____ **6.** The sun shines all night in Iceland in the summer.

B FORM

The Simple Present

Think Critically About Form

A. Read the sentences and complete the tasks below.

1a. I <u>sell</u> bathing suits.
1b. He <u>sells</u> bathing suits.
1c. We <u>sell</u> bathing suits.

2a. You <u>don't buy</u> fruit.
2b. She <u>doesn't buy</u> fruit.
2c. They <u>don't buy</u> fruit.

1. **COMPARE AND CONTRAST** Look at the affirmative verb forms in 1a–1c. What is different about the form in 1b?
2. **COMPARE AND CONTRAST** Look at the negative verb forms in 2a–2c. What is different about the form in 2b?
3. **IDENTIFY** Look back at the quiz on page 4 and the answers on page 5. Two affirmative forms are underlined, and two negative forms are circled. Find two more examples of each form.
4. **ANALYZE** Look at the questions below. Which is a *Yes/No* question? Which is an information question? How are they different? How are they the same?

   a. Does it snow in the winter?
   b. Where do they get the fruit and vegetables?

B. Discuss your answers with the class and read the Form charts to check them.

ONLINE PRACTICE

AFFIRMATIVE STATEMENTS		
SUBJECT	**BASE FORM OF VERB OR BASE FORM OF VERB + *-S/-ES***	
I You	**eat**	fresh fruit.
He She It	**eats**	
We You They	**eat**	

NEGATIVE STATEMENTS			
SUBJECT	***DO/DOES + NOT***	**BASE FORM OF VERB**	
I You	**do not** **don't**	**eat**	fresh fruit.
He She It	**does not** **doesn't**		
We You They	**do not** **don't**		

***YES/NO* QUESTIONS**			
DO/DOES	**SUBJECT**	**BASE FORM OF VERB**	
Do	you		
Does	she	**eat**	fresh fruit?
Do	they		

SHORT ANSWERS					
YES	**SUBJECT**	***DO/DOES***	***NO***	**SUBJECT**	***DO/ DOES+ NOT***
	I	**do**.		I	**don't**.
Yes,	she	**does**.	**No,**	she	**doesn't**.
	they	**do**.		they	**don't**.

INFORMATION QUESTIONS				
***WH-* WORD**	***DO/DOES***	**SUBJECT**	**BASE FORM**	
Who	**do**	you	**teach**	on Tuesdays?
What	**does**	he	**eat?**	
When				
Where				
Why	**do**	they	**travel**	in the winter?
How				

***WH-* WORD (SUBJECT)**			**BASE FORM OF VERB + *-S/-ES***	
Who			**works**	on Tuesdays?
What			**happens**	there?

- In affirmative statements, add *-s* or *-es* to the base form of the verb when the subject is third-person singular (*he, she,* or *it*). See Appendices 1 and 2 for the spelling and pronunciation of verbs ending in *-s* and *-es.* See also Pronunciation Notes on page 9.
- Use *does* in negative statements and questions when the subject is third-person singular. For all other persons, use *do*.

  She **doesn't play** golf. **I don't play** golf.
  Does he **play** golf? **Do** they **play** golf?

> **!** Do not use *do* or *does* in information questions when *who* or *what* is the subject.
>
> Who **lives** here? **X** Who does live here? (INCORRECT)

- *Have* and *be* are irregular in the simple present.

  I have a problem. She **has** a red car. We **have** dinner at 6:00.
  I am busy. He **is** a musician. They **are** home.

> **!** Do not use *do/does* in negative statements or in questions with *be.*
>
> You **aren't** late. **Is** he ready?

B1 Listening for Form

CD1 T3 **Listen to this paragraph. Write the verb forms you hear.**

Many people in Hawaii ___live___ (1) in two different worlds—the world of traditional Hawaiian culture and the world of modern American culture. Keenan Kanaeholo ________ (2) a typical Hawaiian. He ________ (3) on the island of Oahu. Like many Hawaiians, Keenan ________ (4) two languages. At home, he and his family ________ (5) English. They ________ (6) to each other in Hawaiian. Keenan ________ (7) in a large hotel. At work, he ________ (8) English. Keenan's wife, Emeha, ________ (9) in the hotel. She ________ (10) at an elementary school. Both Keenan and Emeha ________ (11) to dance. They ________ (12) dancing on the weekends. Emeha also ________ (13) the hula, but Keenan ________ (14).

B2 Working on Affirmative and Negative Statements

Complete this paragraph with the correct form of the verbs in parentheses. Use contractions where possible.

An okapi

An okapi ___looks___ (1) (look) like the child of a zebra and a giraffe, but it ________ (2) (not/be). It ________ (3) (have) stripes like a zebra, and it ________ (4) (have) a body like a giraffe. The okapi's stripes ________ (5) (hide) it from its enemies. The okapi ________ (6) (be) a relative of the giraffe, but it ________ (7) (not/have) a long neck. It ________ (8) (not/need) one to find food because it ________ (9) (eat) fruit and leaves near the ground. Okapis ________ (10) (play) in a strange way. They ________ (11) (put) their heads down, ________ (12) (move) their tails, and ________ (13) (run) in circles. Okapis ________ (14) (live) only in Central Africa and ________ (15) (be) very rare.

Pronunciation Notes

Pronunciation of Verbs Ending in *-s* or *-es*

The letters *-s* or *-es* at the end of third-person singular verbs are pronounced in three different ways, depending on the final sound of the base form of the verb.

1. The *-s* or *-es* is pronounced /s/ if the base form of the verb ends with the sound /p/, /t/, /k/, or /f/.

   stop — stops /stɑps/ like — likes /laɪks/ laugh — laughs /læfs/

2. The *-s* or *-es* is pronounced /z/ if the base form of the verb ends with the sound /b/, /d/, /ɥ/, /v/, /ð/, /m/, /n/, /ŋ/, /l/, /r/, or a vowel sound.

   leave — leaves /livz/ run — runs /rʌnz/ go — goes /goʊz/

3. The *-es* is pronounced /ɪz/ if the base form of the verb ends with the sound /s/, /z/, /ʃ/, /ʒ/, /tʃ/, /dʒ/, or /ks/. This adds an extra syllable to the word.

   notice — notices /ˈnoʊt̬əsɪz/ buzz — buzzes /ˈbʌzɪz/ watch — watches /ˈwatʃɪz/

B3 Pronouncing Verbs Ending in *-s* or *-es*

CD1 T4 **A. Listen to the pronunciation of each verb. What ending do you hear? Check (✓) the correct column.**

		/s/	/z/	/ɪz/
1.	lives		✓	
2.	practices			
3.	works			
4.	closes			
5.	arranges			
6.	tells			

B. Work with a partner. Take turns reading these sentences aloud. Be sure to pronounce the verb endings correctly.

1. Pablo lives in San Diego.
2. The team practices every day.
3. The computer works just fine.
4. My mother closes the window at night.
5. Tony arranges all the meetings.
6. Sheryl tells everyone's secrets.

B4 Forming *Yes/No* Questions

A. Use these words and phrases to form *Yes/No* questions. Punctuate your sentences correctly.

1. study/do/a lot/you Do you study a lot?
2. teacher/does/your/speak/language/your does your teacher speak your language?
3. have/do/homework/you/a lot of do you have a lot of homework?
4. a/do/use/you/dictionary do you use a dictionary?
5. speak/you/do/English/of/class/outside do you speak English outside of class?
6. your/computers/school/does/have/many does your school have many computers?

B. Work with a partner. Take turns asking and answering the questions in part A.

A: Do you study a lot?

B: Yes, I do. OR *No, I don't.*

B5 Changing Statements into Questions

A. Write an information question about each underlined word or phrase.

1. Water freezes at 32° Fahrenheit. What freezes at 32° Fahrenheit?
2. Kim has a test today. has kim a test today?
   who has a test today?
3. A power plant makes electricity. does a power plant makes electricity?
   what does a power plant make?
4. Niagara Falls is in North America. is Niagara Falls in North America?
   where is Niagara Falls?
5. Dan drives Lee to school every day. does dan drives Lee to school every day?
   who does Dan drive to school every day?
6. Dan drives Lee to school every day. Who drives Lee to school every day?
7. It is hot in Chicago in the summer. Is it hot in Chicago in the summer?
   when is it hot in Chicago?
8. The eucalyptus tree is from Australia. Is the eucalyptus from Australia?
   where is the eucalyptus tree from?

B. In your notebook, write a *Yes/No* question about each sentence in part A.

Does water freeze at 32° Fahrenheit?

2. Does Kim have a test today?
3. Does power plant make electricity?
4. Is Niagara Falls in North America?
5. Does Dan drive Lee to school everyday?
6. Does "
7. Is it hot in Chicago in the summer?
8. Is the eucalyptus tree from Australia?

C MEANING AND USE

The Simple Present

Think Critically About Meaning and Use

A. Read the sentences and answer the questions below.

a. Thailand has three seasons: a hot season, a cold season, and a rainy season.
b. Maria doesn't like her new roommate.
c. My teacher always arrives at school before class starts.

1. **EVALUATE** Which sentence talks about a repeated activity? c.
2. **EVALUATE** Which sentence talks about factual information that you can find in a book? a.
3. **EVALUATE** Which sentence talks about a feeling? b.

B. Discuss your answers with the class and read the Meaning and Use Notes to check them.

Meaning and Use Notes

ONLINE PRACTICE

Repeated Activities

▶ 1 Use the simple present to talk about activities that happen repeatedly (again and again). These events can be personal habits or routines (for example, activities at home or at work), or scheduled events.

Habits or Routines

I always **eat** cereal for breakfast.

He **takes** the bus to work every day.

Scheduled Events

School **starts** at 8:00 and **finishes** at 3:00.

The club **meets** in the library every Friday.

Factual Information

▶ 2 Use the simple present to talk about factual information, such as general truths, scientific facts, or definitions.

General Truths

Doctors **study** for many years.

Scientific Facts

Iceland **has** more than 100 volcanoes.

Definitions

The word *brilliant* **means** "very intelligent."

(Continued on page 12)

States or Conditions

▶ 3 Use the simple present with stative verbs (verbs that do not express action) to talk about states or conditions, such as physical descriptions, feelings, relationships, knowledge, beliefs, or possession. Some common stative verbs are *be, have, seem, like, want, know, understand, mean, believe, own,* and *belong*. See Appendix 7 for a list of common stative verbs.

He **is** tall and **has** dark hair.
She **seems** angry.
You **like** sports.
They **want** a new car.
She **knows** the answer.
I don't **understand**.
I **believe** you.
We **belong** to the soccer club.

Adverbs of Frequency with the Simple Present

▶ 4 Use adverbs of frequency with the simple present to express how often something happens. Adverbs of frequency usually come before the main verb, but after the verb *be*.

She **always** has ballet from 3:00 to 6:00 P.M.
The cafeteria food is **usually** bad.
My mother **often** cooks for us.
It **sometimes** rains here in the summer.
My brother and I **seldom** fight.
He **never** cleans his room.

C1 Listening for Meaning and Use

▶ Notes 1, 2

CD1 T5 Listen to each statement. Is the speaker describing a personal routine or a general truth? Check (✓) the correct column.

	PERSONAL ROUTINE	GENERAL TRUTH
1.		✓
2.	✓	
3.		✓
4.	✓	
5.	✓	
6.		✓

C2 Talking About Routines

▶ Notes 1, 4

A. Read these statements. Check (✓) the ones that are true for you.

____ **1.** I always wash the dishes after dinner.

____ **2.** I often ride the bus in the morning.

____ **3.** My friends sometimes visit me on Saturdays.

____ **4.** I often get up at 7:00 A.M.

____ **5.** I usually recycle paper.

____ **6.** I never go to bed before midnight.

____ **7.** My friends and I sometimes study together in the evenings.

____ **8.** I never stay home on Saturday nights.

B. Work with a partner. Look at the statements in part A that you did not check. Take turns talking about them.

A: *I don't always wash the dishes after dinner. I sometimes leave them for the next day.*

B: *I seldom ride the bus in the morning. I have a car.*

C3 Asking for Definitions

▶ Note 2

A. Work with a partner. How much do you remember from the quiz about Iceland on page 4? Take turns asking and answering questions about the meaning of these words. If you don't remember the meaning of a word, look at the definitions on page 5.

1. tundra

A: *What does the word* tundra *mean?*

B: *The word* tundra *means "a large, flat area of frozen land."*

2. glacier

3. greenhouse

4. climate

5. geyser

6. volcano

B. Look back at the quiz on page 4. Find a word that is new to you and ask your partner what it means. If your partner doesn't know, look in a dictionary.

C4 Expressing Factual Information

▶ Notes 2, 3

A. Complete this paragraph with the correct form of the verbs in parentheses.

Bobsledding ______(1) (be) a dangerous sport. A bobsled ______(2) (weigh) about 600 pounds and ______(3) (carry) four people. Each person on a bobsled team ______(4) (have) an important job. First, all four people ______(5) (move) the sled back and forth. When it ______(6) (start) to move, they ______(7) (push) it very hard, and the pilot ______(8) (jump) into the bobsled to steer. Then, the person on each side ______(9) (jump) in. The brakeman ______(10) (stay) at the back and ______(11) (push) for a few more seconds. Then he or she ______(12) (get) in, too. The bobsled ______(13) (be) very fast. It ______(14) (go) up to 90 miles per hour.

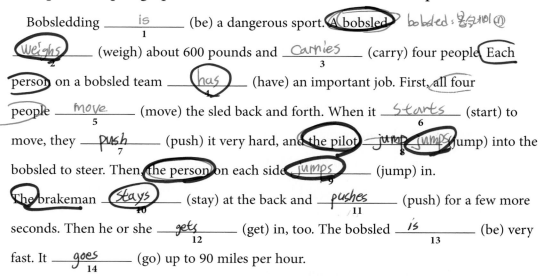

B. Describe another sport. In your notebook, write five or six facts about the sport, using the simple present.

Ice hockey is a popular sport in cold places like Canada and the northeastern United States. This game has two teams of players. The players wear ice skates and play on an ice-skating rink...

WRITING Write a Factual Paragraph

Think Critically About Meaning and Use

A. Look at these topics. Check (✓) the ones you can discuss or write about using the simple present.

____ **1.** Traditions in your country

____ **2.** Your childhood

____ **3.** A concert you went to last night

____ **4.** The geography of a country

____ **5.** The life of a 19th-century politician

____ **6.** A vacation you took

____ **7.** How a machine works

____ **8.** Your best friend's personality

B. Discuss these questions in small groups.

1. **GENERATE** Create two simple present sentences about one of the topics.
2. **SYNTHESIZE** What are some other topics to discuss in the simple present?

Edit

Find the errors in this paragraph and correct them.

Which large American city are on three islands? New York City! New York is on Manhattan Island, Long Island, and Staten Island. Most people thinks of Manhattan when they think of New York City. This is because Manhattan have the tall buildings that New York is famous for. Sometimes people travel from Staten Island to Manhattan by boat. However, most people in New York not use boats to go from one part of the city to another. Large bridges connects the islands. Trains and cars also uses long tunnels under the water to move between the islands. In fact, New Yorkers usually forget that they lives on an island.

Write

Write a factual paragraph about an unusual animal. Follow the steps below to write the paragraph. Use the simple present.

1. **BRAINSTORM** Think about an unusual animal and research it on the Internet. Look for information about the animal and its habits. Take notes about what you want to say. Use these questions to help you.
   - What does this animal look like?
   - Where does it live?
   - What does it eat?
   - When and where does it sleep?
   - What are its habits?
   - How is this animal unusual and interesting?

2. **WRITE A FIRST DRAFT** Before you write your draft, read the checklist below. Write your draft using the simple present.

3. **EDIT** Read your work and check it against the checklist below. Circle grammar, spelling, and punctuation errors.

DO I ...	YES
give basic facts and show how the animal is unusual?	☐
use the simple present?	☐
include at least one positive statement?	☐
include at least one negative statement?	☐
use correct forms for irregular *have* and *be*?	☐

4. **PEER REVIEW** Work with a partner to decide how to fix your errors and improve the content.

5. **REWRITE YOUR DRAFT** Using the comments from your partner, write a final draft.

Moles are small mammals. They live in North America, Europe, and Asia. They are usually underground. A mole has tiny eyes and doesn't see much...

CHAPTER

2

Imperatives

A. GRAMMAR IN DISCOURSE: Dos and Don'ts with Bears 18

B. FORM: Imperatives 20

Open your books.

C. MEANING AND USE: Imperatives 22

Common Uses of Imperatives

Imperatives and Politeness

Using *You* or Names in Imperatives

WRITING: Write a Recipe 27

A GRAMMAR IN DISCOURSE

Dos and Don'ts with Bears

A1 Before You Read

Discuss these questions.

Do you like to walk in the woods? Are there wild animals in the woods in your area? Are they dangerous?

A2 Read

CD1 T6 **Read the webpage on the following page to find out about what to do if you see a bear.**

A3 After You Read

Write *T* for true or *F* for false for each statement.

__F__ **1.** Bears often attack cars.

____ **2.** If a bear attacks you, you should run.

____ **3.** Bears attack when they feel threatened.

____ **4.** Bears are great tree climbers.

____ **5.** Garbage attracts bears because they think it is food.

____ **6.** Bears are slow and weak.

www.blackbearmountainpark.us

BLACK BEAR MOUNTAIN PARK

Dos and Don'ts with Bears

About 250 black bears live in Black Bear Mountain Park. If you run into a bear in the park, it is important to know what to do.

- Talk loudly, sing, or clap as you walk through the woods. Bears don't like surprises. Singing or clapping will probably frighten the bears off before you even see them.
- Don't hike through the woods at night. Bears are most active at nighttime.
- If you are in a car and see a bear, stay inside. Close the windows. Most bears will not attack a car, so you are safest inside. Don't get out to take a photograph.
- If you are outside and see a bear, stay calm. Stand still and don't run. Slowly move backward. Bears are nervous animals. They are more likely to attack you if they feel threatened.
- If a bear attacks you, don't fight. Lie still and be quiet. Maybe the bear will lose interest and wander off.

- Do not climb a tree to get away from a bear. Bears are great tree climbers!
- Do not keep food or cosmetics in your tent. Put them in a bag and hang them in a tree that is at least 100 yards from your tent. Bears like anything that resembles food. Remove food, cosmetics, and toothpaste from your tent so you won't attract their attention.
- Burn food waste. Bears cannot tell the difference between food and garbage. They will go after both.

Remember bears are dangerous animals. They are very fast and very strong. Be safe. Don't be sorry!

---

attract: to cause someone or something to feel interest

dos and don'ts: rules about what you should and should not do in a situation

resemble: to be like or to look like

run into: meet by chance

wander off: to walk away from a place

B FORM

Imperatives

Think Critically About Form

A. Read the sentences and complete the tasks below.

a. Bears are nervous animals.
b. Do not climb a tree.
c. Most bears do not attack cars.
d. Lie still and be quiet.

1. **IDENTIFY** Underline the verbs. Circle the subjects. Which sentences do not seem to have a subject? These are imperatives.
2. **RECOGNIZE** Look back at the webpage on page 19. Find five imperatives.

B. Discuss your answers with the class and read the Form charts to check them.

ONLINE PRACTICE

AFFIRMATIVE IMPERATIVES	
BASE FORM OF VERB	
Open	your books.
Drive	carefully.
Be	here at six.

NEGATIVE IMPERATIVES		
DO + NOT	**BASE FORM OF VERB**	
Do not **Don't**	**open**	your books.
	leave	yet.
	be	late.

- The subject of an imperative is *you* (singular or plural), even though we don't usually say or write the subject.
- The imperative has the same form whether we talk to one person or more than one.
  Teacher to Student: Sit down, please. **Teacher to Class: Sit** down, please.
- In spoken English, *don't* is more common than *do not* in negative imperatives.

B1 Listening for Form

CD1 T7 **Listen to these sentences. Write the verb forms you hear.**

1. Don't leave. It's early.
2. __________ right at the corner.
3. __________ in the kitchen.
4. __________ home before dinner.
5. __________ angry with me, please.
6. Please __________ off the light.

B2 Forming Sentences with Imperatives

Use these words and phrases to form sentences with affirmative and negative imperatives. Punctuate your sentences correctly.

1. take/you/your/with/book Take your book with you.
2. notebook/leave/your/home/at/don't ______
3. tomorrow/be/for/test/ready/the ______
4. questions/to/the/answer/all/try ______
5. not/the/during/talk/test/do ______

B3 Working on Affirmative and Negative Imperatives

A. Read the tips below. Check (✓) the ones that you think are bad advice.

✓ **1.** Don't write English definitions for new words.

____ **2.** Keep a vocabulary notebook.

____ **3.** Don't try to use new words in conversation.

____ **4.** Look up every new word you read.

____ **5.** Try to guess the meaning of new words.

____ **6.** Write a translation of every new word.

B. Now change the bad advice to good advice. Compare answers with a partner.

Write English definitions for new words.

B4 Building Sentences

Build ten imperative and simple present sentences. Use a word or phrase from each column, or from the second and third columns only. Punctuate imperatives with an exclamation point.

Imperative: *Listen to him!* Simple Present: *She goes to class.*

she	goes	to class
don't	listen	gum
they	speak	late
	chew	to him
	is	Korean

C MEANING AND USE

Imperatives

Think Critically About Meaning and Use

A. Read the sentences and answer the questions below.

a. Walk to the corner and turn left. The post office is right there.
b. Watch out! There's ice on the road.
c. Are you getting coffee now? Buy me a coffee, too, please.
d. Talk to the teacher. She can help you.

1. **IDENTIFY** Which underlined sentence gives advice?
2. **IDENTIFY** Which underlined sentence makes a request?
3. **IDENTIFY** Which underlined sentence gives directions?
4. **IDENTIFY** Which underlined sentence gives a warning?

B. Discuss your answers with the class and read the Meaning and Use Notes to check them.

Meaning and Use Notes

ONLINE PRACTICE

Common Uses of Imperatives

▶ 1A An imperative tells someone to do something. Common uses include:

Giving Commands:	**Stop** the car!
Giving Advice:	**Don't worry** about it.
Making Requests:	Please **come** home early.
Giving Directions:	**Turn** left. **Walk** three blocks.
Giving Instructions:	First, **peel** the potatoes. Then, **boil** the water.
Giving Warnings:	**Be** careful! The floor is wet.
Making Offers:	Here. **Have** another piece of cake, Gina.

▶ 1B Although we usually leave out the subject *you* (singular or plural), it is understood as the subject of an imperative.

Boss to Employee	Boss to Several Employees
Come to my office, please.	**Come** to my office, please.

Imperatives and Politeness

▶ 2A Use *please* to make an imperative sound more polite or less authoritative. We often use imperatives with *please* in formal situations when we speak to strangers or to people in authority. In less formal situations, especially with friends and family members, *please* is often used to soften the tone of an imperative. If *please* comes at the end of a sentence, we put a comma before it.

Train Conductor to Passenger

Please **watch** your step.

Child to Parent

Mom, **hand** me a towel, please. I spilled my drink.

▶ 2B You can also make an imperative sound more polite by using polite forms such as *sir, ma'am,* or *miss*. In written English, the polite form of address is separated from the rest of the sentence with a comma.

Sir, **watch** your step!

Stay calm, ma'am. Help is on the way.

Using *You* or Names in Imperatives

▶ 3A Although we usually leave out the subject *you*, we sometimes use it to make it clear who we are speaking to. We can also add the person's name with or without *you* as the stated subject.

A Roommate to Two Other Roommates

You **sweep** the hall, you **vacuum** the living room, and I'll clean the bathroom.

Maria, you **sweep** the hall. Mei, you **vacuum** the rug. I'll clean the bathroom.

C1 Listening for Meaning and Use

▶ Notes 1–3

CD1 T8 **Listen to each conversation. Who are the speakers? Choose the correct answer.**

1. **a.** a boss and an employee
   (b.) two co-workers
   c. two strangers
2. **a.** a teacher and a student
   b. two family members
   c. two strangers
3. **a.** two strangers
   b. two friends
   c. two family members
4. **a.** two family members
   b. two strangers
   c. a boss and an employee
5. **a.** a boss and an employee
   b. two family members
   c. two strangers
6. **a.** a teacher and a student
   b. two friends
   c. two strangers

C2 Giving Warnings and Commands

▶ Notes 1A, 1B, 2A

Look at the pictures. Match the warnings and commands to the pictures.

Stop! Police!	**Please put your seat belt on.**	**Watch out for the ball!**
Look out!	**Don't step on the truck!**	**Sit down and be quiet.**

1. Look out!

4. ______________________

2. ______________________

5. ______________________

3. ______________________

6. ______________________

C3 Making Requests

▶ Notes 1A, 1B, 2A, 2B

Work with a partner. Write a request that you might hear in each place below.

1. (in a classroom) Please give your papers to me.
2. (in an office) ______
3. (in an airport) ______
4. (at the dinner table) ______
5. (at home) ______
6. (at a movie theater) ______

C4 Giving Advice

▶ Notes 1A, 1B

Read each problem. In your notebook, write two sentences of advice: one with an affirmative imperative and one with a negative imperative. Then compare answers with a partner.

1. The light doesn't work.
   Don't touch the lightbulb. Turn the light off first.
2. My son is sick.
3. The gas tank is almost empty.
4. I can't sleep at night.
5. I don't have many friends.
6. I have a headache.

C5 Giving Instructions

▶ Note 1A, 1B, 2A

Work with a partner. You are leaving on vacation, and a friend is going to stay in your apartment. Take turns telling your friend what to do while you are away. Use affirmative and negative imperatives.

cat	**mail**	**newspaper**	**rent**	**voice**	**mail**
lights	**neighbors**	**plants**	**trash**	**windows**	

Don't forget to feed the cat.

Please leave the lights on at night.

C6 Understanding Uses of the Imperative

▶ Notes 1–3

A. Write an appropriate affirmative or negative imperative sentence for each situation.

1. Your friend is new in town. Tell him how to go to the post office:
   Go down three blocks and turn left at the traffic light.
2. You are a bus driver. A man is getting off the bus. Tell him to watch his step.
   ____
3. You are going on vacation with some friends. Your mother is worried. Reassure her.
   ____
4. You are a salesperson. Tell your customer to sign the credit card receipt.
   ____
5. You want your roommates to help you clean the apartment. Give each person a chore.
   ____
6. You dropped a glass on the floor. Warn your roommate.
   ____
7. Josh, a close friend, is visiting your home. Offer him something to eat.
   ____
8. Your uncle looks very tired. Give him some advice.
   ____
9. You are going out to dinner with some co-workers. Tell them to wait for you in the lobby.
   ____
10. You are crossing a busy street with your cousin. Give her a warning.
    ____

B. Would you use *you* in any of the situations in part A? Why or why not? Discuss your ideas with a partner.

WRITING Write a Recipe

Think Critically About Meaning and Use

A. Read what each person says. Is the imperative appropriate for the situation? If it is not appropriate, rewrite it.

1. (a police officer to a driver) Please pull over immediately. You're blocking the ambulance.

   Pull over immediately! You're blocking the ambulance.

2. (a cook to his assistant) Bake the chicken at 375°F for one hour.

   ____

3. (one stranger to another on the street) Please look out! A car is coming!

   ____

4. (a young girl to her grandmother) Sit down!

   ____

5. (an adult to a child) Turn off the television, sir.

   ____

B. Discuss these questions in small groups.

1. **EVALUATE** Why were the imperatives that you rewrote not appropriate?
2. **DRAW A CONCLUSION** In what situation would the inappropriate imperative in 1 be appropriate?

Edit

Some of these sentences have errors. Find the errors and correct them.

1. ~~You don't worrying~~ [*Don't worry*] about your memory.
2. Be not noisy!
3. Don't to listen to her.
4. Megan, closes the door, please.
5. Study the vocabulary for tomorrow's test.
6. Leave not now!

Write

Write a recipe for a favorite food. Follow the steps below to write the recipe, including the ingredients and the steps for making the food. Use imperatives.

1. **BRAINSTORM** Think about a favorite food that you know how to cook or bake. Think about how to prepare the food. Use these questions to help you.
   - What ingredients does this recipe use? How much of each ingredient? Make a list.
   - What is the first step in the recipe? What are the next steps? What is the last step? Write the steps in order.
   - Is there anything else people need to know about the recipe? Include that information.
   - Is there anything people should be careful *not* to do?

2. **WRITE A FIRST DRAFT** Before you write your draft, read the checklist below. Write your draft using imperatives.

3. **EDIT** Read your work and check it against the checklist below. Circle grammar, spelling, and punctuation errors.

DO I ...	YES
give all the steps in the recipe?	☐
give all the ingredients and amounts?	☐
give clear directions?	☐
use imperatives correctly?	☐

4. **PEER REVIEW** Work with a partner to decide how to fix your errors and improve the content.

5. **REWRITE YOUR DRAFT** Using the comments from your partner, write a final draft.

My favorite recipe is my mother's chocolate cake. First, beat two eggs in a bowl. Then, add a cup of milk and stir well. Next...

CHAPTER

3

The Present Continuous

A. GRAMMAR IN DISCOURSE: **Long-Distance Voyager** 30

B. FORM: **The Present Continuous** 32

She is **working** today.

C. MEANING AND USE: **The Present Continuous** 36

Activities in Progress

Stative Verbs and the Present Continuous

Vocabulary Notes: Adverbs and Time Expressions with the Present Continuous

WRITING: **Write a Description of Your Current Activities** 43

PART 1 TEST: **The Present** 45

A GRAMMAR IN DISCOURSE

Long-Distance Voyager

A1 Before You Read

Discuss these questions.

Do you think exploring space is important? Why or why not? What do you think we can learn by exploring space?

A2 Read

CD1 T9 **Read the magazine article on the following page to find out about a famous spacecraft.**

A3 After You Read

Write *T* for true or *F* for false for each statement.

__T__ **1.** *Voyager* is a spacecraft.

____ **2.** *Voyager* is traveling through space.

____ **3.** *Voyager* is coming back to Earth soon.

____ **4.** *Voyager* is reaching the end of the solar system.

____ **5.** We aren't getting information from *Voyager* now.

____ **6.** *Voyager* signals go to large antennas.

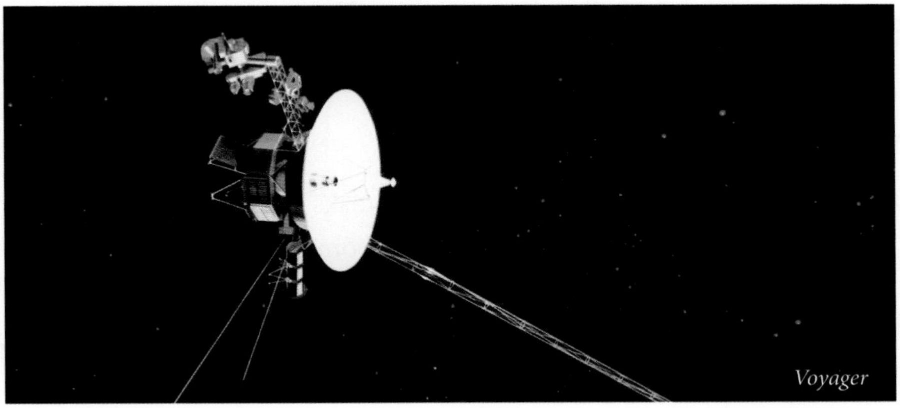
Voyager

LONG-DISTANCE

Voyager

Voyager 1 is a spacecraft that left Earth in 1977. Its purpose was to explore our solar system. Scientists expected to receive information about Jupiter and Saturn from *Voyager* for ten to fifteen years. They were wrong. They are still receiving messages from *Voyager* today. *Voyager* is currently moving away from Earth at a speed of over 38,000 miles per hour (over 61,000 kilometers per hour). Now it is so far away that its messages take over fifteen hours to travel to Earth.

How far away is *Voyager 1* now and what is it exploring? *Voyager* is many billions of miles from us. It is farther from Earth than any other human-made object. It is traveling in a part of our solar system beyond all the planets. In fact, it is approaching the outer boundaries of our solar system. These days, *Voyager*'s messages are giving us information about this most distant part of our solar system. Large antennas on Earth are receiving its signals.

Soon *Voyager* will leave our solar system. Then it will send us information about interstellar space—the space between our Sun and other stars. *Voyager* will continue into interstellar space, and we will continue to learn from *Voyager*. Finally, sometime between about 2020 and 2025, *Voyager* will stop sending information and will travel silently through space.

antenna: equipment that receives signals
outer boundaries: far borders
solar system: the Sun and the planets that move around it
spacecraft: a vehicle that can travel in space
voyager: somebody or something that travels

B FORM

The Present Continuous

Think Critically About Form

A. Read the sentences and complete the tasks below.

a. *Voyager* is many billions of miles from us.
b. It is traveling in a part of our solar system beyond all the planets.

1. **IDENTIFY** Underline the verbs. Which is simple present? Which is present continuous?
2. **DEFINE** How many words are necessary to form the present continuous? What ending is added to the base form of the verb?
3. **RECOGNIZE** Look back at the article on page 31. Find three examples of the present continuous.

B. Discuss your answers with the class and read the Form charts to check them.

ONLINE PRACTICE

AFFIRMATIVE STATEMENTS			
SUBJECT	*BE*	BASE FORM OF VERB + *-ING*	
I	**am**	**working**	today.
You	**are**		
He She It	**is**		
We You They	**are**		

CONTRACTIONS		
I**'m**	**working**	today.
You**'re**		
He**'s**		
They**'re**		

NEGATIVE STATEMENTS				
SUBJECT	*BE*	*NOT*	BASE FORM OF VERB + *-ING*	
I	**am**	**not**	**working**	today.
You	**are**			
He She It	**is**			
We You They	**are**			

CONTRACTIONS		
I**'m not**	**working**	today.
You**'re not** You **aren't**		
He**'s not** He **isn't**		
They**'re not** They **aren't**		

***YES/NO* QUESTIONS**			
BE	**SUBJECT**	**BASE FORM OF VERB + *-ING***	
Are	you	**working**	now?
Is	it		
Are	they		

SHORT ANSWERS				
YES	**SUBJECT**	***BE***	***NO***	**SUBJECT + *BE* + *NOT***
Yes,	I	**am**.	No,	I**'m not**.
	it	**is**.		it **isn't**.
	they	**are**.		they **aren't**.

INFORMATION QUESTIONS			
***WH-* WORD**	***BE***	**SUBJECT**	**BASE FORM OF VERB + *-ING***
How	**am**	I	**doing**?
Who	**are**	you	**calling**?
What	**is**	he	**studying**?
Where	**are**	they	**working**?
Who			**visiting**?

***WH-* WORD (SUBJECT)**	***BE***		**BASE FORM OF VERB + *-ING***
Who	**is**		**laughing**?
What			**happening**?

- See Appendix 3 for the spelling of verbs ending in *-ing*.
- See Appendix 16 for more contractions with *be*.

! Do not use contractions in affirmative short answers.

Yes, I **am**. ✗ Yes, I'm. (INCORRECT)

! Do not use a subject pronoun in information questions when *who* or *what* is the subject.

What is happening? ✗ What is it happening? (INCORRECT)

B1 Listening for Form

CD1 T10 **Listen to each sentence. Choose the verb form you hear.**

1. a. is living
   b. isn't living
   c. are living
   d. aren't living

2. a. am trying
   b. am not trying
   c. are trying
   d. are not trying

3. a. is meeting
   b. is not meeting
   c. are meeting
   d. are not meeting

4. a. am sleeping
   b. am not sleeping
   c. is sleeping
   d. is not sleeping

5. a. is working
   b. isn't working
   c. are working
   d. aren't working

6. a. am cooking
   b. am not cooking
   c. are cooking
   d. aren't cooking

B2 Forming Statements and *Yes/No* Questions

A. Form sentences in the present continuous from these words and phrases. Use contractions where possible, and punctuate your sentences correctly.

1. in Canada/Maria and Hector/live

   Maria and Hector are living in Canada.

2. Hector/in a factory/work

   ____

3. not/Maria/in a factory/work

   ____

4. she/Spanish/teach

   ____

5. English/Hector/at night/study

   ____

6. not/live/they/in an apartment

   ____

7. rent/a small house/they

____

8. learn/Maria and Hector/about life in Canada

____

B. Work with a partner. Take turns asking and answering *Yes/No* questions about the sentences in part A.

A: Are Maria and Hector living in Canada?
B: Yes, they are. OR

A: Are Maria and Hector living in the United States?
B: No, they're not. They're living in Canada.

B3 Writing Information Questions

Write an information question about each underlined word or phrase.

1. <u>The rice</u> is burning!
   What is burning?

2. <u>Carol</u> is talking on the telephone.
   ____

3. Ben is reading <u>the newspaper</u>.
   ____

4. Eric is studying at <u>the library</u>.
   ____

5. Their children are playing <u>a game</u>.
   ____

6. The children are yelling <u>because they're excited</u>.
   ____

7. He's feeling <u>sad</u> today.
   ____

8. They're doing <u>their homework</u> now.
   ____

C MEANING AND USE

The Present Continuous

Think Critically About Meaning and Use

A. Read the sentences and answer the questions below.

a. The earth's climate is becoming warmer.
b. I'm eating dinner now. Can I call you back?
c. I'm taking a computer programming course this semester.

1. **EVALUATE** Which sentence describes an activity that is happening at the exact moment the speaker is talking?
2. **EVALUATE** Which sentence describes an activity that is in progress, but not happening at the exact moment the speaker is talking?
3. **EVALUATE** Which sentence describes a changing situation?

B. Discuss your answers with the class and read the Meaning and Use Notes to check them.

Meaning and Use Notes

ONLINE PRACTICE

Activities in Progress

▶ 1A Use the present continuous for activities that are in progress (or happening) at the exact moment the speaker is talking. You can use time expressions such as *now* or *right now* to emphasize that an action is happening currently (and may end soon).

Activities in Progress at This Exact Moment

Look! It**'s snowing**!

She**'s making** dinner <u>now</u>.

Steve can't come to the phone <u>right now</u>. He**'s taking** a bath.

▶ 1B Use the present continuous for activities that are in progress, but not happening at the exact moment the speaker is talking. You can use time expressions such as *this week* or *these days* to show when the action is happening.

Activities in Progress, but Not Happening at This Exact Moment

I**'m looking** for a cheap car. Do you have any ideas?

I**'m painting** my house <u>this week</u>. It**'s taking** a long time.

▶ **1C** Use the present continuous for changing situations.

Changing Situations

My grades **are improving** this semester.

Computers **are getting** cheaper all the time.

Stative Verbs and the Present Continuous

▶ **2A** Many stative verbs are not generally used in the present continuous. They are usually used in the simple present. Some of these verbs are *know, mean, own, seem,* and *understand*. See Appendix 7 for a list of more stative verbs.

Simple Present	Present Continuous
Do you **know** the answer?	x Are you knowing the answer? (INCORRECT)
What **does** *solar system* **mean**?	x What is *solar system* meaning? (INCORRECT)
We **don't own** a car.	x We're not owning a car. (INCORRECT)

▶ **2B** Some stative verbs can be used in the present continuous, but they are used as action verbs and have a different meaning from their simple present meaning. Some of these verbs are *have, look, see, taste, think,* and *weigh*.

Simple Present	Present Continuous
They **have** a large house. (They own a large house.)	They**'re having** a good time. (They're experiencing a good time.)
Mark **looks** very unhappy. (Mark seems unhappy.)	Mark **is looking** for his car keys. (Mark is searching for his car keys.)
I **see** Lisa. She's behind Bob. (I'm looking at Lisa.)	**I'm seeing** a physical therapist for my back pain. (I'm going to a physical therapist.)
The soup **tastes** salty. (The soup has a salty taste.)	The chef **is tasting** the soup. (The chef is trying the soup.)
I **think** that's a great idea. (I believe that's a great idea.)	**I'm thinking** about Lisa. I'm worried about her. (Lisa is in my thoughts right now.)
The package **weighs** two pounds. (Its weight is two pounds.)	The postal worker **is weighing** the package. (The postal worker is using a scale.)

▶ **2C** Stative verbs that refer to physical conditions can occur in the simple present or present continuous with no difference in meaning. Some of these verbs are *ache, feel,* and *hurt*.

Simple Present	Present Continuous
I **don't feel** well.	**I'm not feeling** well.
My throat **hurts**.	My throat **is hurting**.

C1 Listening for Meaning and Use

▶ Note 1A

CD1 T11 **Listen to the announcements. Where would you hear each one?**

in an airport	on an airplane	on a train
in a store	on a ship	on television or the radio

1. on an airplane
2. on a train
3. in an airport
4. in a store
5. on television or the radio
6. on a ship

C2 Understanding Meaning and Use

▶ Notes 1A–1C

Read each conversation and look at the underlined verb form. Is the statement that follows true or false? Write *T* for true or *F* for false. Then discuss your answers with a partner.

1. **Carol:** Thanks for the ride, Marta. You seem really tired. Are you OK?
   Marta: Well, I'm working a lot of extra hours these days. I guess I am pretty tired.

   F Marta is working in the office right now.

2. **Dan:** I need to find a cheap apartment, and it's not easy.
   Lee: I know. Rents here are getting higher every year.

   T The cost of renting an apartment is changing.

3. **Amy:** How's school this semester?
   Emily: Great! I'm studying physics, and I really like it.

   F Emily is studying physics at this exact moment.

4. **Nesha:** Please answer the phone, Nicole.
   Nicole: I'm sorry. I can't. I'm helping a customer.

   T Nicole is helping a customer right now.

5. **Steve:** How's your new kitten?
   Jenny: Don't ask! She's ruining everything in my apartment.

   T The kitten is ruining everything these days.

6. **Mei:** What's wrong, Hanna? You don't look happy.
   Hanna: I'm getting a cold.

   F Hanna woke up with a bad cold.

C3 Describing Activities in Progress ▶ Note 1A

Look at the pictures. How are they different? In your notebook, write as many sentences as you can. Use the verbs below and the present continuous. (You can use some verbs more than once.)

chase enter help look run shout wait walk

In picture 1, the police officer is helping the woman.

In picture 2, he isn't helping the woman. He's chasing a thief.

1

2

Vocabulary Notes

Adverbs and Time Expressions with the Present Continuous

***Still* and the Present Continuous** *Still* is an adverb that is often used with the present continuous. *Still* emphasizes that the activity or state is in progress. It often suggests surprise that the activity or state has not ended. Place *still* after *be* in affirmative statements, before *be* in negative statements, and after the subject in questions.

Affirmative Statement	**Negative Statement**
He is **still** living with his parents.	He **still** isn't living on his own.
***Yes/No* Question**	**Information Question**
Is he **still** living with his parents?	Why is he **still** living with his parents?

Time Expressions with the Present Continuous Time expressions are also commonly used with the present continuous. Some time expressions refer to an exact moment in the present. These include *now, right now,* and *at the moment.*

Others refer to a longer time period that includes the present moment. These include *this morning, this afternoon, this evening, this week, this month, this semester, this year, these days,* and *nowadays.*

Time expressions can occur at the beginning or end of a sentence.

Exact Moment	**Longer Time Period**
Now I'm making dinner.	She's working hard **this morning**.
He's sleeping **right now**.	**This week** I'm doing research at the library.
He's taking a shower **at the moment.** 바로지금	She's feeling much better **these days**.

C4 Using Adverbs and Time Expressions with the Present Continuous

In your notebook, write sentences about yourself and people you know. Use the present continuous and these subjects and time expressions.

1. I/right now
   I am studying English right now.
2. My best friend/these days
3. Some of my friends/still
4. My English class/right now
5. My family/nowadays
6. I/still
7. I/this year
8. My neighbor/still

C5 Contrasting Routines with Activities in Progress ▶ Note 1A

Look at the pictures. In your notebook, use these words and phrases to write sentences about the people's jobs and what they are doing now.

1. Tom/drive a taxi/watch TV
   Tom drives a taxi. Now he's watching TV.

2. Celia/teach filmmaking/shop for food

3. Linda and Kendra/wait on tables/go to the movies

4. Greg/teach math/play the violin

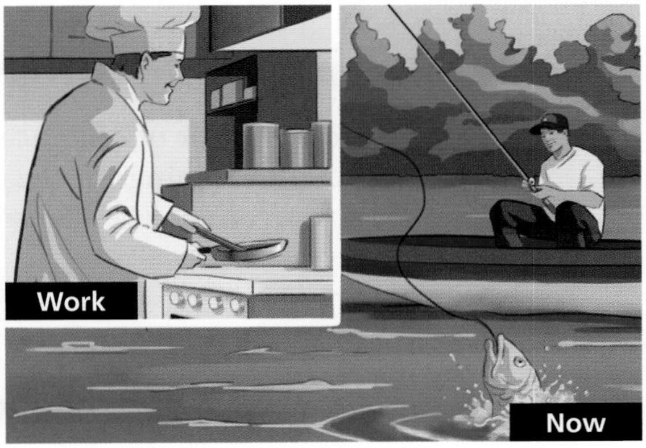

5. David/cook in a restaurant/fish

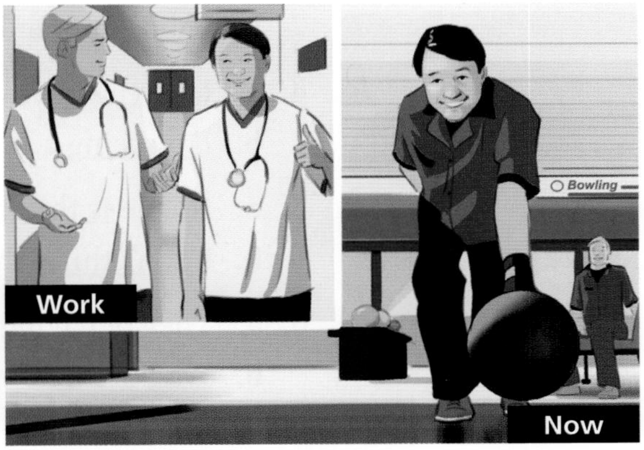

6. Ed and Riku/work in a hospital/bowl

C6 Distinguishing Between States and Actions

▶ Notes 2A–2C

A. Complete this conversation with the correct form of the verbs in parentheses. Use the simple present or present continuous. More than one answer is sometimes possible.

Doctor: What seems (1) (seem) to be the problem?

Rita: I don't know (2) (not/know). My head hurts (3) (hurt), and my stomach aches (4) (ache).

Doctor: You look (5) (look) pale. I think (6) (think) it's probably the flu.

Rita: Oh, no! I'm having (7) (have) a hard time at work right now. I can't get sick now!

Doctor: I'm thinking (8) (think) about your health right now, not your work.

B. Practice the conversation in part A with a partner.

C7 Distinguishing Differences in Meaning

▶ Notes 2B–2C

A. Read each pair of sentences and look at the underlined verbs. Do the verbs have different meanings or the same meaning? Write *D* for different or *S* for same. Discuss your answers in small groups.

D **1. a.** You look really nice today.
b. We're looking at some photos right now.

D **2. a.** I weigh 150 pounds.
b. The clerk is weighing the bananas.

S **3. a.** I need to go home because I don't feel well.
b. Paul says that he's not feeling well.

D **4. a.** I see the boys. There they are!
b. I'm seeing a doctor about my back pain. He's helping me a lot.

D **5. a.** Nicole is thinking about moving.
b. I don't think that's a good plan.

D **6. a.** They're having a good time on their vacation.
b. We have a new TV.

WRITING Write a Description of Your Current Activities

Think Critically About Meaning and Use

A. Complete each conversation.

1. A: Stop her! She ____ !
B: What's the matter?
a. leaves
b. is leaving
c. leave

2. A: Why ____ he ____ German?
B: He's not studying enough.
a. does/fail
b. is/failing
c. does/failing

3. A: How ____ the soup ____?
B: It's delicious.
a. is/tasting
b. is/taste
c. does/taste

4. A: What ____?
B: My parents. I'm worried about them.
a. do you think
b. do you think about
c. are you thinking about

B. Discuss these questions in small groups.

1. **EVALUATE** Which conversation uses a stative verb as an action verb? What is the verb?

2. **ANALYZE** Which two conversations use the present continuous for an activity in progress at the exact moment the speaker is talking? Which conversation uses the present continuous for an activity in progress that is not happening at the exact moment the speaker is talking?

Edit

Find the errors in this email and correct them.

Hi Donna,

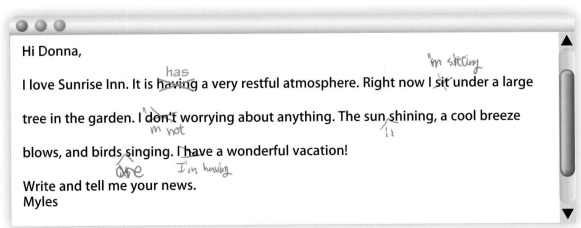

I love Sunrise Inn. It is having a very restful atmosphere. Right now I sit under a large tree in the garden. I don't worrying about anything. The sun shining, a cool breeze blows, and birds singing. I have a wonderful vacation!

Write and tell me your news.
Myles

Write

Imagine that you are updating your profile on a social-networking site. Follow the steps below to write a description of your current activities. Use the present continuous.

1. **BRAINSTORM** Make a list of things that you are doing these days. Include some details about each of these activities. Use these categories to help you.
   - classes and other school activities
   - work activities
   - activities with friends
   - activities with family members
   - other free-time activities
   - unexpected situations

2. **WRITE A FIRST DRAFT** Before you write your draft, read the checklist below. Write your draft using the present continuous.

3. **EDIT** Read your work and check it against the checklist below. Circle grammar, spelling, and punctuation errors.

DO I ...	YES
tell about various activities?	☐
use the present continuous?	☐
include at least one time expression?	☐
use the simple present for stative verbs?	☐

4. **PEER REVIEW** Work with a partner to help you decide how to fix your errors and improve the content.

5. **REWRITE YOUR DRAFT** Using the comments from your partner, write a final draft.

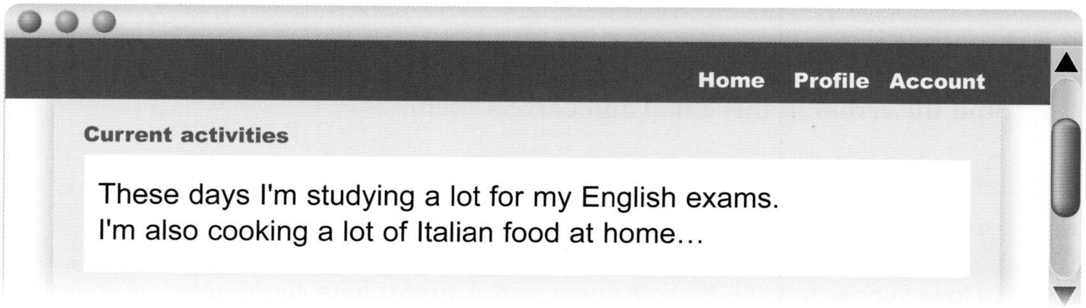
Home
Profile
Account
Current activities
These days I'm studying a lot for my English exams.
I'm also cooking a lot of Italian food at home...

Choose the correct word or words to complete each sentence.

1. ____b____ write in the margins of your test booklet, class.

a. Doesn't **c.** Not

b. Don't **d.** No

2. Please ____a____ the bottom of this form, sir.

a. sign **c.** signing

b. signs **d.** to sign

3. Many economists believe the world economy ____b____ right now.

a. am shrinking **c.** are shrinking

b. is shrinking **d.** shrinking

4. Naomi and Emily ____d____ two brothers.

a. are having **c.** has

b. having **d.** have

5. If you lose something, ____a____ the lost and found.

a. check **c.** to check

b. checks **d.** be checking

6. ____a____ the vocabulary for tomorrow's test.

a. Study **c.** Studies

b. Does study **d.** Is studying

7. Solar energy ____c____ cause pollution. It is very clean. "doesn't cause"

a. doesn't **c.** isn't

b. don't **d.** aren't

8. How many people ____b____ in Moscow?

a. lives **c.** does live

b. live **d.** do live

9. Who ____b____ to right now?

a. Diego and Carl are talking **c.** Diego and Carl talk

b. are Diego and Carl talking **d.** Diego and Carl do talk

10. Mr. and Mrs. Warren __________ much money on electronics this year.

a. not spending **c.** aren't spending

b. isn't spending **d.** don't spend

11. When do __________ publish the economic reports for the quarter?

a. it **c.** they

b. he **d.** she

Choose the correct word or words to complete each conversation.

12. **A:** Is Irina coming to the meeting?

B: (She's thinking / She thinks) about it.

13. **A:** What is Stefan doing this morning?

B: He (is taking / takes) his car to the mechanic.

14. **A:** The weather doesn't look good at all.

B: Don't forget your (glasses / umbrella).

15. **A:** Let's go to the movies tonight.

B: (I'm thinking / I think) that's a great idea.

16. **A:** I'm going to the post office now.

B: (Do you mail / Are you mailing) that card?

Match the sentence parts.

_____ **17.** Our instructor

_____ **18.** The word *humorous*

_____ **19.** A lot of birds

_____ **20.** College fees in the United States

a. ends next week.

b. fly south for the winter.

c. are very interesting.

d. means "funny."

e. are very high.

f. is an MP3 player.

g. is always on time.

h. usually stars in action films.

PART

2

The Past

CHAPTER

4

The Simple Past

A. **GRAMMAR IN DISCOURSE: The Decade That Made a Difference** . . . 48

B. **FORM 1: The Simple Past** . . . 50

I **arrived** yesterday.

Pronunciation Notes: Pronunciation of Verbs Ending in *-ed*

Informally Speaking: Reduced Form of *Did You*

C. **MEANING AND USE 1: The Simple Past** . . . 57

Actions or States Completed in the Past

Vocabulary Notes: Time Expressions with the Simple Past

Beyond the Sentence: Using Time Expressions with Tense Changes

D. **FORM 2: *Used To*** . . . 62

She **used to** arrive late.

E. **MEANING AND USE 2: The Habitual Past with *Used To*** . . . 65

Comparing the Past and the Present

WRITING: Write a Post for a History Class Blog . . . 67

A GRAMMAR IN DISCOURSE

The Decade That Made a Difference

A1 Before You Read

Discuss these questions.

What do you know about the 1960s? What were some important events? Do you have a good opinion or a bad opinion about this decade?

A2 Read

CD1 T12 **Read the excerpt on the following page to find out about the 1960s.**

A3 After You Read

Write *T* for true or *F* for false for each statement.

__F__ **1.** John F. Kennedy led the Civil Rights movement in the United States in the 1960s.

__T__ **2.** Hippies did not agree with the values of society.

__F__ **3.** The peace symbol started with the hippies in San Francisco.

__T__ **4.** In the 1960s, people became concerned about the environment.

__F__ **5.** The changes of the 1960s happened only in North America and Europe.

__T__ **6.** The "space race" involved the Soviet Union and the United States.

A hippie

The Decade That Made A Difference

In the United States and other countries around the world, the 1960s was the decade that made a difference. It was a time of hope and, especially, of great change. When it ended, the world was a very different place than before.

Consider the 1960s in the United States. John F. Kennedy became president. Martin Luther King, Jr., led the Civil Rights movement. Women's groups demanded equal rights. Young people listened to new kinds of music, including the music of the Beatles and other British bands. "Hippies" had long hair and wore strange, colorful clothes. They called for peace instead of war and questioned many of the values of American society, especially the focus on money.

Britons march against nuclear weapons

In many countries around the world, people wanted the freedom to be themselves and express themselves. They did not want to be limited because they were women or black or for any other reason. They wanted everyone to have the same opportunities and they wanted to be able to explore different possibilities and ways of living. Cities such as London, Paris, Amsterdam, and San Francisco were centers of these new ideas. But many people in other cities and countries shared these ideas, too.

Around the world, people also felt growing concern for the planet Earth. In Britain, for example, one group argued for an end to nuclear weapons. This group created the most famous symbol of the 1960s—the peace symbol. People also became more and more concerned about the effects that humans have on the environment. In fact, "Earth Day" first started in 1969.

The 1960s was also, of course, a time for technological advances. A symbol of these advances is the "space race" between the United States and the Soviet Union. At the start of the decade, in 1961, Russian astronaut Yuri Gagarin was the first person in outer space. At its end, in 1969, American astronauts Neil Armstrong and Buzz Aldrin were the first people to walk on the moon. Over 500 million people watched the moon walk on TV—another symbol of technological change.

Civil Rights movement: political and social actions to gain equal rights for African Americans

concern: worry

decade: a period of ten years (for example, 1960–1969)

opportunity: chance

technological: applying science to discover and create useful things

value: a belief about what is right or wrong

B FORM 1

The Simple Past

Think Critically About Form

A. Read the sentences and complete the tasks below.

a. Young people questioned the values of American society.
b. People wanted freedom.
c. One group argued for an end to nuclear weapons.

1. **IDENTIFY** Underline the verbs.
2. **SUMMARIZE** All of these verbs are regular verbs in the simple past. How do we form the simple past of regular verbs?
3. **COMPARE AND CONTRAST** Look back at the excerpt on page 49. Find the simple past of the irregular verbs below. How are they different from the verbs in sentences a, b, and c?

make   become   have   lead   feel

B. Discuss your answers with the class and read the Form charts to check them.

ONLINE PRACTICE

AFFIRMATIVE STATEMENTS		
SUBJECT	**BASE FORM OF VERB + *-D/-ED* OR IRREGULAR FORM**	
I You He She It We You They	**arrived** **worked** **came**	yesterday.

NEGATIVE STATEMENTS			
SUBJECT	***DID* + *NOT***	**BASE FORM OF VERB**	
I You He She It We You They	**did not** **didn't**	**arrive** **work** **leave**	yesterday.

***YES/NO* QUESTIONS**			
DID	**SUBJECT**	**BASE FORM OF VERB**	
	you	**arrive**	
Did	he	**work**	yesterday?
	they	**leave**	

SHORT ANSWERS					
YES	**SUBJECT**	***DID***	***NO***	**SUBJECT**	***DID + NOT***
	I			I	
Yes,	he	**did.**	**No,**	he	**didn't.**
	they			they	

INFORMATION QUESTIONS				
***WH-* WORD**	***DID***	**SUBJECT**	**BASE FORM OF VERB**	
Who		you	**see**	
What		he	**do**	
Where		she	**go**	
When	**did**	we	**study**	yesterday?
Why		you	**leave**	
How		they	**feel**	
***WH-* WORD (SUBJECT)**			**VERB + *-D/-ED* OR IRREGULAR FORM**	
Who			**left**	yesterday?
What			**happened**	

- To form the simple past of most regular verbs, add *-ed* to the base form. If the base form of a regular verb ends in *e,* add *-d.* See Appendices 4 and 5 for the spelling and pronunciation of verbs ending in *-ed.* See also Pronunciation Notes on page 53.
- Some verbs are irregular in the simple past. See Appendix 6 for a list of irregular verbs and their simple past forms.

> **!** Do not use *did* in information questions when *who* or *what* is the subject.
>
> What happened yesterday?
>
> The verb *be* has two irregular simple past forms: *was* and *were.*
>
> I **was** at the concert. You **were** at the mall. He **was** a musician. They **were** home.

> **!** Do not use *did* in negative statements or questions with *was/were.*
>
> **I wasn't there.** Why **was** she late? **We weren't** angry. **Were you at the concert?**

B1 Listening for Form

CD1 T13 **Listen to these sentences. Write the simple past verb forms you hear.**

1. Dan ___invited___ us to the movies.
2. They ____________ to the hockey game.
3. She ____________ 20 dollars on the street.
4. They ____________ the store at nine.
5. I ____________ to work by car every day last week.
6. He ____________ baseball for the New York Mets.
7. You ____________ a haircut! It looks great!
8. We ____________ chocolate cake at the restaurant.

B2 Working on Regular Verb Forms

Complete this paragraph with the simple past form of the verbs below.

carry   listen   live   talk   study   support   want

I was a college student in the 1960s. I ___studied___ (1) history at a university in Chicago. I ____________ (2) in an apartment near the university with four classmates. Like many other students, we ____________ (3) about why war was bad, and we ____________ (4) signs that said "Peace." We ____________ (5) to change the world. We also ____________ (6) the Civil Rights movement and ____________ (7) to speeches by its leader, Martin Luther King, Jr.

Martin Luther King, Jr., 1963

Pronunciation Notes

Pronunciation of Verbs Ending in *-ed*

The regular simple past ending *-ed* is pronounced in three different ways, depending on the final sound of the base form of the verb.

1. The *-ed* is pronounced /t/ if the verb ends with the sound /p/, /k/, /tʃ/, /f/, /s/, /ʃ/, or /ks/.

   work — worked /wərkt/   wash — washed /wɑʃt/   watch — watched /wɑtʃt/

2. The *-ed* is pronounced /d/ if the verb ends with the sound /b/, /g/, /dʒ/, /v/, /ð/, /z/, /ʒ/, /m/, /n/, /ŋ/, /l/, or /r/.

   plan — planned /plænd/   judge — judged /dʒʌdʒd/   bang — banged /bæŋd/
   bathe — bathed /beɪðd/   massage — massaged /mə'sɑʒd/   rub — rubbed /rʌbd/

3. The *-ed* is also pronounced /d/ if the verb ends with a vowel sound.

   play — played /pleɪd/   sigh — sighed /saɪd/   row — rowed /roʊd/
   bow — bowed /baʊd/   sue — sued /sud/   free — freed /frid/

4. The *-ed* is pronounced as an extra syllable, /ɪd/, if the verb ends with the sound /d/ or /t/.

   guide — guided /'gaɪdɪd/   remind — reminded /ˌri'maɪndɪd/
   rent — rented /'rɛntɪd/   invite — invited /ˌin'vaɪtɪd/

B3 Pronouncing Verbs Ending in *-ed*

CD1 T14 Listen to the pronunciation of each verb. Which ending do you hear? Check (✓) the correct column.

		/t/	/d/	/ɪd/
1.	waited			✓
2.	walked	✓		
3.	rained		✓	
4.	played		✓	
5.	coughed	✓		
6.	decided			✓
7.	jumped	✓		
8.	answered		✓	

* k, p, s, ch, sh + -ed = "t" 발음!!!

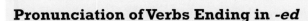

B4 Working on Irregular Verb Forms

A. Read about the first airplane flight by Wilbur and Orville Wright. Complete the paragraph with the verbs in parentheses and the simple past.

The first airplane flight ___took___ (1) (take) place in Kitty Hawk, North Carolina, on December 17, 1903. Orville Wright __________ (2) (lie) face down in the middle of the airplane, and his brother, Wilbur Wright, __________ (3) (run) alongside it. Near the end of the runway, the plane __________ (4) (rise) smoothly into the air. It __________ (5) (fly) for several seconds, but then it __________ (6) (fall) to the ground. This 12-second flight __________ (7) (make) history, but no one __________ (8) (pay) attention to the Wright brothers at first. However, after they __________ (9) (give) many public demonstrations of their flying machine, the Wright brothers __________ (10) (become) famous.

B. In your notebook, write three *Yes/No* and three *Wh-* questions about the paragraph in part A.

Did the first airplane flight take place in North Carolina?

OR

Where did the first airplane flight take place?

C. Work with a partner. Take turns asking and answering your questions from part B.

A: *Did the first airplane flight take place in North Carolina?*

B: *Yes, it did.*

OR

A: *Where did the first airplane flight take place?*

B: *In North Carolina.*

B5 Building *Yes/No* Questions in the Simple Past

Build eight logical *Yes/No* questions. Use a word or phrase from each column. Punctuate your sentences correctly.

Did it rain yesterday?

	it	rain yesterday
	the concert	first
did	the test	nervous (형) 불안해 하는
was	Maria	fun
were	you	win
	the children	leave
	they	difficult
	your team	start on time

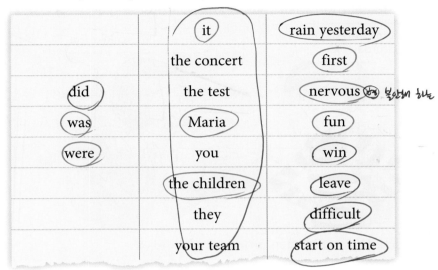

B6 Working on *Yes/No* Questions and Short Answers in the Simple Past

A. Complete this conversation with *did*, *didn't*, *was*, *wasn't*, *were*, or *weren't*.

Lynn: Did (1) you go to the basketball game last night?

Gary: Yes, I did (2).

Lynn: was (3) it exciting?

Gary: Yes, it was (4) great. Maple Valley ~~didn't~~ (5) win until the last minute. What did (6) you and Bill do last night?

Lynn: We were (7) tired, so we didn't (8) go out.

Gary: did (9) you watch that new television show?

Lynn: Yes, we did (10) but we didn't (11) like it. It was (12) really boring!

B. Practice the conversation in part A with a partner.

Informally Speaking

Reduced Form of *Did You*

CD1 T15 Look at the cartoon and listen to the conversation. How is the underlined form in the cartoon different from what you hear?

Did you forget my birthday? It was Saturday.
Oh, no! I'm really sorry!

In informal speech, *Did you* is often pronounced /ˈdɪdʒə/.

Standard Form	What You Might Hear
Did you work yesterday?	"/ˈdɪdʒə/ work yesterday?"
Did you eat yet?	"/ˈdɪdʒə/ eat yet?"

B7 Understanding Informal Speech

CD1 T16 **Listen and write the standard form of the words you hear.**

1. A: Did you go (1) on the hike?
   B: Yes, I did.
   A: Did you have (2) a good time?
   B: Yes, but today I'm very tired.
2. A: Did you eat (1) lunch yet?
   B: Yes, I did.
   A: What did you have (2)?
   B: A burger and fries.
3. A: did you stay (1) home last night?
   B: No, I went to a movie.
   A: Did you like (2) it?
   B: No, it wasn't very good.
4. A: Why did you work (1) so late?
   B: My boss needed help on a report.
   A: Did you finish (2) it?
   B: Yes, it wasn't difficult.

C MEANING AND USE 1

The Simple Past

Think Critically About Meaning and Use

A. Read the sentences and answer the questions below.

a. I walk a mile every day.
b. During my childhood we lived in Morocco.
c. I went to Jake's house last night.

ANALYZE Which sentence talks about the present? Which sentences talk about situations that started and ended in the past? Which sentence talks about a situation that happened a short time ago? A long time ago?

B. Discuss your answers with the class and read the Meaning and Use Notes to check them.

Meaning and Use Notes

ONLINE PRACTICE

Actions or States Completed in the Past

▶ 1A Use the simple past for actions or states that started and ended in the past. Use time expressions to describe the time period.

I **lived** in Boston in 2007.
We **went** shopping yesterday.
They **played** baseball on Saturdays.
The garden **was** beautiful last year.

▶ 1B The actions or states can happen in the recent past (a short time ago) or the distant past (a long time ago).

Recent Past
He **called** five minutes ago.
She **felt** tired yesterday.

Distant Past
They **got married** in 1983.
He **was** very sick ten years ago.

▶ 1C The actions or states can last for a long or short period of time.

Long Period of Time
I **worked** there for many years.
She **was** ill for six months.

Short Period of Time
It **rained** hard all afternoon.
He **seemed** happy to see me.
~하는 것처럼 보였다 (과거) "seem의 과거"

▶ 1D The actions or states can happen once or repeatedly.

Happened Once
I **graduated** on June 5, 2009.

Happened Repeatedly
He always **studied** hard before a test.

C1 Listening for Meaning and Use

▶ Notes 1A–1D

CD1 T17 **A. Listen to each conversation. Listen carefully for the phrases in the chart. Is the second speaker talking about the recent past or the distant past? Check (✓) the correct column.**

		RECENT PAST	DISTANT PAST
1.	grandmother died	✓	
2.	walked to school		
3.	saw Kedra		
4.	bought the dress		
5.	studied French		

CD1 T18 **B. Listen again. Is the second speaker referring to a situation that happened once or repeatedly? Check (✓) the correct column.**

		HAPPENED ONCE	HAPPENED REPEATEDLY
1.	grandmother died	✓	
2.	walked to school		
3.	saw Kedra		
4.	bought the dress		
5.	studied French		

C2 Making Excuses

▶ Notes 1A–1D

A. You were supposed to meet your friend for lunch yesterday, but you didn't. Use these words and phrases to make excuses.

1. go/the wrong restaurant
   I'm sorry. I went to the wrong restaurant.
2. forget/the name of the restaurant
3. have/an important meeting at work
4. my car/run out of gas
5. my watch/stop
6. have/a terrible headache

B. Now think of three more excuses. Use your imagination.

C3 Guessing What Happened

▶ Notes 1A–1D

Work with a partner. Look at the pictures and guess what happened. Use *maybe* or *perhaps* and the simple past to make two sentences for each picture.

1

Maybe she didn't study for the test.
Perhaps she forgot about the test.

2

Maybe She didn't like the food
perhaps

3

perhaps he won a lot of money

4

Maybe he is calling with someone.
perhaps he had a car accident

5

Maybe he got the Grade A
perhaps he
Maybe their son got excellent grades in School.

6

Maybe he is reading a letter.
perhaps he received bad news.

Vocabulary Notes

Time Expressions with the Simple Past

Time expressions are commonly used with the simple past. These words and phrases often refer to an exact point in time in the past or to a past time period. Time expressions can occur at the beginning or end of a sentence.

yesterday	I saw Silvio **yesterday**.
the day before yesterday	We didn't go to school **the day before yesterday**.
this morning/afternoon	**This morning** she stayed home.
last night/week/month/year	Where did they go **last month**?
recently	Did you move **recently**?
a few/several/many years ago	**A few years ago** he lost his job.
a long time ago/a while ago	Rick graduated **a long time ago**.

C4 Using Time Expressions with the Simple Past

A. In your notebook, write sentences about yourself in the simple past with these time expressions and the phrases below. You can use a time expression more than once.

a while ago	**recently**	**this ...**
last ...	**the day before yesterday**	**yesterday**

1. write a paper

   I wrote a paper last night.

2. wash the dishes

   I washed the dishes a while ago.

3. talk to a friend on the telephone

   I talked to a friend on the telephone last night.

4. eat in a restaurant

   I ate steak in a restaurant yesterday.

5. speak English outside of class

   I spoke English outside of class

6. go to a movie

   I went to a movie the day before yesterday.

7. receive a package

   I received a package this week.

8. take a vacation

   I took a vacation recently

B. Work with a partner. Take turns asking and answering information questions about the sentences you wrote in part A.

A: *When was the last time you wrote a paper?*

B: *I wrote a paper last week.*

Beyond the Sentence

Using Time Expressions with Tense Changes

In stories and descriptions, we often use the simple past and the simple present to contrast situations in the past and present. We use time expressions to clarify the change of tenses.

Compare the paragraphs below. The paragraphs on the left are confusing because they do not use time expressions to show the change from the past to the present or the present to the past. The paragraphs on the right are clear because they use time expressions to clarify the tense change in each paragraph.

Without Time Expressions	**With Time Expressions**
Sally **walked** home in the rain. She **feels** sick and **doesn't want** to go to work.	Sally **walked** home in the rain <u>yesterday</u>. <u>Now</u> she **feels** sick and **doesn't want** to go to work.
I usually take a **walk**. It **was** cold, and I **didn't want** to go outside. So I **stayed** home.	I usually take a **walk** <u>in the evening</u>. <u>This evening</u> it was cold, and I **didn't want** to go outside. So I **stayed** home.

C5 Using Time Expressions with Tense Changes

Complete these sentences with one of the time expressions below. There is more than one correct answer for each sentence.

last night	**now**	**recently**	**these days**
last week	**nowadays**	**the day before yesterday**	**this morning**

1. My parents rarely leave home, but ______recently______ they decided to visit Washington, D.C.
2. A couple of weeks ago, I found a shorter way to go to school. ____________ I go that way every time.
3. My two brothers don't always get along. ____________ I found them arguing about something again.
4. My neighbors are very noisy. They often keep me up until late at night. ____________ I finally called the police.
5. I was on my college swim team last year. However, ____________ I don't have time for sports. I have too much homework.
6. I celebrated my birthday ____________, and Jim didn't even send me a card.

D FORM 2

Used To

*원형

* 의문 Did로 물을때 use to로 묻고, 대답할땐 used to 로 대답한다. 뒤는 동사원형이 온다.

Think Critically About Form

* used to + ⓥ : ~하곤 했었다 / 지금은 안함.아님
* didn't use to + ⓥ : ~하지 않았었다 / 지금은 함.
* used to be fat : 살이 쪘었다 (상태나타낼때)
* be used to + 동명사 : ~하는것에 익숙하다
* get used to + " : ~하는것에 익숙해지다.
* have got used to + " : ~하는것에 익숙해 졌다.

A. Read the sentences and complete the tasks below.

a. He didn't use to visit his parents so often.
b. Did she use to like the class?
c. We used to swim every morning.
d. Where did you use to live?

1. IDENTIFY Underline *used to* or *use to* in each sentence. Circle all the examples of *did* or *didn't.*

2. APPLY When do we use the form *used to*? When do we use the form *use to*?

B. Discuss your answers with the class and read the Form charts to check them.

ONLINE PRACTICE

AFFIRMATIVE STATEMENTS			
SUBJECT	***USED TO***	**BASE FORM OF VERB**	
I			
You			
He She It	**used to**	**arrive**	late.
We			
You			
They			

NEGATIVE STATEMENTS				
SUBJECT	***DID + NOT***	***USE TO***	**BASE FORM OF VERB**	
I				
You				
He She It	**did not** **didn't**	**use to**	**arrive**	late.
We				
You				
They				

YES/NO QUESTIONS				
DID	**SUBJECT**	***USE TO***	**BASE FORM OF VERB**	
	you			
Did	he	**use to**	**arrive**	late?
	they			

SHORT ANSWERS					
YES	**SUBJECT**	***DID***	***NO***	**SUBJECT**	***DID + NOT***
	I			I	
Yes,	he	**did.**	**No,**	he	**didn't.**
	they			they	

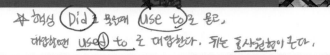

INFORMATION QUESTIONS					
***WH-* WORD**	***DID***	**SUBJECT**	***USE TO***	**BASE FORM OF VERB**	
Why		you		**arrive**	early?
When	**did**	she	**use to**	**go**	to school here?
Where		they		**live**	in Chicago?

***WH-* WORD (SUBJECT)**			***USED TO***	**BASE FORM OF VERB**	
Who			**used to**	**live**	across the street?
What				**happen**	on New Year's Eve?

- Use *used to* in affirmative statements.
- Use *use to* in negative statements with *didn't*, in *Yes/No* questions, and in information questions with *did*.
- The forms *used to* and *use to* have the same pronunciation: /'yustu/.

> **!** Do not use *did* in information questions when *who* or *what* is the subject. Use *used to* with these questions.
>
> Who used to take you to school? ✗ Who did used to take you to school? (INCORRECT)

D1 Listening for Form

CD1 T19 Listen to each sentence. Which form of *used to* does the speaker use? Check (✓) the correct column.

	USED TO	*DIDN'T USE TO*	*DID ... USE TO*
1.	✓		
2.		✓	
3.			✓
4.	✓		
5.			✓
6.	✓		
7.		✓	
8.	✓		

D2 Rewriting Statements and Questions with *Used To*

Rewrite these simple past sentences and questions with the correct form of *used to*.

1. They walked to the park every Sunday.

   They used to walk to the park every Sunday.

2. Were you on a baseball team?

   ____

3. I didn't go to the movies very often.

   ____

4. He wasn't a good student in high school.

   ____

5. Did your family rent a beach house every summer?

   ____

6. We visited our parents on weekends.

   ____

D3 Completing Conversations with *Used To*

Complete these conversations with the words in parentheses and the correct form of *used to*. Then practice the conversations with a partner.

Conversation 1

A: Where did you use to live (1) (you/live)?

B: In Chicago. ______ (2) (we/have) an apartment on Lake Shore Drive.

Conversation 2

A: ______ (1) (Satomi/be) Eva's roommate?

B: No, she didn't, but ______ (2) (they/study) English together.

Conversation 3

A: ______ (1) (I/not/like) Kevin.

B: Yeah. ______ (2) (he/not/be) nice to me, but now we are good friends.

E MEANING AND USE 2

The Habitual Past with *Used To*

Think Critically About Meaning and Use

A. Read the sentences and answer the questions below. Then discuss your answers and read the Meaning and Use Notes to check them.

1a. We used to walk five miles to school.
1b. One morning the bus didn't come, and we walked five miles to school.
2a. Mary used to swim. Now she ice skates.
2b. Mary swam every day. She enjoyed it very much.

1. **EVALUATE** Look at 1a and 1b. Which one refers to a repeated action in the past? 1a.
2. **INTERPRET** Look at 2a and 2b. Which suggests that Mary's present situation is different from the past? Which doesn't suggest anything about Mary's present situation? Mary used to swim everyday. She used to enjoy it very much. but now she ice skats.

B. Discuss your answers with the class and read the Meaning and Use Notes to check them.

Meaning and Use Notes

ONLINE PRACTICE

Comparing the Past and the Present

▶ 1A *Used to* suggests that a habit or situation was true in the past, but is not true now. Use *used to* for repeated (or habitual) actions or states that started and finished in the past. Do not use it for actions or states that happened only once. Adverbs of frequency and other time expressions with *used to* emphasize the repeated actions or states.

We often **used to visit** my grandparents during summer vacation. We don't anymore.

Did you **use to travel** a lot for work?

She **used to be** unfriendly. She never smiled.

This city **didn't use to have** a subway system in the old days.

▶ 1B You can use the simple present with time expressions to say how a present situation is different from the past.

I often **used to watch** TV after school. Now I don't have time to do that.

In the 1930s people **used to get** their news from newspapers or the radio. These days most people get their news from TV or the Internet.

E1 Listening for Meaning and Use

▶ Notes 1A, 1B

CD1 T20 **Listen to each statement. Choose the sentence that best follows it.**

1. **a.** Now I'm married and have a son.
   b. I enjoyed having a lot of people in the house.
2. **a.** We added two rooms last year.
   b. Now there isn't enough room.
3. **a.** Now we don't talk to each other.
   b. Now we see each other every day.
4. **a.** We always ate in restaurants together.
   b. Now we eat out twice a week.
5. **a.** Now they don't want to go.
   b. They always complained about their teachers.
6. **a.** I always did everything myself.
   b. We cleaned together every Saturday.
7. **a.** But we changed our minds.
   b. But we decided to have six.

E2 Comparing the Past and the Present

▶ Notes 1A, 1B

Work with a partner. Look at these facts about the past. How is the present different? Write two sentences for each fact. In the first, rewrite the fact using the correct form of *used to*. In the second, use the simple present with a time expression and the word or phrase in parentheses.

1. Few people had cars. (many)
   In the past, few people used to have cars. Now many people have cars.
2. Women didn't work outside the home. (have jobs)
3. Most people didn't go to college. (many)
4. Supermarkets didn't stay open late. (24 hours)
5. People didn't move away from their families. (live far away)
6. Most people got married very young. (many/in their thirties)

E3 Remembering Your Past

▶ Note 1A

Work with a partner. Talk about your past habits and routines. Use *used to* and other simple past verbs.

A: *I used to play basketball after school with my friends. We always had a lot of fun together, but we were extremely competitive.*

B: *I used to travel...*

Think Critically About Meaning and Use

A. Choose the best answer to complete each conversation.

1. A: Did you go to school yesterday?
   B: ________
   a. Yes, I go today.
   b. No, I was sick.

2. A: I went to the soccer game last night.
   B: ________
   a. Who won?
   b. Is it fun?

3. A: When I was young, I used to climb trees.
   B: ________
   a. Did you climb trees?
   b. Did you ever fall out of one?

4. A: Julie finished law school last year.
   B: ________
   a. Is she still in school?
   b. Did she enjoy it?

5. A: It rained here last night.
   B: Really? ________
   a. It didn't rain here.
   b. It isn't raining here.

6. A: She didn't use to live alone.
   B: ________
   a. Did she like living with other people?
   b. Did she like living alone?

B. Discuss these questions in small groups.

1. **EVALUATE** Why are the wrong answers in 1, 2, 4, and 5 wrong?
2. **DRAW A CONCLUSION** In 3 and 6, why does speaker A use *used to*?

Edit

Some of these sentences have errors. Find the errors and correct them.

1. I used to graduate from high school in 1997.
2. We didn't needed any help.
3. Ana taked the cake to Milly.
4. Where did they went?
5. He failed his driving test three times!
6. Who give you a present?
7. When left he?
8. You didn't answer my question.
9. The test were on Saturday.
10. What did happened here?

Write

Write a post for a history class blog. Write your post about a famous person from the past. Follow the steps below to write the blog post. Use the simple past, *used to*, and time expressions.

1. **Brainstorm** Choose a famous person from the 1960s or another time in history. Research this person on the Internet. Take notes about what you want to say. Use these questions to help you.
   - Who is the person? When and where did he or she live?
   - What did he or she do?
   - What were some important events that he or she was involved in?
   - What changes did this person cause? Is anything different today than it was at that time because of this person? How?

2. **Write a First Draft** Before you write your draft, read the checklist below. Write your draft using the simple past, *used to*, and time expressions.

3. **Edit** Read your work and check it against the checklist below. Circle grammar, spelling, and punctuation errors.

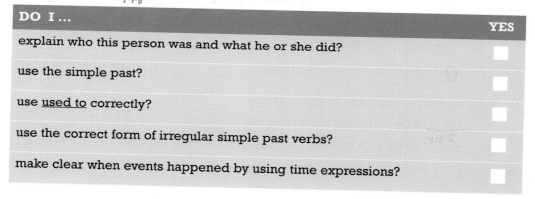

DO I ...	YES
explain who this person was and what he or she did?	☐
use the simple past?	☐
use <u>used to</u> correctly?	☐
use the correct form of irregular simple past verbs?	☐
make clear when events happened by using time expressions?	☐

4. **Peer Review** Work with a partner to help you decide how to fix your errors and improve the content.

5. **Rewrite Your Draft** Using the comments from your partner, write a final draft.

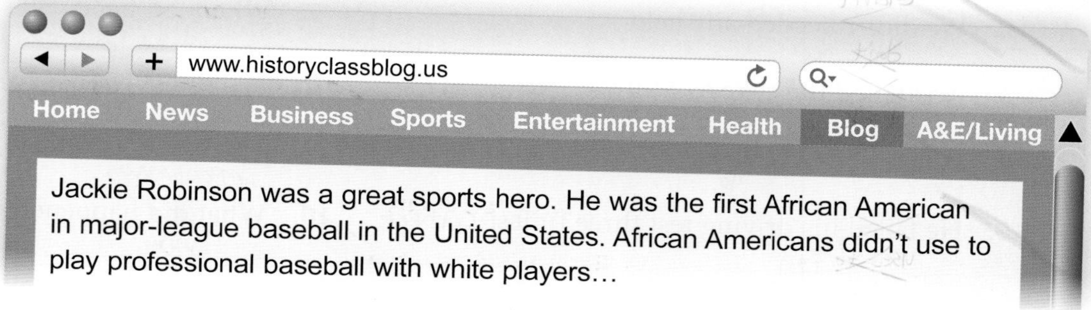

www.historyclassblog.us
Home
News
Business
Sports
Entertainment
Health
Blog
A&E/Living
Jackie Robinson was a great sports hero. He was the first African American in major-league baseball in the United States. African Americans didn't use to play professional baseball with white players…

CHAPTER

5

The Past Continuous and Past Time Clauses

A. GRAMMAR IN DISCOURSE: **Galveston's Killer Hurricane** 70

B. FORM 1: **The Past Continuous** 72

You **were living** there.

C. MEANING AND USE 1: **The Past Continuous** 76

Activities in Progress in the Past

Stative Verbs and the Past Continuous

Beyond the Sentence: Introducing Background Information with the Past Continuous

D. FORM 2: **Past Time Clauses** 80

After the play ended, everyone clapped.

I was eating dinner **when the house collapsed**.

E. MEANING AND USE 2: **Past Time Clauses** 83

Simultaneous Events

Interrupted Events

Events in Sequence

WRITING: **Write About a Natural Disaster** 86

A GRAMMAR IN DISCOURSE

Galveston's Killer Hurricane

A1 Before You Read

Discuss these questions.

Do you have bad storms where you live? Do they cause a lot of damage? What do people in your city or town do to prepare for bad weather?

A2 Read

CD1 T21 **Read this excerpt from a history textbook to find out about how much damage occurred during the worst storm in U.S. history.**

Galveston's Killer Hurricane

The worst weather disaster in the history of the United States was a hurricane that hit the city of Galveston on September 8, 1900. Galveston is on an island near the Texas coast. At that time it was the richest city in Texas, and about 38,000 people were living there.

Galveston before the hurricane

On the morning of Tuesday, September 6, 1900, the head of the Galveston weather station, Isaac Cline, received a telegram about a storm. It was moving north over Cuba and coming toward Galveston. Cline didn't worry when he got the news. Galveston often had bad storms. However, by the next afternoon Cline became concerned. The wind was getting stronger, the ocean waves were getting larger, and the tide was much higher than normal.

On the morning of September 8, Cline began to tell people to leave the island. However, few people listened. Most of them just went to friends' and relatives' houses away from the water. By 4:00 that afternoon, the storm was much worse.

The tide was getting higher and higher when a four-foot wave went through the town. A twenty-foot wave followed it.

Cline was at his house with a lot of other people. While the storm was going on, he was making careful notes of the water's height around his house. Suddenly, a huge wave hit the house and it collapsed. Everyone went into the water. For the next three hours, they floated on the waves. "While we were drifting," he later wrote, "we had to protect ourselves from pieces of wood and other objects that were flying around."

After the storm ended, the city was in ruins. More than 7,000 people were dead. The storm also destroyed more than 3,600 buildings. As a result, the people of Galveston built a seawall. It was 3 miles long, 17 feet high, and 16 feet thick.

Today the people of Galveston depend on weather satellites and other technology to give them hurricane warnings, but they still talk about the great hurricane of 1900.

Galveston after the hurricane

---

collapse: to suddenly fall down
concerned: worried
disaster: an event that causes a lot of damage
drift: to be carried along by moving water
satellite: a man-made object that travels around the Earth and sends back information
tide: the regular rise and fall of the level of the ocean

A3 After You Read

Answer these questions in your notebook.

1. What happened on September 8, 1900?
2. Where is Galveston?
3. What did most of the people of Galveston do before the storm hit?
4. Why did Isaac Cline's house collapse?
5. What did the people of Galveston do to protect themselves from other storms?

B FORM 1

The Past Continuous

Think Critically About Form

A. Look back at the excerpt on page 70 and complete the tasks below.

1. **IDENTIFY** An example of the past continuous is underlined. Find four more examples.
2. **DEFINE** How many words are necessary to form the past continuous? What two forms of the verb *be* are used? What ending is added to the base form of the verb?

B. Discuss your answers with the class and read the Form charts to check them.

ONLINE PRACTICE

AFFIRMATIVE STATEMENTS			
SUBJECT	*WAS/WERE*	BASE FORM OF VERB *-ING*	
I	**was**	**living**	there.
You	**were**		
He She It	**was**		
We You They	**were**		

NEGATIVE STATEMENTS			
SUBJECT	*WAS/WERE* + *NOT*	BASE FORM OF VERB + *-ING*	
I	**was not** **wasn't**	**living**	there.
You	**were not** **weren't**		
He She It	**was not** **wasn't**		
We You They	**were not** **weren't**		

YES/NO QUESTIONS			
WAS/ WERE	SUBJECT	BASE FORM OF VERB + *-ING*	
Were	you	**living**	there?
Was	he		
Were	they		

SHORT ANSWERS					
YES	SUBJECT	*WAS/ WERE*	*NO*	SUBJECT	*WAS/WERE* + *NOT*
Yes,	I	**was.**	**No,**	I	**wasn't.**
	he			he	
	they	**were.**		they	**weren't.**

INFORMATION QUESTIONS			
***WH-* WORD**	***WAS/WERE***	**SUBJECT**	**BASE FORM OF VERB + *-ING***
Who	**were**	you	**watching**?
What	**was**	she	
When			
Where	**were**	they	**traveling**?
Why			
How			

***WH-* WORD (SUBJECT)**	***WAS/WERE***		**BASE FORM OF VERB + *-ING***
Who	**was**		**leaving**?
What			**happening**?

- See Appendix 3 for the spelling of verbs ending in *-ing*.

> **!** Do not use a subject pronoun when *who* or *what* is the subject of an information question.
>
> What was happening? ✗ What was it happening? (INCORRECT)

B1 Listening for Form

CD1 T22 **Listen to these sentences. Choose the verb forms you hear.**

1. **a.** are living
   (b.) were living
   c. was living
2. **a.** wasn't raining
   b. was raining
   c. isn't raining
3. **a.** were leaving
   b. weren't leaving
   c. are leaving
4. **a.** aren't going
   b. were going
   c. weren't going
5. **a.** are … going
   b. were … going
   c. was … going
6. **a.** was … crying
   b. is … crying
   c. wasn't … crying

B2 Forming Statements and *Yes/No* Questions in the Past Continuous

A. **Look at the picture. Write sentences about what the people were doing at Kevin and Kim's house last night.**

1. Paulo and Dan were playing music.
2. Alex was looking paulo and Dan. / was watching a show
3. Myles and Reiko were talking
4. Kevin was opening refrigerator.
5. Kalin and Kim were seeing album.
6. Nicole and Linda were watching TV

B. **Work with a partner. Take turns asking and answering *Yes/No* questions about the people in the picture.**

A: Was Paulo playing the guitar? No, He wasn't.

B: No, he wasn't. He was playing the drums.

B3 Forming Information Questions in the Past Continuous

In your notebook, form information questions from these words and phrases. Punctuate your sentences correctly.

1. four o'clock/happening/what/was/yesterday afternoon/at

   What was happening at four o'clock yesterday afternoon?

2. feeling/how/your/was/grandfather/last night
3. the/this morning/leading/meeting/who/was
4. was/what/Mr. Gonzalez/last semester/teaching
5. you/living/five years ago/were/where
6. Dan and Ben/were/on Saturday/fighting/why

B4 Asking and Answering Information Questions in the Past Continuous

Work with a partner. Take turns asking and answering questions with these time expressions and the past continuous.

1. two hours ago

   A: What were you doing two hours ago?

   B: I was making dinner.

2. at three o'clock yesterday afternoon
3. last night at midnight
4. at seven o'clock this morning
5. at six o'clock yesterday evening
6. ten minutes ago

B5 Building Past Continuous and Simple Past Sentences

Build as many logical sentences as you can in the past continuous or simple past. Use a word or phrase from each column. Punctuate your sentences correctly.

Past Continuous: *Carlos was sleeping.*　　Simple Past: *Carlos had a cold.*

Carlos	was	sleeping
you	had	call
Ana and Rose	didn't	studying
	weren't	a cold
		early

C MEANING AND USE 1

The Past Continuous

Think Critically About Meaning and Use

A. Read the sentences and answer the questions below.

a. This morning I took a walk and then I ate breakfast.
b. At seven o'clock this morning, I was taking a walk and my sister was making breakfast.

1. **EVALUATE** Which sentence shows two past activities in progress at the same time?
2. **EVALUATE** Which sentence shows two completed past activities?

B. Discuss your answers with the class and read the Meaning and Use Notes to check them.

Meaning and Use Notes

ONLINE PRACTICE

Activities in Progress in the Past

▶ 1A Use the past continuous to talk about activities that were in progress (happening) at a specific time in the past. This may be an exact moment in the past or a longer period of time in the past.

It **wasn't raining** at lunchtime. It **was snowing**.

You **were acting** strangely last night.

I **was studying** at Tokyo University in 2010.

▶ 1B The past continuous is often used to talk about several activities that were in progress at the same time.

At six o'clock she **was making** a phone call, and we **were eating** dinner.

▶ 1C The past continuous expresses an ongoing past activity that may or may not be completed. In contrast, the simple past usually expresses a completed past activity.

Past Continuous	Simple Past
At 5:45 Greg **was making** dinner in the kitchen. (He was in the middle of making dinner.)	At 5:45 Greg was in the kitchen. He **made** dinner. Then he washed the dishes. (He completed dinner preparations.)

Stative Verbs and the Past Continuous

▶ **2A** Many stative verbs are used in the simple past but not in the past continuous. Some of these verbs are *know*, *own*, *mean*, *seem*, and *understand*.

Simple Past

I **knew** all the answers.	x I was knowing all the answers. (INCORRECT)
They **owned** three cars in 2008.	x They were owning three cars in 2008. (INCORRECT)

▶ **2B** Some stative verbs are used in the past continuous, but they are used as action verbs with a different meaning. Some of these verbs are *have*, *think*, *taste*, and *weigh*.

Simple Past	Past Continuous
Did you **have** a car?	We **were having** a good time at the basketball game.
(Did you own a car?)	(We were experiencing a good time.)
I **thought** it was a great idea.	I **was thinking** about Jenny recently.
(I believed it was a good idea.)	(Jenny was in my thoughts.)

C1 Listening for Meaning and Use

▶ Notes 1A–1C

CD1 T23 **Listen to each statement. Look at the phrases in the chart. Is the speaker talking about an ongoing past activity or a completed past activity? Check (✓) the correct column.**

		ONGOING	COMPLETED
1.	live in Japan		✓
2.	write a book	✓	
3.	paint the house		✓
4.	fix the air conditioner		✓
5.	write a paper		✓
6.	take flying lessons	✓	

C2 Describing Activities in Progress at the Same Time

▶ Notes 1A–1C

Think about a time when you arrived late for an event. In your notebook, write about what was happening when you arrived. Then read your description to the class.

I arrived at the soccer game late. My favorite team was winning. The crowd was standing and everyone was cheering...

C3 Describing Past Situations

▶ Notes 1A–C, 2A, 2B

A. Complete these conversations with the correct form of the verbs in parentheses. Use the past continuous or the simple past where appropriate.

Conversation 1

Chris: Where were you during the summer of 2007?

Matt: I ___was traveling___ (1) (travel) around the United States.

Chris: How? By plane?

Matt: No, by car. I ___was owning___ (2) (own) a car then.

Conversation 2

Paul: How well ___were___ (1) you ___knowing___ (2) (know) Takeshi before this year?

Eric: Not very well. I ______ (3) (arrive) at school in the middle of the year. Takeshi ___was taking___ (4) (take) several courses at that time, but we ___weren't___ (5) (not/be) in the same classes.

Conversation 3

Josh: You ~~were missing~~ missed (1) (miss) the turn! Now we're on the wrong road.

Amy: Oops. I'm sorry. I ___wasn't pay___ (2) (not/pay) attention. I ___was thinking___ (3) (think) about something else.

Conversation 4

Celia: I ___saw___ (1) (see) Susan at the library yesterday.

Maria: What ___was___ (2) she ___doing___ (3) (do) there?

Celia: She ___was looking___ (4) (look) for information for her English project.

B. Practice the conversations in part A with a partner.

Beyond the Sentence

Introducing Background Information with the Past Continuous

The past continuous and simple past often occur together in the same story. The past continuous is used at the beginning of a story to describe background activities that are happening at the same time as the main events of the story. The simple past is used for main events.

> Yesterday was beautiful. The sun **was shining**, the birds **were singing**, and I **was walking** in a valley. Suddenly, the sky became dark. From nowhere, a storm arrived. The rain fell harder and harder. And there were no buildings nearby.

C4 Introducing Background Information with the Past Continuous

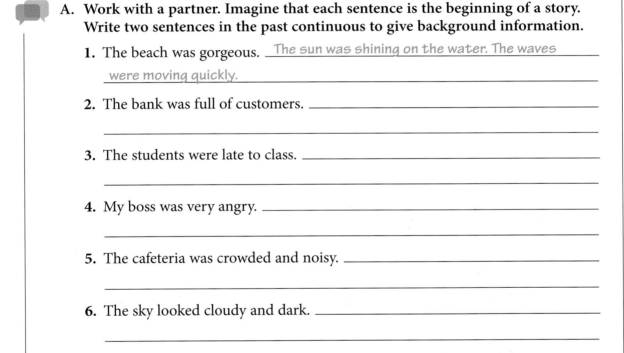

A. Work with a partner. Imagine that each sentence is the beginning of a story. Write two sentences in the past continuous to give background information.

1. The beach was gorgeous. The sun was shining on the water. The waves were moving quickly.
2. The bank was full of customers. ______
3. The students were late to class. ______
4. My boss was very angry. ______
5. The cafeteria was crowded and noisy. ______
6. The sky looked cloudy and dark. ______

B. Complete one of the story beginnings in part A. Use the past continuous to add more background information, and use the simple past for main events.

> The beach was gorgeous. The sun was shining on the water. The waves were moving quickly. Suddenly, a swimmer yelled for help. A lifeguard dove into the water...

D FORM 2

Past Time Clauses

Think Critically About Form

A. Read the sentences and complete the tasks below.

a. At that time, Galveston was the richest city in Texas.
b. Cline didn't worry when he got the news.
c. After the storm ended, the city was in ruins.

1. **IDENTIFY** Underline the verbs. Which sentences have two verbs?
2. **RECOGNIZE** Look at the sentences with two verbs. Each verb is part of a clause. There is a main clause and a past time clause. A past time clause begins with a word such as *before, when, while,* or *after*. Circle the past time clauses.

B. Discuss your answers with the class and read the Form charts to check them.

ONLINE PRACTICE

SENTENCES WITH PAST TIME CLAUSES

PAST TIME CLAUSE			MAIN CLAUSE	
	SUBJECT	VERB	SUBJECT	VERB
Before	**the storm**	**hit,**	everyone	was sleeping.
When	**the house**	**collapsed,**	I	was eating dinner.
While	**I**	**was sleeping,**	the phone	rang.
After	**the play**	**ended,**	everyone	clapped.

POSITION OF PAST TIME CLAUSES

PAST TIME CLAUSE	MAIN CLAUSE
When the house collapsed,	I was eating dinner.
After the play ended,	everyone clapped.

MAIN CLAUSE	PAST TIME CLAUSE
I was eating dinner	**when the house collapsed.**
Everyone clapped	**after the play ended.**

Overview

- A clause is a group of words that has a subject and a verb.
- A main clause can stand alone as a complete sentence.
- A dependent clause cannot stand alone and must be used with a main clause.

Past Time Clauses

- Past time clauses are dependent clauses. They begin with words such as *before, when, while,* and *after*.
- The verbs in a past time clause and main clause can be in the simple past or in the past continuous.
- A past time clause can come before or after the main clause with no change in meaning. If the past time clause comes first, it is separated from the main clause by a comma.

D1 Listening for Form

CD1 T24 **Listen to these sentences. Write the past time clauses you hear.**

1. Some people left town ___before the storm began___.
2. The weather forecaster warned us about the storm ___before it hit___.
3. ___After the people left___, the tornado hit the house.
4. ___When the storm began___, we went into the basement.
5. The river overflowed ___when it rained___.
6. The sky was beautiful ___after the storm indeed?___.

D2 Forming Sentences with Past Time Clauses

Match the clauses to make logical sentences. Pay attention to punctuation.

__f__ **1.** He went to bed	**a.** several people were still outside.
__a__ **2.** When the storm hit,	**b.** while I was waiting for the train.
__e__ **3.** After we visited Chicago,	**c.** he made a speech.
__b__ **4.** I made a phone call	**d.** when he was taking her picture.
__c__ **5.** Before Steve gave Alan the award,	**e.** we went to Cleveland.
__d__ **6.** She closed her eyes	**f.** before I came home.

D3 Practicing Punctuation with Past Time Clauses

Read this paragraph. Underline the time clauses. Add commas where necessary.

A terrible storm hit last night while my friend was staying at my house. All the lights went out when lightning struck the house. While I was looking for matches, I tripped over a rug. I heard a knock on the door. I went to the door and answered it. A strange man was standing outside. He was wearing a hood. The wind was blowing the trees back and forth while the storm was raging. When I saw the stranger, I became nervous. Then, when he began to speak, I recognized his voice. It was my friend's father.

D4 Changing the Position of Past Time Clauses

Change the order of the clauses in these sentences. Add or delete commas where necessary.

1. Alex saw Maria when he went to the laundromat.
   When Alex went to the laundromat, he saw Maria.
2. While Reiko was swimming, she got a cramp in her leg.
   She got a cramp in her leg while Reiko was swimming.
3. When my sister woke up this morning, she ate pizza for breakfast.
   She ate pizza breakfast when my sister woke up
4. It started to rain while I was driving to work.
   While I was driving to work, It started to rain.
5. Eva became a lawyer after she finished high school.
   After she finised high school, Eva became a lawyer.

E MEANING AND USE 2

Past Time Clauses

Think Critically About Meaning and Use

A. Read the sentences and complete the tasks below.

a. I was taking a nap when the mailman knocked on the door.
b. I put on suntan lotion before I went to the beach.
c. We were playing soccer while Josh was studying for an exam.

1. **EVALUATE** Which sentence shows that two events were happening at exactly the same time?
2. **EVALUATE** Which sentence shows that one event interrupted the other?
3. **EVALUATE** Which sentence shows that one event happened after the other?

B. Discuss your answers with the class and read the Meaning and Use Notes to check them.

Meaning and Use Notes

ONLINE PRACTICE

Simultaneous Events

▶ 1 Sentences with past time clauses describe the order in which two past events occurred. When the verbs in both the time clause and the main clause are in the past continuous, the events were simultaneous (happening at exactly the same time). *When* or *while* introduces the time clause.

Past Continuous	Past Continuous
When I was sleeping,	the children were watching TV.
I was sleeping	**while the children were watching TV.**

Interrupted Events

▶ 2 When one verb is in the simple past and the other is in the past continuous, it shows that one event interrupted the other. The event in the past continuous started first and was interrupted by the simple past event. *When* or *while* begins the time clause, which uses the past continuous.

Past Continuous (First Event)	Simple Past (Second Event)
When I was sleeping,	the telephone rang.
While I was sleeping,	the telephone rang.

(Continued on page 84)

Events in Sequence

▶ 3 When the verbs in both the time clause and the main clause are in the simple past, one event happened after the other (in sequence). *Before*, *when*, or *after* introduces the time clause and indicates the order of events.

Simple Past (First Event)	Simple Past (Second Event)
I walked past my sister	**before I recognized her.**
When the phone rang,	I answered it.
After he gave me the diploma,	I shook his hand.

E1 Listening for Meaning and Use

▶ Notes 1–3

CD1 T25 **Listen to each conversation. Is the second speaker talking about simultaneous events, an interrupted event, or events in sequence? Check (✓) the correct column.**

	SIMULTANEOUS	INTERRUPTED	IN SEQUENCE
1.		✓	
2.			
3.			
4.			
5.			

E2 Understanding Time Clauses

▶ Notes 2, 3

Work with a partner. Discuss why these sentences are not logical. Then change the time clause in each sentence to make it logical.

1. Before Carlos threw the ball, I caught it.

   A: Sentence 1 isn't logical. You can't catch a ball before someone throws it.

   B: It should be "After Carlos threw the ball, I caught it."

2. While Ben found his car keys, he drove away.
3. When the sun came up, it was very dark.
4. Everyone listened before he began to talk.
5. After we went swimming, they filled the pool with water.

E3 Writing About Events in Sequence

▶ Note 3

Read each situation. Then complete each sentence with a clause in the simple past.

1. Silvio and Maria bought a new house last month.

   Before they bought the house, they saved a lot of money.

   When they saw the house for the first time, ______________________________

   After they moved in, ______________________________

2. Megan went to a great concert last night.

   Before she went to the concert, ______________________________

   When she arrived at the concert, ______________________________

   After she left the concert, ______________________________

3. Paul traveled to Europe last summer for his vacation.

   Before ______________________________

   When ______________________________

   After ______________________________

E4 Expressing Simultaneous, Interrupted, and Sequential Events

▶ Notes 1–3

Complete the time clauses. Use the simple past or the past continuous.

1. Donna and I made dinner together last night. While Donna was chopping the vegetables, I was baking a cake for dessert.
2. We were watching the movie when ______________________________
3. I'm sorry I didn't answer the phone this morning. It rang while ______________________________

   ____
4. Last night while I was watching TV, ______________________________
5. At first Lauren wasn't a good student. After ______________________________

   ______________________________, her grades improved.
6. Why did you leave class so early? It was so interesting! After you left,

   ____

WRITING Write About a Natural Disaster

Think Critically About Meaning and Use

A. Read each sentence and answer the questions that follow with ***Yes, No,*** or ***It's not clear***.

1. We ran out of the building when the fire alarm started to ring.

___Yes___ a. Were they in the building before the fire alarm started to ring?

___No___ b. After the fire alarm rang, did they stay in the building for a long time?

2. Lynn was sleeping while Holly was cleaning the house.

___No___ a. Did Lynn help Holly clean the house?

___yes___ b. Did Lynn fall asleep before Holly started cleaning the house?

3. Luis saw Jake this morning. He was walking down the street.

___No___ a. Did Luis walk down the street with Jake?

___Yes___ b. Did Jake continue walking after Luis saw him?

4. Jake was working on the roof when he fell off.

___yes___ a. Did he hurt himself badly?

___yes___ b. Did he work after he fell?

5. When he left the house, he wasn't carrying his umbrella.

___No___ a. Did he take his umbrella with him?

___yes___ b. Was it raining when he left the house?

6. The fire started after we left the building.

___No___ a. Were we in danger?

___No___ b. Did we start the fire?

7. She was unlocking the door when she heard a loud noise.

___No___ a. Did she hear the noise before she unlocked the door?

___yes___ b. Did she hear the noise at the same time as she was unlocking the door?

8. Don was waiting in the car while Helen was buying stamps.

___No___ a. Did Don go into the post office?

___No___ b. Did Don and Helen both buy stamps?

9. Mike left before the game ended.

   ______ a. Did Mike see the end of the game?

   ______ b. Did the game end after Mike left?

B. Discuss these questions in small groups.

1. **ANALYZE** If we change both verbs in 7 to the simple past, how does the meaning of this sentence change?
2. **GENERATE** Create a sentence with two past continuous verbs and a sentence with one past continuous and one simple past verb.

Edit

Some of these sentences have errors. Find the errors and correct them.

1. I feel terrible. I was breaking my favorite necklace when I put it on this morning.
2. I'm so sorry about your mug. I was dropping it.
3. They were owning a house before they had children.
4. It snowing when we went to school.
5. While we were shopping, they were cleaning the house.
6. After he was throwing the ball, it hit the window.
7. What did he say to you while you watched the movie?
8. Where were you going when I was seeing you yesterday?
9. She was reading after she fell asleep.
10. He hit his head when he had the car accident.

Write

Write a paragraph about a hurricane, flood, or other natural disaster. Follow the steps below to write the paragraph. Use the simple past and the past continuous.

1. **BRAINSTORM** Think of some recent and past natural disasters. Research one of these disasters. Take notes. Use these questions to help you.
   - What was the disaster? When and where did it occur?
   - What, if anything, did people do to prepare for the disaster?
   - What did they do when the disaster struck?
   - What damage occurred during the disaster?
   - What happened after the disaster?

2. **WRITE A FIRST DRAFT** Before you write your draft, read the checklist below and look at the reading on page 70. Write your draft using the simple past and the past continuous.

3. **EDIT** Read your work and check it against the checklist below. Circle grammar, spelling, and punctuation errors.

DO I ...	YES
give the basic information and some details about the disaster?	☐
use the simple past?	☐
use the past continuous?	☐
use the simple past for stative verbs?	☐
include at least one sentence with a time clause?	☐
use correct punctuation in sentences with time clauses?	☐

4. **PEER REVIEW** Work with a partner to decide how to fix your errors and improve the content.

5. **REWRITE YOUR DRAFT** Using comments from your partner, write a final draft.

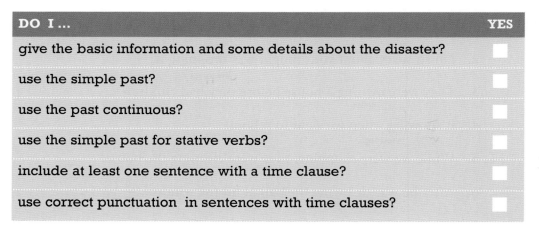

A terrible earthquake hit my country last year. When it hit, people were working at their jobs and children were studying at school. It seemed like a normal day...

CHAPTER

6

The Present Perfect

A. **GRAMMAR IN DISCOURSE: Tales of a World Traveler** 90

B. **FORM: The Present Perfect** 92

She **has traveled** to Paris.

Informally Speaking: Reduced Forms of *Have* and *Has*

C. **MEANING AND USE 1: Continuing Time Up to Now** 97

Continuing Time Up to Now

For* and *Since

D. **MEANING AND USE 2: Indefinite Past Time** 100

Indefinite Past Time

Using *Ever* with Indefinite Past Time

Vocabulary Notes: More Adverbs with the Present Perfect

WRITING: Write About Someone You Admire . . . 106

PART 2 TEST: The Past 109

A GRAMMAR IN DISCOURSE

Tales of a World Traveler

A1 Before You Read

Discuss these questions.

Do you like to travel? What are some good and bad things about traveling? Name some countries you have visited. Where else do you want to go?

A2 Read

CD1 T26 **Read this online magazine article to find out about world traveler Charles Veley.**

Travel

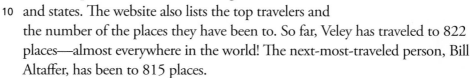

The World's Most-Traveled Man

Charles Veley is only in his mid-40s, but he has been to more places than anyone else in the world. You can see this on the website of the group he started, Most Traveled People. Members of this group have listed the world's places—872 of them, including all the countries plus islands, territories, regions, and states. The website also lists the top travelers and the number of the places they have been to. So far, Veley has traveled to 822 places—almost everywhere in the world! The next-most-traveled person, Bill Altaffer, has been to 815 places.

When Veley was a boy, he wanted to travel, but he never left the United States—his family didn't have much money. But things changed. As a young man, he started a software company and became a millionaire. When he was 25, he got married, and he and his wife Kimberly decided to travel around the world for a year. They had a great time, so one year became four. And Veley has traveled ever since.

Veley has experienced it all! He's traveled 1,686,953 miles. He's traveled to remote places. For example, he went to Bouvet Island, near Antarctica. Very few people have ever been there. He's faced danger.

For example, his canoe tipped over in the Zambezi River. The river was filled with hippopotamuses.

Where hasn't Veley been? The very few places include Navassa Island, a small island in the Caribbean; Oeno Island, a small island in the South Pacific; and Jan Mayen, in the Arctic.

Not surprisingly, Veley has many favorite places, all over the world. These include Lord Howe Island, Australia; Kauai, Hawaii; and the Lauterbrunnen Valley, in Switzerland.

How has he done it? Having the money to travel, of course, is part of the answer. Veley has spent a little over $1 million just for plane tickets! Another part, he says, is being patient and having a good attitude. Veley has learned a lot from his travels, and he has this advice for other travelers:

- "Travel light—pack only the basics." Many of Veley's best experiences (and souvenirs) have come because he needed something."
- "Each place has its own beauty. You need to go there and discover it."
- "Go everywhere at least twice." Veley follows his own advice. He has returned to places again and again to make new discoveries.

---

canoe: a light, narrow kind of boat
hippopotamus: a large, heavy African animal, often in water
patience: the quality of being able to deal with delays and problems in a calm way
remote: very far from other places
territory: an area of land that belongs to a country

A3 After You Read

A. Circle the places that Charles Veley has *not* visited.

Bouvet Island	**Lauterbrunnen Valley**	**Oeno Island**
Jan Mayen	**Lord Howe Island**	**Navassa Island**

B. Match each number with the correct description.

_a_ **1.** 872
____ **2.** a little over 1 million
____ **3.** 822
____ **4.** 815
____ **5.** 1,686,953

a. the number of places Most Traveled People has listed on its website
b. the number of places Bill Altaffer has visited
c. the number of miles Charles Veley has traveled
d. the amount of money Charles Veley has spent on plane tickets
e. the number of places Charles Veley has visited

B FORM

The Present Perfect

Think Critically About Form

A. Read the sentences and complete the tasks below.

1a. He has crossed the Atlantic many times.
1b. He crossed the Atlantic in 2009.

2a. They flew to Paris last night.
2b. They have flown to Paris many times.

1. **IDENTIFY** Which two sentences are in the simple past? Which two sentences are in the present perfect? How many words are necessary to form the present perfect?
2. **RECOGNIZE** Underline the verb forms that follow *has* and *have*. These are past participles. Which form resembles the simple past? Which form is irregular?
3. **LABEL** Look back at the article on page 90. Find five examples of the present perfect.

B. Discuss your answers with the class and read the Form charts to check them.

ONLINE PRACTICE

AFFIRMATIVE STATEMENTS			
SUBJECT	***HAVE/HAS***	**PAST PARTICIPLE**	
I You	**have**	**traveled** **flown**	to Paris.
He She It	**has**		
We You They	**have**		

NEGATIVE STATEMENTS				
SUBJECT	***HAVE/HAS***	***NOT***	**PAST PARTICIPLE**	
I You	**have**	**not**	**traveled** **flown**	to Paris.
He She It	**has**			
We You They	**have**			

CONTRACTIONS		
I**'ve**	**traveled**	to Paris.
She**'s**		
They**'ve**		

CONTRACTIONS			
I	**haven't**	**traveled**	to Paris.
She	**hasn't**		
They	**haven't**		

YES/NO QUESTIONS			
HAVE/ HAS	**SUBJECT**	**PAST PARTICIPLE**	
Have	you	**traveled** **flown**	to Paris?
Has	he		
Have	they		

SHORT ANSWERS					
YES	**SUBJECT**	***HAVE/ HAS***	***NO***	***SUBJECT***	***HAVE/HAS + NOT***
Yes,	I	**have**.	**No,**	I	**haven't**.
	he	**has**.		he	**hasn't**.
	they	**have**.		they	**haven't**.

INFORMATION QUESTIONS				
***WH-* WORD**	***HAVE/HAS***	**SUBJECT**	**PAST PARTICIPLE**	
Who	**have**	you	**seen**?	
What				
Why	**has**	she	**been**	in the hospital?
How long	**have**	they		
***WH-* WORD (SUBJECT)**	***HAS***	**SUBJECT**	**PAST PARTICIPLE**	
Who	has		**traveled**	to Paris?
What			**happened**?	

- The past participle of a regular verb has the same form as the simple past (verb + *-d/ -ed*). See Appendices 4 and 5 for the spelling and pronunciation of verbs ending in *-ed*.
- Irregular verbs have special past participle forms. See Appendix 6 for a list of irregular verbs and their past participles.

! Do not confuse the contraction of *is* with the contraction of *has* in the present perfect.

He**'s traveling** a lot = He is traveling a lot.

He**'s traveled** a lot = He has traveled a lot.

- See Appendix 16 for more contractions with *have*.

! Do not use a subject pronoun in information questions when the *wh-* word is the subject.

What has happened? **X** What has it happened? (INCORRECT)

B1 Listening for Form

CD1 T27 **Listen to these sentences. Write the present perfect verb forms you hear. You will hear both contracted and full forms.**

1. I ___have worked___ here for three years.
2. We ______________ Yuji since August.
3. I'm sorry. Mr. O'Neill ______________ for the day.
4. Our class ______________ the exam yet.
5. It ______________ every day this week!
6. Don't leave yet. You ______________ your breakfast.

B2 Working on Irregular Past Verb Forms

Complete the chart. See Appendix 6 if you need help.

	BASE FORM	SIMPLE PAST	PAST PARTICIPLE
1.	know	knew	known
2.		got	
3.			taken
4.		bought	
5.	leave		
6.			cost
7.		showed	
8.	be		
9.			gone
10.	eat		
11.			made
12.		did	
13.		saw	
14.			thought
15.		grew	
16.			spent

Informally Speaking

Reduced Forms of *Have* and *Has*

CD1 T28 Look at the cartoon and listen to the conversation. How is the underlined form in the cartoon different from what you hear?

Wow... Sandra has changed a lot!
She's gotten her hair cut. She looks great!

In informal speech, we often reduce *have* and *has* with names and other nouns.

Standard Form	What You Might Hear
Mark **has** changed.	"/mɑrks/ changed."
The cities **have** grown.	"The /ˈsɪtizəv/ grown."

We also often reduce *have* and *has* with *wh-* words in informal speech.

Standard Form	What You Might Hear
Why **has** he left?	"/waɪz/ he left?"
Where **have** you been?	"/ˈwɛrəv/ you been?"

B3 Understanding Informal Speech

CD1 T29 **Listen and complete these sentences with the standard form of the words you hear.**

1. John ___has been___ here for a long time.
2. Kedra and Rick ________________ the movie already.
3. Paul ________________ a new racing bicycle.
4. The guests ________________ home.
5. The police ________________ the thief.
6. Where ________________ she ________________?
7. Fresno ________________ bigger since the 1930s.
8. Why ________________ it ________________ so long?

B4 Completing Conversations with the Present Perfect

A. Complete these conversations with the words in parentheses and the present perfect. Use contractions where possible.

Conversation 1

Silvio: How long ____have____ (1) you ____lived____ (2) (live) here?

Victor: Five years. ________ (3) you ________ (4) (be) here long?

Silvio: No, I ________ (5) (not). I ________ (6) only ________ (7) (be) here for six months.

Conversation 2

Gina: Hi, Julie. I ________ (1) (not/see) you for a long time.

Julie: Hi, Gina. I think it ________ (2) (be) almost three years since we last met. How ________ (3) your family ________ (4) (be)?

Gina: Oh, there ________ (5) (be) a lot of changes. My older brother, Chris, ________ (6) (get) married, and Tony and his wife, Marta, ________ (7) (have) two children.

B. Practice the conversations in part A with a partner.

B5 Building Sentences

A. Build eight logical sentences: four in the present perfect and four in the simple past. Punctuate your sentences correctly.

Present Perfect: *She has been a good friend.*
Simple Past: *She went to a restaurant.*

she	have	been	for a long time
they	has	waited	to a restaurant
		learned	a good friend
		went	English

B. Rewrite your sentences as negative statements.

C

MEANING AND USE 1

Continuing Time Up to Now

Think Critically About Meaning and Use

A. Read the sentences and answer the questions below.

1a. Hiro has lived in New York since 1989.

1b. Hiro lived in Chicago for three years.

2a. Rosa has been a teacher for ten years.

2b. Rosa was a nurse for one year.

1. **ANALYZE** Which sentences show situations that began and ended in the past? What tense do they use?
2. **ANALYZE** Which sentences show situations that began in the past and have continued up to the present time. What tense do they use?

B. Discuss your answers with the class and read the Meaning and Use Notes to check them.

Meaning and Use Notes

ONLINE PRACTICE

Continuing Time Up to Now

▶ **1** The present perfect connects the past with the present. Use the present perfect for actions or states that began in the past and have continued up to the present time. These actions or states may continue into the future.

He**'s worked** here for five years.

She**'s lived** in the same town since 2001.

For and *Since*

Sentences expressing continuing time up to now often use *for* and *since*.

▶ **2A** *For* + a length of time tells how long an action or state has continued up to the present time.

I've worked here **for** a long time.

I've lived here **for** ten years.

▶ **2B** *Since* + a point in time tells when an action or state began.

I've worked here **since** 2000.

I've been here **since** Tuesday.

Since can also introduce a time clause. When it does, the verb in the time clause is usually in the simple past.

I've lived here **since** I was 20.

I've worked here **since** I left home.

C1 Listening for Meaning and Use

▶ Note 1

CD1 T30 Listen to each sentence. Is the speaker talking about a past situation that continues to the present, or a situation that began and ended in the past? Check (✓) the correct column.

	PAST SITUATION THAT CONTINUES TO THE PRESENT	SITUATION THAT BEGAN AND ENDED IN THE PAST
1.	✓	
2.		
3.		
4.		
5.		
6.		
7.		
8.		

C2 Contrasting *For* and *Since*

▶ Note 2

A. Complete these sentences with *for* or *since*.

1. Alex has climbed mountains ___since___ he was 15 years old.
2. They've been out of town __________ Saturday.
3. My boss has been in a meeting __________ a long time.
4. He has worked in Brazil __________ last September.
5. That restaurant has been closed __________ a week now.
6. I've known Matt __________ we were in high school.
7. They've studied French __________ a few months.
8. Lisa has lived in New York __________ ten years.
9. Keiko has liked winter sports __________ she was a child.
10. We've been here __________ half an hour.

B. **Use these words and phrases to write sentences. Use the present perfect with *for* or *since*.**

1. Sue/live/Rome/2009

   Sue has lived in Rome since 2009. ______________________

2. Betty/work/at Happy Systems/ten years

   ____

3. Paul/study/French/two semesters

   ____

4. I/be married/to Kalin/last August

   ____

5. Liz and Sheryl/know/Celia/many years

   ____

C3 Talking About How Long

▶ Notes 1–2

A. **Work with a partner. Look at the timeline. Use the phrases below and the present perfect to ask and answer questions about Gary's life. Use contractions where possible.**

be a U.S. citizen	**have a business**	**live in the U.S.**
be married	**know his best friend**	**own a house**

A: How long has he been a U.S. citizen?

B: He's been a U.S. citizen since 2003. OR *He's been a U.S. citizen for . . . years*

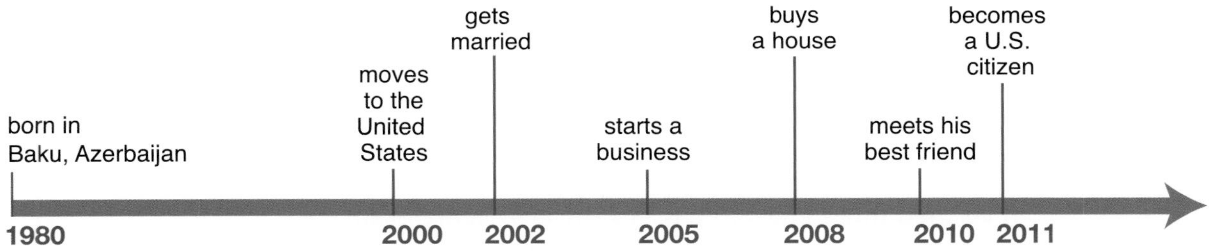

B. **Make a list of questions about your partner's life. Use the present perfect with *for* and *since*. Take turns asking and answering each other's questions. Use contractions where possible.**

A: How long have you studied English?

B: I've studied English for five years.

B: How long have you lived in this city?

A: I've lived here since 2010.

D MEANING AND USE 2

Indefinite Past Time

Think Critically About Meaning and Use

Read the sentences and answer the questions below.

1a. I've flown in an airplane.
1b. I flew to Rome last month.

2a. There have been many car accidents on this road.
2b. There was an accident here yesterday.

1. **EVALUATE** Which sentences talk about an indefinite (not exact) time in the past? Which form of the verb is used in these sentences?
2. **EVALUATE** Which sentences talk about a definite (exact) time in the past? Which form of the verb is used in these sentences?

B. Discuss your answers with the class and read the Meaning and Use Notes to check them.

Meaning and Use Notes

ONLINE PRACTICE

Indefinite Past Time

▶ 1A Use the present perfect to talk about actions or states that happened at an indefinite (not exact) time in the past.

A: Have you met Bob?
B: Yes, I**'ve met** him. He's really nice.

▶ 1B Actions or states in the present perfect can happen once or repeatedly.

He**'s visited** Hawaii <u>once</u>.
I've tried <u>three times</u> to pass my driver's license exam.

▶ 1C Do not use the present perfect with time expressions that express a definite (exact) time in the past. When you mention the definite time an event happened, use the simple past.

I **went** to Europe in 2009. x I've gone to Europe in 2009. (INCORRECT)

Using *Ever* with Indefinite Past Time

▶ 2 The adverb *ever* means "at any time." Use *ever* in present perfect questions to ask if an action took place at any time in the past.

A: **Have** you **ever been** in a helicopter?

B: Yes, I have. OR
No, I haven't.

> ! We usually do not use *ever* in present perfect affirmative statements.
> I have been in a helicopter. X I have ever been in a helicopter. (INCORRECT)

D1 Listening for Meaning and Use

▶ Notes 1A, 1C

CD1 T31 **Listen to each sentence. Does it refer to a definite time in the past or an indefinite time in the past? Check (✓) the correct column.**

	DEFINITE TIME IN THE PAST	INDEFINITE TIME IN THE PAST
1.		✓
2.		
3.		
4.		
5.		
6.		
7.		
8.		
9.		
10.		

D2 Contrasting Definite and Indefinite Past Time

▶ Notes 1A–1C

A. Each of these situations begins with a sentence about the indefinite past. Complete the second sentence with an example expressing the definite past.

1. I've met a lot of famous people. For example, last year I _spoke to Bill Gates in an elevator at the Plaza Hotel._
2. I've met some interesting people since I moved here. For example, this year I ______________
3. My friend has done a lot of crazy things. Last month ______________
4. My parents have helped me a lot. When I was younger, they ______________
5. I had a difficult professor a while ago. For example, once ______________

B. Now write sentences about an indefinite time in the past. Use the present perfect to introduce each situation.

1. _My parents have traveled a lot_. Last summer they went to Thailand and South Korea, and they visited Brazil and Peru in October.
2. ______________. He worked in a restaurant for one year, he sold cars for six months, and he worked as a bank teller for only one month!
3. ______________. She danced in a Broadway musical last December, and she sang in another show in Chicago this year.
4. ______________. This morning I cleaned the house, washed the clothes, and even worked in the garden!
5. ______________. They lived in Venezuela for two years, they stayed in Mexico for six months, they lived in Seattle for one year, and now they live in Tucson, Arizona.

D3 Asking Questions About Indefinite Past Time ▶ Notes 1A, 2

Write two *Yes/No* questions for each of these situations. Use the present perfect.

1. Your friends have traveled a lot. You want to find out about their trips.

   Have you ever been to Egypt? Have you seen the pyramids?

2. You are thinking about buying a used car. You meet a woman who is trying to sell her car.

   ____

3. You want to hire a babysitter. You are interviewing a teenager for the job.

   ____

4. You are looking for a new roommate. Someone comes to see your apartment.

   ____

5. Your friend, Lee, has moved to a new town. You want to find out about his experiences.

   ____

D4 Describing Progress ▶ Notes 1A, 1B

Paul has made a list of things to do before he moves to his new apartment. Look at the list and make statements about his progress so far.

He's called the moving company.

He hasn't cleaned the apartment.

TO DO

✔ call the moving company

clean apartment

✔ Disconnect computer

Pack clothes

Throw away trash

Contact the post office

✔ call mom and give her new address

say goodbye to neighbors

Leave key with superintendent

Vocabulary Notes

More Adverbs with the Present Perfect

Never means "not ever" or "not at any time." We can use *never* instead of *not* in negative statements. Do not use *never* with *not*. *Never* comes before the past participle.

She has **never** been to Greece.

Already means "at some time before now." Use *already* with questions and affirmative statements. It comes before the past participle or at the end of a sentence.

She has **already** left. Have they **already** eaten? What has he **already** done?
She has left **already**. Have they eaten **already**? What has he done **already**?

Yet means "up to now." Use *yet* with negative statements and *Yes/No* questions. It comes at the end of a sentence.

They haven't arrived **yet**. Have you met him **yet**?

Still also means "up to now." It has a similar meaning to *yet*, but with the present perfect is used only in negative statements. It comes before *have* or *has*.

She **still** hasn't called. (= She hasn't called **yet**.)

So far means "at any time up to now." Use *so far* in affirmative and negative statements and in questions. It comes at the beginning or end of a sentence.

So far he's spent $500. How much money have you spent **so far**?
So far I haven't had a good time. Have you had a good time **so far**?

D5 Using Adverbs with the Present Perfect

A. **Rewrite these sentences. Place the word or words in parentheses in an appropriate position in each sentence. Use contractions where possible.**

Conversation 1

A: Have you asked Sheryl to help you (yet)?
Have you asked Sheryl to help you yet? (1)

B: No, I haven't asked her (still).
________________ (2)

Conversation 2

A: Have you played golf (ever)?

____
1

B: No, I've played golf (never).

____
2

Conversation 3

A: Has she bought the tickets (yet)?

____
1

B: No. She's made the reservations (already), but I don't think that she has paid for the tickets (yet).

____
2

Conversation 4

A: How's the fund drive going? Have you raised any money (yet)?

____
1

B: Yes. We've raised $2,000 (so far). We haven't finished (still).

____
2

Conversation 5

A: Has Rick left (yet)?

____
1

B: Yes, he has left (already).

____
2

Conversation 6

A: Have you made any friends at school (yet)?

____
1

B: No, I've been too busy (so far).

____
2

B. Practice the conversations in part A with a partner.

Think Critically About Meaning and Use

A. Choose the best answer to complete each conversation.

1. A: He visited Sweden four years ago.
B: ___________
a. Where is he staying?
(b.) Did he have a good time?

2. A: Emily has worked for the school for a long time.
B: ___________
a. Is she going to retire soon?
b. Why did she leave?

3. A: I've already cooked dinner.
B: ___________
a. Can I help you?
b. What did you cook?

4. A: It has rained only once this month.
B: ___________
a. Does it usually rain more?
b. Has it rained a lot?

5. A: I haven't been to Europe yet.
B: ___________
a. Do you want to go sometime?
b. When did you go?

6. A: Have you ever flown a plane?
B: ___________
a. No, I didn't.
b. No, not yet.

7. A: So far I've spent $100 on course books.
B: ___________
a. Do you think you'll need to buy more?
b. You're lucky you don't need any more.

B. Discuss these questions in small groups.

1. **EVALUATE** In 2 and 3, can speaker A use the simple past instead of the present perfect? If so, does the meaning change?

2. **EXPLAIN** Look at 2, 3, 5, and 7. How does Speaker A use the present perfect: for time up to now or the indefinite past?

Edit

Find the errors in this paragraph and correct them. Use the simple present, the simple past, and the present perfect.

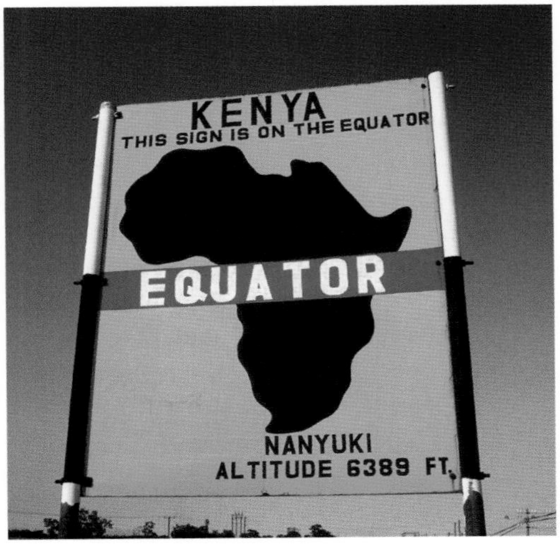

Rita and Bob ~~have been~~ are the most-traveled people I know. They went almost everywhere. Rita has been a photographer, and Bob has been a travel writer, so they often travel for work. They been to many countries, such as Nepal and India. They have also travel to Turkey, Greece, and Bulgaria. They have see some places yet, though. For example, they still haven't visited New Zealand. This year they've been already away from home a total of three months, and it has been only June. In January Rita has gone to Kenya while Bob has toured Indonesia. Then they both have traveled to Argentina and Norway. Right now they're at home. They were here for two weeks already. Two weeks at home is like a vacation for Rita and Bob.

Write

Write a paragraph about someone you admire. Follow the steps below. Use the present perfect.

1. **Brainstorm** Think about a person you admire. This person must still be alive. He or she can be someone you know or someone you know about. Take notes about what you want to say. Use these questions to help you.
   - Who is this person and why do you admire him or her?
   - What are some basic facts of this person's life? For example, where has this person lived and worked?
   - What has the person done that seems special to you? For example, has he or she worked somewhere special or helped other people?
   - How has the person influenced you?

2. **Write a First Draft** Before you write your draft, read the checklist below. Write your draft using the present perfect, the simple past, and simple present.

3. **Edit** Read your work and check it against the checklist below. Circle grammar, spelling, and punctuation errors.

DO I ...	YES
describe what this person has done and show why I admire him or her?	☐
use the present perfect?	☐
use the simple past?	☐
use the simple present?	☐
include *for, since,* and adverbs with the present perfect?	☐

4. **Peer Review** Work with a partner to help you decide how to fix your errors and improve the content.

5. **Rewrite Your Draft** Using the comments from your partner, write a final draft.

I admire my uncle Tomás. He is a doctor. He has worked with poor people since he graduated from college twenty years ago...

PART 2 TEST | The Past

Choose the correct word or words to complete each sentence.

1. Who __________ the Nobel Peace Prize in 2001?
   a. win **b.** won **c.** used to win **d.** use to win
2. Did New York __________ be the capital of the United States?
   a. used to **b.** use to **c.** did **d.** was
3. My aunt and uncle __________ a new house near the beach last year.
   a. has bought **b.** bought **c.** buys **d.** is buying
4. Have you __________ your report yet?
   a. wrote **b.** written **c.** write **d.** have written
5. It's 3:00, and we __________ lunch yet.
   a. not eaten **b.** don't eat **c.** haven't eaten **d.** didn't use to eat
6. The city __________ this building and the land around it.
   a. use to own **b.** owning **c.** used to own **d.** didn't use to
7. Chris was standing near the telephone when he __________ it ring.
   a. was hearing **b.** were hearing **c.** heard **d.** has heard
8. Joon-ho __________ when I called.
   a. not studying **b.** wasn't studying **c.** hasn't studied **d.** isn't studying

Choose the correct word or words to complete each conversation.

9. **A:** How many fish have you caught (yet / so far)?
   B: I haven't caught any.
10. **A:** I've already mowed the lawn.
    B: (How long did it take? / Can I help you do it?)
11. **A:** He's worked at the high school for 20 years.
    B: (I guess he likes it. / Why did he leave?)

12. **A:** She didn't use to live alone.
    B: Did she like living (with other people / alone)?

13. **A:** Bob (starts his new job tomorrow / started his new job last week).
    B: He seems to like it.

14. **A:** I'm sorry. I didn't know you (were using / used) the computer.
    B: That's okay. I'll be done soon.

15. **A:** What (did you do last night / were you doing at 3:00 yesterday)?
    B: I was sleeping. I was feeling sick.

16. **A:** Have you traveled a lot?
    B: Yes, I (have / did).

Complete each sentence with the affirmative or negative past continuous form of the word or words in parentheses. Use contractions for the negative past continuous form.

17. Tim and Frank ______________________ (play) baseball on Sunday. Their team won.
18. It was cold and cloudy yesterday. The sun ______________________ (not/shine).
19. Why did you wake me? I ______________________ (have) a great dream.
20. I ______________________ (talk) to Elsa after class. She's really nice.

PART

3

The Future

CHAPTER

7

Future Time: *Be Going To, Will,* and the Present Continuous

A. GRAMMAR IN DISCOURSE: The Election 112

B. FORM 1: The Future with *Be Going To* and the Present Continuous 114

The Future with *Be Going To*
He **is going to help** later.

The Present Continuous as Future
She **is helping** later.

Informally Speaking: Reduced Form of *Going To*

C. MEANING AND USE 1: *Be Going To* and the Present Continuous as Future 119

Intentions and Plans with *Be Going To* and the Present Continuous

Predictions with *Be Going To*

Vocabulary Notes: Future Time Expressions

D. FORM 2: The Future with *Will* 125

She **will leave** tomorrow.

Informally Speaking: Reduced Form of Will

E. MEANING AND USE 2: *Will* vs. *Be Going To* 130

Predictions with *Will* and *Be Going To*

Quick Decisions vs. Advance Plans

Promises with *Will*

WRITING: Write a Comment to Post on Your School's Website 134

A GRAMMAR IN DISCOURSE

The Election

A1 Before You Read

Discuss these questions.

Are you interested in politics? Do you vote? Why or why not?

A2 Read

CD1 T32 **Read this feature article from an online news website to find out about four people's opinions of candidates in an election for governor.**

THE ELECTION

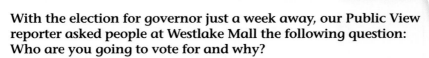

With the election for governor just a week away, our Public View reporter asked people at Westlake Mall the following question: Who are you going to vote for and why?

I'm voting for Greta Monroe. She's the best candidate. She's honest, hardworking, and intelligent. Just think, we are going to have our first woman governor! I am sure that she'll do a great job. For one thing, she's fair. She wants to help poor people, but she isn't going to raise taxes for the rest of us. She's also very interested in education, and that's important to me.

Diane Marshall, 67
retired teacher

I'm not voting. I used to vote in every election and nothing changed. I'm not going to waste my time anymore. In fact, I am leaving for Chicago the day before the election, so I'm not even going to be here. Besides, I'm sure Overmeyer is going to win. He's not a politician; he's a businessman. He started his own company and now it's one of the state's largest employers. All the business people will vote for him. The others don't have a chance.

Richard Chen, 26
accountant

I'm undecided. I'm not voting for Monroe, that's for sure. So I still have to decide between either Overmeyer or Kelly. Overmeyer has made a lot of promises, but will he keep them? He says that he is going to help bring jobs to the state. But how is he going to do that? And what kind of jobs will they be? Are they going to be jobs for skilled workers at good salaries, or will they be minimum-wage jobs for teenagers? And Kelly? Well, I'm not sure about him, either. He's done a good job as mayor, but running a state is a lot more difficult than running a city.

Steve Corum, 38
unemployed mechanic

I'm new here and I don't know enough about the candidates to make a decision. People say that Kelly will probably raise taxes, Monroe won't be able to do the job, and Overmeyer will only help businesses. I've received a lot of information in the mail about all three. I'm going to sit down this weekend and read it. I hope I can make a decision after that.

Marcy Willis, 28
chef

governor: the head of a state government
candidate: a person who people can vote for in an election
running: managing, directing
mayor: the head of a city government
skilled: trained
minimum wage: the lowest amount an employer can pay a worker for an hour's work

A3 After You Read

Look at the questions in the chart. Check (✓) the correct column.

	WHICH CANDIDATE . . .	MONROE	OVERMEYER	KELLY
1.	isn't going to raise taxes?	✓		
2.	is a woman?	✓		
3.	runs a large company?		✓	
4.	promises to bring jobs to the state?		✓	
5.	is a mayor?			✓
6.	wants to raise taxes?			✓

B FORM 1

The Future with *Be Going To* and the Present Continuous

Think Critically About Form

A. Look back at the article on page 112 and complete the tasks below.

1. **IDENTIFY** An example of *be going to* + verb is underlined. Find three more affirmative examples.
2. **RECOGNIZE** What form of *be going to* is used with *we*? with *he*? with *I?*
3. **LABEL** An example of the present continuous as future (*be* + verb + *-ing*) is circled. Find one more affirmative example.

B. Discuss your answers with the class and read the Form charts to check them.

▶ The Future with *Be Going To*

ONLINE PRACTICE

AFFIRMATIVE STATEMENTS

SUBJECT	*BE*	*GOING TO*	BASE FORM OF VERB	
I	**am**	**going to**	**help**	later.
You	**are**			
He She It	**is**			
We	**are**			
You				
They				

NEGATIVE STATEMENTS

SUBJECT	*BE*	*NOT*	*GOING TO*	BASE FORM OF VERB	
I	**am**	**not**	**going to**	**help**	later.
You	**are**				
He She It	**is**				
We	**are**				
You					
They					

***YES/NO* QUESTIONS**

BE	SUBJECT	*GOING TO*	BASE FORM OF VERB	
Are	you	**going to**	**help**	later?
Is	she			
Are	they			

SHORT ANSWERS

YES	SUBJECT	*BE*	*NO*	SUBJECT + *BE* + *NOT*
Yes,	I	**am.**	**No,**	**I'm not.**
	she	**is.**		she **isn't**.
	they	**are.**		they **aren't**.

INFORMATION QUESTIONS					
WH- WORD	*BE*	SUBJECT	*GOING TO*	BASE FORM OF VERB	
Who	**are**	you		**call**	later?
What	**is**	she	**going to**	**do**	tomorrow?
When	**are**	they		**study**	at the library?

WH- WORD (SUBJECT)	BE		*GOING TO*	BASE FORM OF VERB	
Who	**is**		**going to**	**win**	the election?
What				**happen**	next?

- See Appendix 16 for contractions with *be going to*.

> **!** Do not use contractions with affirmative short answers.
>
> Yes, I **am** ✗ Yes, I'm. (INCORRECT)

▶ The Present Continuous as Future

AFFIRMATIVE STATEMENTS			
SUBJECT	*BE*	BASE FORM OF VERB + *-ING*	
She	**is**	**helping**	later.

NEGATIVE STATEMENTS				
SUBJECT	*BE*	*NOT*	BASE FORM OF VERB + *-ING*	
She	**is**	**not**	**helping**	later.

YES/NO QUESTIONS			
BE	SUBJECT	BASE FORM OF VERB + *-ING*	
Are	they	**helping**	later?

INFORMATION QUESTIONS				
WH- WORD	*BE*	SUBJECT	BASE FORM OF VERB + *-ING*	
When	**are**	they	**helping**?	

- See Chapter 3 for more information on the present continuous.

B1 Listening for Form

CD1 T33 A. **Listen to these sentences. Write the subjects and future verb forms you hear.**

1. She's going to start school next year.
2. ____________ home tonight. The airline canceled our flight.
3. Where ____________ tonight?
4. Take your umbrella. ____________.
5. ____________ TV tonight?
6. They hate that hotel so ____________ there again.
7. ____________ on vacation tomorrow.
8. ____________ to the office next week. I'm on vacation.
9. Study hard, or ____________ the test.
10. I'm really excited. ____________ on a business trip to Brazil next month.

B. **Work with a partner. Look at each sentence again. Which future form is used: *be going to* or the present continuous as future?**

B2 Working on *Be Going To*

Complete these sentences with the correct forms of *be going to* and the words in parentheses. Use contractions where possible.

1. Soo-jin is going to study (study) in the United States next year.
2. She and her classmates are going to take (take) language exams in December.
3. She is not going to apply (not/apply) to many schools—just a few in Boston.
4. She knows that it is going to be (be) difficult to study abroad.
5. Her parents aren't worried, because she is not going to be (not/be) alone.
6. She is going to stay (stay) with relatives there.
7. She is going to live (live) with her aunt and uncle.
8. Soo-jin and her relatives are very close so they are going to enjoy (enjoy) living together.

B3 Building Present Continuous Sentences

Build six logical sentences with the present continuous as future. Use a word or phrase from each column. Punctuate your sentences correctly.

I am taking a test tomorrow.

I	am	giving	a test	next summer
my friends	is	taking	to Europe	tomorrow
our teacher	are	going	to a restaurant	tonight

B4 Forming Questions with *Be Going To*

Complete each conversation with a *Yes/No* question or information question. Use *be going to* and the words and phrases in parentheses.

1. A: Is he going to study tonight? (study/tonight)

   B: Yes, he is.

2. A: Are they going to call tomorrow? (call/tomorrow)

   B: No, they aren't.

3. A: Are you going to graduate this semester? (graduate/this semester)

   B: No, I'm not.

4. A: Are you going to move to Canada? (move/to Canada)

   B: No, I'm not.

5. where A: Is he going to study tonight? (he/study/tonight)

   B: In the library.

6. when A: Are they going to call? (they/call)

   B: Tonight.

7. A: When are you ~~graduat~~ going to graduate? (you/graduate)

   B: Next semester.

8. A: where are you going ~~to~~ move? (you/move)

   B: To Japan.

Informally Speaking

Reduced Form of *Going To*

CD1 T34 Look at the cartoon and listen to the conversation. How are the underlined forms in the cartoon different from what you hear?

Are you going to see Mary tonight?
No, I'm going to study. I have a lot of homework.

In informal speech, *going to* is often pronounced /gənə/.

Standard Form	**What You Might Hear**
They are **going to** call.	"They're /gənə/ call."
He is **going to** buy a new phone.	"He's /gənə/ buy a new phone."
I am **going to** stay home.	"I'm /gənə/ stay home."

B5 Understanding Informal Speech

CD1 T35 **Listen and write the standard form of the words you hear.**

1. We ___are going to make___ dinner soon.
2. I ______________________ to the beach.
3. We ______________________ him in Seattle.
4. Our class ______________________ next Wednesday.
5. The store ______________________ in five minutes.
6. Mark ______________________ at Lincoln University.
7. The children ______________________ happy about this.
8. They ______________________ the test tomorrow.

C

MEANING AND USE 1

Be Going To and the Present Continuous as Future

Think Critically About Meaning and Use

A. Read the sentences and answer the questions below.

a. I'm going to buy my father a book for his birthday.
b. I think we're going to have a storm tonight.
c. We're taking a trip next month.

1. **EVALUATE** Which two sentences talk about an intention (something you're thinking about doing) or a plan?
2. **EVALUATE** Which sentence makes a prediction (a guess about the future)?

B. Discuss your answers with the class and read the Meaning and Use Notes to check them.

Meaning and Use Notes

ONLINE PRACTICE

Intentions and Plans with *Be Going To* and the Present

▶ 1A Use *be going to* to talk about intentions or future plans.

I'**m going to study** hard for the test.

I'**m going to visit** Greece this summer.

A: What **is** Josh **going to study** at college?

B: He'**s going to study** chemistry.

▶ 1B You can also use the present continuous to talk about intentions or future plans. A future time expression is usually used with the present continuous to show that the sentence refers to the future (and not something happening right now). The verbs *go*, *come*, *do*, and *have*, as well as verbs related to travel, are especially common with the present continuous as future.

When **are** you **coming** to see me?

I'**m visiting** Greece this summer.

My flight **is arriving** in the afternoon. My father **is meeting** me at the airport.

A: What **are** you **doing** tomorrow?

B: I'**m having** lunch with friends. Then we'**re going** to a movie.

(Continued on page 120)

▶ 1C The present continuous often refers to more definite plans than *be going to*. With *be going to*, the speaker often has not decided on the details.

Present Continuous as Future (Details Definite)

I'**m taking** a 3:00 flight to Chicago. In Chicago, I'**m changing** planes and **flying** on to Miami.

***Be Going To* (Details Not Definite)**

A: I'**m going to buy** a car.

B: What kind **are** you **going to get**?

A: I don't know yet.

Predictions with *Be Going To*

▶ 2 Use *be going to* for predictions (guesses about the future), especially when there is evidence that something is just about to happen. The present continuous is not used to make predictions.

Be careful! That glass **is going to fall**!

It's cloudy. I think it'**s going to rain** tonight.

x It's cloudy. I think it's raining tonight. (INCORRECT)

C1 Listening for Meaning and Use

▶ Notes 1A,1B, 2

CD1 T36

Listen to each sentence. Is the speaker talking about an intention or plan, or making a prediction? Check (✓) the correct column.

	INTENTION/PLAN	PREDICTION
1.		✓
2.	✓	
3.	✓	
4.		✓
5.		✓
6.	✓	
7.		✓
8.	✓	

C2 Making Predictions with *Be Going To*

▶ Note 2

Work with a partner. Look at the pictures and make two predictions about what is going to happen in each situation. Use *be going to*.

I think she's going to take a trip.

I think she's going to travel to a cold place.

He's going to prepose to her

He's going to give ~~a ring to~~ her the ring

He's going to write a letter.

He's going to play with his friend

She's going to cut her hair.

She's going to catch a ball.

Vocabulary Notes

Future Time Expressions

The future time expressions below are commonly used in sentences about the future.

Today/Tonight/Tomorrow	***This* + Time Period**	***Next* + Time Period**
today	this afternoon	next Sunday
tonight	this Sunday	next week
tomorrow	this week	next August
the day after tomorrow	this year	next month
tomorrow morning/ afternoon/night	this spring	next year
They're arriving **tomorrow**.	I'm leaving **this week**.	**Next week** I'm visiting Ana.

***IN* + QUANTITY OF TIME**	***THE* + TIME PERIOD + *AFTER NEXT***
in five minutes	the week after next
in a few days	the weekend after next
in a few weeks	the month after next
in a few months	the year after next
He's going to call **in a few hours**.	We're having a test **the week after next**.

C3 Using Future Time Expressions

Work with a partner. Take turns asking and answering questions with *when* and *be going to* or the present continuous as future. Use *be going to* for intentions and the present continuous as future for more definite plans. Use future time expressions in your answers.

1. you/study
   A: When are you going to study?
   B: I'm going to study tonight.
   OR
   A: When are you studying?
   B: I'm studying this afternoon.
2. your best friend/visit you
3. you/finish your homework
4. your friends/moving to Rio
5. you/check your email
6. your history teacher/give a test
7. your family/take a vacation
8. you/clean your apartment

C4 Talking About Intentions and Plans

▶ Notes 1A–1C

A. Write sentences about what you intend or plan to do at the future times in parentheses. Use *be going to* for intentions and the present continuous as future for more definite plans.

1. (next weekend) Next weekend I'm going to visit my parents.
2. (the day after tomorrow) I'm going to movies the day after tomorrow.
3. (next spring) I'm going to Vancouver next year
4. (in six months) I'm going to go home in six months to see my parents.
5. (next year) I'm studying Italian next year.
6. (in an hour) I'm leaving in an hours.

B. Work with a partner. Ask your partner about his or her intentions or plans. Use future time expressions in your questions.

A: What are you doing next weekend?

B: I'm visiting my parents.

C5 Thinking About Intentions and Plans

▶ Notes 1A–1C

A. Think about these possible events. Check (✓) the events that you can plan.

✓ 1. learn to drive a car

___ 2. have bad weather

✓ 3. shop for clothes

✓ 4. go to college

___ 5. get sick

___ 6. have a car accident

✓ 7. look for a job

✓ 8. go camping

✓ 9. have an eye exam

✓ 10. get married

___ 11. win the lottery

✓ 12. watch a movie

B. Work with a partner. Talk about the things you plan to do. You can use the events you checked in part A or others. Use *be going to* for intentions or the present continuous as future for more definite plans. Use future time expressions.

A: I'm going to learn to drive this summer. My brother is going to teach me.

B: I'm watching a movie with some friends tonight. My friend Silvia is renting a video, and everyone is coming to my house at 7:00.

C6 Planning a Meeting

▶ Notes 1B–1C

A. Fill in the chart below with your schedule for the next week.

	Monday	Tuesday	Wednesday	Thursday	Friday
8:00 A.M.					
9:00 A.M.					
10:00 A.M.					
11:00 A.M.					
12:00 P.M.					
1:00 P.M.					
2:00 P.M.					
3:00 P.M.					
4:00 P.M.					
5:00 P.M.					

B. Now work with three other students to find a time for a two-hour meeting, a lunch date, and a one-hour work-out at the gym. Use the present continuous as future and time expressions to talk about your future plans.

A: *What is the easiest subject you have ever studied?*

B: *I'm free next Tuesday at 9 A.M.*

C: *I'm not. I'm working all morning.*

D: *What are you doing next Thursday at one?*

C: *I'm not doing anything until three.*

D FORM 2

The Future with *Will*

Think Critically About Form

A. Read the sentences and complete the tasks below.

a. I will decide in a few weeks.
b. He will probably raise taxes.
c. They will vote for him.
d. Will Overmeyer keep his promises?

1. **IDENTIFY** Underline *will* + verb in each sentence. Circle the subjects.
2. **APPLY** Does the form of *will* change with different subjects?
3. **APPLY** Does *will* go before or after the subject in a question?

B. Discuss your answers with the class and read the Form charts to check them.

ONLINE PRACTICE

AFFIRMATIVE STATEMENTS			
SUBJECT	*WILL*	BASE FORM OF VERB	
I You He She It We You They	**will**	**leave**	tomorrow.

CONTRACTIONS		
I**'ll** She**'ll** They**'ll**	**leave**	tomorrow.

NEGATIVE STATEMENTS				
SUBJECT	*WILL*	*NOT*	BASE FORM OF VERB	
I You He She It We You They	**will**	**not**	**leave**	tomorrow.

CONTRACTIONS			
I She They	**won't**	**leave**	tomorrow.

(Continued on page 126)

YES/NO QUESTIONS			
WILL	**SUBJECT**	**BASE FORM OF VERB**	
Will	you	**leave**	tomorrow?
	she		
	they		

SHORT ANSWERS					
YES	**SUBJECT**	***WILL***	***NO***	**SUBJECT**	***WILL* + *NOT***
Yes,	I	**will.**	**No,**	I	**won't.**
	she			she	
	they			they	

INFORMATION QUESTIONS				
***WH-* WORD**	***WILL***	**SUBJECT**	**BASE FORM OF VERB**	
Who	**will**	he	**see**	at the wedding tomorrow?
What		they	**do**	later?

***WH-* WORD (SUBJECT)**	***WILL***		**BASE FORM OF VERB**	
Who	**will**		**leave**	first?
What			**happen**	next?

- Use the same form of *will* with every subject. See Appendix 16 for contractions with *will.*

> **!** Do not use contractions with affirmative short answers.
>
> Yes, I **will.** ✗ Yes, I'll. (INCORRECT)

D1 Listening for Form

CD1 T37 Listen to each sentence. Which form is used to talk about the future: *be going to*, the present continuous, or *will*? Check (✓) the correct column.

	BE GOING TO	PRESENT CONTINUOUS	*WILL*
1.		✓	
2.			
3.			
4.			
5.			
6.			
7.			

D2 Completing Conversations with *Will*

Complete these conversations with the words in parentheses and *will* or *won't*. Use contractions where possible. Then practice the conversations with a partner.

Conversation 1

Susan: I don't believe all these predictions (예측, 예견). In the next ten years ___we won't have___ (1) (we/not/have) hydrogen-powered cars.

Bob: Oh, I think ___we will___ (2) (we).

Conversation 2

Jenny: ___will we be___ (1) (we/be) friends in five years?

Keiko: Of course, ___we will be___ (2) (we/be) friends.

Conversation 3

Lauren: Take your jacket or ___you will be___ (1) (you/be) cold.

Dan: No, ___I won't___ (2) (I/not). It's not cold outside.

Conversation 4

Paul: ___I'll do___ (1) (I/do) my homework in the morning. I promise, Mom.

Mom: No, ___you won't___ (2) (you/not). You're always too tired in the morning. Do it now.

Conversation 5

Carol: ___I'll never learn___ (1) (I/never/learn) how to download files to my new MP3 player.

Betty: I have the same one. ___I'll show___ (2) (I/show) you.

Conversation 6

Robin: Do you think ___~~will you find~~ you'll find___ (1) (you/find) an apartment in San Francisco?

Kedra: That's a good question. ___It will be___ (2) (it/be) difficult. Maybe ___I'll try___ (3) (I/try) Oakland, too.

D3 Asking *Yes/No* Questions with *Will*

A. **Imagine that this is the first day of your new English class. You are feeling very nervous. Use these phrases to write *Yes/No* questions to ask your teacher. Use *will* in your questions.**

1. (get homework every night) Will we get homework every night?
2. (have a final exam) will we have a final exam?
3. (get grades for class participation) Will we get grades for class participation?
4. (use a textbook) will we use a textbook?
5. (have a lot of tests) will we have a lot of tests?
6. (use the language lab) will we use the language lab?

B. **Work with a partner. Think of two more questions to ask your teacher.**

Will we use the Internet in class?

C. **Take turns asking and answering the questions in parts A and B.**

A: Will we get homework every night?

B: Yes, you will. It will help you a lot.

D4 Building Sentences

Build six logical information questions with *will*. Use each *wh-* word at least once. Remember that *wh-* (subject) questions do not need an item from the third column. Punctuate your sentences correctly.

What will you talk about at the meeting?

what	will	dinner	talk about	from college
when		you	be	after class today
where		your boss	go	at the meeting
who			graduate	ready

Informally Speaking

Reduced Form of *Will*

CD1 T38 Look at the cartoon and listen to the conversation. How are the underlined forms in the cartoon different from what you hear?

Who will pick up the kids from school?
I will. My boss will let me leave early.

In informal speech, *will* is often contracted with nouns and *wh-* words.

Standard Form	What You Might Hear
Jake will be late.	"/ˈdʒeɪkəl/ be late."
The **children will** be here soon.	"The /ˈtʃɪldrənəl/ be here."
How will you get to Boston?	"/ˈhaʊəl/ you get to Boston?"
Where will you live?	"/ˈwɛrəl/ you live?"

D5 Understanding Informal Speech

CD1 T39 **Listen and write the standard form of the words you hear.**

1. What will ________ you say to him tonight?
2. ________ Tony be home?
3. The ________ need paper and pencils for the test.
4. ________ help me carry these bags?
5. ________ help you with your homework.
6. After the test, the ________ grade our papers.
7. ________ get the job. He's so qualified.
8. The ________ be over at ten o'clock.

E MEANING AND USE 2

Will vs. *Be Going To*

Think Critically About Meaning and Use

A. Read the conversations and answer the questions below.

a. **Waiter:** Our special today is chicken salad.
Customer: I think I'll have a tuna sandwich instead, please.

b. **Father:** I'm very angry with you.
Daughter: I'm sorry. I'll never lie to you again.

c. **Wife:** What time are your parents arriving?
Husband: They'll probably be here by six.

1. **ANALYZE** In which conversation is the second person making a prediction?
2. **ANALYZE** In which conversation is the second person making a quick decision?
3. **ANALYZE** In which conversation is the second person making a promise?

B. Discuss your answers with the class and read the Meaning and Use Notes to check them.

Meaning and Use Notes

ONLINE PRACTICE

Predictions with *Will* and *Be Going To*

▶ 1A Use *will* or *be going to* to make predictions (guesses about the future). You can also use *probably* and other adverbs with *will* and *be going to* to express certainty or uncertainty.

Will	*Be Going To*
Electric cars **will become** popular in the next ten years.	Electric cars **are going to become** popular in the next ten years.
They**'ll** probably **win** the championship.	They**'re** probably **going to win** the championship.

▶ 1B With predictions, the meanings of *will* and *be going to* are not exactly the same. Use *be going to* when you are more certain that an event will happen because there is evidence. Do not use *will* in this situation.

She**'s going to have** a baby!   x She'll have a baby! (INCORRECT)

Quick Decisions vs. Advance Plans

▶ 2 In statements with *I*, *will* and *be going to* have different meanings. *Will* is often used to express a quick decision made at the time of speaking (such as an offer to help). *Be going to*, however, shows that you have thought about something in advance. Do not use *be going to* for quick decisions.

***Will* for Quick Decisions**

A: I don't have a fork.
B: **I'll ask** the waiter to bring you one.

A: Someone is at the door.
B: **I'll get** it.

***Be Going To* for Advance Plans**

A: Do we have plastic forks for the picnic?
B: No. **I'm going to ask** Lisa to bring some.

A: Have you decided to buy the car?
B: Yes. **I'm going to get** it tomorrow.

Promises with *Will*

▶ 3 In statements with *I*, *will* is often used to express a promise.

A: Chris, please clean your room.
B: **I'll do** it later, Mom. I promise.

E1 Listening for Meaning and Use

▶ Notes 1A, 1B, 2, 3

CD1 T40 **Listen to each sentence. Is the speaker making a promise, a prediction, or a quick decision? Check (✓) the correct column.**

	PROMISE	PREDICTION	QUICK DECISION
1.		✓	
2.			
3.			
4.			
5.			
6.			

E2 Contrasting *Be Going To* and *Will*

▶ Notes 1B, 2

Complete each conversation with the words in parentheses and the correct form of *be going to* or *will*. Use contractions where possible.

Conversation 1

A: Are you going (1) (you/go) to Jake's soccer practice?

B: I can't. I'm going to visit (2) (I/visit) my grandmother this weekend.

Conversation 2

A: Did you hear? Maria is going to have (1) (Maria/have) a baby in February!

B: That's great news!

Conversation 3

A: Oh, there's the doorbell.

B: Don't worry. I'll answer (1) (I/answer) it.

Conversation 4

A: Maria, I have to ask you something important.

Will you marry (1) (you/marry) me?

B: Yes, of course, I will (2) (I), Luis.

E3 Making Quick Decisions

▶ Note 2

Complete each conversation with an offer of help. Use *will* and a contraction.

Conversation 1

A: My cat is stuck in the tree again! I'll never get it down.

B: Don't worry! I'll get it down for you.

Conversation 2

A: I can't open the door. I'm carrying too many groceries.

B: It's ok. I'll open the door. for you.

Conversation 3

A: Oh no! I don't have enough money to pay for dinner.

B: Don't worry. I'll pay for dinner. or I'll lend you some money.

빌려주다.

Conversation 4

A: I'll never have time to clean this apartment before my mom comes over.

B: ~~I'll clean this apartment~~ I'll help you clean it.

Conversation 5

A: I lost my math notes and I need them to study for the quiz.

B: I'll give my math notes for you. I'll lend you my notes.

E4 Making Promises

▶ Note 3

Read the situations. Write promises *with* will or *won't*.

1. Tony got bad grades this semester. His parents are angry. What does he promise them?

   I'll study much harder next semester.

2. Derek went away on vacation. He forgot to lock his house. Thieves came in and stole everything. What does he promise himself?

   I'll lock my house next time. I'll never forget to lock the house again.

3. Pedro forgot his essay. What does he promise his professor?

   I won't forget my ~~essay next time~~ homework again.

4. Dr. Smith is about to give Sara an injection. What does he promise her?

   ~~I'll give an injection~~ I promise you it won't hurt.

5. Eve is on the telephone with the manager of the local telephone company. She hasn't paid her bill for three months. What does she promise?

   I'll pay ~~my bill for three months~~. the whole bill next month.

E5 Making Predictions

▶ Note 1A

Work in small groups. Look at these topics. Make predictions using *be going to* and *will*. Then discuss your predictions with the rest of the class.

1. medicine

   Medical care is going to become more expensive, but more people will have health insurance.

2. space travel
3. technology
4. cars and planes
5. education
6. wealth and poverty

Think Critically About Meaning and Use

A. Complete each conversation.

1. A: ___________

B: I'm getting up early, packing a lunch, and taking a bus to the beach.

a. What are you doing now?

b. What are you going to do tomorrow?

2. A: I don't need an umbrella. It's not raining.

B: ___________

a. But it's raining this afternoon.

b. But it's going to rain this afternoon.

3. A: Tomorrow's election is going to be close.

B: ___________

a. Yes, but I think O'Casey's winning.

b. Yes, but I think O'Casey will win.

4. A: Next Monday is Pat's birthday.

B: ___________

a. Yes. We're going to invite her to dinner.

b. Yes. We'll invite her to dinner.

5. A: This box is very heavy. I can't carry it any longer.

B: ___________

a. Don't worry. I'm going to carry it.

b. I'll carry it. You carry the lighter one.

6. A: We're going on a Caribbean cruise.

B: ___________

a. Wow! You're having a great time.

b. Wow! You're going to have a great time.

7. A: Does Lisa know whether she's going to have a boy or a girl?

B: ___________

a. Yes, the doctor told her. She will have a boy.

b. Yes, the doctor told her. She's going to have a boy.

B. Discuss these questions in small groups.

1. COMPARE AND CONTRAST Compare the use of the present continuous in 1 and 2. What is the difference?

2. GENERATE In 3, how else could speaker B state the response?

Edit

Some of these sentences have errors. Find the errors and correct them.

1. Betty going to college this fall.
2. What she is going to study?
3. She is going to study cooking because she wants to be a chef.
4. Betty studying with some famous chefs next year.
5. Someday maybe Betty is being a famous chef, too.
6. Betty is also going to take some business classes.
7. After these classes she certainly wills know all about restaurant management.
8. Maybe in a few years Betty owns a restaurant.
9. What kind of food her restaurant will serve?
10. I predict it is serving Chinese.

Write

Imagine that there is a problem in your school, and you have a plan to solve it. Follow the steps to write a comment about the problem to post on your school's website. Use *be going to*, the present continuous as future, and *will*.

1. **Brainstorm** Think about a problem at your school and how you (or others) can solve it. Use these questions to help you.
   - What is the problem?
   - What are you and/or others going to do to fix the problem?
   - What will the results be? How will the situation improve?

2. **Write a First Draft** Before you write your draft, read the checklist below. Write your draft using different ways of expressing future time.

3. **Edit** Read your work and check it against the checklist below. Circle grammar, spelling, and punctuation errors.

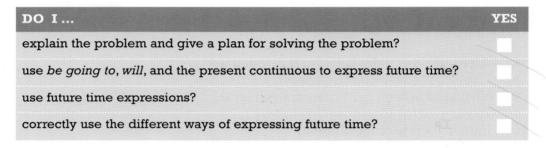

DO I ...	YES
explain the problem and give a plan for solving the problem?	☐
use *be going to*, *will*, and the present continuous to express future time?	☐
use future time expressions?	☐
correctly use the different ways of expressing future time?	☐

4. **Peer Review** Work with a partner to help you decide how to fix your errors and improve the content.

5. **Rewrite Your Draft** Using the comments from your partner, write a final draft.

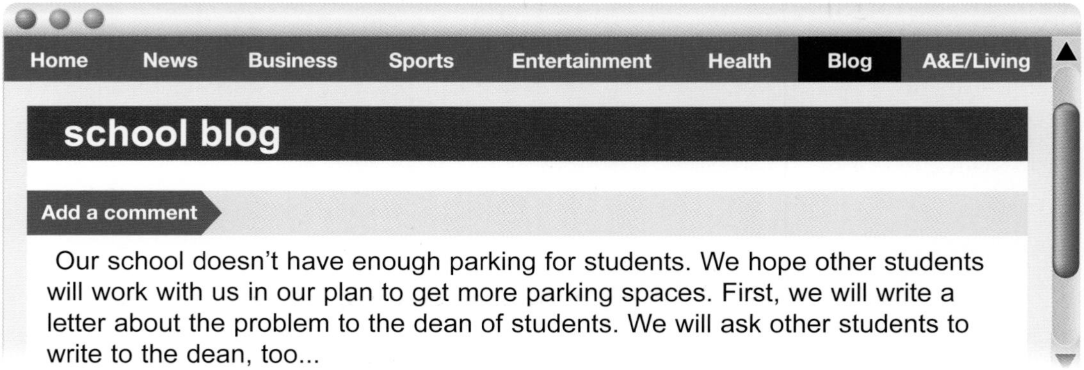

Home
News
Business
Sports
Entertainment
Health
Blog
A&E/Living
school blog
Add a comment
Our school doesn't have enough parking for students. We hope other students will work with us in our plan to get more parking spaces. First, we will write a letter about the problem to the dean of students. We will ask other students to write to the dean, too...

CHAPTER

8

Future Time Clauses and *If* Clauses

A. **GRAMMAR IN DISCOURSE: What Will Happen in the Future?** 138

B. **FORM: Future Time Clauses and *If* Clauses** 140

Future Time Clauses

Before I **go** to the movies, I**'m going to do** my homework.

I**'m going to do** my homework **before** I **go** to the movies.

***If* Clauses**

If it **rains** tomorrow, (then) they**'ll cancel** the picnic.

They**'ll cancel** the picnic **if** it **rains** tomorrow.

C. **MEANING AND USE 1: Using Future Time Clauses for Events in Sequence** 144

Future Events in Sequence

D. **MEANING AND USE 2: Expressing Future Possibility with *If* Clauses** 146

Cause-and-Effect Relationships

Expressing Advice, Warnings, Promises, and Predictions

Possibility vs. Certainty

WRITING: Write a Campaign Flyer 150

PART 3 TEST: The Future 153

A GRAMMAR IN DISCOURSE

What Will Happen in the Future?

A1 Before You Read

Discuss these questions.

Do you think about life in the future? What will be different in the future? Will the world be a better or worse place than it is today? Why?

A2 Read

CD1 T41 **Read this magazine article to find out if your predictions about the future match one expert's predictions.**

What Will Happen in the Future?

In the year 2020 our computers will be very good at communicating with us. Because they will understand everything we say, and we will understand everything they say, we won't need a keyboard or mouse when we use them. At work, at school, and in stores, computers will be our assistants. With computers really talking, many of life's tasks will become much easier for us.

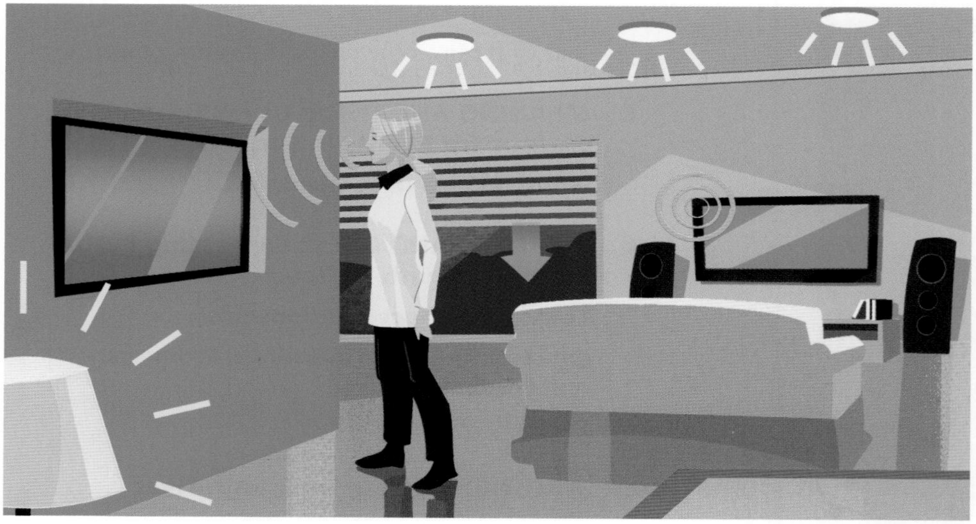

Computers of the future will communicate with us.

In the year 2025 some people will live in "smart" houses. These houses will use less energy and will be more environmentally friendly than the houses of today. If a room is empty, the lights and TV will go off. When the weather is cold, windows will shut automatically. They will open when the weather is hot. The windows will also change the energy of the sun into electricity. Some people say that smart houses are not going to be very popular because we will prefer our traditional houses. Others say that smart houses will change our way of life completely and everyone will love them.

In the year 2040 traveling by car will also be easier and more environmentally friendly. Smart cars will do the driving themselves. And more cars will run on electricity instead of gasoline. Countries will start to build underground automated highways (UAHs)—special roads under the ground for these smart cars. When we have these underground highways, we will be able to travel quickly between large cities.

In the year 2045 humans will orbit Mars in a spaceship. Some years later, humans will land on Mars and explore the planet.

---

assistant: helper

environmentally friendly: something that is good for the environment

task: job, something that needs to be done

orbit: go around

A3 After You Read

Check (✓) the predictions that the writer makes in the article.

_✓_ **1.** In 2020 we will have computers that talk to us.

____ **2.** In 2020 many people will have a computer for a boss.

____ **3.** In 2030 underground roads will connect most cities.

____ **4.** In 2025 smart houses will use energy from the sun.

____ **5.** People in smart houses will not need electricity.

____ **6.** People will orbit and explore Mars.

B FORM

Future Time Clauses and *If* Clauses

Think Critically About Form

A. Read the sentences and complete the tasks below.

a. I'll see him before I leave.
b. When they graduate, they're going to look for work.
c. We're going to have dessert after we finish dinner.

1. **IDENTIFY** Underline the main clause and circle the dependent clause in each sentence. What form of the verb is used in each main clause?
2. **RECOGNIZE** Look at each dependent clause. What is the first word? What form of the verb is used? These are future time clauses.
3. **RECOGNIZE** Look at this sentence. What is the first word of the dependent clause? This is an *if* clause.
   If I go to the store, I'll buy the groceries.
4. **LABEL** Look back at the article on page 138. Find two future time clauses and one *if* clause.

B. Discuss your answers with the class and read the Form charts to check them.

▶ Future Time Clauses

ONLINE PRACTICE

FUTURE TIME CLAUSE				MAIN CLAUSE
	SUBJECT	**VERB**		
Before	I	**go**	to the movies,	I'**m going to do** my homework.
When	she	**gets**	to work,	she'**ll make** some phone calls.
After	we	**finish**	dinner,	we'**ll wash** the dishes.

MAIN CLAUSE	FUTURE TIME CLAUSE			
		SUBJECT	**VERB**	
I'**m going to do** my homework	before	I	**go**	to the movies.
She'**ll make** some phone calls	when	she	**gets**	to work.
We'**ll wash** the dishes	after	we	**finish**	dinner.

Overview

- A clause is a group of words that has a subject and a verb.
- A main clause can stand alone as a complete sentence.
- A dependent clause cannot stand alone and must be used with a main clause.

Future Time Clauses

- Future time clauses are dependent time clauses. They begin with words such as *before, when, while,* and *after*.
- A future time clause can come before or after the main clause with no change in meaning. If the future time clause comes first, then it is separated from the main clause by a comma.
- Use *will* or *be going to* in the main clause.
- The verb in the future time clause is in the simple present even though it has a future meaning.

> **!** Do not use *be going to* or *will* in the future time clause.
>
> After I **finish** my work, I'll watch TV. ✗ After I will finish my work, I'll watch TV. (INCORRECT)

▶ *If* Clauses

IF CLAUSE					MAIN CLAUSE
IF	**SUBJECT**	**VERB**		***(THEN)***	
If	you	**exercise**	every day,	(then)	you'**ll feel** better.
	it	**rains**	tomorrow,		they'**ll cancel** the picnic.
	we	**don't score**	soon,		we'**re going to lose** the game.

MAIN CLAUSE	*IF* CLAUSE			
	IF	**SUBJECT**	**VERB**	
You'**ll feel** better	**if**	you	**exercise**	every day.
They'**ll cancel** the picnic		it	**rains**	tomorrow.
We'**re going to lose** the game		we	**don't score**	soon.

(Continued on page 142)

If Clauses

- *If* clauses are dependent clauses. They must be used with a main clause.
- An *if* clause can come before or after the main clause with no change in meaning. When the *if* clause comes first, it is separated from the main clause by a comma.
- When the *if* clause comes first, *then* can be added before the main clause with no change in meaning.
- Use *will* or *be going to* in the main clause.
- The verb in the *if* clause is in the simple present even though it has a future meaning.

> Do not use *be going to* or *will* in the *if* clause.
>
> If I **finish** my work, I'll watch TV. ✗ If I'll finish my work, I'll watch TV. (INCORRECT)

B1 Listening for Form

CD1 T42 **Listen to these sentences. Write the verb forms you hear.**

1. When I ___*see*___ Elena, I ___*'ll give*___ her the message.
2. We ____________ more time if the test ____________ very difficult.
3. Marcus and Maria ____________ to Budapest after they ____________ Prague.
4. She ____________ us when she ____________ here.
5. If Matt ____________ a loan from the bank, he ____________ a new car.

B2 Building Sentences

Build five logical sentences with future time clauses and *if* clauses. Use a clause from each column. Use the correct form of the verbs in parentheses. Punctuate your sentences correctly.

After Megan finishes class, she'll have lunch.

after Megan (finish) class	we (get) a lot of money
before she (leave) the house	she (have) lunch
if we (win) the award	you (pass) the test
if you (study) hard	she (call) you
when we (get) to the movies	we (save) you a seat

B3 Working on Future Time Clauses and *If* Clauses

A. **Complete each sentence with a future time clause or a main clause. Use the words and phrases in parentheses and the correct punctuation.**

1. When I get a job_, I'll buy a car.___ (I/buy/a car)
2. ________________ (after/she/graduate) she's going to move to L.A.
3. After we save some money ________________ (we/look/for a house)
4. ________________ (they/visit/the Eiffel Tower) before they leave Paris.

B. **Complete each sentence with an *if* clause or a main clause. Use the words and phrases in parentheses and the correct punctuation.**

1. We'll take her out to dinner _if she visits.___ (if/she/visit)
2. ________________ (I/call) if I hear any news.
3. If I feel better ________________ (I/go/to work)
4. ________________ (if/you/not/study) you won't do well on the test.

B4 Completing Sentences with Future Time Clauses and *If* Clauses

Complete this email with the correct form of the verb in parentheses.

From: George
To: Vinh
Subject: surprise party

Hi Vinh,

We're planning a surprise for Dan's graduation. Here are the plans.

Alex __will bring__ (1) (bring) me their house key after Dan ________ (2) (leave) for work on Friday. I ________ (3) (cook) before I ________ (4) (go) to class. I ordered a cake from the bakery. Stefan ________ (5) (get) it when he ________ (6) (go) shopping on Friday afternoon. But we need your help. If Dan ________ (7) (come) home right after work, we ________ (8) (not/be) ready. Will you ask him to drive you home after work? If you ________ (9) (ask) him to take you home, he ________ (10) (not/be) suspicious. Then, when everyone ________ (11) (be) here, I ________ (12) (call) you on your cell.

George

C

MEANING AND USE 1

Using Future Time Clauses for Events in Sequence

Think Critically About Meaning and Use

A. Read the sentences and complete the task below.

a. We'll give you the information when we get the results.
b. Before you take the test, the teacher will review the homework.
c. He'll need help after he comes home from the hospital.

IDENTIFY Look at each sentence. Underline the event that happens first. Which word or words in each sentence tell you the order of the events?

B. Discuss your answers with the class and read the Meaning and Use Notes to check them.

Meaning and Use Notes

ONLINE PRACTICE

Future Events in Sequence

▶ **1** Future time clauses show the time relationship between two events or situations in a sentence. When a time clause begins with *when* or *after*, the event in the time clause happens first. When a time clause begins with *before*, the event in the time clause happens second.

First Event	Second Event
When I get home,	I'll call you.
After they get married,	they're going to move to California.
I'm going to water the plants	**before I go on vacation.**

C1 Listening for Meaning and Use

▶ Note 1

CD1 T43 **Listen to each sentence. Which event happens first and which happens second? Write *1* next to the first event and *2* next to the second.**

__1__	**1.** I look for a job.	__2__	I graduate.
__2__	**2.** He gets here.	__1__	We make dinner.
__2__	**3.** We go to the park.	__1__	We go to the museum.
__2__	**4.** I call you.	__1__	They leave.
__2__	**5.** I clean the house.	__1__	I go shopping.

C2 Talking About Two Future Events ▶ Note 1

A. **Complete these sentences with future time clauses or main clauses.**

1. When I finish school, my family will be happy.
2. After I finish this English class, I'm going to enter a Fanshawe College.
3. After I finish work, I'll take a vacation.
4. I'll buy a new car after I get my driver's license.
5. When I finish ELF courses, I'll speak English.
6. I'll be happy when I take a vacation.

B. **Work with a partner. In your notebook, write two main clauses and two future time clauses. Have your partner complete each one.**

I'll call you after I finish work.

When my friend visits me, I'll be happy.

C3 Describing Future Events in Sequence ▶ Note 1

Think about your day tomorrow. Write two sentences for each part of the day. Use future time clauses with *before, when,* and *after*.

1. (tomorrow morning)

   I'll get up when my alarm rings.

   After my alarm rings, I'll get up.

2. (tomorrow afternoon)

   I'll study ~~when~~ before I go to excercise.

   After I go to excercise, I'll do homework.

3. (tomorrow evening)

   I'll go shopping when I get ~~paycheck~~ salary.

4. (tomorrow night)

   I'll sleep early after I do homework.

D MEANING AND USE 2

Expressing Future Possibility with *If* Clauses

Think Critically About Meaning and Use

A. Read the sentences and complete the tasks below.

1a. If you take some aspirin, you'll feel better.
1b. I'll take you out to dinner if you help me with the housework.
2a. If Ben leaves, call me.
2b. When Ben leaves, call me.

1. **EVALUATE** Look at 1a and 1b. Underline the *if* clauses. Circle the main clauses. Which clause in each sentence describes a possible situation? Which clause in each sentence describes a possible result of that situation?
2. **INTERPRET** Look at 1a and 1b again. Which sentence gives advice? Which sentence makes a promise?
3. **APPLY** Look at 2a and 2b. In which sentence is it more certain that Ben will leave?

B. Discuss your answers with the class and read the Meaning and Use Notes to check them.

Meaning and Use Notes

ONLINE PRACTICE

Cause-and-Effect Relationships

▶ 1 Sentences with an *if* clause show a cause-and-effect relationship. The *if* clause introduces a possible situation (the cause). The main clause talks about the possible result (the effect) of that situation. The cause and effect can come in either order.

***If* Clause (Cause)**	**Main Clause (Effect)**
If she gets that job,	her salary will increase.
If you press the red button,	the elevator will stop.
Main Clause (Effect)	***If* Clause (Cause)**
Her salary will increase	**if she gets that job.**
The elevator will stop	**if you press the red button.**

Expressing Advice, Warnings, Promises, and Predictions

▶ 2 Sentences with an *if* clause and a main clause with *be going to* or *will* have several common uses:

Giving Advice: If you rest now, you'll feel better later.

Giving a Warning: If you don't tell the truth, you're going to be sorry.

Making a Promise: If you elect me, I won't raise taxes.

Making a Prediction: If he moves to the city, he won't be happy.

Possibility vs. Certainty

▶ 3 Use an *if* clause if you think something is possible, but you are not sure it will happen. Use a future time clause with *when* if you are certain something will happen.

If **Clause (Possible)**	**Future Time Clause (Certain)**
If it goes on sale, I'll buy it.	**When it goes on sale,** I'll buy it.
I'll visit the Taj Mahal **if I go to India**.	I'll visit the Taj Mahal **when I go to India**.

D1 Listening for Meaning and Use

▶ Note 3

CD1 T44 Listen to each conversation. Does the second speaker think the situation is possible or certain? Check (✓) the correct column.

	SITUATION	POSSIBLE	CERTAIN
1.	She and Amy will see a movie.	✓	
2.	He will go to the store.		
3.	It will snow this weekend.		
4.	He will go to Mexico.		
5.	Mark will ask Celia to marry him.		
6.	Jake will rent the apartment.		

D2 Giving Warnings ▶ Notes 1, 2

Complete each warning with an *if* clause or a main clause.

1. If you don't stop at a red light, you'll get a ticket.
2. You'll burn your hand if your hand into a fire.
3. The electricity will shut down if you don't pay your electric bill.
4. If you go swimming in cold weather, you'll have a cold.
5. You'll be hungry if you don't eat breakfast.
6. You'll be tired if you stay up all night. (늦게까지 안자는것) 꼬박새다, 안자다
7. You'll lose your job if you don't work hard.
8. If you exercise excessively, you'll break your leg.

D3 Giving Advice ▶ Notes 1, 2

Write two pieces of advice for the person in each situation. Each piece of advice should include an *if* clause and a main clause.

1. Your friend is always late for school.
   a. If you leave home on time, you won't be late for school.
   b. ______
2. Your brother wants to go to a good university.
   a. If your brother get a good grade, he'll go to a good university.
   b. ______
3. Your sister doesn't get along with a co-worker.
   a. If your mind open first, you'll get along with a co-worker.
   b. ______
4. Your cousin wants to move to a new apartment, but he doesn't have much money.
   a. If you save the money, you'll move a new apartment.
   b. ______

D4 Making Promises

▶ Notes 1, 2

Work with a partner. Read these situations. Take turns making promises. Each promise should include an *if* clause and a main clause. Switch roles after each situation.

1. **Student A:** You are a student. You need help with your English homework.
   Student B: You are the student's best friend.

   A: If you help me with my English homework, I'll help you with your math.
   B: I'll help you with your homework if you let me ride your motorcycle.

2. **Student A:** You are a teenager. You want to borrow the family car.
   If you borrow the family car, I'll drive safe.
   Student B: You are the teenager's parent.
   I'll borrow the family car if you drive safe.
3. **Student A:** You are a driver. You were speeding.
   If I were speeding, police offcer will give a ticket.
   Student B: You are a police officer.
   I'll give a ticket if you are speeding.
4. **Student A:** You are an employee. You are often late for work.
   If I go to work late, I'll lose my job.
   Student B: You are the employee's boss.
   You'll lose your job if you are often late for work.

D5 Making Predictions

▶ Notes 1, 2

Look at the picture. Write predictions about what will happen. Include an *if* clause and a main clause in each prediction.

If the man trips over the telephone cord, he'll fall.
~에 발이 걸려 넘어지다.

If the man pass through the telephon cord, she'll drop the phone.
The dishes will brake if she lose a balance.
If the child lower the fish, the cat will ~~eat~~ catch the fish.

WRITING Write a Campaign Flyer

Think Critically About Meaning and Use

A. Read each sentence and the statements that follow. Check (✓) the statement that has the same meaning.

1. He'll come and get us when the program starts.

____ a. The program will start, and then he'll come and get us.

____ b. He'll come and get us, and then the program will start.

2. Before you graduate, you'll need another math course.

____ a. You can't graduate without another math course.

____ b. You'll graduate, and then you'll take another math course.

3. He'll leave before I leave.

____ a. I'll leave when he leaves.

____ b. He'll leave, and then I'll leave.

4. He'll be happy if he gets the job.

____ a. He'll get the job, and then he'll be happy.

____ b. It's possible that he'll get the job. If he does, he'll be happy.

5. We're going to buy a house when we get married.

____ a. We feel certain that we'll buy a house after we marry.

____ b. We don't feel certain that we'll get married and buy a house.

6. If the store is open, I'll buy some milk.

____ a. The store will be open, so I'll buy some milk.

____ b. Maybe the store will be open, and I'll buy some milk.

7. I'll help you when I finish making lunch.

____ a. I'll make lunch. Then I'll help you.

____ b. I'll help you. At the same time, I'll make lunch.

8. She'll cook dinner when her husband comes home.

____ a. Dinner will not be ready when he arrives.

____ b. Dinner will be ready when he arrives.

9. I'll see Ben if I go to the café.

___ a. I'm not certain that I'm going to the café.

___ b. Ben isn't certain that he's going to the café.

B. Discuss these questions in small groups.

1. **EVALUATE** In 1, what change can you make to the time clause to make the other option correct?
2. **COMPARE AND CONTRAST** In 5, how does the meaning change if we use *if* instead of *when*?

Edit

Some of these sentences have errors. Find the errors and correct them. There may be more than one error in some sentences.

1. When I will see Debbie, I'll give her the book.
2. If I won't feel better soon, I'll go to the doctor.
3. If I get an A on the final, then I'll get an A for the course.
4. I'm going to check the prices online before I'm going to buy a camera.
5. We won't have time to see a movie after we go shopping.
6. He's going to drive to Dallas if the weather will improve.
7. When I'll get my paycheck, I'll pay my bills.
8. They cancel the picnic if it will rain tomorrow.
9. When the phone is going to ring, I'll answer it.
10. She'll email her friends tonight if she has time.

Write

Imagine you are running for election as mayor of your town or city. Follow the steps below to write a campaign flyer to tell voters why they should vote for you. Use future time clauses and *if* clauses.

1. **Brainstorm** Think about the needs of your town or city and about the changes that you will make as mayor. Take notes about what you want to say. Use these questions to help you.
   - What will you do in your city or town if people elect you?
   - What will you NOT do if people elect you?
   - How will the town or city improve if you are mayor? How will people's lives change?
   - What bad things won't happen in the city or town if you are mayor?

2. **Write a First Draft** Before you write your draft, read the checklist below. Write your draft using future time clauses and *if* clauses.

3. **Edit** Read your work and check it against the checklist below. Circle grammar, spelling, and punctuation errors.

DO I ...	YES
explain why people should vote for me for mayor?	☐
make predictions and promises?	☐
use future time clauses for events in sequence?	☐
use *if* clauses to express future possibility?	☐
use correct verb forms in all clauses?	☐

4. **Peer Review** Work with a partner to help you decide how to fix your errors and improve the content.

5. **Rewrite Your Draft** Using the comments from your partner, write a final draft.

On November 7,
vote for Jenna Zabala for mayor!

Ten good reasons to vote for me:

- **If you elect me, I will build new parks.**
- **When I am mayor, I won't raise city taxes.**
- **I will always be available if people want to talk to me.**

PART 3
TEST | The Future

Choose the correct word or words to complete each sentence.

1. We'll let you know about an interview __________ the manager reviews your résumé.

a. while **b.** before **c.** after **d.** until

2. The director isn't going to promote Amy if her evaluations __________ good.

a. won't be **b.** aren't **c.** isn't **d.** will be

3. Many reporters predict that the mayor __________ the election next year.

a. is not winning **b.** is not going to win **c.** not win **d.** doesn't win

4. __________ practicing with the team tomorrow?

a. Is Jada **b.** Will Jada **c.** Is Jada going to **d.** Won't Jada

5. If you eat that whole pizza, you __________ to walk!

a. aren't able **b.** won't be able **c.** not able **d.** isn't able

6. If the history class ______ full, I'm going to take Spanish.

a. is **b.** will be **c.** is going to be **d.** is being

7. When Hiro __________, we will start the dinner.

a. will be coming **b.** will come **c.** comes **d.** is going to come

8. The team __________ the game without Kedra.

a. not winning **b.** will not win **c.** not win **d.** win

9. Tomek __________ a lecture next month.

a. give **b.** is going to give **c.** going to give **d.** to give

10. Fumiko __________ to have dinner with Reiko on Friday night.

a. go **b.** are going **c.** is going **d.** will

Choose the correct word or words to complete each conversation.

11. A: We are (going to buy a new house some day / moving into our new house next week).
B: Is it big?

12. A: I need to pay off my credit card debt.
B: (I'll help you with a payment plan. / Will this purchase be cash or charge?)

13. A: So what is your prediction about the election tomorrow?
B: Adams is (winning / going to win).

14. A: Why are they moving to a bigger apartment?
B: Julia (is having / will have) a baby in a few months.

15. A: I can't carry all these shopping bags!
B: (I'm going shopping for bags next week. / I'll help you. Give me that big one.)

16. A: If it rains, they'll cancel the game.
B: I just heard the forecast. It's not (going to rain / raining).

17. A: I'm going to make dinner when you get home.
B: Good. (I'm glad it'll be ready. / I'll have time for a shower.)

Match the sentence parts.

____ **18.** If you get more sleep,	**a.** if you leave it out.
____ **19.** The milk will spoil	**b.** if I find my checkbook.
____ **20.** I'll pay the rent	**c.** you won't be so tired.
	d. if the snow doesn't stop.
	e. your hands will be cold.
	f. I'll open the window.
	g. he'll miss his family.
	h. I'll cook dinner.

PART

4

Modals

CHAPTER

9

Modals of Ability and Possibility

A. **GRAMMAR IN DISCOURSE: Two Amazing People** 156

B. **FORM 1: Modals of Ability: *Can* and *Could*; *Be Able To*** ... 158

***Can* for Present and Future Ability**

He **can play** the piano.

***Could* for Past Ability**

He **could read** in kindergarten.

***Be Able To* for Past, Present, and Future Ability**

He **was able to work** yesterday.
He **is able to work** today.
He **will be able to work** tomorrow.

C. **MEANING AND USE 1: Past, Present, and Future Ability** .. 162

Present Ability with *Can*

Future Ability with *Be Able To* and *Can*

Past Ability with *Could* and *Be Able To*

Vocabulary Notes: *Know How To*

D. **FORM 2: Modals of Future Possibility** 167

They **may leave** tomorrow.

E. **MEANING AND USE 2: Future Possibility** 170

Expressing Future Possibility with *Could, Might,* and *May*

Expressing Strong Certainty with *Will*

WRITING: Write an Email About Your Future After College 174

A GRAMMAR IN DISCOURSE

Two Amazing People

A1 Before You Read

Discuss these questions.

Who is someone you think is amazing? What makes this person amazing?

A2 Read

CD1 T45 **Read this magazine article to find out about two amazing people and why they are so amazing.**

feature story

Two Amazing People

Stephen Wiltshire

Some people have exceptional abilities–they can do things that ordinary people cannot do. And for a very few people these abilities come with a lack of ability to do some other things that ordinary people take for granted.

Think about Stephen Wiltshire. He is able to draw a city after flying over it for a half hour or so in a helicopter. He has drawn huge pictures of cities including London, New York, Moscow, Tokyo, Rome, and Shanghai. In addition to drawing with great accuracy and detail from memory (such as the right number of columns on the Pantheon in Rome), Stephen is able to show the feeling of each city. And yet Stephen has autism, a condition that affects various abilities, including language, intelligence, and the ability to interact with other people.

As a young child in London, Stephen could not speak. But he could draw amazing pictures. At the special school he attended, his artistic ability was clear by the time he was five years old. His first word was "paper"—he wanted drawing paper. At 13, he published a book of drawings. He went on to study at the City and Guilds of London Art School. Since then, he has published three other books and has drawn and shown his art in cities around the world.

Tony DeBlois is an exceptionally talented jazz pianist. And he's not just a pianist. He also can play 21 other instruments, many of them very well. He can sing in 11 languages and is able to play over 8,000 pieces of music from memory.

Tony is autistic and has been blind from birth. His musical ability emerged when he was two. He wasn't able to sit up, so his mother bought him a toy piano to encourage him. Music has been important to Tony in many ways. He learned to brush his teeth by learning to play the violin, and he learned to brush his hair by learning to play drums. He couldn't button his clothes until he was 26, and he still can't buckle his belt or tie his shoes.

Nevertheless, after attending a school for the blind, Tony went on to the Berklee College of Music in Boston, Massachusetts. He graduated with honors, and ever since he has been playing the piano—and inspiring audiences and other musicians.

---

accuracy: being correct
condition: illness
emerge: come out
inspire: give someone strong positive feelings
interact: to communicate and mix with, relate to
take for granted: to assume without thinking about

A3 After You Read

Write *T* for true or *F* for false for each statement.

__T__ **1.** Stephen Wiltshire usually draws cities.

_____ **2.** Stephen Wiltshire draws cities after studying them for many days.

_____ **3.** As a young child, Stephen drew pictures before he learned to speak.

_____ **4.** Jazz pianist Tony DeBlois knows how to play only the piano.

_____ **5.** Both Stephen Wiltshire and Tony DeBlois are autistic.

B FORM 1

Modals of Ability: *Can* and *Could*; *Be Able To*

Think Critically About Form

A. Look back at the article on page 156 and complete the tasks below.

1. **IDENTIFY** Look at the underlined examples of *can* + verb and *could* + verb. What form of the verb follows *can* and *could*?
2. **RECOGNIZE** Find the negative forms of *can* + verb and *could* + verb on the first page. What is unusual about the negative form of *can* + verb? What are the contracted negative forms of *can* and *could*?

B. Discuss your answers with the class and read the Form charts to check them.

▶ *Can* for Present and Future Ability

ONLINE PRACTICE

AFFIRMATIVE STATEMENTS			
SUBJECT	**MODAL**	**BASE FORM OF VERB**	
I	can	**play**	the piano.
He			
They		**work**	tomorrow.

NEGATIVE STATEMENTS			
SUBJECT	**MODAL + *NOT***	**BASE FORM OF VERB**	
I	**cannot** **can't**	**play**	the piano.
He			
They		**work**	tomorrow.

YES/NO QUESTIONS			
MODAL	**SUBJECT**	**BASE FORM OF VERB**	
Can	you	**play**	the piano?
	he	**work**	tomorrow?
	they		

SHORT ANSWERS					
YES	**SUBJECT**	**MODAL**	***NO***	**SUBJECT**	**MODAL + *NOT***
Yes,	I	**can.**	**No,**	I	**can't.**
	he			he	
	they			they	

INFORMATION QUESTIONS				
***WH-* WORD**	**MODAL**	**SUBJECT**	**BASE FORM OF VERB**	
What	**can**	you	**play**?	
How long		he	**work**	tomorrow?

***WH-* WORD (SUBJECT)**	**MODAL**		**BASE FORM OF VERB**	
Who	**can**		**work**	tomorrow?
What			**fly**?	

- *Can* is a modal. Like all modals, it is followed by the base form of a verb and has the same form for all subjects.
- The negative form of *can* is *cannot*. Notice that *cannot* is written as one word.
- It is often difficult to hear the difference between *can* and *can't* because the final *t* in *can't* is not clearly pronounced. In sentences with *can* + verb, the vowel sound in *can* is very short and the stress is on the verb that follows *can*: I /kən/ gȯ. In sentences with *can't* + verb, the stress is on *can't* and the *a* is pronounced like the *a* in *ant*: I /kǣnt/ go.

▶ *Could* for Past Ability

AFFIRMATIVE STATEMENTS			
SUBJECT	**MODAL**	**BASE FORM OF VERB**	
I	**could**	**read**	in kindergarten.
He			
They			

NEGATIVE STATEMENTS			
SUBJECT	**MODAL + *NOT***	**BASE FORM OF VERB**	
I	**could not** **couldn't**	**read**	in kindergarten.
He			
They			

***YES/NO* QUESTIONS**			
MODAL	**SUBJECT**	**BASE FORM OF VERB**	
Could	you	**read**	in kindergarten?

SHORT ANSWERS					
YES	**SUBJECT**	**MODAL**	***NO***	**SUBJECT**	**MODAL + *NOT***
Yes,	I	**could**.	**No,**	I	**couldn't**.

(Continued on page 160)

INFORMATION QUESTIONS				
WH- WORD	MODAL	SUBJECT	BASE FORM OF VERB	
What	could	she	read	in kindergarten?

WH- WORD (SUBJECT)	MODAL		BASE FORM OF VERB	
Who	could		read	in kindergarten?

- *Could* is a modal. Like all modals, it is followed by the base form of a verb and has the same form for all subjects.

▶ *Be Able To* for Past, Present, and Future Ability

AFFIRMATIVE STATEMENTS			
SUBJECT	*BE ABLE TO*	BASE FORM OF VERB	
He	was able to	work	yesterday.
	is able to		today.
	will be able to		tomorrow.

NEGATIVE STATEMENTS			
SUBJECT	*BE + NOT + ABLE TO*	BASE FORM OF VERB	
He	was not able to	work	yesterday.
	is not able to		today.
	will not be able to		tomorrow.

- *Be able to* is not a modal, but it has the same meaning as *can* and *could*. The verb *be* in *be able to* changes form and agrees with the subject.
- See Appendix 16 for contractions with *be* and *will*.

B1 Listening for Form

CD1 T46 **Listen to this paragraph. Write *can* or *can't*.**

Michael is blind. He __can't__(1) see. He ______(2) do amazing things, however. He lives in Chicago, and he ______(3) walk around the city alone. Of course, he ______(4) read the street signs, so sometimes he asks for help. After he has been somewhere with a friend, he ______(5) go there again by himself. Michael is good at sports, too. He's the best player on his bowling team, even though he ______(6) see the bowling pins.

B2 Building Sentences with *Can* and *Can't*

Build three logical sentences with *can* and three logical sentences with *can't*. Use a word from each column.

People can climb trees.

people	can	climb trees
fish	can't	bark
dogs		swim

B3 Forming Statements and Questions with *Can* and *Could*

In your notebook, write a statement and a question for each set of words and phrases. Punctuate your sentences correctly.

1. Emily/house/can/our/come/to
   Emily can come to our house.
   Can Emily come to our house?
2. them/airport/could/we/the/take/to
3. his/languages/can/parents/speak/several
4. sister/your/can/Mandarin/speak
5. problem/us/can/she/this/with/help

B4 Completing Conversations with *Be Able To*

Complete these conversations with the words in parentheses and the correct form of *be able to*. Use contractions where possible.

1. **A:** ___Were___(1) you ___able to finish___(2) (finish) the test yesterday?
   B: No, ______________(3) (not), but I ______________(4) (do) 45 out of the 50 questions.
2. **A:** Did David help you clean the attic?
   B: No, he ______________(1) (not/come) on Saturday. But I think he ______________(2) (help) me this weekend.
3. **A:** __________(1) Susan ______________(2) (practice) the piano at college last year?
   B: Well, not in the dorm, but she ______________(3) (play) at the Student Center.
4. **A:** __________(1) you ______________(2) (call) me later?
   B: No. I'm busy tonight, but I ______________(3) (see) you tomorrow.

C MEANING AND USE 1

Past, Present, and Future Ability

Think Critically About Meaning and Use

A. Read the sentences and answer the questions below.

a. Carl can type 40 words a minute.
b. Last year Carl could type 20 words a minute.
c. When Carl's typing class ends, he will be able to type 60 words a minute.

1. **EVALUATE** Which sentence talks about an ability that Carl has at the present time?
2. **EVALUATE** Which sentence talks about an ability Carl doesn't have yet?
3. **EVALUATE** Which sentence talks about an ability Carl had in the past?

B. Discuss your answers with the class and read the Meaning and Use Notes to check them.

Meaning and Use Notes

ONLINE PRACTICE

Present Ability with *Can*

▶ **1A** *Can* is used to talk about an ability in the present.

The baby **can walk**, but she **can't talk** yet.
Strong winds **can cause** a lot of damage.

▶ **1B** *Be able to* also describes an ability in the present, but *can* is more commonly used.

Less Common	More Common
He **is able** to speak French and Arabic.	He **can speak** French and Arabic.

Future Ability with *Be Able To* and *Can*

▶ **2A** Use *will be able to* to talk about a skill or other ability that you don't have yet but will have in the future. Do not use *can* to describe an ability that you will have only in the future.

After I complete this class, **I'll be able to type** 60 words a minute.
X After I complete this class, I can type 60 words a minute. (INCORRECT)

I **will be able to see** better after I get new glasses.
X I can see better after I get new glasses. (INCORRECT)

▶ **2B** Use *will be able to* or *can* to express ability that relates to decisions and arrangements for the future.

She {**'ll be able to** / **can**} **meet** you at the airport at 3:00.

I'm busy now, but I {**'ll be able to** / **can**} **help** you in ten minutes.

Past Ability with *Could* and *Be Able To*

▶ **3A** Use *could* or *was/were able to* to talk about an ability that existed for a long period of time in the past.

Long Period of Time

When I was young, I {**was able to** / **could**} **eat** dessert every night, and I didn't gain weight.

▶ **3B** In affirmative statements with action verbs, do not use *could* to talk about an ability related to a single event. Use only *was/were able to.*

Single Event with Action Verb (Affirmative)

Yesterday I **was able to finish** my homework quickly.

X Yesterday I could finish my homework quickly. (INCORRECT)

▶ **3C** In affirmative statements with certain stative verbs such as *see, hear, feel, taste, understand,* and *remember,* use *could* or *was/were able to* to talk about ability related to a single event in the past.

Single Event with Stative Verb (Affirmative)

Last night the sky was clear and we {**were able to** / **could**} **see** for miles.

▶ **3D** In negative statements, use *couldn't* or *wasn't/weren't able to* for both ability during single events and ability over a long period of time.

Single Event (Negative)

Yesterday I {**wasn't able to** / **couldn't**} finish my homework quickly.

Long Period of Time

When I was younger, I {**wasn't able to** / **couldn't**} **finish** my homework quickly.

C1 Listening for Meaning and Use

▶ Notes 1–3

CD1 T47 **Listen to each speaker. Choose the correct response.**

1. **a.** OK, let's go today.
   (b.) OK, we'll go tomorrow.
2. **a.** No, they can't. It's raining.
   b. Why not?
3. **a.** Were they very high?
   b. How disappointing!
4. **a.** Well, at least she tries.
   b. Of course she can. Her dad's a coach.
5. **a.** So what did they do?
   b. When did they learn?
6. **a.** Is she able to walk now?
   b. Will she be able to walk tomorrow?

C2 Talking About Future Abilities

▶ Note 2A

Complete the sentences with *will/won't + be able to.* Use your own ideas.

1. Next year *I'll be able to drive.*
2. In 20 years people ______
3. In 50 years doctors ______
4. By 2030 scientists ______
5. In 10 years I ______
6. In 100 years humans ______

C3 Distinguishing Between *Can* and *Be Able To*

▶ Notes 2A, 2B

In your notebook, rewrite these sentences with *can* where possible.

1. The teacher will be able to help you with your homework this afternoon.
   The teacher can help you with your homework this afternoon.
2. Paul will be able to drive us to school tomorrow morning.
3. Larry will be able to get a job when he learns how to create websites.
4. Will you be able to swim after you finish this swimming class?
5. The doctor will be able to see you at three o'clock this afternoon.
6. He will be able to walk again after the operation.

C4 Talking About Past Abilities

▶ Notes 3A–3D

A. **Work with a partner. Look at the topics below, and think about how people lived fifty years ago. Take turns making sentences with *could(n't)* and *was/were (not) able to.***

education	food	housing	relationships
energy	health	leisure time	transportation

A: Fifty years ago many people weren't able to go to college.

B: Fifty years ago you could buy a house for ten thousand dollars.

B. **Share your ideas with your classmates.**

C5 Comparing Long Periods of Time and Single Events

▶ Notes 3A–3D

A. **In your notebook, rewrite these sentences with *could* or *couldn't* where possible. Do not change the meaning.**

1. For many years, we were able to take long vacations.

   For many years, we could take long vacations.

2. They were able to get tickets for the game this morning.
3. Before he hurt his knee, he was able to run five miles a day.
4. Even as a young child, she was able to swim well.
5. We weren't able to get to the concert on time last night.
6. Were you able to see the fireworks from your window the other night?
7. Matt wasn't able to find his keys this morning.
8. I was able to park the car in front of the restaurant this morning.

B. **Look back at the sentences in part A. Which sentences cannot be rewritten? Why?**

Vocabulary Notes

Know How To

You can use *know how to* instead of *can* to talk about a skill (a particular ability that you develop through training or practice).

Know How To	*Can*
They **know how to** speak Portuguese.	They **can** speak Portuguese.
She **doesn't know how to** drive a car.	She **can't** drive a car.

We do not use *know how to* to talk about abilities that do not require training or practice. We use *can* instead.

Can

Hurricanes **can** cause damage.
X Hurricanes know how to cause damage. (INCORRECT)

The doctor **can** see you now.
X The doctor knows how to see you now. (INCORRECT)

C6 Talking About Skills

A. **Ask your classmates questions to find out who has the skills on the list. Ask four questions with *can* and four questions with *know how to.***

1. play chess
   Can you play chess? OR
   Do you know how to play chess?
2. change a tire
3. create a podcast
4. sew on a button
5. play the guitar
   (or other instrument)
6. ice skate
7. speak French
8. drive a motorcycle

B. **Work in small groups. Talk about your classmates' abilities. Use *can* and *know how to.***

Carlos can play chess, but Mei Ling can't. OR
Carlos knows how to play chess, but Mei Ling doesn't.

D FORM 2

Modals of Future Possibility

Think Critically About Form

A. Read the sentences and complete the tasks below.

a. He might walk again.
b. He has the strength of one hundred men.
c. Researchers may find a cure.

1. **IDENTIFY** Which sentences contain modals? Underline them. Which sentence contains a verb in the simple present?
2. **COMPARE AND CONTRAST** Change all the sentences to negative statements. How are the negative statements with modals different from the negative statement in the simple present?

B. Discuss your answers with the class and read the Form charts to check them.

▶ *Can* for Present and Future Ability

ONLINE PRACTICE

AFFIRMATIVE STATEMENTS			
SUBJECT	MODAL	BASE FORM OF VERB	
I You He They	**might** **may** **could** **will**	**leave**	tomorrow.

NEGATIVE STATEMENTS			
SUBJECT	MODAL + *NOT*	BASE FORM OF VERB	
I You He They	**might not** **may not** **won't**	**leave**	tomorrow.

YES/NO QUESTIONS
FUTURE FORM
Are you going to leave next weekend? Will you leave next weekend? Are you leaving next weekend?

SHORT ANSWERS	
AFFIRMATIVE	NEGATIVE
I **may**.	I **may not**.
I **might**.	I **might not**.
I **could**.	I **may not**. / I **might not**.

(Continued on page 168)

- *Could not (couldn't)* is not usually used to express future possibility.
- *May not* and *might not* are not contracted in American English.
- *Yes/No* questions about future possibility are not usually formed with *may, might,* or *could*. Instead, they are formed with *be going to, will*, or the present continuous as future. You can use *may, might*, or *could* in short answers.
- Use modal + *be* in short answers to questions with *be*.

  A: Will you **be** home next weekend?
  B: I **might be**.
- Information questions about future possibility are also usually asked with future forms. You can answer with *may, might,* or *could*.

  A: When are you leaving?
  B: I'm not sure. I **may leave** next weekend.

  A: When is he going to call?
  B: He **might call** today.

D1 Listening for Form

CD1 T48 **Listen to these conversations. Write the correct form of the modals you hear.**

1. **A:** What will you do when you finish college?

   B: I __might__(1) look for a job, or I ________(2) go to graduate school instead.
2. **A:** The traffic is moving very slowly. We won't get to the theater on time.

   B: We ________(1). We still have plenty of time.
3. **A:** When is the package arriving?

   B: It ________(1) be here tomorrow, or it ________(2) arrive until the next day.
4. **A:** Will there be many people at the meeting?

   B: I don't know. There ________(1) be just a few of us.
5. **A:** What do you think? Is it going to snow tonight?

   B: Well, according to the weather report, there ________(1) be a lot of snow, but the storm ________(2) hit us at all.

D2 Forming Affirmative and Negative Statements

A. **Form affirmative statements from these words and phrases. Punctuate your sentences correctly.**

1. fail/the/I/might/test

   I might fail the test.

2. game/you/win/next/could/the/Saturday

   ____

3. might/Bob and Carol/married/get/year/next

   ____

4. rain/could/tomorrow/it

   ____

5. tonight/cook/Sheryl/dinner/will

   ____

6. on/we/go/may/Sunday/beach/the/to

   ____

7. will/Yuji/at six o'clock/come

   ____

8. buy/Kim and Josh/a/house/might

   ____

9. Lynn/graduate/could/next semester

   ____

10. stay/may/home/Victor/next weekend

    ____

B. **In your notebook, rewrite the sentences as negative statements. Which three sentences cannot be made negative? Why? Discuss your answers with a partner.**

I might not fail the test.

E MEANING AND USE 2

Future Possibility

Think Critically About Meaning and Use

A. Read the sentences and answer the questions below.

a. Ana could leave tomorrow, or she could leave today.
b. Ana will leave tomorrow. She's ready to go.
c. Ana may leave tomorrow. She's ready to go, but it depends on the weather.
d. Maybe Ana will leave tomorrow. I'm not certain.
e. Ana might leave tomorrow. I'm not sure.

ANALYZE Which sentence is the most certain? Which sentences are less certain?

B. Discuss your answers with the class and read the Meaning and Use Notes to check them.

Meaning and Use Notes

ONLINE PRACTICE

Expressing Future Possibility with *Could, Might,* and *May*

▶ 1A *Could, might (not),* and *may (not)* express possibility about the future. *Could* and *might* sometimes express more uncertainty than *may*.

I **could get** an A or a B in the course. It depends on my final paper.

I **may take** history next semester. It seems like a good idea.

▶ 1B You can talk about future possibility and future ability together with *might/may (not) + be able to*. You cannot use *might/may (not) + can*.

It's already April, but I **might be able to go** skiing one more time.

If I learn to speak Portuguese, I **may be able to get** a job in Brazil.
X If I learn to speak Portuguese, I may can get a job in Brazil. (INCORRECT)

▶ 1C Do not confuse *may be* and *maybe*. *May be* is the modal *may* and the verb *be*. *Maybe* is an adverb. It comes at the beginning of a sentence, and it is written as one word. *Maybe* can be used with *will* to express future possibility.

***May Be* (Modal + *Be*)**		***Maybe* (Adverb)**
We **may be** away next week.	=	**Maybe** we'**ll be** away next week.

▶ 1D Use *will* in *Yes/No* questions about future possibility. You can use *might,* but it will sound overly formal. Do not use *may.*

Will	*Might/May*
Will he come home soon?	**Might** he come home soon? (OVERLY FORMAL)
	x May he come home soon? (INCORRECT)

Expressing Strong Certainty with *Will*

▶ 2 Use *will* when you are certain about something. If you are not certain, you can weaken *will* by adding the adverbs *probably, maybe,* and *perhaps.*

Certain	Not Certain
They**'ll move** in the summer.	They**'ll probably move** in the summer.
She**'ll find** a new job.	**Maybe** she**'ll find** a new job.

E1 Listening for Meaning and Use

▶ Notes 1A, 1B, 2

CD1 T49 **Listen to the conversation. Check (✓) the places that Mark and Dan are definitely going to see on their trip to Florida. Put a question mark (?) next to the places that they aren't sure about.**

__✓__ **1.** Disney World
_____ **2.** Epcot Center
_____ **3.** Cape Canaveral
_____ **4.** Miami Beach
_____ **5.** the Everglades
_____ **6.** Key West

The Colony Hotel, Miami Beach

E2 Using Modals for Future Possibility ▶ Notes 1–2

Complete this conversation by choosing the appropriate word or phrase in parentheses.

A: So what's your daughter Lisa going to do this summer?

B: She's not sure, but she (could / 'll) probably work for an architect. What's your son going to do? (Will / May) he have the same job as last summer?
(1) (2)

A: He isn't sure. He (might / 'll) work in a movie theater again. But there aren't many jobs available, so he (couldn't / might not) find one.
(3) (4)

B: They (can / might) be able to give him a job at my office. I'll speak to my boss. (Maybe / May be) there will be an opening.
(5) (6)

A: Oh, thank you! That (maybe / may be) a better way for him to spend the summer. I (can / 'll) probably be able to convince him to apply.
(7) (8)

E3 Contrasting *May Be* and *Maybe* ▶ Notes 1C, 2

Rewrite each sentence in your notebook. If the sentence uses *maybe*, rewrite it with *may be*. If it uses *may be*, rewrite it with *maybe*. Make all other necessary changes.

1. Lee's family may be in town next week.
   Maybe Lee's family will be in town next week.
2. Maybe the weather will be better on the weekend.
3. Maybe we'll be able to get tickets to the baseball game.
4. This may be an exciting game.
5. Maybe they won't be home this evening.
6. The final exam may not be very difficult.
7. He may be stuck in traffic.
8. Maybe they'll be able to help us clean the attic.

E4 Expressing Future Possibility

▶ Notes 1A–2

A. Use your imagination to complete these conversations. Use a modal of future possibility and a verb.

Conversation 1

A: What are your roommates going to do tonight?

B: I don't know. They ___might go to the movies___ (1), but they ___may stay home and watch the game on TV___ (2).

Conversation 2

A: Can you come to Europe with us this summer?

B: I don't have much money, but I ____________ (1).

Conversation 3

A: Tomorrow's Monday again! I don't want to go to school!

B: ____________ (1). Then we won't have to go to school.

Conversation 4

A: What are we having for dinner tonight?

B: We have a couple of choices. We ____________ (1), or we ____________ (2).

Conversation 5

A: Where will you go on your next vacation?

B: I'm not sure. ____________ (2).

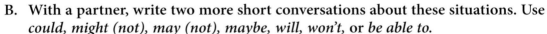

B. With a partner, write two more short conversations about these situations. Use *could, might (not), may (not), maybe, will, won't,* or *be able to.*

A student asks a teacher about finishing a paper late.

A reporter asks an athlete about the next Olympics.

WRITING Write an Email About Your Future After College

Think Critically About Meaning and Use

A. Choose the best answer to complete each conversation.

1. A: At that time, she could speak Japanese fluently.
B: ___________
a. Maybe she can teach me.
(b.) How did she learn it?

2. A: He won't be able to leave the hospital for a long time.
B: ___________
a. Who's going to take care of him at home?
b. I'll try to visit him every day.

3. A: The whole house is clean.
B: ___________
a. It's amazing that you were able to do it by yourself.
b. Who could help you?

4. A: We might go out to dinner tonight.
B: ___________
a. OK. I was able to meet you there.
b. Where do you think you'll go?

5. A: Do you know how to swim?
B: ___________
a. Yes, but not very well.
b. No, it's too cold today.

6. A: Were you able to go to the meeting last night?
B: ___________
a. Yes, I could.
b. Yes, I was.

7. A: What will you be able to do after this English class?
B: ___________
a. I'll be able to speak English more fluently.
b. I can speak English more fluently.

B. Discuss these questions in small groups.

1. **EVALUATE** Why is the incorrect answer in 6 wrong?
2. **ANALYZE** In 1, 2, 5, 6, and 7, is speaker A talking about past, present, or future ability?

Edit

Find the errors in this paragraph and correct them.

My friend Jen might take~~s~~ us to the beach this weekend. The beach isn't far from her house. Jen can to walk there. She is a great swimmer. She could swim when she was three years old! My roommate Nicole doesn't know to swim, so I will probably teach her this weekend. Nicole will able to swim by the end of the summer if she practices every day. May be we'll go sailing this weekend, too. Last Saturday Jen and I was able to go sailing because the weather was great. We could see dolphins near the boat. They were beautiful. Unfortunately, we couldn't touch them. If we're lucky, we can see some dolphins this weekend.

Write

Imagine that you're going to graduate from college soon, and you want to write an email to a friend in another country talking about your plans for the future. Follow the steps below to write the email. Use modals of ability and possibility.

1. **Brainstorm** Think about your plans for the future. Take notes about what you want to say. Use these questions to help you.
   - What are you going to do when you finish college?
   - What things will you be able to do? What useful skills and abilities will you have?
   - What kind of work will you definitely do? What kind of work won't you do?
   - Where do you think you will live?
   - What do you think you'll probably do in your free time? What do you think you won't do?

2. **Write a First Draft** Before you write your draft, read the checklist below. Write your draft using modals of ability and possibility.

3. **Edit** Read your work and check it against the checklist below. Circle grammar, spelling, and punctuation errors.

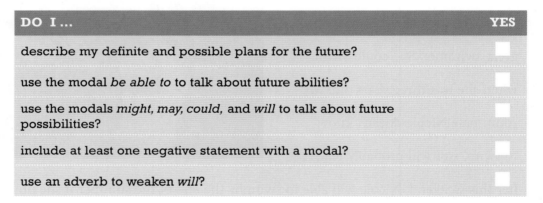

DO I ...	YES
describe my definite and possible plans for the future?	☐
use the modal *be able to* to talk about future abilities?	☐
use the modals *might, may, could,* and *will* to talk about future possibilities?	☐
include at least one negative statement with a modal?	☐
use an adverb to weaken *will*?	☐

4. **Peer Review** Work with a partner to help you decide how to fix your errors and improve the content.

5. **Rewrite Your Draft** Using the comments from your partner, write a final draft.

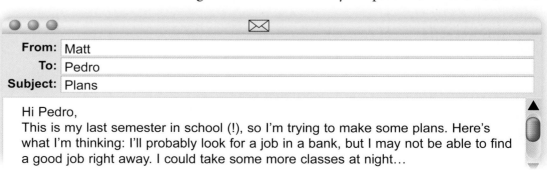

From: Matt
To: Pedro
Subject: Plans

Hi Pedro,
This is my last semester in school (!), so I'm trying to make some plans. Here's what I'm thinking: I'll probably look for a job in a bank, but I may not be able to find a good job right away. I could take some more classes at night…

CHAPTER

10

Modals and Phrases of Request, Permission, Desire, and Preference

A. **GRAMMAR IN DISCOURSE: How *Not* to Ask for a Raise** . 178

B. **FORM: Modals of Request; Modals of Permission; *Would Like, Would Prefer,* and *Would Rather*** 180

Modals of Request

Can/Could/Will/Would you **close** the window?

Modals of Permission

You **can/may borrow** my car.

Would Like, Would Prefer,* and *Would Rather

I **would rather leave**.

I **would prefer/would like to leave**.

I **would prefer/would like some tea**.

C. **MEANING AND USE 1: Modals of Request** 186

Making Requests

Agreeing to and Refusing Requests

D. **MEANING AND USE 2: Modals of Permission** 190

Asking for Permission

Giving and Refusing Permission

E. **MEANING AND USE 3: *Would Like, Would Prefer,* and *Would Rather*** 193

Stating Desires and Making Requests with *Would Like*

Making Offers with *Would Like*

Accepting and Refusing Offers with *Thank You*

Stating Preferences with *Would Like, Would Prefer,* and *Would Rather*

WRITING: Write an Email Involving a Request 197

A GRAMMAR IN DISCOURSE

How *Not* to Ask for a Raise

A1 Before You Read

Discuss these questions.

Have you ever asked for a raise (an increase in pay)? How did you ask? What did your boss say? What are some good ways to ask for a raise?

A2 Read

CD1 T50 **Read this excerpt from an e-book to find out about good and bad ways to ask for a raise.**

How *Not* to Ask for a Raise

A Case Study

As the manager of her own company, Rachel Franz has been asked for raises by many employees. Sometimes she has agreed and sometimes she hasn't. Franz's decision is often influenced by how an employee asks. Here is a typical request for a raise. Find the mistakes that the employee makes in this situation.

Robert: Ms. Franz, could I speak to you for a few minutes?

Ms. Franz: Can we talk another time? It looks like we have a big problem with our computer system and...

Robert: I would rather talk to you now, if possible. It will only take a few minutes.

Ms. Franz: Well, OK, come in.

Robert: I don't know if you know this, but I'm getting married next month.

Ms. Franz: No, I didn't know that, Robert. Congratulations!

Robert: Thank you. Of course, getting married is quite expensive. Would you consider giving me a raise?

Ms. Franz: Well, Robert, your performance review is coming up in six months. I would like to wait until your review.

Robert: But six months is a long time. Could we discuss a raise sooner?

Ms. Franz: We usually don't give raises between reviews, Robert. Now please excuse me. I have to find out about this computer problem. Can you please ask Kristen to come into my office when you leave?

Analysis

Robert made several errors. First of all, it is best to make an appointment with your boss in advance. Second, try to speak to your boss when things are going well, not badly. Listen when your boss says that it isn't a good time to talk, and arrange to speak to him or her later. Third, give your boss a good reason to give you a raise. Explain that you have more responsibilities at work now, or that you are working longer hours. Show your boss how important you are to the company, not how badly you need the money. Last, do your homework. Robert didn't know that the company doesn't give raises between reviews. Robert didn't get a raise, and he has probably hurt his chances of getting one in the future!

Adapted from *Executive Female*

---

consider: to think about

do your homework: to prepare for something by finding out important information

influence: to have an effect on someone's behavior

performance review: a meeting in which a boss and an employee discuss the employee's work

responsibilities: things that you must do as part of your job

A3 After You Read

The writer says that Robert made several errors. Check (✓) the four errors that Robert made, according to the Analysis in the e-book excerpt.

__✓__ **1.** Robert didn't make an appointment with his boss in advance.

____ **2.** Robert didn't speak politely to his boss.

____ **3.** Robert chose a bad time to speak to his boss.

____ **4.** Robert walked into his boss's office without her permission.

____ **5.** Robert didn't have a good reason for his boss to give him a raise.

____ **6.** Robert didn't know the company rules about raises before he spoke to his boss.

B FORM

Modals of Request; Modals of Permission; *Would Like, Would Prefer,* and *Would Rather*

Think Critically About Form

A. Look back at the conversation in the e-book excerpt on page 178 and complete the tasks below.

1. **IDENTIFY** Find questions with the modals *can, could,* and *would.* (An example is underlined.) What is the subject of each question? What form of the verb follows the subject?
2. **CATEGORIZE** Find the expressions *would rather* and *would like.* Which one is followed by the base form of the verb? Which one is followed by an infinitive (*to* + verb)?

B. Discuss your answers with the class and read the Form charts to check them.

▶ Modals of Request

ONLINE PRACTICE

***YES/NO* QUESTIONS**			
MODAL	**SUBJECT**	**BASE FORM OF VERB**	
Can	you	close	the window?
Could			
Will		give	me a raise?
Would			

SHORT ANSWERS					
YES	**SUBJECT**	**MODAL**	***NO***	**SUBJECT**	**MODAL + *NOT***
Yes,	I	can.	No,	I	can't.
		will.			won't.

- Modals of request are usually used in questions with *you.*
- We usually use *can* and *will* in affirmative short answers. *Could* and *would* are less common.
- We usually avoid using *won't* in negative short answers because it sounds very impolite and angry.

▶ Modals of Permission

AFFIRMATIVE STATEMENTS			
SUBJECT	**MODAL**	**BASE FORM OF VERB**	
You	**can**	**borrow**	my car.
	may		

NEGATIVE STATEMENTS			
SUBJECT	**MODAL + *NOT***	**BASE FORM OF VERB**	
You	**cannot** **can't**	**borrow**	my car.
	may not		

YES/NO QUESTIONS			
MODAL	**SUBJECT**	**BASE FORM OF VERB**	
Can	I we	**borrow**	your car?
Could			
May			

SHORT ANSWERS					
YES	**SUBJECT**	**MODAL**	***NO***	**SUBJECT**	**MODAL + *NOT***
Yes,	you	**can.**	**No,**	you	**can't.**
		may.			**may not.**

INFORMATION QUESTIONS				
***WH-* WORD**	**MODAL**	**SUBJECT**	**BASE FORM OF VERB**	
What	**can**	I	**call**	you?
When	**could**	we	**make**	a reservation?
Where	**may**	I	**put**	my coat?

- Modals of permission are most often used in questions with *I* and *we* and in statements with *you*.
- Use *can* and *may* in statements and short answers. Do not use *could*.
- Use *can, could,* and *may* in *Yes/No* questions.
- There is no contracted form of *may not*.

(Continued on page 182)

▶ *Would Like, Would Prefer,* and *Would Rather*

AFFIRMATIVE STATEMENTS

SUBJECT	*WOULD RATHER*	BASE FORM OF VERB
I	would rather	leave.

SUBJECT	*WOULD PREFER/ WOULD LIKE*	INFINITIVE OR NOUN PHRASE
I	would prefer would like	to leave. some tea.

NEGATIVE STATEMENTS

SUBJECT	*WOULD RATHER + NOT*	BASE FORM OF VERB
I	would rather not	leave.

SUBJECT	*WOULD PREFER + NOT*	INFINITIVE
I	would prefer not	to leave.

***YES/NO* QUESTIONS**

WOULD	SUBJECT	*RATHER*	BASE FORM OF VERB
Would	you	rather	leave?

WOULD	SUBJECT	*PREFER/ LIKE*	INFINITIVE OR NOUN PHRASE
Would	you	prefer like	to leave? some tea?

SHORT ANSWERS

YES,	SUBJECT	*WOULD*	*NO,*	SUBJECT	*WOULD + NOT*
Yes,	I	would.	No,	I	wouldn't.

YES,	SUBJECT	*WOULD*	*NO,*	SUBJECT	*WOULD + NOT*
Yes,	I	would.	No,	I	wouldn't.

INFORMATION QUESTIONS

WH- WORD	*WOULD*	SUBJECT	*RATHER*	BASE FORM OF VERB
What	would	you	rather	eat?

WH- WORD	*WOULD*	SUBJECT	*PREFER/LIKE*	INFINITIVE
What	would	you	prefer like	to eat?

- *Would rather* is similar to a modal verb. It is followed by the base form of the verb.
- Unlike modals, *would like* and *would prefer* are followed by the infinitive (*to* + verb). They can also be followed by a noun phrase.
- *Would like* is not usually used in negative statements. Use *don't/doesn't want* instead.

  I **don't want** to leave.   I **don't want** tea.
- For contractions with *would*, combine the subject pronoun + *'d*.

B1 Listening for Form

CD1 T51 **Listen to these conversations. Write the form of the modals you hear.**

1. **A:** Kevin, ___will___(1) you start dinner? I'm going shopping.

   B: Hmm… __________(2) you get some chocolate ice cream?

   A: I __________(3) buy more ice cream. You know we're both on a diet.
2. **A:** __________(1) I speak with Mrs. Thompson, please?

   B: No, I'm sorry. She's in a meeting. __________(2) you call back in an hour?
3. **A:** __________(1) you __________(2) a cup of coffee?

   B: No, thanks. I __________(3) a cup of tea.
4. **A:** I __________(1) to go to the beach with my friends this weekend, but I don't have any money. __________(2) I borrow $50?

   B: No, you __________(3). You already owe me $100!

B2 Building Questions with Modals

Build eight logical questions. Use a word or phrase from each column.

Can I come with you?

can	I	give	to leave now
could	you	come	with you
would		prefer	me a ride
		like	eat later
		rather	some coffee

B3 Completing Conversations

Complete these conversations using the words in parentheses. Use contractions where possible. Then practice the conversations with a partner.

1. **Guard:** Excuse me, sir. The sign says ___visitors may not take___ (1) (not/take/may/visitors) pictures inside the museum.

   Visitor: Oh, I'm sorry. I didn't see it. ______________ (2) (leave/I/can/where) my camera?

2. **Salesclerk:** ______________ (1) (I/help/may) you?

   Customer: Yes. I'm looking for a gift for my husband. ______________ (2) (like/I/get/would/to) him something special.

3. **Visitor:** ______________ (1) (I/park/can) here?

   Guard: No, I'm sorry. ______________ (2) (can/visitors/park/not) in this section.

4. **Husband:** ______________ (1) (you/will/answer) the phone, please? My hands are wet.

   Wife: Sorry, ______________ (2) (I/not/can). I'm busy. They can leave a message on the answering machine.

5. **Father:** ______________ (1) (you/go/would/like/to) skiing with us this weekend?

   Daughter: No, thanks. ______________ (2) (rather/I/stay/would) home.

6. **Waitress:** ______________ (1) (order/like/you/would/to) now?

   Customer: Yes, I'll have the broiled chicken.

   Waitress: ______________ (2) (you/would/prefer) soup or salad as an appetizer?

B4 Working on Negative Sentences

Write the negative form of each sentence. Use contractions where possible. Remember to avoid the negative form of *would like.*

1. I would rather stay home tonight.

   I'd rather not stay home tonight.

2. We would prefer to exercise in the morning.

   ____

3. I would like to call you later.

   ____

4. They would rather live in the suburbs.

   ____

5. He would prefer to buy a new computer.

   ____

6. He would like to finish his work now.

   ____

B4 Writing Short Conversations

In your notebook, write short conversations with information questions and answers using these words and phrases. Punctuate your sentences correctly.

1. where/would rather/live/in Hong Kong/in New York City

   A: Where would you rather live, in Hong King or in New York City?

   B: I'd rather live in Hong Kong.

2. who/would prefer/meet/a famous athlete/a famous writer
3. where/would like/eat dinner tonight/at home/in a restaurant
4. what/would rather/do tonight/watch TV/go out
5. how/would rather/travel/by car/by plane
6. what/would like/buy/a laptop computer/desktop computer
7. what/would rather/eat/cookies/cake
8. where/would prefer/live/in a big city/in a small town

C MEANING AND USE 1

Modals of Request

Think Critically About Meaning and Use

A. Read the sentences and answer the questions below.

a. Will you open the door?
b. Would you open the door, please?
c. Can you open the door, please?

EVALUATE Which request is the most polite? Which request is the least polite?

B. Discuss your answers with the class and read the Meaning and Use Notes to check them.

Meaning and Use Notes

ONLINE PRACTICE

Making Requests

▶ 1A Use *can, could, will,* and *would* to make requests. *Can* and *will* are less formal than *could* and *would*. We usually use *can* and *will* in informal conversations with friends and family. We use *could* and *would* to make polite requests in formal situations when we speak to strangers or to people in authority.

Less Formal	More Formal
To a Friend: **Can** you **tell** me the time?	To a Stranger: **Could** you **tell** me the time?
Mother to Child: **Will** you **be** quiet?	To a Boss: **Would** you **look** at my report?

▶ 1B Add *please* to a request to make it more polite.

Can you tell me the time, **please**?

Would you **please** look over my report?

Agreeing to and Refusing Requests

▶ 2A Use *will* and *can* to agree to requests. Do not use *would* or *could*. We generally use *can't* to refuse a request. *Won't* is used for strong refusals, and sounds impolite.

Agreeing to a Request

A: **Will** you help me for a minute?
B: **Yes**, I **will**.

A: **Could** you **spell** your name for me?
B: **Yes**, I **can**. It's C-L-A-R-K-E.

Refusing a Request

A: **Can** you **help** me with the laundry?
B: Sorry. I **can't** right now. (polite)

A: Holly, will you clean up this room?
B: **No**, I **won't**. (impolite)

▶ **2B**	Instead of *can* or *will*, we often use expressions such as *OK*, *sure*, or *certainly* when agreeing to a request. A: Will you help me for a minute? B: **OK**. A: Could you spell your name for me? B: **Sure**. It's C-L-A-R-K-E.
▶ **2C**	We often say *I'm sorry* and give a reason in order to make our refusal more polite. A: Can you help me with the laundry? B: **I'm sorry**, but I can't right now. **I have a doctor's appointment**.

C1 Listening for Meaning and Use

▶ Notes 1A,1B

CD1 T52 **A. Listen to each conversation. Is the request you hear informal or formal? Check (✓) the correct column.**

	INFORMAL	FORMAL
1.	✓	
2.		
3.		
4.		
5.		

CD1 T53 **B. Listen to the conversations again. Who are the speakers? Look at the choices, and write the correct letter for each conversation. Then discuss your answers with your classmates.**

1. __a__ a. mother and daughter
2. ______ b. two strangers
3. ______ c. two friends
4. ______ d. student and teacher
5. ______ e. employee and boss

C2 Using the Telephone

▶ Notes 1–2

A. **Choose the best response to complete each telephone conversation.**

1. **Student:** Could you connect me with Professor Hill's office?
   Secretary: ________
   a. No, I won't. He's busy.
   b. I'm sorry. He's not in right now. Would you like to leave a message?

2. **Secretary:** Good morning, History Department.
   Student: I'd like to register for History 201. Is it still open?
   Secretary: ________
   a. Yes. Give me your name.
   b. Yes, it is. Could you give me your name, please?

3. **Jenny's friend:** Will you please tell Jenny that I called?
   Jenny's sister: ________
   a. No, I won't. I'm going out.
   b. I won't be here when she gets home, but I'll leave her a note.

4. **Mark's friend:** Hi. Is Mark there?
   Mark's brother: ________
   a. Sure. Can you hold on a minute?
   b. Certainly. Would you hold, please?

5. **Client:** Would you please ask Ms. Banes to call me this afternoon?
   Secretary: ________
   a. I'm sorry, but she's out of the office until next week.
   b. Sorry, I can't.

6. **Student:** Could you send me some information about scholarships?
   Secretary: ________
   a. Certainly.
   b. No, I can't. That's impossible right now.

B. **Discuss your answers with a partner. Why did you choose each response? Why was the other response inappropriate?**

C. **Now practice the conversations with your partner.**

C3 Making Formal and Informal Requests ▶ Notes 1A, 1B

A Work with a partner. Complete the requests with *can*, *will*, *could*, or would. (More than one answer is possible for each situation.)

1. **Neighbor A:** ___Can___ you take in our mail while we're away?
   Neighbor B: I'm sorry, but I can't. I'll be away then, too.
2. **Young Woman:** Excuse me, officer. ________ you please help me?
   Police Officer: Of course. What's the problem?
3. **Parent:** ________ you help me for a minute?
   Child: OK.
4. **Customer:** ________ you put that in a box, please?
   Salesclerk: I'm sorry, ma'am. I don't have any boxes.
5. **Employee:** When you get a chance, ________ you please show me how to use this new computer program?
   Manager: Certainly. How about right now?

B. Work with a different partner. Compare your answers. Be prepared to explain the modals you choose.

C4 Agreeing to and Refusing Requests ▶ Notes 1, 2

Work with a partner. Read each situation. Then take turns making and responding to requests. Use *can*, *will*, *could*, or *would* in your requests. Use expressions such as *OK*, *sure*, *certainly*, and *I'm sorry* in your responses, and give reasons for refusals.

1. You are at a supermarket. You want the cashier to give you change for a dollar.

   A: Could you give me change for a dollar, please?

   B: Certainly.

   OR

   I'm sorry. The manager doesn't allow us to make change.
2. You are moving to a new apartment. You want your friend to help you move.
3. You would like your friend to lend you $50 until next week.
4. You are on vacation. You want the hotel desk clerk to give you a larger room.
5. You missed class yesterday, and you want your classmate to lend you her notes.
6. You would like your mechanic to repair your car by the end of the week.

D MEANING AND USE 2

Modals of Permission

Think Critically About Meaning and Use

A. Read the sentences and answer the questions below.

1a. Can I look at your book?

1b. Can you speak Russian?

2a. May I borrow your book?

2b. Can I borrow your book?

1. **EVALUATE** Look at 1a and 1b. Which question asks for permission to do something? Which question asks about ability?
2. **INTERPRET** Look at 2a and 2b. Which question is more formal?

B. Discuss your answers with the class and read the Meaning and Use Notes to check them.

Meaning and Use Notes

ONLINE PRACTICE

Asking for Permission

▶ 1A Use *can, could,* and *may* to ask for permission. *Can* and *could* are less formal than *may*. We usually use *may* in formal situations when we speak to strangers or to people in authority. You can use *please* to make your request more polite.

Less Formal

Child to Parent: **Can** I **go** outside and play now?

Friend to Friend: **Could** I **borrow** your pen for a minute?

More Formal

Business Call: A: **May** I **speak** to Ms. Jones, **please**?

B: Certainly. **May** I **ask** who's calling?

▶ 1B Because *may* is more formal, it is often used in announcements and signs or other printed materials.

Announcement: Flight 26 has arrived. Passengers **may proceed** to Gate 2B for boarding.

Sign: Visitors **may not park** in numbered spaces.

	Giving and Refusing Permission
▶ 2A	Use *may/may not* or *can/can't* to give or refuse permission. Do not use *could*. **Giving Permission** A: Could I hand in my homework tomorrow? B: **Yes, you may.** Just put it on my desk. **Refusing Permission** A: Could I hand in my homework tomorrow? B: **No, you can't.** It's due today.
▶ 2B	Instead of answering with *can* or *may*, we often use expressions such as *sure, go (right) ahead,* or *certainly* when giving permission. A: Can I use the computer now? B: **Sure**. I'm finished with it. A: Could I turn on the radio? B: **Go right ahead.**
▶ 2C	We often say *I'm sorry* and give a reason to make a refusal sound more polite. A: Could I hand in my homework tomorrow? B: **I'm sorry,** but you can't. **It's due today.**

D1 Listening for Meaning and Use

▶ Notes 1A, 1B

CD1 T54

Listen to these conversations. In each, the first speaker is asking for permission. Who is the second speaker? Look at the choices and write the correct letter for each conversation.

1. d
2. ____
3. ____
4. ____
5. ____
6. ____
7. ____
8. ____

a. a boss
b. a stranger
c. a mother
d. a friend
e. a police officer
f. a salesclerk
g. a brother
h. a teacher

D2 Asking For Permission

▶ Note 1A

Look at the pictures. Make sentences to ask permission. Use informal and formal modals as appropriate.

May I go in front of you?

D3 Asking For and Giving or Refusing Permission

▶ Notes 1–2

Work with a partner. Take turns asking for and giving or refusing permission in these situations. Use *can*, *may*, or *could* in your questions. Use expressions such as *sure*, *go (right) ahead*, *certainly*, and *I'm sorry* in your responses.

1. You need to use your classmate's pencil.

   A: Can I use your pencil for a minute?

   B: Sure. Here you are.

2. You want to rent an apartment. The landlord shows it to you at night. You want to see it again in the daytime.
3. You want to borrow your friend's car this afternoon.
4. You are hungry, and your roommate has some leftover pizza in the refrigerator.
5. You are paying your bill at a restaurant. You want to pay with a credit card.

E MEANING AND USE 3

Would Like, Would Prefer, and *Would Rather*

Think Critically About Meaning and Use

A. Read the sentences and complete the tasks below.

1a. I want the check now.
1b. I'd like the check, please.

2a. Do you like ice cream?
2b. Would you like ice cream?

1. **EVALUATE** Compare 1a and 1b. Which sounds more polite?
2. **EVALUATE** Compare 2a and 2b. Which is an offer? Which asks about likes or dislikes?

B. Discuss your answers with the class and read the Meaning and Use Notes to check them.

Meaning and Use Notes

ONLINE PRACTICE

Stating Desires and Making Requests with *Would Like*

▶ **1A** *Would like* has the same meaning as *want*. It is often used to talk about desires.

Stating a Desire with *Would Like*
I'd like to go to China next year. (= I **want** to go to China next year.)

▶ **1B** *Would like* is also used to make requests. In making requests, *would like* is more polite than *want*. Add *please* to make the request even more polite.

Making a Request with *Would Like*
I'd like the check, please. ✗ I want the check. (NOT POLITE)

Making Offers with *Would Like*

▶ **2** Use *would like* in a question to make a polite offer.

A: **Would** you **like** some coffee?
B: Yes, please. With milk and sugar.

> ! Be careful not to confuse *would like* and *like*.
>
> *Would Like* (to Make an Offer)
> A: **Would** you **like** some coffee?
> B: Yes, please. With milk and sugar.
>
> *Like* (to Ask About Likes and Dislikes)
> A: Do you **like** coffee?
> B: Yes, I do. I drink it every morning.

(Continued on page 194)

Accepting and Refusing Offers with *Thank You*	
▶ 3	Use *thank you* to accept and refuse offers. We often give a reason to make our refusal more polite.

Accepting an Offer

A: Would you like a seat?

B: Yes, **thank you.**

Refusing an Offer

A: Would you like a seat?

B: No, **thanks**. I'm getting off at the next stop.

Stating Preferences with *Would Like, Would Prefer,* and *Would Rather*	
▶ 4A	Use *would like, would prefer,* or *would rather* to ask about and state preferences.

A: **Would** you {**like** to / **prefer** to / **rather**} walk home or take the bus?

B: I**'d like** to walk.

C: I**'d rather** take the bus. It's too far to walk.

▶ **4B** Use *would rather* with *than* to compare two actions.

I**'d rather** walk **than** take the bus.

I**'d rather** play basketball **than** (play) football.

E1 Listening for Meaning and Use

▶ **Notes 1, 2, 4A, 4B**

CD1 T55

Listen to each statement. Is the speaker making a request, making an offer, or stating a preference? Check (✓) the correct column.

	REQUEST	OFFER	PREFERENCE
1.			✓
2.			
3.			
4.			
5.			
6.			
7.			

E2 Making Offers and Stating Preferences

▶ Notes 2, 3, 4A

Work with a partner. Look at the pictures and take turns making offers, asking about preferences, and responding appropriately. Use *would like, would prefer,* or *would rather.*

1

A: *Would you like some help?*

B: *Yes, thank you.* OR
No, thanks. I can carry them myself.

2

3

4

5

6

E3 Asking About and Stating Preferences

▶ Notes 4A, 4B

Work with a partner. Read each situation. Take turns asking and answering questions with *would prefer*, *would rather*, and *would like*.

1. You and your friend are making plans for the evening. You could see a movie, or you could go to a concert.

   A: Would you rather see a movie or go to a concert?

   B: I'd rather see a movie.

   OR

   A: Would you prefer to see a movie or go to a concert?

   B: I'd prefer to go to a concert.

2. You and your roommate are trying to decide what to eat for dinner: chicken or fish.
3. You need to finish a project by tomorrow. Your boss asks if you want to stay late today or come in early tomorrow.
4. You are making arrangements to travel from Paris to Rome. The travel agent asks you if you want to fly or go by train.
5. You want your roommate to help with the housework. You give her a choice: do the dishes or vacuum.

E4 Discussing Preferences

▶ Notes 4A–4C

Work with a small group. Look at these winter vacation ideas and choose where you would like to go. Then discuss your preferences by explaining what you would like to do. Use *would prefer*, *would rather*, and *would like*.

1. Mountain resort	watch ski competitions, go downhill skiing, go cross-country skiing, hike, watch birds, visit nearby towns
2. Caribbean cruise	swim, play volleyball, play tennis, sunbathe, go scuba diving, visit islands, eat fancy buffet dinners
3. Trip to Europe	shop, visit art museums, try foreign foods, speak foreign languages, visit cities, see famous buildings, take photographs

I'd prefer to go on a Caribbean cruise because I'd rather be in the tropics than in the mountains. Once I get there, I'd rather play tennis than volleyball. I'd also like to go scuba diving, but I prefer not to eat fancy buffet dinners. I'm on a diet!

WRITING Write an Email Involving a Request

Think Critically About Meaning and Use

A. Choose the best answer to complete each conversation.

1. A: Could you help me?
   B: I'm sorry. _____
   a. I didn't have the time.
   (b.) I'm busy right now.

2. A: Could I borrow your car later?
   B: No, I'm sorry, but _____.
   a. you can't.
   b. you couldn't.

3. A: Would you help me choose a present for my wife?
   B: ___________
   a. Yes, I may.
   b. Certainly.

4. A: Do you like to play soccer?
   B: ___________
   a. Not really.
   b. Yes. I'd love to.

5. A: Could you give me a ride to work?
   B: Sure, _____.
   a. no problem.
   b. no way.

6. A: Would you rather go to the art museum or stay home?
   B: ___________
   a. Yes, I would.
   b. I'd rather stay home tonight.

B. Discuss these questions in small groups.

1. **COMPARE AND CONTRAST** How are the questions in 1, 2, 3, and 5 different from the questions in 4 and 6?
2. **ANALYZE** Why is the correct response in 1 a little more polite than the correct response in 2?

Edit

Some of these sentences have errors. Find the errors and correct them.

1. I would rather ^(have) an apple.
2. You could not borrow my van next week.
3. May we leave now?
4. You mayn't leave until the exam is over.
5. Where you prefer to go this weekend?
6. I'd rather not to go now.
7. She'd like learn to drive.
8. What would you rather do tonight?

Write

Imagine that you want to ask your professor for an extension on a paper. Write an email asking for permission. Follow the steps below. Use modals and phrases of request, permission, and desire.

1. **Brainstorm** Think about what you will say in your email. Take notes about what you will say. Use these categories to help you.
   - opening question (polite request)
   - how much of an extension you want
   - why you deserve an extension
   - what you have done on your paper so far

2. **Write a First Draft** Before you write your draft, read the checklist below. Write your draft using modals and phrases of request, permission, and desire.

3. **Edit** Read your work and check it against the checklist below. Circle grammar, spelling, and punctuation errors.

DO I ...	YES
begin with a polite request using *could* or *may* to ask for an extension?	☐
provide one or more reasons to explain why I need an extension?	☐
use *would like* to express a desire?	☐
use *please* and language that is polite and appropriately formal for the situation?	☐
finish by thanking my professor for considering my request?	☐

4. **Peer Review** Work with a partner to help you decide how to fix your errors and improve the content.

5. **Rewrite Your Draft** Using the comments from your partner, write a final draft.

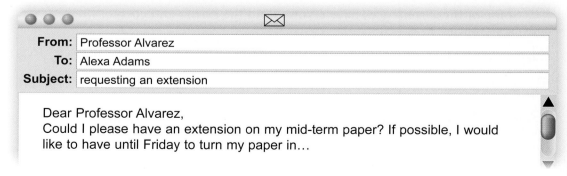

From: Professor Alvarez
To: Alexa Adams
Subject: requesting an extension

Dear Professor Alvarez,
Could I please have an extension on my mid-term paper? If possible, I would like to have until Friday to turn my paper in…

CHAPTER

11

Modals and Phrasal Modals of Advice, Necessity, and Prohibition

A. **GRAMMAR IN DISCOURSE: Tips on Being a Good Dinner Guest** 200

B. **FORM: Modals and Phrasal Modals of Advice, Necessity, and Prohibition** 202

Modals of Advice, Necessity, and Prohibition

You **could/might/should/must buy** a gift.

You **must not buy** a gift.

Phrasal Modals of Advice and Necessity

You **have to/have got to call** him.

I **ought to call** him.

Informally Speaking: Reduced Forms of *Ought To, Has To, Have To, and Have Got To*

C. **MEANING AND USE 1: Modals and Phrasal Modals of Advice** 208

Weak and Strong Advice

Suggestions with *Could* and *Might*

Advice with *Should* and *Ought To*

Warnings with *Had Better*

Strong Advice with *Have To, Have Got To,* and *Must*

D. **MEANING AND USE 2: Modals of Necessity and Prohibition** 214

Necessity

Lack of Necessity vs. Prohibition

WRITING: Write a Memo on Office Rules 218

PART 4 TEST: Modals 221

A GRAMMAR IN DISCOURSE

Tips on Being a Good Dinner Guest

A1 Before You Read

Discuss these questions.

Do you go to dinner at friends' homes and invite friends to your home for dinner? What are these dinners like? What is polite behavior for hosts and guests?

A2 Read

CD1 T56 **Read these tips for some ideas about what to do and not do when you're a dinner guest in another country.**

Tips on Being a Good Dinner Guest

When you travel or live in another country, it's an honor to be invited to dinner at the home of someone from that country. This meal may be the first of many great experiences you'll have in that country. Before accepting a dinner invitation, however, you'd better know the cultural "rules" for guests. Although you don't have to follow these rules, by following them you show respect for your hosts and are more likely to have a really good time.

Every country has its own "rules." Here are some examples:

Turkey

- You must not wear your shoes in the house. Your hosts will offer you slippers.
- You had better not eat too much before you go to dinner. Your hosts will probably offer you a big dinner followed by nuts, fruit, cake, and tea and coffee. You should accept all this food; you shouldn't say that you cannot eat more.

Mexico

- You must not arrive early. In fact, you have to be at least a little late. Your hosts will expect this.
- Don't leave too soon after the meal. Mexicans feel that a good guest ought to stay and talk for a while after all the eating is finished.

China

- You should be on time. This shows respect for your hosts.
- You must take off your shoes before you enter the house.
- You should leave a little food on your plate because you want to show that your hosts are generous.

General

In many countries, you are expected to give your hosts a small gift. Of course, you ought to find out what kind of gift is appropriate.

Finally, because these customs can be so different from country to country and culture to culture, look and listen carefully. Follow the lead of your hosts.

---

honor: something special and a reason for feeling proud

respect: politeness, a feeling that you value and appreciate someone

generous: kind, willing to give a lot to others

A3 After You Read

Write *T* for true or *F* for false for each statement.

__F__ **1.** The tips are for dining in restaurants.

_____ **2.** According to the tips, being on time is especially important in Mexico.

_____ **3.** According to the tips, taking your shoes off before entering the house is important in both Turkey and China.

_____ **4.** In Turkey, when your hosts offer you more food, they expect you to say "no."

_____ **5.** In many countries, guests sometimes bring a small gift.

B FORM

Modals and Phrasal Modals of Advice, Necessity, and Prohibition

Think Critically About Form

A. Look back at the online tips on page 201 and complete the tasks below.

1. **IDENTIFY** An example of the modal *must* is underlined. Find another example. What form of the verb follows *must*?
2. **IDENTIFY** Find an example of the modal *should*. What form of the verb follows it?
3. **IDENTIFY** Find an example of each of these phrasal modals: *have to*, *ought to*, and *had better*. What form of the verb follows each of them?
4. **COMPARE AND CONTRAST** Find the negative forms of *must*, *should*, and *have to*. How is the negative form of *have to* different from the negative forms of *should* and *must*?

B. Discuss your answers with the class and read the Form charts to check them.

▶ Modals of Advice, Necessity, and Prohibition

ONLINE PRACTICE

AFFIRMATIVE STATEMENTS			
SUBJECT	MODAL	BASE FORM OF VERB	
You He They	**could** **might** **should** **must**	**buy**	a gift.

NEGATIVE STATEMENTS			
SUBJECT	MODAL + *NOT*	BASE FORM OF VERB	
You He They	**should not** **shouldn't** **must not**	**buy**	a gift.

YES/NO QUESTIONS			
MODAL	SUBJECT	BASE FORM OF VERB	
Should	I	**buy**	a gift?

SHORT ANSWERS					
YES	SUBJECT	MODAL	*NO*	SUBJECT	MODAL + *NOT*
Yes,	you	**should.**	**No,**	you	**shouldn't.**

INFORMATION QUESTIONS				
WH- WORD	MODAL	SUBJECT	VERB	
Where	**should**	we	**go**	for dinner?

- *Could, might, should,* and *must* are used to give advice. *Should* and *must* are also used to express necessity. *Must not* is used to express prohibition.
- Like all modals, *could, might, should,* and *must* are followed by the base form of the verb and have the same form for all subjects.
- The contracted form *mustn't* is not usually used in American English.
- Do not use *couldn't* in negative statements of advice.
- *Could, might,* and *must* are not usually used in questions of advice.
- We usually use *have to* (see below) instead of *must* in questions of necessity.

Phrasal Modals of Advice and Necessity

AFFIRMATIVE STATEMENTS			
SUBJECT	PHRASAL MODAL	BASE FORM OF VERB	
I	have to have got to	call	him.
She	has to has got to		
They	have to have got to		
CONTRACTIONS			
I've	got to	call	him.
She's			

NEGATIVE STATEMENTS				
SUBJECT	*DO/DOES + NOT*	PHRASAL MODAL	BASE FORM OF VERB	
I	do not don't	have to	call	him.
She	does not doesn't			
They	do not don't			
CONTRACTIONS				
I	don't	have to	call	him.
She	doesn't			

AFFIRMATIVE STATEMENTS			
SUBJECT	PHRASAL MODAL	BASE FORM OF VERB	
I	ought to had better	call	him.
She			
They			
CONTRACTIONS			
I'd better	call	him.	

NEGATIVE STATEMENTS			
SUBJECT	PHRASAL MODAL *+ NOT*	BASE FORM OF VERB	
I	had better not	call	him.
She			
They			
CONTRACTIONS			
I'd better not	call	him.	

(Continued on page 204)

***YES/NO* QUESTIONS**				
DO/DOES	**SUBJECT**	**PHRASAL MODAL**	**BASE FORM OF VERB**	
Do	I	**have to**	**call**	him?
Does	she			
Do	they			

SHORT ANSWERS					
YES	**SUBJECT**	***DO/ DOES***	***NO***	**SUBJECT**	***DO/DOES* + NOT**
Yes,	you	**do.**	**No,**	you	**don't.**
	she	**does.**		she	**doesn't.**
	they	**do.**		they	**don't.**

INFORMATION QUESTIONS				
***WH-* WORD**	***DO/DOES***	**SUBJECT**	**PHRASAL MODAL**	**BASE FORM OF VERB**
Who	**do**	I	**have to**	**pay**?
What				
When	**does**	she		
Why				

- *Have to, have got to, ought to,* and *had better* are used to give advice. *Have to* and *have got to* are also used to express necessity.
- Unlike other phrasal modals, *have to* and *have got to* have different forms for the third-person singular.
- *Had better* looks like a past form, but isn't. It is used to talk about the present and the future.

  You**'d better** call him now. We**'d better** leave tomorrow.
- In spoken English, we usually use contracted forms of *had better* and *have got to.* The contracted form of *had* for all persons is *'d. Have to* does not have a contracted form.

  You**'d better** call him. You**'ve got to** call him ✗ You've to call him. (INCORRECT)
- We do not usually use *have got to* or *ought to* in negative statements or in questions.
- We do not usually use *had better* in questions.

B1 Listening for Form

CD1 T57 **Listen to these sentences. Circle the modal forms you hear.**

1. **a.** should
   (b.) shouldn't
2. **a.** has to
   b. doesn't have to
3. **a.** We'd better
   b. We'd better not
4. **a.** must
   b. must not
5. **a.** have to
   b. don't have to
6. **a.** should
   b. shouldn't
7. **a.** You've got to
   b. You have to

B2 Working on Questions

A. **Rewrite these statements as *Yes/No* questions.**

1. He should buy a new car. Should he buy a new car?
2. We have to eat at 12:00. ______
3. They should bring a gift. ______
4. She has to go to class today. ______
5. You have to get a new passport. ______
6. He should see a doctor. ______

B. **Write an information question about each underlined word or phrase.**

1. <u>Susan</u> should give us the money. Who should give us the money?
2. He has to write <u>a paper for his history class</u>. ______
3. You have to stay in the hospital <u>for two days</u>. ______
4. We should go to the gym <u>on Monday</u>. ______
5. They have to take this form <u>to the Registration Office</u>. ______
6. You should talk to the professor <u>after the class</u>. ______

B3 Writing Contracted Forms

Rewrite these sentences with contractions where possible. If you cannot use a contraction in a sentence, write *No contraction possible.*

1. You had better tell her the truth. You'd better tell her the truth.
2. You have to look for a better job. ______
3. She ought to see a doctor. ______
4. He has got to study more. ______
5. You should not wear jeans to work. ______
6. She has to spend more time with the kids. ______
7. You had better not argue with him. ______
8. You have got to take a trip to the Caribbean! ______
9. He should not waste any more time. ______
10. You do not have to call. ______

B4 Writing Negative Statements

Rewrite these affirmative statements as negative statements. Use contractions where possible.

1. You should ask him to help. You shouldn't ask him to help.
2. Jake has to do his homework now. ______
3. Visitors must park here. ______
4. You had better tell your roommate the news. ______
5. Employees have to attend the sales meeting. ______
6. They should buy their son a car this year. ______
7. You must get on that train. ______
8. You should ask for a raise. ______
9. He had better wait until tomorrow. ______
10. You have to be home early. ______

Informally Speaking

Reduced Forms of *Ought To*, *Has To*, *Have To*, and *Have Got To*

CD1 T58 Look at the cartoon and listen to the conversation. How are the underlined forms in the cartoon different from what you hear?

I ought to get back to the library.
Yeah, I have to go to class, anyway.

In informal speech, *ought to* is often pronounced as /ˈɔt̬ə/, *has to* as /ˈhæstə/, *have to* as /ˈhæftə/, and *have got to* as /hævˈgɑt̬ə/ or /ˈgɑt̬ə/.

Standard Form	**What You Might Hear**
I **ought to** go.	"I /ˈɔt̬ə/ go."
She **has to** do the work.	"She /ˈhæstə/ do the work."
We **have to** see him now.	"We /ˈhæftə/ see him now."
You**'ve got to** finish today.	"You've /ˈgɑt̬ə/ finish today." OR "You /ˈgɑt̬ə/ finish today."

B5 Understanding Informal Speech

CD1 T59 **Matt and Linda are getting married today. Listen to their conversations. Write the standard form of the words you hear.**

Conversation 1: At Matt's house

Matt: It's 9:00. We ___ought to___ (1) leave now.

Friend: The wedding is at 10:00. We don't ______________ (2) leave until 9:30.

Matt: But we ______________ (3) be there before the guests arrive.

Conversation 2: Later, at the ceremony

Linda: Where's Matt? He ______________ (1) come soon! We're getting married in 15 minutes!

Sister: Maybe I ______________ (2) call him at home.

Father: Don't worry. He'll be here. We ______________ (3) stay calm and wait.

C MEANING AND USE 1

Modals and Phrasal Modals of Advice

Think Critically About Meaning and Use

A. Read the sentences and answer the questions below.

a. You ought to take that job.
b. You could take that job now, or you could wait awhile.
c. You had better take that job soon, or someone else will.
d. You have to take that job. You need a job!
e. You should take that job.

1. **EVALUATE** Which two sentences offer advice and have the same meaning?
2. **EVALUATE** Which sentence expresses the strongest advice?
3. **EVALUATE** Which sentence makes two suggestions?
4. **EVALUATE** Which sentence expresses a warning?

B. Discuss your answers with the class and read the Meaning and Use Notes to check them.

Meaning and Use Notes

ONLINE PRACTICE

Weak and Strong Advice

▶ **1** Use *could, might, should (not), ought to, had better (not), have to, have got to,* and *must* to give advice, suggestions, and warnings.

		It's Mary's graduation tomorrow.
Weak	• could, might	You **could buy** her flowers.
↕	• should (not), ought to	You **should ask** her what she wants.
	• had better (not)	You**'d better buy** something before it's too late.
Strong	• have to, have got to, must	You **have to buy** her that new e-book.

Suggestions with *Could* and *Might*

▶ 2 Both *could* and *might* are used to make casual suggestions, especially when there is more than one choice.

If you don't want to drive there, you **might** try taking the bus, or you **could** ride your bike.

You **could** meet for lunch or dinner.

Advice with *Should* and *Ought To*

▶ 3A Use *should (not)* and *ought to* to give advice. *Should (not)* is more common than *ought to.*

You **should get** married in June, when the weather is warm.

You **ought to look** for a new job.

▶ 3B You can also use *should (not)* and *ought to* in general statements to express a personal opinion about something.

People **shouldn't** drive when they're tired.

The President **ought to** do more for the environment.

▶ 3C Use words such as *I think, maybe*, and *perhaps* to soften your advice or opinion.

I think the President **ought to do** more for the environment.

Maybe you **should get** married in June.

Warnings with *Had Better*

▶ 4 *Had better (not)* is stronger than *should (not)* or *ought to*. It is used to give advice with a warning about possible bad consequences. As with *should (not)* or *ought to*, you can use expressions such as *I think, maybe,* and *perhaps* to soften the meaning.

You**'d better study** for the test. If you don't, you'll fail.

You**'d better not make** so many personal phone calls at work, or you'll lose your job.

I think you**'d better see** the doctor, or your cold will get worse.

The roads are really icy. Maybe you**'d better stay** home.

(Continued on page 210)

Strong Advice with *Have To, Have Got To,* and *Must*
▶ **5A** *Have to, have got to,* and *must* are used to give strong advice. They often suggest that the situation is serious or urgent. Your cough sounds terrible. You {**have to** / **'ve got to** / **must**} **see** a doctor immediately.
▶ **5B** Another type of strong advice with *have to, have got to,* and *must* is more casual. It shows that the speaker has a strong opinion about something, even though the situation is not serious. You {**have to** / **'ve got to** / **must**} **try** that new restaurant. I ate there yesterday and the food is great!

C1 Listening for Meaning and Use

▶ Notes 1–5

CD1 T60

Listen to two people give advice. Who gives stronger advice: speaker A or speaker B? Check (✓) the correct column.

	SPEAKER A	SPEAKER B
1.		✓
2.		
3.		
4.		
5.		
6.		
7.		
8.		

C2 Making Suggestions

▶ Note 2

Write two suggestions for each question or statement. Use *could* in one suggestion and *might* in the other.

1. **Friend:** My grades in French are really bad. What should I do?

   You: You could study harder.

   You might get a tutor to help you.

2. **Friend:** I need to earn some extra money this summer. How can I find a job?

   You: ______________________________

   ____

3. **Sister:** Let's go somewhere special for Mom's birthday. Where could we go?

   You: ______________________________

   ____

4. **Friend:** I'm so bored. There's nothing to do around here.

   You: ______________________________

   ____

C3 Giving Your Opinion

▶ Notes 3A–3C

A. Work with a partner. Take turns asking and answering questions using these words and phrases. Use *should* in your questions. Use *should* or *ought to* in your answers. You can soften your opinions with *I think, maybe,* or *perhaps.*

1. college students/take courses in many different subject areas?

   A: Should college students take courses in many different subject areas?

   B: No, they shouldn't. I think college students should take most of their courses in just one subject area.

2. students/have a job while they're in school
3. students/take more online courses
4. teachers/give less work
5. students/spend a semester studying abroad

B. Work on your own. Make up two more opinion questions with *should*. Then ask your classmates for their opinions.

C4 Giving Advice

▶ Notes 3A, 3C, 5A

A. Work with a partner. Give two pieces of advice to the person(s) in each situation. Use *you should* in one and *you ought to* in the other. You can soften your advice with *maybe*, *perhaps*, or *I think*.

1. Sasha has an old car. The car is making a strange noise.

   You ought to buy a new car. Maybe you should fix your car.

2. Today is Monday. Emily has to work today, but she woke up with a sore throat.

   ____

3. Dan isn't doing very well in his math class.

   ____

4. Mr. and Mrs. Chen love their apartment, but it's a little expensive.

   ____

B. The situations have become worse. Give two pieces of strong advice for each situation. Use *you have to*, *you've got to*, or *you must*.

1. Now Sasha's car has broken down.

   You must not fix this car. You've got to buy a new car.

2. It's Monday night. Emily has a high fever. She feels very sick.

   ____

3. Now Dan is failing math. If he fails, he won't graduate.

   ____

4. The Chens' landlord has increased the rent and they can't afford it.

   ____

C. Work by yourself. Write down three situations of your own. Then ask your partner to give advice.

C5 Giving Warnings

▶ Note 4

Look at the pictures and write a warning for each one. Use *had better* or *had better not*.

1. He had better stop the car.

2. ______________________________

3. ______________________________

4. ______________________________

5. ______________________________

6. ______________________________

D MEANING AND USE 2

Modals of Necessity and Prohibition

Think Critically About Meaning and Use

A. Read the sentences and answer the questions below.

1a. Students must show ID to enter the building.
1b. You have to show ID to enter the building.

2a. Students must not bring food into the library.
2b. You shouldn't bring food into the library.

1. **EVALUATE** Which sentence in each pair is formal, and sounds like a rule or a law?
2. **EVALUATE** Which sentence in each pair sounds more conversational?

B. Discuss your answers with the class and read the Meaning and Use Notes to check them.

Meaning and Use Notes

ONLINE PRACTICE

	Necessity
▶ **1A**	*Should, ought to, have to, have got to,* and *must* express necessity. *Must* expresses the strongest necessity and is used in formal or more serious situations. We often use *should, ought to, have to,* and *have got to* in conversation to avoid sounding too formal. Students **should study** their notes before the exam. I **have to hurry**. I'm going to be late! We**'ve got to send** out the invitations today. The award ceremony is next week. You **must take** the final exam if you want to pass the course.
▶ **1B**	Use *must* to express rules, laws, and requirements, especially in written documents. Bicyclists **must obey** all traffic lights in the city. All couples **must apply** for a marriage license in person.
▶ **1C**	*Should, have to,* and *have got to* are often used instead of *must* to talk about rules and laws in less formal English. The manual says that cyclists **should obey** all traffic lights in the city. I found out that we **have to apply** for a marriage license in person.

Lack of Necessity vs. Prohibition

▶ 2 *Don't/doesn't have to* and *must not* have very different meanings. *Don't/doesn't have to* means that something is not necessary—there is a choice of whether to do it or not. *Must not* means that something is prohibited (not allowed). There is no choice involved.

***Don't/Doesn't Have To* (Not Necessary)**

Your children **don't have to take** these vitamins. If they eat a healthy diet, they'll be fine.

***Must Not* (Prohibited)**

Your children **must not take** these vitamins. They are for adults only.

D1 Listening for Meaning and Use

▶ Notes 1A,1B, 2

CD1 T61 **Listen to these conversations between an employee at the Department of Motor Vehicles and people who call with questions. What does the employee say about each of the topics in the chart? Check (✓) the correct column.**

		NECESSARY	NOT NECESSARY	PROHIBITED
1.	take an eye test	✓		
2.	take the eye test at the Department of Motor Vehicles			
3.	need a California license to drive in California			
4.	pay with a credit card			
5.	go to driving school			
6.	drive alone with a learner's permit			

D2 Explaining Signs

▶ Notes 1B, 2

A. **Read these public signs. Then explain the signs by completing the statements with *must, don't have to,* or *must not.***

1. SWIMMING POOL FOR APARTMENT RESIDENTS ONLY

   This means that you ___have to___ be a resident of the apartment building to swim in the pool.

2. NO BICYCLES ALLOWED

   This means that you ________________ ride your bike in the park.

3. CHILDREN UNDER 12 FREE

   This means that children under 12 years old ________________ pay to go in.

4. NO APPOINTMENT NECESSARY

   This means that you ________________ make an appointment.

5. NO EXIT

   This means that you ________________ go out this door.

6. ID REQUIRED

   This means that you ________________ show identification.

7. HOSPITAL ZONE—NO HORNS

   This means that you ________________ blow your car horn in this area.

8. NO FOOD OR GLASS BOTTLES

   This means that you ________________ take food into this place, but you ________________ take a plastic bottle.

B. **Work with a partner. Discuss the signs in part A. Where do you think you might find each one?**

D3 Writing About Rules and Laws ▶ Notes 1B, 1C, 2

A. Look at each sign and write a sentence to explain its meaning. Use *must* and *must not*.

1. You must wear a seat belt.
3. ______________________
5. ______________________

2. ______________________
4. ______________________
6. ______________________

B. Work with a partner. What other signs have you seen? Write down the words. Draw the images and show them to your classmates. Explain each sign using *have to*, *have got to*, or *must not*.

You have to turn right.

D4 Stating Necessity, Lack of Necessity, and Prohibition ▶ Notes 1A, 2

Work with a partner. Think about your English class. Write sentences about what is necessary, what is not necessary, and what is not allowed. Use *have got to*, *have to*, *don't have to*, *must*, and *must not*.

1. We have to speak English in class.
2. ____
3. ____
4. ____
5. ____

WRITING Write a Memo on Office Rules

Think Critically About Meaning and Use

A. Choose the best answer to complete each conversation.

1. A: Emergency Room. How can I help you?

B: My daughter fell down the stairs and she's unconscious! Should I bring her in?

A: _____ wait for an ambulance.

a. You'd better (circled)

b. You could

2. A: Do you like my new dress?

B: __________.

a. Not really. You shouldn't wear that color.

b. Yes, you don't have to wear that color.

3. A: I'd like to pick up my car. Is it ready?

B: Yes, but you _____ come right away. We're closing in a few minutes.

a. might

b. should

4. A: I don't have my glasses. What does that sign say?

B: It says, "Visitors _____ check in at the front desk."

a. must

b. ought to

5. A: Can we put posters on the wall in our dorm room?

B: Yes, but you _____ make holes in the walls. It's against the rules.

a. don't have to

b. shouldn't

6. A: My boss will fire me if I come late again.

B: __________

a. Then you'd better be on time from now on.

b. Then maybe you must not be late.

7. A: What do you want for dinner?

B: I don't care. __________

a. You should make hot dogs.

b. We could have spaghetti.

8. A: Look at all those people at the exit. We'll never get out.

B: We _____ use that exit. There's another one in the back.

a. don't have to

b. must not

B. Discuss these questions in small groups.

1. **ANALYZE** Look at conversations 1, 3, 4, and 7. Which three use strong modals of advice? Which uses a weaker modal of advice?
2. **EVALUATE** Look at B's reponses in 5 and 8. Which gives a warning about something that might have bad consequences? Which expresses lack of necessity?

Edit

Find the errors in this paragraph and correct them.

There are many wedding traditions in the United States. One of them is that the bride ought ^to wear "something old, something new, something borrowed, something blue, and a sixpence in her shoe." The old, new, borrowed, and blue parts are easy enough. However, a sixpence is an old English coin. It is impossible to find these days, so most people feel that the bride doesn't has to use a sixpence—any coin will do. Another tradition is that the groom must not to see the bride before the wedding. People think that it is bad luck. Many people think that brides ought wear white. However, less traditional brides feel they must not do that. One final tradition is that when people get married, they've to save and freeze a piece of their wedding cake to eat on their first anniversary.

Write

Imagine that you are the director of a small company. Follow the steps below to write a memo explaining the office rules to new employees. Use modals of advice, necessity, and prohibition.

1. **BRAINSTORM** Think about all the things a new employee needs to know. Make notes about what you want to say. Use these categories to help you.
   - office hours
   - lateness
   - appropriate clothing
   - lunch breaks
   - vacation policy
   - sick leave
   - personal phone calls
   - personal emails and Internet use

2. **WRITE A FIRST DRAFT** Before you write your draft, read the checklist below. Write your draft using modals and phrasal modals to express advice, necessity, and prohibition.

3. **EDIT** Read your work and check it against the checklist below. Circle grammar, spelling, and punctuation errors.

DO I ...	YES
clearly explain the office rules to new employees in an appropriately organized memo?	☐
express rules, advice, and suggestions with modals and phrasal modals such as *must*, *had better*, *should*, *ought to*, *might*, and *could*?	☐
express prohibition with *must not* and lack of necessity with *don't have to*?	☐
use modals of the appropriate strength?	☐
use appropriate form for modals?	☐

4. **PEER REVIEW** Work with a partner to help you decide how to fix your errors and improve the content.

5. **REWRITE YOUR DRAFT** Using the comments from your partner, write a final draft. Remember to include these features of a business memo.

To: All New Employees
From: Bob Chang
Re: Office rules

CC: Vilma Rodriguez
Date:

1. Office hours are 9:00 to 5:00. If you are going to be late, you should always...

PART 4 TEST | Modals

Choose the correct word or words to complete each sentence.

1. In the early 20th century, doctors __________ bacterial infections because antibiotics did not exist.
   a. cannot treat   b. could not treat   c. may treat   d. will be able to treat
2. There is no guarantee, but medical researchers __________ a cure for cancer someday.
   a. can be able to find   b. are able to find   c. will be able to find   d. may be able to find
3. I think Alex would __________ have Chinese food tonight.
   a. prefer to   b. prefers to   c. to prefer   d. prefer
4. Could you __________ me your car tomorrow?
   a. will lend   b. lending   c. lend   d. to lend
5. Joe __________ work the late shift.
   a. doesn't have   b. don't have to   c. doesn't have to   d. don't have
6. Takeshi __________ get to work on time every day or his boss will fire him.
   a. have to   b. had better   c. might   d. could
7. __________ Holly on Sunday?
   a. Should Carla visit   b. Ought Carla visit   c. Should Carla visiting   d. Ought to Carla visit
8. I'm not feeling well. I'd rather __________ go to the show.
   a. no   b. not   c. don't   d. not to
9. I think Naomi would __________ become the new manager.
   a. rather prefer   b. like to   c. prefer   d. likes to
10. __________ join us for dinner?
    a. Pedro would prefer   b. Pedro should   c. Could Pedro   d. Would Pedro like
11. Can Ana __________ our study group?
    a. to join   b. joins   c. join   d. joining
12. Library patrons __________ books from the reference section without permission.
    a. removing   b. may   c. may not remove   d. to remove

Choose the correct response to complete each conversation.

13. A: Is Keiko going on vacation next month?

B: ________________ but I'm not sure.

a. She might be, **c.** She will be going to,

b. Maybe she can, **d.** She is going to,

14. A: I'm sorry, but the attorney can't interview the witness today.

B: ________________

a. When will she be able to interview him? **c.** When was she able to interview him?

b. When will she know how to interview him? **d.** Why doesn't she know how to interview him?

15. A: ________________ hear the music?

B: Yes, it's beautiful.

a. May you **c.** Might you

b. Can you **d.** May be you

16. A: Could you help me with this?

B: I ________________ right now. I'll be there in a few minutes.

a. can't **c.** may not

b. couldn't **d.** might not

17. A: Would you rather drive or walk to school today?

B: ________________ It's beautiful out.

a. Yes, I would. **c.** No, I wouldn't rather.

b. I'd rather walk. **d.** Yes, thanks for asking me.

Match the response to the statement below.

_____ **18.** The vacuum is overheating.

_____ **19.** You shouldn't eat a lot of salt.

_____ **20.** I'm taking the bus today.

a. I don't care. We could eat Greek food.

b. I know. It's bad for your health.

c. Good. Then I don't have to order them online.

d. You'd better study a lot.

e. You should hurry. It's coming in a few minutes.

f. You'd better not eat this dessert.

g. Yes. According to the law, you have to be at least 16 years old

h. You'd better unplug it.

PART

5

Tag Questions and Other Additions

CHAPTER

12

Tag Questions

A. **GRAMMAR IN DISCOURSE: Women's Language and Men's Language** **224**

B. **FORM: Tag Questions** **226**

Tag Questions with *Be*, *Have*, or Modal

I'm right, **aren't** I?

We **have** finished, **haven't** we?

They **should** come, **shouldn't** they?

Tag Questions with *Do*

You **live** nearby, **don't** you?

Subject Pronouns in Tag Questions

John seems shy, doesn't **he**?

Informally Speaking: Reduced Statements with Tag Questions

C. **MEANING AND USE: Tag Questions** **231**

Tag Questions vs. *Yes/No* Questions

Intonation Patterns and Certainty

Negative Words in Affirmative Statements

Vocabulary Notes: Other Ways of Answering Tag Questions

Beyond the Sentence: Beginning Conversations Using Statements with Tag Questions

WRITING: Write a Conversation with Tag Questions .. **237**

A GRAMMAR IN DISCOURSE

Women's Language and Men's Language

A1 Before You Read

Discuss these questions.

In your opinion, are conversations between female friends different from conversations between male friends? How?

A2 Read

CD2 T2 **Read this article from an online magazine to find out about the different ways in which men and women talk to their friends.**

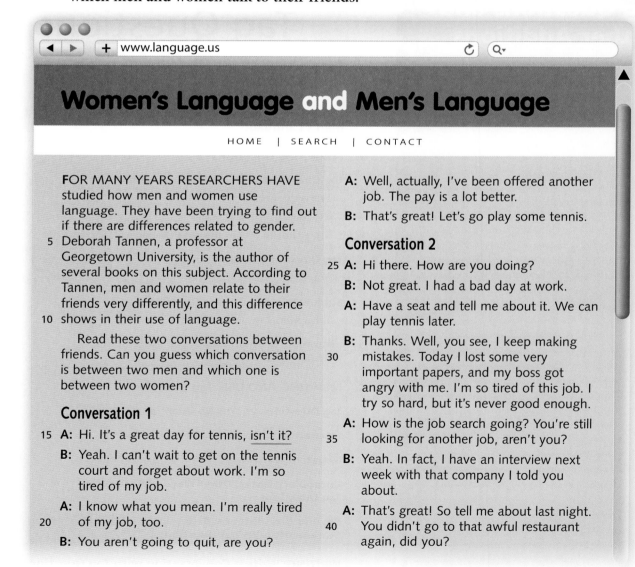

www.language.us

Women's Language and Men's Language

HOME | SEARCH | CONTACT

FOR MANY YEARS RESEARCHERS HAVE studied how men and women use language. They have been trying to find out if there are differences related to gender. Deborah Tannen, a professor at Georgetown University, is the author of several books on this subject. According to Tannen, men and women relate to their friends very differently, and this difference shows in their use of language.

Read these two conversations between friends. Can you guess which conversation is between two men and which one is between two women?

Conversation 1

A: Hi. It's a great day for tennis, <u>isn't it?</u>

B: Yeah. I can't wait to get on the tennis court and forget about work. I'm so tired of my job.

A: I know what you mean. I'm really tired of my job, too.

B: You aren't going to quit, are you?

A: Well, actually, I've been offered another job. The pay is a lot better.

B: That's great! Let's go play some tennis.

Conversation 2

A: Hi there. How are you doing?

B: Not great. I had a bad day at work.

A: Have a seat and tell me about it. We can play tennis later.

B: Thanks. Well, you see, I keep making mistakes. Today I lost some very important papers, and my boss got angry with me. I'm so tired of this job. I try so hard, but it's never good enough.

A: How is the job search going? You're still looking for another job, aren't you?

B: Yeah. In fact, I have an interview next week with that company I told you about.

A: That's great! So tell me about last night. You didn't go to that awful restaurant again, did you?

Did you guess that Conversation 1 was between two men and Conversation 2 was between two women? The conversations show very different communication styles.

According to Tannen, the differences in the ways that men and women relate to friends begin in childhood. Little girls usually spend a lot of time talking and sharing their feelings. A girl's best friend is the person who knows all her secrets. Talk is the "glue" that holds the female friendship together. However, this is not true for boys. A boy's best friend is a person that he does everything with. Although a boy will defend his friend in a fight, he often doesn't know his best friend's secrets or private feelings. Tannen says that women often tell their friends the intimate details of their lives, but men rarely do this. Male friendships focus on activities; female friendships focus on talk.

Female friendships focus on talk.

Male friendships focus on activities.

defend: fight to protect someone or something
gender: being male or female
intimate: private, personal
relate: to interact or have a relationship with

A3 After You Read

Write *T* for true or *F* for false for each statement.

__F__ **1.** Women's friendships are the same as men's friendships.

_____ **2.** Differences in the way men and women relate to friends begin in childhood.

_____ **3.** Women don't usually tell each other how they feel.

_____ **4.** Men tell their friends everything about their lives.

_____ **5.** For men, doing things together is more important than talking.

B FORM

Tag Questions

Think Critically About Form

A. Look back at the online magazine article on page 224 and complete the tasks below.

1. **IDENTIFY** An example of a tag question is underlined. Find three more.
2. **RECOGNIZE** Look at the statement that comes before each tag question. What kind of tag question follows an affirmative statement? What kind of tag question follows a negative statement?

B. Discuss your answers with the class and read the Form charts to check them.

▶ Tag Questions with *Be, Have,* or Modal

ONLINE PRACTICE

AFFIRMATIVE STATEMENT	NEGATIVE TAG		SHORT ANSWERS	
STATEMENT WITH *BE, HAVE,* OR MODAL	*BE, HAVE,* OR MODAL + *NOT*	SUBJECT	AFFIRMATIVE	NEGATIVE
I'**m** right,	**aren't**	I?	**Yes**, you **are**.	**No**, you **aren't**.
He **was** tired,	**wasn't**	he?	**Yes**, he **was**.	**No**, he **wasn't**.
It **was** raining,	**wasn't**	it?	**Yes**, it **was**.	**No**, it **wasn't**.
We **have** finished,	**haven't**	we?	**Yes**, you **have**.	**No**, you **haven't**.
They **should** come,	**shouldn't**	they?	**Yes**, they **should**.	**No**, they **shouldn't**.

NEGATIVE STATEMENT	AFFIRMATIVE TAG		SHORT ANSWERS	
STATEMENT WITH *BE, HAVE,* OR MODAL	*BE, HAVE,* OR MODAL	SUBJECT	AFFIRMATIVE	NEGATIVE
I'**m not** right,	**am**	I?	**Yes**, you **are**.	**No**, you **aren't**.
He **wasn't** tired,	**was**	he?	**Yes**, he **was**.	**No**, he **wasn't**.
It **wasn't** raining,	**was**	it?	**Yes**, it **was**.	**No**, it **wasn't**.
We **haven't** finished,	**have**	we?	**Yes**, you **have**.	**No**, you **haven't**.
They **shouldn't** come,	**should**	they?	**Yes**, they **should**.	**No**, they **shouldn't**.

Overview

- A tag question (or tag) is an addition to a sentence. It is a short *Yes/No* question that is added to the end of a statement. It is separated from the statement by a comma.
- Use a negative tag after an affirmative statement. A negative tag is usually contracted.
- Use an affirmative tag after a negative statement. An affirmative tag is never contracted.

Tag Questions with *Be*, *Have*, and Modals

- After statements where *be* is a main verb, use the correct form of *be* in the tag.

  He **was** tired, **wasn't** he?
  They**'re** here, **aren't** they?

  He **wasn't** tired, **was** he?
  They **aren't** here, **are** they?

- Note that affirmative statements with *I am* are followed by the negative tag *aren't I?*

  I'm right, **aren't** I?

- After statements with verb tenses formed with *be*, *have*, or a modal + a main verb, use the correct form of *be*, *have*, or the modal in the tag. Do not repeat the main verb.

  It **was** raining, **wasn't** it?
  We **have** finished, **haven't** we?
  They **should** come, **shouldn't** they?

  It **wasn't** raining, **was** it?
  We **haven't** finished, **have** we?
  They **shouldn't** come, **should** they?

- We form answers to tag questions in the same way that we form answers to *Yes/No* questions.

  A: You're not tired, are you?
  B: **Yes, I am.** OR **No, I'm not.**

  A: We haven't finished, have we?
  B: **Yes, you have.** OR **No, you haven't.**

▶ Tag Questions with *Do*

AFFIRMATIVE STATEMENT	NEGATIVE TAG	
SIMPLE PRESENT OR SIMPLE PAST STATEMENT	*DO* + *NOT*	SUBJECT
I **play** badly,	**don't**	I?
It **costs** a lot,	**doesn't**	it?
You **live** nearby,	**don't**	you?
They **sang** well,	**didn't**	they?

SHORT ANSWERS	
AFFIRMATIVE	NEGATIVE
Yes, you **do**.	**No**, you **don't**.
Yes, it **does**.	**No**, it **doesn't**.
Yes, we **do**.	**No**, we **don't**.
Yes, they **did**.	**No**, they **didn't**.

(Continued on page 228)

NEGATIVE STATEMENT	AFFIRMATIVE TAG		SHORT ANSWERS	
SIMPLE PRESENT OR SIMPLE PAST STATEMENT	***DO***	**SUBJECT**	**AFFIRMATIVE**	**NEGATIVE**
I **don't play** badly,	**do**	I?	**Yes**, you **do**.	**No**, you **don't**.
It **doesn't cost** a lot,	**does**	it?	**Yes**, it **does**.	**No**, it **doesn't**.
They **didn't sing** well,	**did**	they?	**Yes**, they **did**.	**No**, they **didn't**.

- After simple present and simple past statements with all verbs except *be*, use the correct form of *do* in the tag.

  You **live** nearby, **don't** you?
  They **sang** well, **didn't** they?
  It **doesn't cost** a lot, **does** it?
  They **didn't sing** well, **did** they?

- Answer tag questions with *do* in the same way you answer *Yes/No* questions with *do*.

  A: It costs a lot, doesn't it?
  B: **Yes, it does.** OR **No, it doesn't.**

  A: They didn't sing well, did they?
  B: **Yes, they did.** OR **No, they didn't.**

▶ Subject Pronouns in Tag Questions

STATEMENT	TAG
He seems shy,	doesn't **he**?
John seems shy,	doesn't **he**?
This is fun,	isn't **it**?
That's true,	isn't **it**?
These are Ana's,	aren't **they**?
Those are mine,	aren't **they**?
There's more hot water,	isn't **there**?

- When a personal pronoun is used in the statement, it is always repeated in the tag.
- When a noun is used in the statement, use the appropriate pronoun in the tag.

  Gina is nice, **isn't she?**   **His car** is really old, **isn't it?**

- When *this* or *that* is used in the statement, substitute *it* in the tag.
- When *these* or *those* is used in the statement, substitute *they* in the tag.
- When *there* is used in the statement, repeat *there* in the tag.

B1 Listening for Form

CD2 T3 **Listen to each conversation. Choose the tag question you hear.**

1. (a.) aren't you? b. are you?
2. a. did you? b. didn't you?
3. a. does he? b. doesn't he?
4. a. can you? b. can't you?
5. a. are there? b. is there?
6. a. am I? b. aren't I?

B2 Working on Tag Questions

Complete these conversations with tags. Then practice them with a partner.

1. **A:** There's no one home, ___is there___?
   B: No, there's not.
2. **A:** I'm going to drive downtown.
   B: You couldn't give me a ride, ________?
3. **A:** He didn't tell you the answers, ________?
   B: No, he didn't.
4. **A:** Ben, I want to discuss your test.
   B: I did okay, ________?
5. **A:** The traffic was terrible. I'm not late, ________?
   B: No, you're not.
6. **A:** Rita came in late last night, ________?
   B: I'm not sure. Ask Beth.

B3 Asking and Answering Tag Questions

A. Work with a partner. Add a tag to each statement.

1. You aren't hungry, ___are you___?
2. You're studying English, ________?
3. You like this class, ________?
4. You've flown, ________?
5. You have a car, ________?
6. You don't live alone, ________?

B. Take turns asking and answering the questions in part A.

A: You aren't hungry, are you?
B: No, I'm not. OR *Yes, I am.*

Informally Speaking

Reduced Statements with Tag Questions

CD2 T4 Look at the cartoon and listen to the conversation. How are the underlined forms in the cartoon different from what you hear?

He's not very good, is he?
No, he's absolutely awful.

In informal speech, we often leave out subject pronouns and forms of *be* in statements with tag questions.

Standard Form	What You Might Hear
It's hot in here, isn't it?	"Hot in here, isn't it?"
She's not a good speaker, is she?	"Not a good speaker, is she?"
You're leaving at six, aren't you?	"Leaving at six, aren't you?"

B4 Understanding Informal Speech

CD2 T5 **Listen to these reduced statements with tag questions. What subject pronoun + form of *be* does the speaker leave out at the beginning of each statement? Choose the correct answer.**

1. **a.** It's
b. They're

2. **a.** She's
b. She was

3. **a.** They're
b. It's

4. **a.** They aren't
b. They're

5. **a.** You're
b. You aren't

6. **a.** It's
b. It has been

C MEANING AND USE

Tag Questions

Think Critically About Meaning and Use

A. Read the sentences and answer the questions below.

1a. Is dinner at six?
1b. Dinner is at six, isn't it?

2a. It's a nice day, isn't it?
2b. You couldn't give me that pen, could you?

1. **EVALUATE** Look at 1a and 1b. Which sentence shows that the speaker has a previous idea about the time of dinner? Which sentence shows that the speaker has no previous idea about the time of dinner?
2. **EVALUATE** Look at 2a and 2b. In which sentence is the speaker making a request? In which sentence is the speaker expecting agreement?

B. Discuss your answers with the class and read the Meaning and Use Notes to check them.

Meaning and Use Notes

ONLINE PRACTICE

Tag Questions vs. *Yes/No* Questions

▶ **1** Tag questions are different from *Yes/No* questions. Use a tag question when you have a previous (earlier) idea or opinion about something and want to confirm it. Use a *Yes/No* question when you have no previous idea or opinion. Tag questions are more common in spoken English than in written English.

Tag Question	***Yes/No* Question**
You**'re** a student, **aren't** you?	Are you a student?
(I think you're a student.)	(I have no idea.)

Intonation Patterns and Certainty

▶ **2A** Use tag questions with falling intonation if you are very certain of your previous idea or opinion. Use tag questions with rising intonation if you are less certain.

Falling Intonation	**Rising Intonation**
He makes a lot of money, **doesn't he?** ↘	He makes a lot of money, **doesn't he?** ↗
(I'm sure he makes a lot of money.)	(I think he makes a lot of money, but I'm not sure.)

(Continued on page 232)

▶ **2B** We often use tag questions with rising intonation to express doubt or surprise. We also use them to make polite requests with modals, especially when we're not sure that the listener will agree to our request.

Expressing Doubt or Surprise

That box won't fit in the trunk, **will it?**

Making a Polite Request

You couldn't lend me five dollars, **could you?**

▶ **2C** We often use tag questions with falling intonation to confirm information we are already sure of, or to ask for agreement.

Confirming Information

We've met before, **haven't we?**

Asking for Agreement

We haven't had rain for a long time, **have we?**

Negative Words in Affirmative Statements

▶ **3** An affirmative statement that uses a negative adverb of frequency (such as *rarely, hardly, seldom*, and *never*) or a word with *no* (such as *nobody, nowhere*, and *nothing*) has a negative meaning. It requires an affirmative tag.

You <u>never</u> go to class, **do** you?

There's <u>nobody</u> here, **is** there?

C1 Listening for Meaning and Use

▶ Notes 1–3

CD2 T6 **A. Listen to these statements with tag questions. Draw arrows to show falling or rising intonation.**

1. We spent too much money, didn't we?
2. That's a very expensive restaurant, isn't it?
3. You didn't walk here, did you?
4. He has Ms. Walker for history, doesn't he?
5. You couldn't watch my children for an hour, could you?
6. You've never met the Smiths, have you?

CD2 T7 B. Listen again. Is the speaker certain or uncertain? Check (✓) the correct column.

	CERTAIN	UNCERTAIN
1.	✓	
2.		
3.		
4.		
5.		
6.		

C2 Practicing the Intonation of Tag Questions

▶ Note 2A

A. Read each conversation. Think about the meaning and decide if the tag question expresses certainty or uncertainty. Draw an arrow over each tag question to show falling (certain) or rising (uncertain) intonation.

1. **A:** Sam got an A in calculus.

   B: He's really smart, isn't he?

2. **A:** I'm sorry, but Mark left.

   B: He's coming back, isn't he?

3. **A:** I've got some bad news. Your car needs a new engine.

   B: Oh, no! It's going to be really expensive, isn't it?

4. **A:** Look how cloudy it is outside!

   B: It's going to rain, isn't it?

5. **A:** Thanks for inviting us to dinner.

   B: You're welcome. You eat meat, don't you?

6. **A:** Can you believe it? My boss asked me to take work home over the holiday.

   B: You didn't agree, did you?

B. Work with a partner. Practice the conversations in part A. Use the correct intonation.

C3 Expressing Doubt

▶ Note 2B

Work with a partner. Take turns expressing doubt about these incorrect facts. Use negative statements with affirmative tags and rising intonation. Reply with the correct fact, using the information in parentheses.

1. Columbus sailed to America in 1489. (1492)

   A: Columbus didn't sail to America in 1489, did he?

   B: No, he didn't. He sailed to America in 1492.

2. Africa is the largest continent. (Asia)
3. Saturn is the farthest planet from the sun. (Neptune)
4. Toronto is the capital of Canada. (Ottawa)
5. There are 31 days in November. (30)
6. They use pesos in Japan. (yen)
7. Albert Einstein invented the telegraph. (Samuel Morse)
8. One yard is equal to 24 inches. (36)

C4 Making Polite Requests

▶ Note 2B

Read each situation. Then make a polite request. Use a negative statement with an affirmative tag and rising intonation.

1. You are a waiter. You can't work tomorrow, and you hope your friend can take your place. You ask your friend.

   You couldn't take my place tomorrow, could you?

2. You have a doctor's appointment, and you need a ride to the clinic. You ask your roommate.
3. You need someone to take care of your son after school today. You ask your neighbor.
4. You need help tonight with your paper for English class. You ask your sister.
5. You're going on vacation. You need someone to feed your cats next week. You ask your neighbor.
6. You want to go away for the weekend, but you don't have a car. Maybe your father can lend you his car. You ask him.

Vocabulary Notes

Other Ways of Answering Tag Questions

Using short answers is not the only way to respond to tag questions. We can also use other expressions to show agreement or disagreement. In negative responses, we often correct the speaker's statement.

A: The movie starts at six, doesn't it?

B: That's right. OR No, it starts at seven.

A: You don't like your new roommate, do you?

B: Not really. OR Actually, I think she's great!

C5 Using and Answering Tag Questions

A. **Work with a partner. Use the questions as a guide to help you confirm what you know about each other. Take turns using and answering tag questions. Use appropriate intonation in your tag questions and a variety of expressions and short answers in your responses.**

1. How does your partner get to school?

   A: You drive to school, don't you?

   B: That's right. OR *No, I don't. Actually, I usually walk.*

2. Where does your partner live?
3. Where is your partner from?
4. How long has your partner studied English?
5. What other languages does your partner speak?
6. Does your partner work?
7. Does your partner like classical music?
8. Does your partner have brothers and sisters?
9. Does your partner play tennis?
10. Does your partner like to swim?

B. **Think of two more pieces of information to confirm with your partner. Then ask your partner to confirm the information using statements with tag questions.**

A: Pizza is your favorite food, isn't it?

B: Not really. Actually, I prefer Mexican food.

Beyond the Sentence

Beginning Conversations Using Statements with Tag Questions

Using statements with tag questions is a good way to begin a conversation with someone that you do not know. We often do this by using a statement with a tag question to comment on a shared experience. Using a statement with a tag question is an effective way to begin a conversation because the listener is expected to respond.

At a Train Station

A: These trains never come on time, do they?
B: No, they don't. And I'm always late for work.

In a Cafeteria

A: The cafeteria is very crowded today, isn't it?
B: Yes, it is. This line is really long.

C6 Beginning Conversations

A. Work with a partner. How would you begin a conversation in each situation?

1. You're leaving the classroom after the first day of class. The teacher has told you that you have to read 50 pages for the next class.

   She gives a lot of homework, doesn't she?

2. You're standing at a bus stop on a beautiful spring day, waiting for a bus.

   ____

3. You're in a very long line at the supermarket. The cashier is very slow.

   ____

4. You're at a soccer game. The home team is playing well.

   ____

5. You're on an airplane eating dinner. The food isn't very good.

   ____

6. You're at a conference. There are a lot of people there.

   ____

B. Now think of two more situations. Write them down and ask your partner to think of a statement with a tag question to begin each conversation.

WRITING Write a Conversation with Tag Questions

Think Critically About Meaning and Use

A. Choose the best answer to complete each conversation.

1. A: You always study hard, don't you?
B: ________
a. Yes, I did.
b. No, not always.

2. A: You couldn't lend me your car, could you?
B: ________
a. Of course I couldn't.
b. Sure. When do you need it?

3. A: It's a beautiful day, isn't it?
B: ________
a. Yes. We're having great weather.
b. I'm not sure.

4. A: We didn't pay the phone bill, did we?
B: ________
a. Oh, no! You're right, we didn't.
b. Why not?

B. Discuss these questions in small groups.

1. **EVALUATE** Why does speaker A use a tag question instead of a *Yes/No* question in 2? In 3?

2. **DRAW A CONCLUSION** In 3, why is the right answer better than the wrong answer?

Edit

Some of these sentences have errors. Find the errors and correct them.

1. Tom has been here before, ~~is~~ hasn't he?

2. I shouldn't tell the teacher, could I?

3. There are many French-speaking people in Canada, aren't they?

4. I'm not going to see you again, are I?

5. He never visits his parents on Saturday, doesn't he?

6. Frank didn't get married, did Frank?

7. Barbara isn't traveling alone, will she?

8. Your sneakers don't fit, don't they?

Write

Imagine that two people meet at school. They think they have met before, but they aren't sure where. They ask questions about places where they think they have seen each other. Follow the steps below to write a conversation between the two people. Use tag questions.

1. **Brainstorm** Think about some questions for the conversation. What are some possible places and situations for a previous meeting? Make notes about what you want to say. Use these categories to help you.
   - at another school
   - on vacation
   - at a summer job
   - at a friend's house
   - at an event like a concert or game
   - in a public place like a library or café
   - while traveling on a train, bus, or plane
   - through a family member

2. **Write a First Draft** Before you write your draft, read the checklist below. Write your draft using tag questions and answers to tag questions.

3. **Edit** Read your work and check it against the checklist below. Circle grammar, spelling, and punctuation errors.

DO I ...	YES
write a conversation appropriate for the situation?	☐
use various questions including tag questions?	☐
include appropriate responses to the tag questions?	☐
use correct form for the tag questions and responses?	☐

4. **Peer Review** Work with a partner to help you decide how to fix your errors and improve the content.

5. **Rewrite Your Draft** Using the comments from your partner, write a final draft.

A: Haven't I met you before? You used to work at the library, didn't you?

B: No, I never worked at the library... I know! You were at Cindy's wedding last year, weren't you?

A: That's right. Now I remember. You were a college friend of hers, weren't you?

CHAPTER

13

Additions with Conjunctions

A. GRAMMAR IN DISCOURSE: Josh's Travel Blog **240**

B. FORM 1: Additions with *And ... Too, And ... Either,* and *But* **242**

Bob is angry, **and** Amy is **too**.

Bob isn't angry**, and** Amy isn't **either**.

Bob is angry, **but** Amy isn't.

C. FORM 2: Additions with *And So* and *And Neither* .. **247**

I could go, **and so** could you.

We haven't eaten, **and neither** has he.

D. MEANING AND USE: Expressing Similarities and Differences **250**

Expressing Similarities

Expressing Differences

Informally Speaking: Pronouns in Short Responses

Beyond the Sentence: Combining Ideas

WRITING: Write a Paragraph Describing Two People or Things **256**

PART 5 TEST: Tag Questions and Other Additions ... **259**

A GRAMMAR IN DISCOURSE

Josh's Travel Blog

A1 Before You Read

Discuss these questions.

Think of two cities you know well. How are these two cities similar? How are they different?

A2 Read

CD2 T8 **Read this American student's blog to see what he thinks about London and Athens.**

www.joshblog.us

Josh's travel blog

HOME | ARCHIVE | CONTACT

I can't believe it! My year at University College London is over, and here I am in Athens for three weeks. Strangely enough, Athens reminds me of London in many ways. I guess that's not totally surprising. London is the capital city, the largest city, and the cultural and economic center of the country, and Athens is too. And London played an important role in world history, and so did Athens. As an American, I'm so impressed by the amount of history in both cities—the Tower of London and Buckingham Palace in London, and now the Acropolis with the Parthenon! London is a city of many different neighborhoods, and Athens is too. And, as in London, the different neighborhoods in Athens are very different from each other. For example, Plaka, beneath the Acropolis, has lots of tourists and tourist shops,

but Exarcheia doesn't. Exarcheia seems to have lots of students and a lot of bookstores and cafés. London has something for everyone, and Athens does too. London isn't perfect of course, and neither is Athens. Both cities can seem overcrowded—with locals and tourists—as well as dirty and polluted. But in London you can get away from it all without leaving the city, and in Athens you can too. In London, I often go to Hyde Park or St James's Park, and this morning I went to the National Garden of Athens, right in the center of the city. In both places, it's also easy to get around. In London, I take the Tube everywhere, and the last few days I've used the Athens Metro a lot. The London Underground is really old (the oldest subway in the world), but the Athens Metro isn't. It was mostly built in the 1990s and is incredibly modern. I'm not sure about walking here, though. In London, drivers typically wait for pedestrians to cross, but in Athens they don't. I almost got run over this morning, but I'm learning fast!

get away from it all: escape from something routine or not pleasant

locals: people who live in a place

overcrowded: when there are too many things or people in a place

pedestrian: someone who is walking

polluted: air, water, and soil that are extremely dirty and unsafe

the Tube: the London Underground

A3 After You Read

Read these statements. Check (✓) the ones you think the writer would agree with.

__✓__ **1.** London and Athens have many similarities.

_____ **2.** London has many historical buildings.

_____ **3.** All parts of Athens look basically the same.

_____ **4.** Athens seems like a perfect city.

_____ **5.** Athens drivers often don't wait for people to cross the street.

_____ **6.** The subway in Athens looks a lot like the subway in London.

B FORM 1

Additions with *And ... Too, And ... Either,* and *But*

Think Critically About Form

A. Read the sentences and complete the tasks below.

a. Derek is busy, but Joe isn't. (= Derek is busy. Joe isn't busy.)
b. Derek is busy, and Joe is too. (= Derek is busy. Joe is busy.)
c. Derek isn't busy, and Joe isn't either. (= Derek isn't busy. Joe isn't busy.)
d. Joe isn't busy, but Derek is. (= Joe isn't busy. Derek is busy.)

1. **ANALYZE** Which sentence is a combination of two affirmative sentences? What two words connect the second clause to the first clause?
2. **ANALYZE** Which sentence is a combination of two negative sentences? What two words connect the second clause to the first clause?
3. **ANALYZE** Which sentences are a combination of an affirmative sentence and a negative sentence (in either order)? What word connects the second clause to the first clause in both sentences?
4. **IDENTIFY** Look back at the underlined examples in the blog on page 240. Circle the connecting words. Do they connect two affirmative clauses, two negative clauses, or an affirmative and a negative clause?

B. Discuss your answers with the class and read the Form charts to check them.

ONLINE PRACTICE

AND ... TOO					
AFFIRMATIVE			**AFFIRMATIVE**		
SUBJECT	**VERB PHRASE**	***AND***	**SUBJECT**	***BE, HAVE,* MODAL, OR *DO***	***TOO***
Bob	**is** angry,	and	Amy	**is**	too.
He	**was** running,		they	**were**	
We	**have** eaten,		he	**has**	
I	**could** go,		you	**could**	
You	**like** sports,		he	**does**	
We	**sang** well,		they	**did**	

AND ... EITHER					
NEGATIVE			NEGATIVE		
SUBJECT	**VERB PHRASE + *NOT***	***AND***	**SUBJECT**	***BE, HAVE,* MODAL, OR *DO* + *NOT***	***EITHER***
Bob	**isn't** angry,	**and**	Amy	**isn't**	**either**.
He	**wasn't** running,		they	**weren't**	
We	**haven't** eaten,		he	**hasn't**	
I	**couldn't** go,		you	**couldn't**	
You	**don't like** sports,		he	**doesn't**	
We	**didn't sing** well,		they	**didn't**	

BUT				
SUBJECT	**VERB PHRASE**	***BUT***	**SUBJECT**	***BE, HAVE,* MODAL, OR *DO* + *NOT***
Bob	**is** angry,	**but**	Amy	**isn't**.
He	**was** running,		they	**weren't**.
We	**have** eaten,		he	**hasn't**.

SUBJECT	**VERB PHRASE + *NOT***	***BUT***	**SUBJECT**	***BE, HAVE,* MODAL, OR *DO***
I	**couldn't** go,	**but**	you	**could**.
You	**don't like** sports,		he	**does**.
We	**didn't sing** well,		they	**did**.

- Use the conjunctions *and … too, and … either*, and *but* to combine two sentences with similar verb phrases but different subjects. In the combined sentence, the second clause (the addition) is a shortened form of the second sentence.

  Bob is angry. Amy is angry. → Bob is angry, **and** Amy is **too**.
- Use *and … too* to combine two affirmative sentences. Use *and … either* to combine two negative sentences. Use *but* to combine an affirmative and a negative sentence (in either order).
- To combine two sentences where *be* is the main verb, use a form of *be* in the addition and omit the rest of the verb phrase.
- To combine two sentences with verb tenses formed with *be*, *have*, or a modal, use a form of *be* or *have* or the modal in the addition and omit the rest of the verb phrase.
- To combine two sentences in the simple present or the simple past, use the correct form of *do* in the addition and omit the rest of the verb phrase.

B1 Listening for Form

CD2 T9 Listen to each sentence. Does the speaker use *and ... too*, *and ... either*, or *but*? Check (✓) the form you hear.

	AND ... TOO	AND ... EITHER	BUT
1.			✓
2.			
3.			
4.			
5.			
6.			
7.			
8.			
9.			
10.			

B2 Understanding Additions

Look at the underlined addition in each sentence. Which words are missing? Omit the conjunction and rewrite the addition as a complete sentence.

1. She had fun on the trip, <u>but he didn't</u>.

   He didn't have fun on the trip.

2. Koji is hungry, <u>and I am too</u>.

   ______

3. I watch a lot of television, <u>but he doesn't</u>.

   ______

4. The students needed to leave early, <u>and the teachers did too</u>.

   ______

5. Our computer wasn't working, and <u>theirs wasn't either</u>.

   ______

6. We couldn't speak French, <u>and they couldn't either</u>.

____

7. Pedro enjoys going to the gym, <u>but Holly doesn't</u>.

____

8. I liked the concert, <u>and she did too</u>.

____

9. My aunt has visited Iowa, <u>but my uncle hasn't</u>.

____

10. Kim isn't going to work this summer, <u>and Josh isn't either</u>.

____

B3 Working on Form

Complete each sentence with the correct form of *be*, *have*, a modal, or *do*.

1. I didn't do the homework last night, and Alex ___didn't___ either.
2. Our neighbors have a swimming pool, and we __________ too.
3. Rita lives in an apartment, but Ben __________. He owns a house.
4. Miguel is worried about the test, and Sheryl __________ too.
5. My friend couldn't go to the café last night, and I __________ either.
6. Steve wasn't at home when I called, but his wife __________. I left him a message.
7. My roommate has been to Thailand, but I __________. I'd like to go someday.
8. I wasn't listening to the teacher, and my partner __________ either. What did she say?
9. I got to work late, and Rick __________ too.
10. Larry will come tonight, but Eva __________.
11. You shouldn't drink so much coffee, and I __________ either.
12. Lee and Chang have learned Chinese, but their sister __________.

B4 Combining Sentences

Combine each pair of sentences. Use *and … too*, *and … either*, or *but*.

1. Koji fell asleep during the movie. Yuji didn't fall asleep during the movie.

   Koji fell asleep during the movie, but Yuji didn't.

2. I don't like getting up early. Jane doesn't like getting up early.

   ____

3. Dan has a car. Rita has a car.

   ____

4. She was feeling sick. He wasn't feeling sick.

   ____

5. I didn't play sports in high school. Carlos didn't play sports in high school.

   ____

6. He's going to the conference. She's not going to the conference.

   ____

7. Ana doesn't eat meat. I don't eat meat.

   ____

8. Tony has studied chemistry. Won-joon has studied chemistry.

   ____

B5 Completing Sentences

Work in small groups. Complete these statements about yourself and the other members of your group. Use additions with *and … too*, *and … either*, or *but*.

1. I have a __sister__, and __Reiko does too__.
2. I'm wearing ______________, and ______________.
3. I never eat ______________, and ______________.
4. Five years ago I was ______________, but ______________.
5. I'm going to ______________ this weekend, and ______________.
6. I haven't ______________ yet, and ______________.

C FORM 2

Additions with *And So* and *And Neither*

Think Critically About Form

A. Read the sentences and complete the tasks below.

1a. Trains are convenient, and so are buses.
1b. Trains are convenient, and buses are too.
2a. Trains aren't always on time, and neither are buses.
2b. Trains aren't always on time, and buses aren't either.

1. **COMPARE AND CONTRAST** Compare 1a and 1b. Underline the subject and circle the verb in each addition. How is the word order different in these additions?
2. **COMPARE AND CONTRAST** Compare 2a and 2b. Underline the subject and circle the verb in each addition. How is the word order different?
3. **ANALYZE** Does *and so* connect two affirmative or two negative sentences? Does *and neither* connect two affirmative or two negative sentences?

B. Discuss your answers with the class and read the Form charts to check them.

ONLINE PRACTICE

AND SO				
AFFIRMATIVE			AFFIRMATIVE	
SUBJECT	VERB PHRASE	*AND SO*	*BE, HAVE,* MODAL, OR *DO*	SUBJECT
Bob	**is** angry,	**and so**	**is**	Amy.
He	**was** running,		**were**	they.
We	**have** eaten,		**has**	he.
I	**could** go,		**could**	you.
You	**like** sports,		**does**	he.
We	**sang** well,		**did**	they.

(Continued on page 248)

AND NEITHER				
NEGATIVE			AFFIRMATIVE	
SUBJECT	VERB PHRASE + *NOT*	*AND NEITHER*	*BE, HAVE,* MODAL, OR *DO*	SUBJECT
Bob	**isn't** angry,	and neither	**is**	Amy.
He	**wasn't** running,		**were**	they.
We	**haven't** eaten,		**has**	he.
I	**couldn't** go,		**could**	you.
You	**don't** like sports,		**does**	he.
We	**didn't** sing well,		**did**	they.

- The conjunctions *and so* and *and neither* are used to combine two sentences with similar verb phrases but different subjects. They form additions with *be, have,* a modal, or *do,* but the additions have a different word order than additions with *and … too* and *and … either.*
- Use *and so* to combine two affirmative sentences. Notice the word order after *and so. Be, have,* a modal, or *do* comes before the subject.
- Use *and neither* to combine two negative sentences. Since *neither* has a negative meaning, the verb form that follows it is affirmative. Notice the word order after *neither. Be, have,* a modal, or *do* comes before the subject.

> **!** **Do not use *not* in additions with *neither. Neither* expresses the negative meaning.**

C1 Listening for Form

CD2 T10 **Listen to these sentences. Write the additions with *and so* or *and neither.***

1. Los Angeles is a big city, and so is Chicago.
2. He didn't need a hotel room, ______________________________
3. February doesn't have 31 days, ______________________________
4. Teresa should go home, ______________________________
5. Carol can't ski, ______________________________
6. They've left, ______________________________

C2 Combining Sentences

Combine each pair of sentences. Use *and so* and *and neither*.

1. I'm going away to college next year. My friend Paul is going away to college next year.
   I'm going away to college next year, and so is my friend Paul.
2. Science isn't an easy subject for me. Math isn't an easy subject for me.
   ____
3. Children will enjoy that movie. Adults will enjoy that movie.
   ____
4. My sisters don't live at home anymore. My brother doesn't live at home anymore.
   ____
5. The stores here close early. The restaurants here close early.
   ____
6. We didn't know the answer. The teacher didn't know the answer.
   ____

C3 Completing Sentences

A. **Work with a partner and complete these sentences. For sentences 1–4, use *and so* or *and neither* in the addition. For sentences 5–8, use an appropriate first clause.**

1. I don't have a bicycle, and neither does my neighbor.
2. Spaghetti is an Italian food, ______________________________.
3. Children deserve to be happy, ______________________________.
4. Coffee isn't good for you, ______________________________.
5. ______________________________, and so does my best friend.
6. ______________________________, and neither did my parents.
7. ______________________________, and neither have I.
8. ______________________________, and so should I.

B. **In your notebook, write the first clause of two more sentences. Then exchange notebooks with your partner and complete each other's sentences.**

D MEANING AND USE

Expressing Similarities and Differences

Think Critically About Meaning and Use

A. Read the sentences and answer the questions below.

a. Carl lives in Florida, and Lee does too.
b. Carl doesn't live in Florida, and Lee doesn't either.
c. Carl lives in Florida, and so does Lee.
d. Carl doesn't live in Florida, and neither does Lee.

COMPARE AND CONTRAST Which sentences have the same meaning? Does each sentence express a similarity between the two subjects or a difference?

B. Discuss your answers with the class and read the Meaning and Use Notes to check them.

Meaning and Use Notes

ONLINE PRACTICE

Expressing Similarities

▶ 1A Use additions with *and … too, and … either, and so,* and *and neither* to show that the information about the subject of the addition is the same as the information about the subject of the first clause.

We live in Germany, **and** they do **too**.
Lisa has a brother, **and so** does Susan.
I don't like pizza, **and** she doesn't **either**.
He didn't get sick, **and neither** did she.

▶ 1B *And … too* and *and so* have the same meaning. *And … either* and *and neither* have the same meaning.

I have a car, **and she does too**. = I have a car, **and so does she**.
He didn't come, **and she didn't either**. = He didn't come, **and neither did she**.

▶ 1C *Too, so, not either,* and *neither* can be used in conversation to form a response that shows agreement with the speaker. (Such responses are also called rejoinders.) *And* is usually omitted. Use *too* or *so* to agree with an affirmative statement. Use *not either* or *neither* to agree with a negative statement.

Agreeing with an Affirmative Statement	Agreeing with a Negative Statement
A: I thought the test was really hard.	A: I couldn't do the math homework.
B: **I did too. / So did I.**	B: **I couldn't either. / Neither could I.**

Expressing Differences

▶ 2 Use additions with *but* to show that the information about the subject of the addition is different from the information about the subject of the first clause.

I can ice skate, **but** she can't.

Their classroom has a computer, **but** our classroom doesn't.

D1 Listening for Meaning and Use

▶ Notes 1A, 1B, 2

CD2 T11 Listen to each sentence. Do the two clauses contain the same information about the subjects or different information? Check (✓) the correct column.

	SAME INFORMATION	DIFFERENT INFORMATION
1.		✓
2.		
3.		
4.		
5.		
6.		

D2 Expressing Similarities and Differences

▶ Note 1C

A. Complete these statements about yourself.

1. I don't like ______cooking______.
2. I really like ____________.
3. I often ____________ with my friends.
4. I don't usually ____________ on the weekend.
5. When I was a child, I used to ____________.
6. When I was a child, I never ____________.

B. Work with a partner. Take turns making the statements in part A and giving short responses to express your similarities and differences.

A: I don't like cooking.

B: Really? I do. OR *Neither do I.*

Informally Speaking

Pronouns in Short Responses

CD2 T12 Look at the cartoon and listen to the conversation. How are the underlined forms in the cartoon different from what you hear?

I want to try bungee jumping.
I do, too.
I'm not sure about this.
Neither am I!

In informal speech, we often use object pronouns (*me, him, her, us, them*) instead of subject pronouns (*I, he, she, we, they*) in responses with *too*. Informal responses with *either* and *neither* can only begin with *me*.

Standard Form	What You Might Hear
I am too. / I do too.	"Me too."
She is too. / She does too.	"Her too."
He is too. / He does too.	"Him too."
We are too. / We do too.	"Us too."
They are too. / They do too.	"Them too."
I'm not either. / I don't either.	"Me either."
Neither am I. / Neither do I.	"Me neither."

D3 Understanding Informal Speech

CD2 T13 **Listen and choose the standard form of the responses you hear.**

1. **a.** I didn't either.
b. I did too.

2. **a.** We are too.
b. We do too.

3. **a.** So do I.
b. Neither do I.

4. **a.** We are too.
b. So do we.

5. **a.** They are too.
b. They aren't either.

6. **a.** Neither can I.
b. So can I.

7. **a.** She did too.
b. She didn't either.

8. **a.** I am too.
b. Neither am I.

9. **a.** She does too.
b. She is too.

D4 Adding Information to Sentences

▶ Notes 1A, 1B, 2

A. Work with a partner. Take turns choosing categories. Your partner will read a statement to you. Add to the statement, using the noun in parentheses. Use additions with *and ... too, and so, and ... either, and neither*, or *but*.

A: Geography.

B: Egypt has a canal.

A: Egypt has a canal, and Panama does too.

OR

Egypt has a canal, and so does Panama.

Geography

1. Egypt has a canal. (Panama)
2. Brazil isn't in Europe. (France)
3. Guam is an island. (Puerto Rico)
4. Austria isn't near the sea. (Switzerland)

Food

1. Prunes are dried fruit. (raisins)
2. Strawberries are red. (bananas)
3. Fish isn't fattening. (ice cream)
4. Potatoes don't have seeds. (carrots)

Animals

1. Chickens don't swim. (turkeys)
2. Kangaroos can't sing. (birds)
3. Snails have shells. (turtles)
4. Elephants live in Africa. (lions)

B. Work alone. Write two more statements for each category. Then work with your partner. Take turns reading your statements and making additions using *and ... too, and so, and ... either, and neither*, or *but*.

A: Canada has glaciers.

B: Canada has glaciers, and so does Iceland.

D5 Comparing and Contrasting Information

▶ Notes 1A, 1B, 2

Work in small groups. Look at the college scholarship applications. Imagine that your group will give a scholarship to one of the two students. Make sentences comparing and contrasting the students. Use additions with *and ... too, and so, and ... either, and neither*, or *but*. Then make your decision.

Jenny Chang has good grades, and Pedro Gonzalez does too.
Jenny Chang did volunteer work, but Pedro Gonzalez didn't.

College Scholarship Application Form

Name: Jenny Chang

Major: Don't know yet

High School Grades (Average)

English: A
Spanish: A
Science: B
Math: B
History: A

SCHOOL ACTIVITIES

Was student a member of clubs? Yes; Spanish Club, sophomore, junior and senior years

Did student participate in sports? No

Did student participate in student government? Yes; president of senior class

Did student work on online school newspaper? No

Did student receive awards? Yes; Most Outstanding English Student

ACTIVITIES OUTSIDE SCHOOL

Did student do volunteer work? Yes; volunteer language tutor (Spanish, Cantonese) at community center

Did student work? Yes; worked in a camp for children during the summer (3 years)

College Scholarship Application Form

Name: Pedro Gonzalez

Major: Biology, interested in medical research

High School Grades (Average)

English: A
German: B
Science: A
Math: A
History: B

SCHOOL ACTIVITIES

Was student a member of clubs? Yes; Science Club, junior and senior years

Did student participate in sports? No

Did student participate in student government? No

Did student work on online school newspaper? No

Did student receive awards? Yes; first prize in school science fair senior year

ACTIVITIES OUTSIDE SCHOOL

Did student do volunteer work? No

Did student work? Yes; worked at a science laboratory (1 year)

Beyond the Sentence

Combining Ideas

When you compare people or things, it is important to combine your ideas by using additions with *and . . . too, and . . . either, and so, and neither,* and *but.* If you do not combine ideas, your writing will be very repetitive. Compare these two paragraphs. Notice how combining ideas makes the second paragraph sound less repetitive.

Repetitive

My best friend and I have many similarities. I have a sister. Carol has a sister. I like vanilla ice cream. Carol likes vanilla ice cream. I'm not good at math. Carol isn't good at math. There is one big difference. Carol lives in the United States. I don't live in the United States. I live in Costa Rica.

Not Repetitive

My best friend and I have many similarities. I have a sister, **and so does** Carol. I like vanilla ice cream, **and** Carol does, **too**. I'm not good at math, **and neither** is Carol. There is one big difference. Carol lives in the United States, **but** I don't. I live in Costa Rica.

D6 Avoiding Repetition

Read this paragraph. Underline the parts that are repetitive. Then rewrite the paragraph combining sentences where possible.

The United States and the United Kingdom have many similarities and differences. One of the similarities is language. People in the United States speak English. People in the United Kingdom speak English. Some people say that Americans don't speak very clearly. Some people say that the British speak very clearly. American and British food is also similar in some ways. Americans like to eat meat and potatoes. The British like to eat meat and potatoes. The two countries also both have strong traditions of volunteer work. Many Americans give some of their time to help others. Many Britons also give some time to help others. One big difference is the political system. The United Kingdom has a queen. The United States doesn't have a king or a queen. In the United States, voters elect a president. In the United Kingdom, voters don't elect a president. They elect a prime minister.

WRITING Write a Paragraph Describing Two People or Things

Think Critically About Meaning and Use

A. Choose the best answer to complete each conversation.

1. A: You have to take the test, but I don't.
B: ___________
a. That's not fair.
b. Good. Let's study together.

2. A: She's never late.
B: ___________
a. So am I.
b. Neither am I.

3. A: I'm going to get a new computer next month.
B: ___________
a. So am I.
b. Neither am I.

4. A: We have to leave before noon.
B: ___________
a. I do too.
b. I don't either.

5. A: They seldom get to class on time.
B: Well, ___________
a. you don't either.
b. you do too.

6. A: I haven't seen him in years.
B: ___________ I wonder what he's doing these days.
a. I have too.
b. I haven't either.

7. A: I usually go to bed before twelve.
B: ___________
a. Me too.
b. Me neither.

B. Discuss these questions in small groups.

1. **GENERATE** What is a more complete way to state the correct responses in 2 and 3?
2. **GENERATE** What is a more informal way to state the correct responses in 2 and 3?

Edit

Some of these sentences have errors. Find the errors and correct them.

1. I want to go to Hawaii, and so ~~he does~~ does he.
2. They don't have enough money, but we do too.
3. The books cost a lot of money, and the paper was too.
4. She hasn't finished cleaning her room, and I have either.
5. Susan is angry, but I'm not.
6. We are going to go by plane, and so they are.
7. He is doing well in class, but she is.
8. The coffee was hot, and so was the tea.
9. He never gets a raise, and I do too.
10. Megan doesn't exercise every day, and neither doesn't Donna.

Write

Write a paragraph describing two people or things. Follow the steps below to write a description that compares and contrasts the two people or things. Use additions with conjunctions.

1. **BRAINSTORM** Think about two people or things that you know well, and that you can compare and contrast. Use these categories to help you. Then think of some similarities and differences.
   - two places (two cities, countries, parts of a town, shopping centers...)
   - two types of vacations (city and country, mountains and beach)
   - two kinds of food (two dishes, foods from two countries)
   - two people you know (two family members, friends, teachers...)
   - two school subjects
   - two sports (two sports you watch or sports you play)
2. **WRITE A FIRST DRAFT** Before you write your draft, read the checklist below. Write your draft using additions with conjunctions to express similarities and differences.
3. **EDIT** Read your work and check it against the checklist below. Circle grammar, spelling, and punctuation errors.

DO I ...	YES
show the similarities and differences between the two people or things?	☐
use at least one *and ... too* or *and ... so* to show similarities?	☐
use at least one *and ... either* or *and neither* to show similarities?	☐
use *but* to show differences?	☐
use correct shortened form in the additions?	☐

4. **PEER REVIEW** Work with a partner to help you decide how to fix your errors and improve the content.
5. **REWRITE YOUR DRAFT** Using the comments from your partner, write a final draft.

A vacation at the mountain and a vacation at the beach are very different, but they are also similar. Mountains are beautiful places, and so are beaches. Both kinds of vacations give us a chance to be in nature. Mountain vacations are good for walking and exploring, and beaches are too...

PART 5 TEST | Tag Questions and Other Additions

Choose the correct word or words to complete each sentence.

1. Mark's coming back, __________?

a. hasn't he **c.** wasn't he

b. isn't he **d.** doesn't he

2. I'm not on the track team, and Rick isn't __________.

a. neither **c.** too

b. either **d.** so

3. Those shoes are Eva's, aren't __________?

a. them **c.** they

b. those **d.** there

4. Lynn and Matt never played well, __________?

a. didn't they **c.** did they

b. don't they **d.** do they

Choose the correct response to complete each conversation.

5. **A:** I lost my wallet yesterday.

B: ______________

a. You won't cancel your credit cards, did you? **c.** You cancelled your credit cards, did you?

b. You cancelled your credit cards, didn't you? **d.** You didn't cancel your credit cards, didn't you?

6. **A:** I couldn't go to the meeting yesterday.

B: ______________

a. Me too. **c.** Either could I.

b. Neither could I. **d.** So did I.

7. **A:** ______________

B: Sure. When do you want to come in?

a. I changed my appointment, didn't I? **c.** I didn't change my appointment, didn't I?

b. I couldn't change my appointment, could I? **d.** I couldn't change my appointment, couldn't I?

Complete each sentence with the correct tag.

8. You don't live around here, ____________________?
9. I'm not a very good cook, ____________________?
10. Matthew didn't like this course, ____________________?
11. They weren't happy to say good-bye, ____________________?

Complete each sentence with *and so* or *and neither* + the correct verb form.

12. Sue is running for class president, ____________________ Gina and Bob.
13. I couldn't find the tickets, ____________________ Ed.
14. Sam has lost weight, ____________________ Tina and Paul.

Match the tag to the sentence.

_____	**15.** Leonard left yesterday,	**a.** aren't I?
_____	**16.** Sue has been to Brazil,	**b.** shouldn't he?
_____	**17.** Those are lovely shoes,	**c.** aren't they?
		d. hasn't it?
		e. hasn't she?
		f. didn't he?
		g. isn't she?
		h. don't we?

Match the addition to the correct sentence.

_____	**18.** Josh can't swim,	**a.** and so is Koji.
_____	**19.** Al applied for that job,	**b.** and neither will I.
_____	**20.** I need a vacation,	**c.** and so does Robert.
		d. and neither can Stefan.
		e. and so has John.
		f. and neither has Ed.
		g. and so did Ann.
		h. and neither did they.

PART

6

Nouns, Quantity Expressions, and Articles

CHAPTER

14

Nouns and Quantity Expressions

A. GRAMMAR IN DISCOURSE: **Mood Foods** 262

B. FORM: **Nouns and Quantity Expressions** 264

Count and Noncount Nouns

An **egg** has **70** calories.

Four **eggs** have **280** calories.

Juice is sweet.

General Quantity Expressions

There are **many/several/a few/few apples** in the bag.

We have **a great deal of/a little/little food**.

There are **a lot of/some/no apples** on the tree.

Specific Quantity Expressions

There is **a carton of eggs** in the refrigerator.

Informally Speaking: Reducing *Of* in Informal Speech

C. MEANING AND USE 1: **General Quantity Expressions** 270

Expressing Large and Small Amounts

Many* vs. *Much

A Few/A Little* vs. *Few/Little

Expressing None

Emphasizing Amounts

D. MEANING AND USE 2: **Specific Quantity Expressions** 276

Expressing Specific Amounts

WRITING: **Write a Request for Advice** 279

A GRAMMAR IN DISCOURSE

Mood Foods

A1 Before You Read

Discuss these questions.

What is your favorite food? Why do you like it? How do you feel after you eat it? Are there any foods that make you feel sleepy? Are there any foods that give you energy or help you stay awake?

A2 Read

CD2 T14 **Read the chart on the following page to find out how certain foods can affect the way you feel.**

A3 After You Read

Answer these questions according to the information in the magazine article. Use the choices below.

cayenne pepper	**cheese**	**eggs**	**honey**
chamomile tea	**coffee**	**gingko biloba**	**mint**

1. Which two give you long-lasting energy? cheese, eggs
2. Which two calm your nerves? ________________
3. Which one helps you stay awake, but doesn't make you nervous? ________________
4. Which one helps you wake up, but also makes you nervous? ________________
5. Which one may help you concentrate? ________________
6. Which one helps the body absorb calcium? ________________

MOOD FOODS

We all know that the food we eat can affect the way we look physically. But did you know that food can also have an impact on the way you feel?

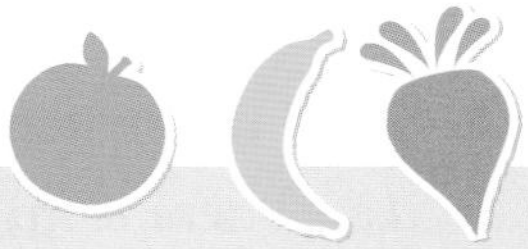

The Situation	The Food	The Result
1. You have little energy in the morning.	Don't eat pancakes or toast. Have some cheese or an egg instead.	Eggs and cheese have a great deal of protein, which builds muscles and gives you long-lasting energy to start your day. Pancakes are high in carbohydrates, which can give you a lot of energy, but only for a short time.
2. You are preparing for an important meeting or for a final exam. You have to stay up late.	Don't have a cup of coffee. Mix one teaspoon of cayenne pepper with a quart of tomato juice. Then drink it.	The caffeine in coffee will keep you awake, but it will also make you nervous. Cayenne pepper gives you energy, but won't make you nervous. The tomato juice just covers up its hot taste.
3. You have looked at a report for three hours, and you can't concentrate anymore.	Take some gingko biloba, eat a few prunes, or drink a cup of ginger tea.	Many nutritional experts say that prunes, gingko biloba, and ginger may improve memory and concentration.
4. It's exam time, and you're really nervous.	Drink chamomile or peppermint tea. If you don't like tea, have a few pieces of mint candy.	Both chamomile and mint calm your nerves. (Some people also say that mint helps your digestion.)
5. You can't sleep, and your interview is only hours away.	Drink a cup of warm milk mixed with one teaspoon of honey.	Milk contains calcium and tryptophan, both of which have a calming effect. Honey may help the body absorb calcium.

absorb: to take something in (e.g., a sponge absorbs water)

concentrate: to focus your thoughts on something

digestion: the body's ability to break down food

gingko biloba: an herbal preparation that comes from the leaves of the gingko tree

impact: effect, influence

nutrition: food science

B FORM

Nouns and Quantity Expressions

Think Critically About Form

A. Read the sentences and complete the tasks below.

1a. There is milk in this drink.
1b. There is a lot of milk in this drink.

2a. There is one calorie in this drink.
2b. There are a lot of calories in this drink.

1. **IDENTIFY** Look at the underlined nouns. Which are count nouns? Which is a noncount noun?
2. **RECOGNIZE** Look back at the nutrition chart on page 263. Find the nouns below and write the quantity expressions that are used with them. (Some appear more than once.)

_________ energy _________ prunes

_________ protein _________ people

B. Discuss your answers with the class and read the Form charts to check them.

▶ Count and Noncount Nouns

ONLINE PRACTICE

COUNT NOUNS			
***A, AN, THE,* NUMBER, OR Ø**	**COUNT NOUN**	**VERB**	
An The One	**egg**	has	70 calories.
The Four	**eggs**	have	280 calories.
Ø	**Eggs**	have	a lot of protein.

NONCOUNT NOUNS			
***THE* OR Ø**	**NONCOUNT NOUN**	**VERB**	
The	**juice**	is	in the refrigerator.
Ø	**Juice**		sweet.

Count Nouns

- Count nouns can be counted. They have both singular and plural forms.

  one **egg** four **eggs**
- *A, an, the,* a number *(one, two, ...)*, or Ø *(no article)* can come before count nouns.
- The plural of a count noun is usually formed by adding *-s* or *-es* to the singular form. See Appendix 1 for the spelling of nouns ending in *-s* or *-es*.
- Some count nouns have irregular plural forms. See Appendix 8 for a list of common irregular plural nouns.

Noncount Nouns

- Noncount nouns cannot be counted. They do not have plural forms.
- *The* or Ø (no article) can come before noncount nouns. *A, an,* or a number cannot come before them.

▶ General Quantity Expressions

PLURAL COUNT NOUNS

	QUANTITY EXPRESSION	COUNT NOUN	
There are	**many** **several** **a few** **few**	**apples**	in the bag.
There aren't	**many**	**eggs**	in the basket.

NONCOUNT NOUNS

	QUANTITY EXPRESSION	NONCOUNT NOUN
We have	**a great deal of** **a little** **little**	**food**.
We don't have	**much**	**milk**.

PLURAL COUNT NOUNS OR NONCOUNT NOUNS

	QUANTITY EXPRESSION	COUNT NOUN	
There are	**a lot of** **some** **no**	**apples**	on the tree.
There aren't	**any**	**grapes**	in the bowl.

	QUANTITY EXPRESSION	NONCOUNT NOUN	
There is	**a lot of** **some** **no**	**food**	in the bag.
There isn't	**any**	**milk**	in the cup.

QUESTIONS WITH *HOW MANY* AND *HOW MUCH*

HOW MANY	COUNT NOUN	
How many	**sandwiches**	should I buy?

HOW MUCH	NONCOUNT NOUN	
How much	**sugar**	do you want?

(Continued on page 266)

General Quantity Expressions with Count Nouns

- Use *many, several, a few,* and *few* before count nouns.

General Quantity Expressions with Noncount Nouns

- Use a *great deal of, much, a little,* and *little* only before noncount nouns.
- *Much* is not usually used in affirmative statements. Use *a lot of* instead.

  This recipe has **a lot of sugar** in it.

  x This recipe has much sugar in it. (INCORRECT)

General Quantity Expressions with Count or Noncount Nouns

- A *lot of, lots of, plenty of, some, any,* and *no* can be used before both plural count nouns and noncount nouns.
- Use *any* before plural count nouns or noncount nouns in negative statements and questions.

Questions with *How Many* and *How Much*

- Use *how many* with plural count nouns to ask about quantity.
- Use *how much* with noncount nouns to ask about quantity.

▶ Specific Quantity Expressions

PLURAL COUNT NOUNS OR NONCOUNT NOUNS			
	QUANTITY EXPRESSION	**COUNT NOUN**	
There is	**a carton of**	**eggs**	in the refrigerator.
There are	**two cartons of**		
	QUANTITY EXPRESSION	**NONCOUNT NOUN**	
There is	**a cup of**	**sugar**	in the recipe.
There are	**three teaspoons of**		

- Many specific quantity expressions end in *of*. They can go before plural count nouns and noncount nouns.

B1 Listening for Form

CD2 T15 **A. Listen to each sentence. Are the nouns you hear count or noncount? Check (✓) the correct column.**

	COUNT	NONCOUNT
1.		✓
2.		
3.		
4.		
5.		
6.		
7.		
8.		

CD2 T16 **B. Complete these conversations with the quantity expressions you hear.**

Conversation 1

A: Do you have any news about those jobs you applied for?

B: Yes. I've had ___several___ (1) interviews. I'm sure I'll get an offer, but I need ________ (2) information about the companies before I decide.

Conversation 2

A: Were there ________ (1) people in the park?

B: There were ________ (2) children! I forgot that summer vacation started last week.

Conversation 3

A: Would you like ________ (1) milk with your sandwich?

B: No, thanks. I'd rather have ________ (2) coffee.

Conversation 4

A: ________ (1) food should I buy?

B: There are ________ (2) people coming. You should buy ________ (3) food.

B2 Working on Form

Choose the correct general quantity expression to complete each sentence.

1. Desserts usually have ____ sugar.
   (**a.**) lots of **b.** many

2. ____ salt often makes food taste better.
   a. A few **b.** A little

3. Does ice cream have ____ calories?
   a. many **b.** much

4. On hot days you should drink ____ water.
   a. plenty of **b.** many

5. One reason junk food isn't good for you is that it has ____ vitamins.
   a. little **b.** few

6. John ate ____ pancakes for breakfast.
   a. a great deal of **b.** a lot of

B3 Asking Questions with *How many...?* and *How much...?*

Work with a partner. Use *How many* and *How much* to ask questions about the list of ingredients in this recipe for chocolate cake.

How many cups of sugar are in the recipe? OR *How much sugar is in the recipe?*

http://www.cookcakes.us

save | share | email | print

Chocolate Cake

Rated: ✻✻✻✻ *[3 of 4 stars]*
47 reviews

Ingredients
1 ½ cups of sugar
5 eggs
1 ½ teaspoons of vanilla extract
1 teaspoon of almond extract
2 cups of sour cream
1 ½ teaspoons of baking powder
¼ teaspoon of salt
4 tablespoons of powdered cocoa
2 cups of chocolate chips
¾ cup of milk
1 stick (8 tablespoons) of butter
¾ cup of flour

Informally Speaking

Reducing *Of* in Informal Speech

CD2 T17 Look at the cartoon and listen to the conversation. How are the underlined forms in the cartoon different from what you hear?

Well, Liz, we have a lot of gas and plenty of time.
Good thing we also have a lot of friends.

In informal speech, we often reduce the word *of* in quantity expressions.

Standard Form	**What You Might Hear**
You need **plenty of** time.	"You need /ˈplɛniə/ time."
There are **a lot of** cars here.	"There are /əˈlɑtə/ cars here."
He has **lots of** money.	"He has /ˈlɑtsə/ money."

B4 Understanding Informal Speech

CD2 T18 **Listen and write the standard form of the words you hear.**

1. ____Lots of____ people enjoy playing golf.
2. ________________ my friends are coming over tonight.
3. This dishwasher uses a great ________________ hot water.
4. Are you hungry? There's ________________ food left over.
5. There are ________________ lakes in Minnesota.
6. He took ________________ classes last year.
7. We won't be late. We have ________________ time.

C MEANING AND USE 1

General Quantity Expressions

Think Critically About Meaning and Use

A. Read the sentences and complete the tasks below.

1a. Ben has many friends.
1b. Eva has few friends.
1c. Josh has lots of friends.
1d. Tony has a lot of friends.
2a. There's little time left. I don't think we can get there by 8:30.
2b. There's a little time left. We can get there by 8:30 easily.

1. **CATEGORIZE** Look at 1a–1d. Underline the quantity expressions. Who has a large number of friends? Who has a small number of friends?
2. **ANALYZE** Look at 2a and 2b. Underline the quantity expressions. In which sentence is there not enough time?

B. Discuss your answers with the class and read the Meaning and Use Notes to check them.

Meaning and Use Notes

ONLINE PRACTICE

Expressing Large and Small Amounts

▶ 1 General quantity expressions are used to refer to larger and smaller amounts. They don't refer to exact amounts. *Many*, *much*, *a lot of*, *lots of*, *plenty of*, and *a great deal of* all have the same meaning, but *lots* of and *plenty of* are more informal and are more commonly used in spoken English.

Larger Amount ↑	• many, much, a lot of, lots of, plenty of, a great deal of	There are **many** calories in potato chips. Milk has **lots of** calcium.
	• some/several	There is **some** juice in the refrigerator.
↓	• a few/a little	There are **a few** people here.
Smaller Amount	• few/little	We have **little** money, so we rarely go on vacation.

Many vs. *Much*

▶ 2A Use *many* in affirmative and negative statements and questions. Use *much* in negative statements and questions.

Many	***Much***
I have **many** friends.	—
I do**n't** have **many** friends.	We do**n't** get **much** rain here.
Do you have **many** friends?	Do you get **much** rain here?

▶ 2B *Much* is not usually used alone in affirmative statements. Use *a lot of* instead.

We get **a lot of** rain here.

A Few/A Little vs. *Few/Little*

▶ 3 Use *a few/a little* or *few/little* to talk about smaller amounts. However, notice the difference in meaning:

Few* vs. *A Few

We have **few** sandwiches left. We'll have to make more.
(We have a small number of sandwiches, but not enough.)

We have **a few** sandwiches left. Would you like one?
(We have a small number of sandwiches, but it's enough.)

Little* vs. *A Little

I can't pay my rent this month. I have **little** money in the bank.
(I have a small amount of money, and it isn't enough.)

I can pay my rent this month. I have **a little** money in the bank.
(I have a small amount of money, but it's enough.)

▶ 3B *Not … many* and *not … much* are more common in speech than *few* and *little.*

We do**n't** have **many** sandwiches left. We'll have to make more.

I can't pay my rent this month. I do**n't** have **much** money in the bank.

Expressing None

▶ 4 Use *no* or *not any* to express *none. No* is used in affirmative statements, but it has a negative meaning. *Not any* is used to form a negative statement. *Not* usually contracts with the verb.

{ There is **no sugar** / There is**n't any** sugar } in this dessert.

{ There are **no eggs** / There are**n't any** eggs } in this recipe.

(Continued on page 272)

Emphasizing Amounts

▶ 5A You can use *so* and *too* before *many* and *much* to emphasize a larger amount. *Too* usually has a negative meaning.

Plural Count Nouns with *Many*

There are **so many** choices on this menu. Isn't it wonderful?

There are **too many** choices on this menu. I can't decide what to eat.

Noncount Nouns with *Much*

She's made **so much** money this year. She's very happy about it.

She's made **too much** money this year. She'll have to pay a lot in taxes.

▶ 5B Use *only* before *a few* or *a little* to emphasize an even smaller amount. Use *quite* with *a few* (but not with *a little*) to emphasize a larger amount.

Plural Count Nouns with *A Few*

Only a few houses are available. (There are a small number of houses.)

Quite a few houses are available. (There are a large number of houses.)

Noncount Nouns with *A Little*

A: Would you like some milk in your coffee?

B: **Only a little,** please.

C1 Listening for Meaning and Use

▶ Notes 1–5

CD2 T19 **Listen to this conversation. Listen carefully for the nouns in the chart. Is the speaker talking about a large quantity of each noun, a small quantity, or none at all? Check (✓) the correct column.**

		LARGE QUANTITY	SMALL QUANTITY	NONE
1.	work	✓		
2.	milk			
3.	cars			
4.	homework			
5.	food			
6.	books			
7.	caffeine			
8.	tests			
9.	money			
10.	friends			

C2 Understanding Quantity Expressions

▶ Notes 1–5

Choose the best answer to complete each conversation.

1. A: I have a little money.

B: __________

(**a.**) So do I. Let's go out to dinner.

b. Then we'd better not go out to dinner. Let's have spaghetti at home.

2. A: Can you help me with my homework?

B: Sorry. I ____ time right now.

a. have much

b. don't have much

3. A: The kids do a lot of work these days.

B: __________

a. That's great! They're finally old enough to help you.

b. That's not good. You should ask them to help you more.

4. A: So far, we have no information.

B: __________

a. I don't, either.

b. I do, too.

5. A: There are too many people here.

B: __________

a. I agree. Why don't we leave?

b. I know. It's wonderful, isn't it?

6. A: Can we still get tickets to the game?

B: I'm not sure. There are ____ a few tickets left.

a. only

b. quite

C3 Talking About Small Quantities

▶ Note 3

Work with a partner. Consider the meaning of each sentence and complete it with *a few*, *few*, *a little*, or *little*.

1. The students thought the exam was very difficult. They complained that ___few___ people got high grades.
2. Amy has to visit a friend in the hospital. She can probably go on Monday because she has __________ time in the afternoon.
3. Not everyone was able to sit down because there were __________ chairs.
4. Diana is trying to teach Gina to play guitar. Gina doesn't practice, so she's making __________ progress. She needs to practice a lot more.
5. Luckily, the school library has __________ computers, so I'll be able to research my history project tonight.
6. Koji's new cell phone isn't working correctly. He calls the store and says, "I'm having __________ trouble with my new phone."

C4 Using Quantity Expressions

▶ Notes 1–3, 5

Rick's office had a picnic. One hundred people attended the picnic. Rick ordered the food, but he made some mistakes. Write sentences about the amounts of food that Rick ordered. Use quantity expressions in affirmative and negative sentences.

100 fish fillets, 30 rolls	1 apple pie, 10 chocolate cakes
50 burgers, 100 burger buns	1 gallon of lemonade, 3 bottles of soda
5 bags of potato chips	10 gallons of coffee, 1 gallon of iced tea
2 bowls of salad	50 cups, 100 plates, 25 napkins

He bought plenty of fish fillets, but he didn't buy many rolls.

C5 Talking and Writing About Foods

▶ Notes 1–4

A. Work with a partner. Look at the charts. Take turns asking and answering questions about the two cereals. Use quantity expressions.

A: Does Healthy Grains have much fiber?

B: Yes, it has plenty of fiber. What about Chocolate Puffies? How much fiber does it have?

A: It has only a little.

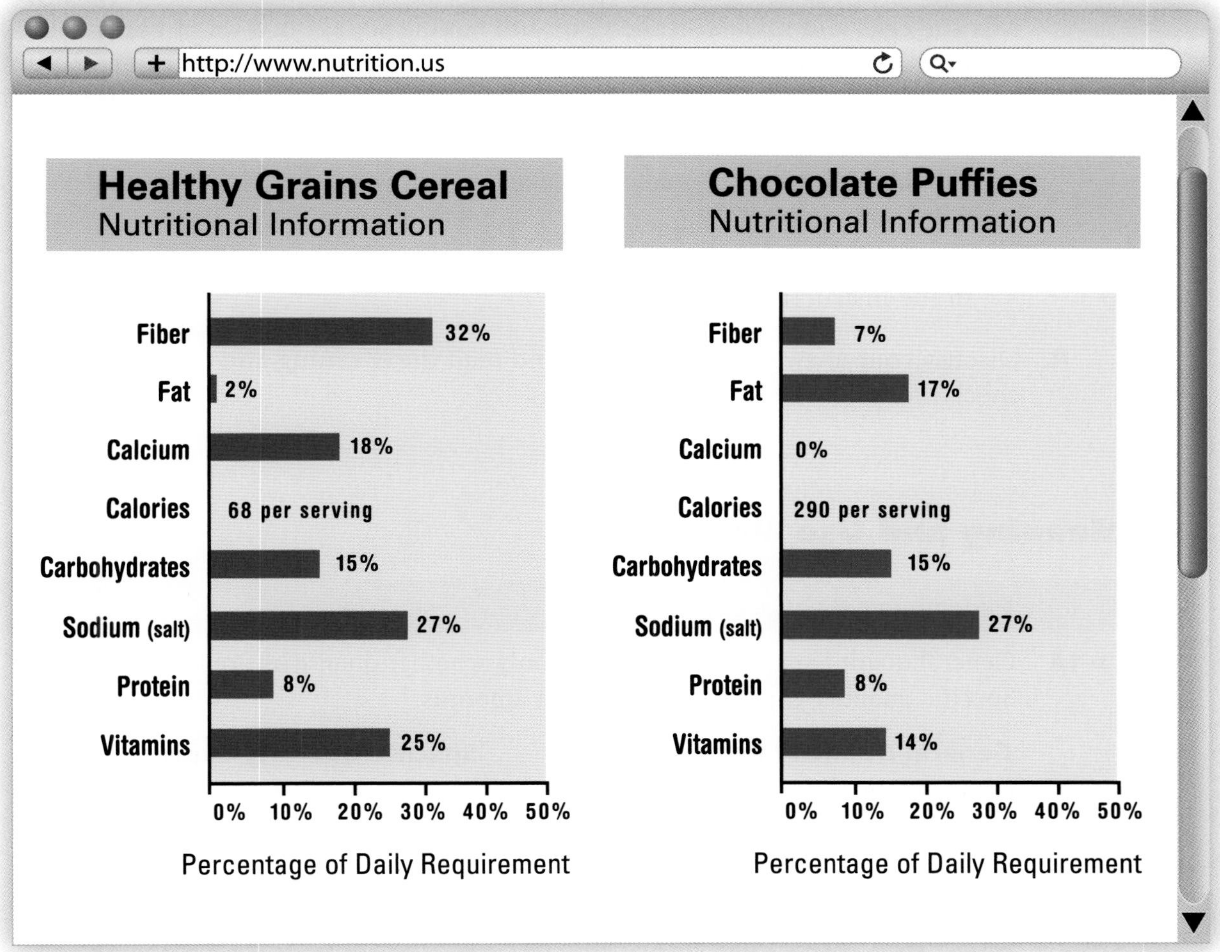

B. Look at the nutritional information on the package of a food that you eat often. Write four sentences about the nutritional value of this food.

Spaghetti has a lot of carbohydrates. It has very little fat and…

D MEANING AND USE 2

Specific Quantity Expressions

Think Critically About Meaning and Use

A. Read the instructions for making pancakes and answer the questions below.

Mix a lot of flour with a little baking powder. Beat some eggs with some milk. Mix the eggs and milk with the flour and baking soda. Put a lot of blueberries in the mix. Add a little vanilla. Melt some butter in a frying pan. Pour in some of the batter. After a while, turn the pancake over. When it is brown, remove it from the pan and serve immediately.

1. **EVALUATE** Can you make pancakes by following these instructions? Why or why not?
2. **GENERATE** Can you think of any specific quantity expressions that should be in the instructions above?

B. Discuss your answers with the class and read the Meaning and Use Notes to check them.

Meaning and Use Notes

ONLINE PRACTICE

Expressing Specific Amounts

▶ 1A General quantity expressions indicate only whether quantities are large or small. Specific quantity expressions give exact amounts.

General Quantity Expression	Specific Quantity Expression
I ate **too much** pizza.	I ate **six slices** of pizza.
He bought **a lot of** potato chips.	He bought **ten bags of** potato chips.

▶ 1B Specific quantity expressions can be used with plural count nouns or noncount nouns.

Plural Count Nouns	Noncount Nouns
a box of matches	a box of cereal
a cup of raisins	a cup of sugar

▶ 1C Specific quantity expressions make noncount nouns countable.

one bowl of milk	**six ounces of** cheese
two cans of soup	**four gallons of** gas

▶ 1D The expression *a piece of* can be used with a number of noncount nouns to express a specific amount.

a piece of { cake / bread / furniture / clothing / advice / news }

▶ 1E There are many different types of specific quantity expressions. Some include:

Containers
a carton of eggs/milk
a jar of mayonnaise
a bag of potato chips
a can of tuna fish
a box of cereal/candy

Portions
a slice of bread
a piece of cake
a bowl of soup
a glass of milk
a cup of coffee

Groups
a bunch of bananas
a dozen eggs
a herd of cattle
a flock of birds
a school of fish

Measurements
a quart/gallon of juice
an inch/foot/yard of cloth
a cup/teaspoon/tablespoon of salt
an ounce/pound of butter

Shapes
a grain of rice/sand
a pile/stack of leaves
a drop of water
a stick of butter

D1 Listening for Meaning and Use

▶ Notes 1A–1E

CD2 T20 **Listen to this description. Listen carefully for each food in the chart. Does the speaker mention a specific or general amount? Check (✓) the correct column.**

		SPECIFIC	GENERAL
1.	tomatoes	✓	
2.	ground beef		
3.	salt		
4.	onions		
5.	cream		
6.	spaghetti		
7.	water		
8.	bread		

D2 Choosing Specific Quantity Expressions

▶ Notes 1A–1E

Work with a partner. Each item has one specific quantity expression that is incorrect. Cross it out.

1. a piece of cloth
   ~~a pound of cloth~~
   a yard of cloth
2. a drop of milk
   a pound of milk
   a quart of milk
3. a piece of bread
   a slice of bread
   a tablespoon of bread
4. a grain of rice
   a bunch of rice
   a cup of rice
5. an ounce of fish
   a pound of fish
   a gallon of fish
6. a slice of cereal
   a cup of cereal
   a box of cereal
7. a bag of peanut butter
   a jar of peanut butter
   a teaspoon of peanut butter
8. a can of food
   a bowl of food
   a yard of food
9. a bunch of bananas
   a pound of bananas
   a quart of bananas
10. a drop of papers
    a pile of papers
    a box of papers

D3 Using Specific Quantity Expressions

▶ Notes 1A–1E

Work with a partner. Look at the shopping list and take turns asking and telling your partner about how much of each item you're going to buy. Use specific quantity words and expressions.

A: How much juice are you going to buy?

B: I think I'll get three quarts of juice.

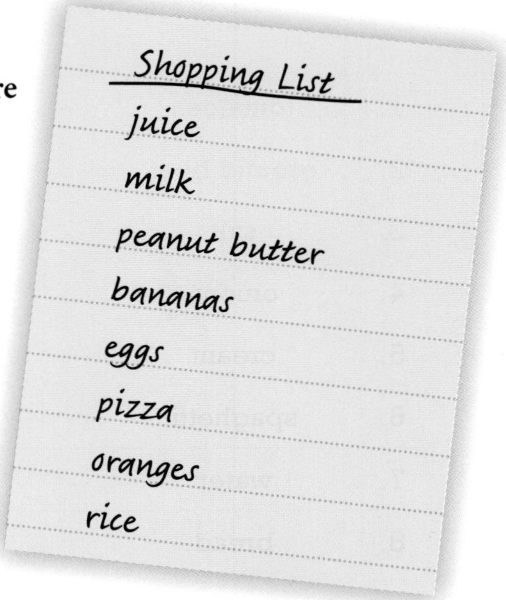

WRITING Write a Request for Advice

Think Critically About Meaning and Use

A. Choose the best answer to complete each conversation.

1. A: We have plenty of food.

B: ___________

a. OK. I'll get some more.

(b.) OK. I won't bring any.

2. A: I have little free time.

B: ___________

a. Oh. Then you can't help me.

b. Good. Then you can help me.

3. A: My car gives me little trouble.

B: ___________

a. Why don't you get it fixed?

b. You're lucky.

4. A: Is a gallon enough for ten people?

B: ___________

a. No. Buy more meat.

b. No. Buy more soda.

5. A: We don't have any milk.

B: ___________

a. Good. I need a cup for this recipe.

b. I'll go buy some.

6. A: It snowed here last night.

B: ___________

a. How many inches did you get?

b. How many quarts did you get?

B. Discuss these questions in small groups.

1. GENERATE How else could speaker A express the same idea in 2? In 3?

2. SYNTHESIZE What are some other possible responses to the question in 4?

Edit

Some of these sentences have errors. Find the errors and correct them.

1. There ~~is several fruit~~ *are several pieces of fruit* in the basket.
2. We bought many food.
3. There isn't much salt in the soup.
4. There isn't much traffic at night.
5. I have little money, so I guess we can go out to dinner tonight.
6. I bought a grain of eggs.
7. How many does a pound of cheese cost?
8. We had foot of snow last night.
9. Could I have a piece of cake?
10. She'll graduate soon. She only has a little more courses to take.

Write

You would like advice from a nutrition website. Follow the steps below to write a comment for the website's message board. Use count and noncount nouns with quantity expressions.

1. **Brainstorm** Think about your eating habits and about what advice you would like to have on foods and healthy eating. Take notes about what you want to say and ask. Use the questions below to help you.
   - What are your usual eating habits?
   - Do you have any specific health needs? For example, do you want to have more energy?
   - Are some meals or times of day a problem for you (breakfast, snacks, late night)?
   - Are some of the foods that you like a lot not healthy? Are there some healthy foods that you never eat?

2. **Write a First Draft** Before you write your draft, read the checklist below. Write your draft using quantity expressions.

3. **Edit** Read your work and check it against the checklist below. Circle grammar, spelling, and punctuation errors.

DO I ...	YES
ask for some specific advice about eating?	☐
include count and noncount nouns with general quantity expressions?	☐
include count and noncount nouns with specific quantity expressions?	☐
include at least one question and one negative with a quantity expression?	☐
use the correct form of quantity expressions?	☐

4. **Peer Review** Work with a partner to help you decide how to fix your errors and improve the content.

5. **Rewrite Your Draft** Using the comments from your partner, write a final draft.

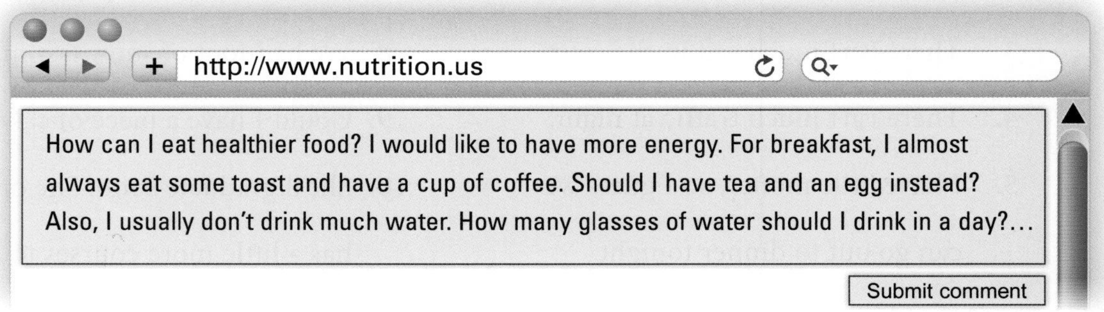
http://www.nutrition.us
How can I eat healthier food? I would like to have more energy. For breakfast, I almost always eat some toast and have a cup of coffee. Should I have tea and an egg instead? Also, I usually don't drink much water. How many glasses of water should I drink in a day?...
Submit comment

CHAPTER

15

Indefinite and Definite Articles

A. **GRAMMAR IN DISCOURSE: Meat-Eating Plants** .. 282

B. **FORM: Indefinite and Definite Articles** 284

a flower	**the** flower
an insect	**the** insect
Ø flowers	**the** flowers
some water	**the** water

C. **MEANING AND USE 1: Indefinite and Definite Articles** 287

The Indefinite Article for Introducing a Noun

The Definite Article for Identifying a Noun

Vocabulary Notes: Phrases such as *In School* and *In the School*

D. **MEANING AND USE 2: Nouns in General Statements** 293

Making General Statements

WRITING: Write a Summary of a Story 297

PART 6 TEST: Nouns, Quantity Expressions, and Articles 299

A GRAMMAR IN DISCOURSE

Meat-Eating Plants

A1 Before You Read

Discuss these questions with your classmates.

Do you know about any unusual plants? What makes them unusual? Have you ever heard of a meat-eating plant? What kind of meat do you think it eats?

A2 Read

CD2 T21 **Read the online article from a science website on the following page to find out how meat-eating plants attract insects and other small animals.**

A3 After You Read

Write *T* for true or *F* for false for each statement.

__T__ **1.** Venus flytraps are one kind of carnivorous plant.

____ **2.** Flies can easily escape from a Venus flytrap.

____ **3.** Carnivorous plants have moving parts.

____ **4.** There are about 450 kinds of carnivorous plants.

____ **5.** Carnivorous plants eat large animals.

____ **6.** Some carnivorous plants smell sweet.

Pitcher plant

Cobra lily

Sundew

http://www.meateatingplants.us

Meat-Eating Plants

A black fly hovers in the air over a strange-looking plant. Attracted by a sweet smell, the fly lands on one of the plant's flat, red leaves. The fly begins to crawl across the leaf. Suddenly, the leaf moves! Before the fly can get away, the leaf closes around it. Two rows of teeth close together. Escape is impossible. The fly tries to get out, but the trap closes more tightly. Soon the fly is dead. In a few days there is nothing left but the hard parts of its body.

The plant that ate this fly is called a Venus flytrap. It is one of about 450 species, or kinds, of carnivorous plants. A plant that is carnivorous actually eats meat. It traps and eats insects and, in some cases, small animals such as frogs and mice.

How do these unusual plants work? They must attract animals.

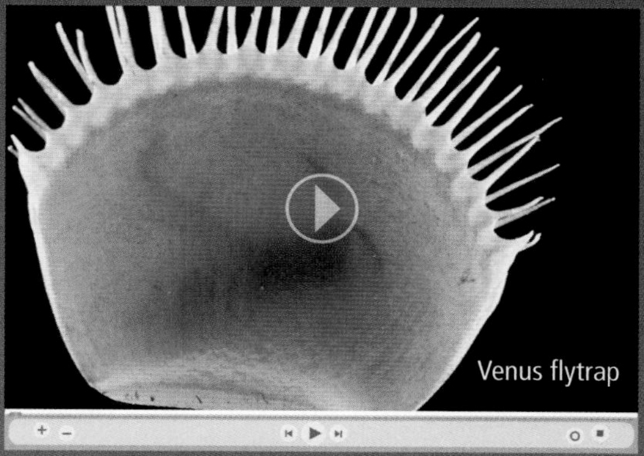

Unlike a frog or a bird, a carnivorous plant cannot reach out and grab an insect. It must wait until an insect comes to it. Some carnivorous plants give off a sweet smell that attracts insects such as flies, bees, and ants. Other carnivorous plants have bright colors and patterns. And one species has leaves covered with sparkling droplets that attract insects with bright color and light, as well as with a sweet smell.

Adapted from *Carnivorous Plants*

---

crawl: to move slowly with the body close to the ground, like a baby

droplet: a very small drop of liquid

grab: to take hold of something quickly

hover: to stay in one position in the air

insect: a small animal such as an ant, fly, or bee

sparkling: shiny and bright from light reflecting off it, like water in sunshine

B FORM

Indefinite and Definite Articles

Think Critically About Form

A. Look back at the online article on page 283 and complete the tasks below.

1. **IDENTIFY** Complete each sentence from the reading with an article *(a, an,* or *the)*.
   a. ____ black fly hovers in ____ air over ____ strange-looking plant.
   b. Suddenly, ____ leaf moves.
   c. In a few days there is nothing left but ____ hard parts of its body.
2. **CATEGORIZE** Look at the underlined nouns in the sentences above. Are they count nouns or noncount nouns? In these examples, which article(s) are used with singular count nouns? Which are used with plural count nouns? Which are used with noncount nouns?

B. Discuss your answers with the class and read the Form charts to check them.

▶ Count and Noncount Nouns

ONLINE PRACTICE

INDEFINITE ARTICLE	
A/AN	**SINGULAR COUNT NOUN**
a	flower uniform
an	insect hour

DEFINITE ARTICLE	
THE	**SINGULAR COUNT NOUN**
the	flower uniform insect hour

Ø OR *SOME*	**PLURAL COUNT NOUN**
Ø some	flowers uniforms insects hours

THE	**PLURAL COUNT NOUN**
the	flowers uniforms insects hours

Ø OR *SOME*	**NONCOUNT NOUN**
Ø some	water information money

THE	**NONCOUNT NOUN**
the	water information money

Indefinite Article

- The indefinite article is *a* or *an*. It can be used before a singular count noun (*a book*) or an adjective + a singular count noun (*an interesting book*).
- Use *a* before words that begin with a consonant sound (*a flower, a uniform*). Use *an* before words that begin with a vowel sound (*an insect, an hour*).
- Do not use *a* or *an* before plural count nouns or noncount nouns. We show this with the symbol Ø, which means "no article."
- *Some* often acts like an indefinite article before plural count nouns and noncount nouns.

Definite Article

- The definite article is *the*. It can be used before singular count nouns, plural count nouns, and noncount nouns.
- The definite article can be used before a noun (*the flower*) or an adjective + noun (*the beautiful flower*).
- When *the* comes before a noun that begins with a consonant sound, it is often pronounced /ðə/. When *the* comes before a noun that begins with a vowel sound, it is often pronounced /ði/.

/ðə/	/ði/
the plant	the insect

B1 Listening for Form

CD2 T22 Listen to these sentences. Listen carefully for the nouns in the chart. Which article do you hear before each noun? Check (✓) the correct column.

		A	*AN*	*THE*	Ø (NO ARTICLE)
1.	scientist	✓			
2.	botany				
3.	plants				
4.	hour				
5.	books				
6.	fork				
7.	apple				
8.	children				
9.	pen				
10.	flowers				

B2 Working on the Indefinite Article

Some of these sentences have errors. Find the errors and correct them.

1. I'd like ~~an~~ a hot drink.
2. Can you give me a example?
3. I waited an whole hour for you. Where were you?
4. If you're going to London, don't forget a umbrella.
5. We saw a huge old elephant at the zoo.
6. You've met the Senator? What a honor!
7. She's thinking about buying an used car.
8. He isn't a honest man.
9. Can I use a one dollar bill in the soda machine?
10. Cornell is an university in New York state.

B3 Working on Singular and Plural Forms

Look at the underlined count nouns in these sentences. Change singular nouns to plural nouns, and plural nouns to singular nouns. Change the form of the verb where necessary.

1. A new <u>store</u> is opening here soon. New stores are opening here soon.
2. Celia is taking a <u>class</u> now. ____________________
3. The <u>sandwich</u> is good. ____________________
4. We saw some interesting <u>movies</u>. ____________________
5. We've been here for <u>hours</u>. ____________________
6. The new <u>people</u> at work are nice. ____________________
7. Mr. Smith has a <u>cow</u> and some <u>horses</u>. ____________________
8. The <u>girls</u> need <u>uniforms</u> for school. ____________________
9. There was an <u>insect</u> in the bathroom. ____________________
10. Some <u>men</u> were talking to my father. ____________________

C MEANING AND USE 1

Indefinite and Definite Articles

Think Critically About Meaning and Use

A. Read the sentences and complete the task below.

1a. Let's go shopping. I need a lamp for my bedroom.
1b. We'll need to use a flashlight. The lamp in the bedroom is broken.

2a. Excuse me, sir. I'm looking for a bank. Do you know where one is?
2b. Excuse me, sir. Where is the bank in this mall?

COMPARE AND CONTRAST Compare the meaning of the underlined articles and nouns in each pair of sentences. In which sentences do the speakers have a specific object or place in mind? In which sentences do the speakers have only a general idea of the object or place they mention?

B. Discuss your answers with the class and read the Meaning and Use Notes to check them.

Meaning and Use Notes

ONLINE PRACTICE

The Indefinite Article for Introducing a Noun

▶ 1A Use *a* or *an* to introduce a singular count noun. *There is* or *there are* often begins a sentence or clause that introduces a noun with an indefinite article.

Woman: Did you see **a little boy** walk by here five minutes ago?
Mall Security Officer: I'm not sure. What does he look like?
Woman: He has brown hair, and there's **a big soccer** ball on his sweatshirt.

▶ 1B Use *some* or Ø (no article) to introduce plural count nouns or noncount nouns.

I downloaded **some** videos from the Internet.
I called for **some information.**
I downloaded **Ø videos** from the Internet.
I called for **Ø information.**

▶ 1C When a speaker uses an indefinite article, the noun is not a specific thing in the mind of the listener. In the speaker's mind, however, sometimes the noun is specific and sometimes it is not.

Bob: I bought **a** new **car**. (Bob has a specific car in mind, but the listener doesn't.)
Bob: I need **a** new **car**. (Neither Bob nor the listener have a specific car in mind.)

(Continued on page 288)

The Definite Article for Identifying a Noun

Use *the* to refer to a noun that both you and a listener can identify. This is possible when you and the listener share information about the noun.

▶ **2A** Use the definite article after a noun has already been introduced with an indefinite article.

Introduced (with Indefinite Article)

I bought Koji a sweater and a watch for his birthday.

Mentioned Again (with Definite Article)

The sweater doesn't fit and **the watch** doesn't work!

▶ **2B** Use the definite article for objects that you can see or hear.

Nouns You Can See or Hear

Could you pass **the butter**, please?

That must be a big fire. I can hear **the sirens** from here!

▶ **2C** Use the definite article when you and a listener share general knowledge about something in your environment.

Noun of General Knowledge

A: Oh, no! **The copy machine** is broken again!

B: I can't believe it!

(Both workers use a particular copy machine, so they know which one is broken.)

▶ **2D** Use the definite article when other information in the sentence identifies the noun.

Noun Identified in Sentence

Turn off **the light** near the door.

(The phrase *near the door* tells which light.)

Please hand me **the book** about England.

(The phrase *about England* tells which book.)

▶ **2E**	Use the definite article with certain nouns (*store, doctor, hospital, movies, bank, park, TV, phone*) that are familiar to you and a listener in everyday life. **Familiar Noun** A: I'm going to **the doctor** this morning. Can I borrow your car? B: Sure. A: Hello. I'm here to see Ms. Stephens. B: I'm sorry, she's on **the phone.** Would you like to sit down and wait?
▶ **2F**	Use the definite article for a noun that is unique (the only one of its type). **Unique Noun** **The moon** revolves around Earth. Tokyo is **the capital** of Japan.

C1 Listening for Meaning and Use

▶ **Notes 1A, 2A, 2C, 2E**

CD2 T23 **Listen to these sentences. Listen carefully for the nouns in the chart. Is each speaker introducing a noun or referring to a noun that the listener can identify? Check (✓) the correct column.**

		INTRODUCING A NOUN	REFERRING TO A NOUN THAT THE LISTENER CAN IDENTIFY
1.	present	✓	
2.	children		
3.	car		
4.	teacher		
5.	restaurant		
6.	bank		
7.	article		
8.	car keys		
9.	meeting		

C2 Choosing the Correct Article

▶ Notes 1, 2A, 2D

Choose the articles that best complete this description.

The Venus flytrap is (a / some)[1] famous carnivorous plant that grows in North and South Carolina. (The / Ø)[2] entire plant is about a foot tall. In spring it has (the / Ø)[3] small white flowers. But the most interesting parts of (a / the)[4] plant are its leaves.

(The / Ø)[5] leaves grow in (a / some)[6] circle around the bottom of (Ø / the)[7] plant. Each leaf opens into two halves. On (the / Ø)[8] surface of the leaves there are (some / the)[9] short hairs. They are called (Ø / some)[10] trigger hairs. If (an / the)[11] insect lands on one of (Ø / the)[12] leaves and touches (a / the)[13] trigger hairs in a certain way, (the / some)[14] two halves of the leaf close tightly around (an / the)[15] insect.

To find more information about (Ø / the)[16] carnivorous plants, look in (Ø / the)[17] plant guides, or on (the / Ø)[18] Internet.

C3 Using Definite and Indefinite Articles

▶ Notes 1–2

Complete each sentence with the, *a*, *an*, or Ø.

1. **A:** Excuse me. Where's Room 203?

   B: Room 203 is ___the___ room at the end of the hall, next to the stairs.

2. Two women are eating lunch. There's a bottle of water on the table. One says, "Please pass me ______ water, Julie."

3. **A:** How do you get to school?

   B: I walk, but it takes too long. I think I'll buy ______ bike next semester.

4. Look at ______ sky! It's beautiful, isn't it?

5. My friend made a cake and a pie. I tasted ______ pie, and it was delicious!

6. Two roommates are cleaning their apartment. One says, "Could you help me move ______ couch? I need to sweep under there."

7. Oh, no! There's ______ fly in my salad.

8. This evening I'm going to visit my aunt. She's in ______ hospital.

9. **A:** Can I borrow your truck tomorrow?

   B: Yes, but you'll need to buy ______ gas.

10. Two co-workers are standing near a printer. One of them says,

   "I think ______ printer is out of paper."

C4 Guessing About Contexts

▶ Notes 1–2

Work with a partner. Discuss the two sentences in each situation. How does the speaker's use of the indefinite or definite article change the meaning? Make guesses about the context of each sentence.

1. Two young women are talking. One says:

   a. "I hope I get the job."

   b. "I hope I get a job."

   A: In the first sentence the definite article means that the job is specific for both her and her friend. Maybe the young woman has applied for a specific job that her friend knows about.

   B: In the second sentence the indefinite article means that she doesn't have a specific job in mind. It sounds as though she isn't working and will take just about any job.

2. A married couple is talking. The man says:

   a. "I bought the book on Tahiti."

   b. "I bought a book on Tahiti."

3. Two young men are talking. One says:

   a. "I got the letter today."

   b. "I got a letter today."

4. A middle-aged woman is talking to her son. She says:

   a. "Did you buy a suit?"

   b. "Did you buy the suit?"

Vocabulary Notes

Phrases Such as *In School* and *In the School*

After the preposition *in,* some nouns change meaning depending on whether they are used with an article or not. Some examples are *school, college, court, bed,* and *class.* Use these nouns without an article to refer to what people usually do in them. Use these nouns with an article to refer to the physical place or object.

Ø Article	With an Article
Are your children **in school**? (Are they students?)	Are your children **in the school**? (Are they in the school building?)
Professor Lee is **in class.** (He's teaching.)	There aren't enough chairs **in the class.** (in the class = in the room)

C5 Using Nouns that Change Meaning

Work with a partner. Complete each sentence with *the* or Ø (no article).

1. He's still in ___Ø___ school, but he's graduating next year.
2. On our tour of ________ school, we saw that huge new student center.
3. Professor Johnson teaches two courses. He's in ________ class all morning, and he has office hours in the afternoon.
4. There is a job opening for a social worker in ________ new high school. They're looking for someone with a lot of experience.
5. Right now, there's no gym in ________ college, so I can't exercise here.
6. As an attorney, she spends a lot of her time in ________ court.
7. When I was in ________ college, I lived at home.
8. I know three people in my history course. Rita, Holly, and Omar are in ________ class.

D MEANING AND USE 2

Nouns in General Statements

Think Critically About Meaning and Use

A. Read the sentences and complete the tasks below.

1a. Students often don't get enough sleep.
1b. How much sleep do the students in your class get?

2a. Plants usually need light and water.
2b. The plants in my garden don't need much water.

COMPARE AND CONTRAST Compare the meaning of the underlined nouns in each pair of sentences. In which sentences do they refer to a group of people or plants in general? In which sentences do the underlined nouns refer to specific people or plants?

B. Discuss your answers with the class and read the Meaning and Use Notes to check them.

Meaning and Use Notes

ONLINE PRACTICE

Making General Statements

▶ 1A Sometimes a noun is used to make a general statement about a whole class or group. These nouns do not identify a specific person, place, or thing. They represent all members of that class or group.

Ants are insects.

Chocolate is made from cacao seeds.

▶ 1B When making general statements about a whole class or group, we use *a/an* with singular count nouns, and Ø with plural count nouns and noncount nouns.

Singular Count Noun

A cheetah can run very fast.

Plural Count Noun

Cheetahs can run very fast.

Noncount Noun

Oxygen is necessary for our survival.

(Continued on page 294)

▶ **1C**	You may also see or hear *the* before singular count nouns in more formal discussions about plants, animals, and machines. Musical instruments usually occur with *the* in general statements. **The giant panda** is an endangered animal. It is difficult to play **the violin**.
▶ **1D**	General statements are often used to classify and define nouns. **A diary** is a daily record of a person's life. **A carnivorous plant** is a plant that eats meat.
▶ **1E**	General statements are also often used to express opinions. **Sharks** are beautiful creatures.

D1 Listening for Meaning and Use

▶ **Notes 1A–1C**

CD2 T24 **Listen to each sentence. Listen carefully for the nouns in the chart. What does each one represent: a specific person, place, or thing, or a whole class or group? Check (✓) the correct column.**

		SPECIFIC PERSON, PLACE, OR THING	WHOLE CLASS OR GROUP
1.	a. teachers		✓
	b. tests		✓
2.	a. girl		
	b. information		
3.	a. dolphin		
	b. animal		
4.	a. radio station		
	b. advertisements		
5.	a. doctor		
	b. hospital		

D2 Classifying and Defining Nouns

▶ Note 1D

A. Look at the pictures. Match each group noun below to the appropriate specific noun.

fish plant insect flower tree vegetable

1. cactus - plant

3. maple - ________

5. pepper - ________

2. butterfly - ________

4. rose - ________

6. shark - ________

B. Work with a partner. Take turns asking for and giving simple definitions of the specific nouns in part A.

A: What's a cactus?

B: A cactus is a plant.

D3 Giving Your Opinion

▶ Note 1E

Work with a partner. Discuss your opinion about the topics below.

cell phones	**football**	**politicians**	**the guitar**
doctors	**housework**	**television**	**video games**

A: Television wasn't a good invention.

B: I agree. People don't read enough books these days. TV has made us lazy.

D4 Using Articles in General Statements

▶ Note 1A-1E

A. **Complete the statements with *a, an,* or Ø. Be sure to capitalize the first word of each sentence where necessary.**

1. __Ø__ ~~rainforests~~ Rainforests are very warm, wet, dense forests. They cover about 6% of Earth's land surface.
2. ______ parrot is a well-known rainforest bird.
3. ______ teak and mahogany are two kinds of exotic wood that come from rainforest trees.
4. ______ jaguars are large beautiful rainforest cats. They are in danger of becoming extinct.
5. ______ rhinoceros beetle is a beetle that has a curved horn on its head. It is one of the more exotic-looking rainforest insects.

B. **Complete these sentences with *a, an, the,* or Ø. Be sure to capitalize the first word of each sentence where necessary.**

1. __Ø__ ~~wolves~~ Wolves usually live in groups.
2. ______ chair is a piece of furniture that you can sit on.
3. ______ flute is my favorite instrument.
4. ______ rice is a popular food in Asia.
5. ______ trumpet is very hard to play.
6. ______ palm trees are common in places that have a tropical climate.
7. ______ calcium is important for strong bones.
8. ______ mango is a tropical fruit.

WRITING Write a Summary of a Story

Think Critically About Meaning and Use

A. Read the conversations and the statements that follow. Write ***True, False,*** or ***It's not clear*** next to each statement.

Conversation 1

A: Have you met the new teacher?
B: No, I haven't.

1. B knows that there is going to be a new teacher. ____True____
2. B knows the new teacher. ________________

Conversation 2

A: Betty works in a department store.
B: Really? Does she like it?

1. A knows the name of the department store.
2. B knows the name of the department store. ________________

B. Discuss these questions in small groups.

1. **EXPLAIN** What reasons can you give for your answers for conversation 2?
2. **ANALYZE** In conversation 2, imagine A uses the definite article. How does this change the answers? Why?

Edit

Find the errors in this paragraph and correct them.

The leaves of Venus flytraps are ~~the~~ clever traps. Each leaf has the "trigger" hairs. When these hairs move, a trap closes. When leaf is open, the trap is set, ready for a insect to come. Plant attracts insects with the sweet smell. When an insect crawls across the leaf, it moves the trigger hairs. This is a signal for a trap to close. But the trap must receive two signals before it closes. It will close only if one hair moves twice or if two hairs move. This way, the plant makes sure that it has caught the live creature and not the piece of grass or a leaf.

Write

Write a summary of a story. Follow the steps below. Use nouns with indefinite and definite articles.

1. **BRAINSTORM** Think about a story to summarize. It can be a true story, a fable, a story from a movie or book, or a story that you make up. Use the questions below to help you.
   - Who or what is the story about?
   - Where does it take place?
   - How does the story begin?
   - What are the main events?
   - How does the story end?

2. **WRITE A FIRST DRAFT** Before you write your draft, read the checklist below. Write your draft using indefinite and definite articles.

3. **EDIT** Read your work and check it against the checklist below. Circle grammar, spelling, and punctuation errors.

DO I ...	YES
summarize the important points in the story?	☐
use noncount nouns and singular and plural count nouns?	☐
use indefinite articles (*a*, *an*, Ø, *some*) to introduce nouns?	☐
use the definite article (*the*) to identify nouns?	☐

4. **PEER REVIEW** Work with a partner to help you decide how to fix your errors and improve the content.

5. **REWRITE YOUR DRAFT** Using the comments from your partner, write a final draft.

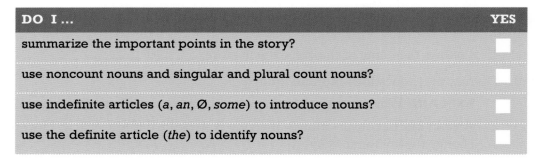

Once upon a time there was a beautiful young girl. The girl lived in a small village. She had a very mean stepmother...

PART 6 TEST | Nouns, Quantity Expressions, and Articles

Choose the correct response to complete each conversation.

1. **A:** Is Jamal playing soccer this year?
B: No, he works after school, so he has _______________ time for practice.

a. little **c.** few
b. a little **d.** a few

2. **A:** I don't have _______________ pictures of you.
B: I'll send you a few tonight. I have some nice ones from the summer.

a. some **c.** much
b. any **d.** a lot

3. **A:** What kind of computer do you have?
B: _______________

a. A laptop. **c.** Laptop.
b. The laptop. **d.** The laptops.

4. **A:** Do you ever buy frozen vegetables?
B: No, I never buy them because _______________ of them taste good.

a. a few **c.** a little
b. few **d.** little

5. **A:** The supermarket has very sweet melons this week.
B: I know. I bought _______ yesterday.

a. it **c.** Ø
b. much **d.** one

Look at the underlined noun in each sentence. Write *count* or *noncount*.

6. After the storm, we had no <u>electricity</u>.

____

7. How many <u>days</u> is she staying with us?

____

8. Only a few <u>people</u> attended the meeting.

____

Choose the correct word or words to complete each sentence.

9. Young-soo dropped __________ bananas on the kitchen floor.

a. a **b.** a bunch of **c.** a loaf of **d.** much

10. There is __________ opportunity to rewrite your term paper.

a. any **b.** few **c.** no **d.** a few

11. I'd like __________ sauce with my noodles.

a. some **b.** any **c.** a great deal **d.** a drop

Identify the use of each underlined article. Choose the correct answer.

12. <u>The</u> bus was late this morning.

a. Speaker introduces noun. **b.** Speaker and listener share knowledge.

13. <u>The</u> sun is hurting my eyes.

a. Speaker introduces noun. **b.** Listener is familiar with noun.

14. Daniela bought <u>a</u> new house.

a. Speaker introduces noun. **b.** Speaker and listener share knowledge.

Reorder each set of words to make a sentence.

15. sandwiches/a/left/few/we/have

____

16. a/money/have/bank/I/little/the/in

____

17. much/rent/pay/does/she/how

____

18. isn't/soup/salt/there/much/the/in

____

Rewrite each sentence using the word in parentheses. Make other changes as needed.

19. I need eggs for the cake. (egg)

____

20. The doctor is here. (doctors)

____

PART

7

Adjectives and Adverbs

CHAPTER

16

Adjectives

A. GRAMMAR IN DISCOURSE: **Unusual Gifts for Unusual People** 302

B. FORM: **Adjectives** 304

Placement of Adjectives

I saw an **entertaining** play last night.

It's nothing **important**.

The sky became **cloudy**.

Formation of Adjectives

The bus driver saw a **speeding** car.

The house had a **broken** window.

She wears **fashionable** clothes.

C. MEANING AND USE: **Describing with Adjectives** 309

Order of Adjectives

Adjectives Ending in *-ing* and *-ed*

WRITING: **Write an Advertisement** 314

A GRAMMAR IN DISCOURSE

Unusual Gifts for Unusual People

A1 Before You Read

Discuss these questions.

Do you ever buy things from mail-order catalogs? Do you ever buy things online? If so, what do you buy? Do you prefer to shop at a store? Why or why not?

A2 Read

CD2 T25 **Read the catalog entries on the following page. Would you buy any of these items?**

A3 After You Read

Choose the answer that best completes each sentence.

1. The crossword puzzle has __________.

a. 91,000 clues **b.** 100 squares (**c.**) 28,000 words

2. The potholders are __________.

a. washable **b.** removable **c.** round

3. The thermometer has __________ balls.

a. wooden **b.** glass **c.** leather

4. Each ball in the thermometer has a __________ tag.

a. silver **b.** black **c.** gold

5. The backpacker guitar is __________.

a. easy to carry **b.** heavy **c.** soft

http://www.unusualgiftsforup.us

Unusual Gifts for Unusual People

The World's Largest Crossword Puzzle

This challenging crossword puzzle can take months to finish. It has 91,000 squares and contains fascinating clues for over 28,000 words. A 100-page clue book provides additional help. The puzzle is printed on strong paper so that you can hang it on any wall. Comes with storage box.

Item #66813

Backpacker Guitar

This extremely light, compact guitar weighs less than three pounds. It is so lightweight and portable that it has gone on trips on the Space Shuttle, to the summit of Mount Everest, and to both the North and South Poles. It has a wooden body and neck, and metal tuners, and it comes with a soft, padded carrying case.

Item #66545

Galileo Liquid Thermometer

Galileo was the first to make this unusual liquid thermometer. The clear glass tube holds a number of handmade glass balls that float in a special liquid. Each colored ball responds to temperature changes by rising or falling. The lowest ball gives you the correct temperature. The temperatures are easy to read because each ball has a gold tag with large numbers.

Item #48210

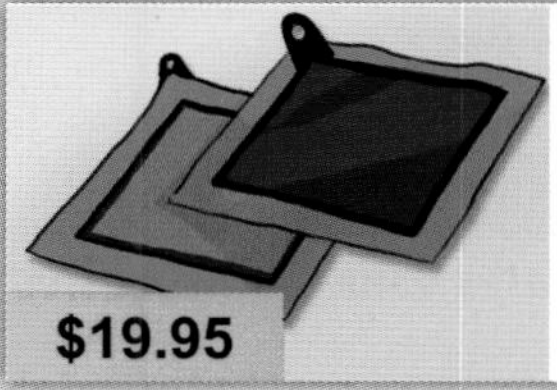

Washable Leather Potholders

These strong, long-lasting potholders are excellent for protecting your hands from heat. The potholders are made from two soft, attractive leather pieces. They're washable, too.

Item #60934

Adapted from the *Hammacher Schlemmer catalog*

challenging: difficult, but exciting and interesting

clue: a piece of information that helps someone solve a puzzle

compact: small and convenient

potholder: a thick piece of material used to handle hot pots, pans, or dishes

summit: the top of a mountain

temperature: measure of how hot or cold something is

B FORM

Adjectives

Think Critically About Form

A. Complete the tasks below.

1. **IDENTIFY** Underline the adjective and circle the noun in each phrase below. Does the adjective come before or after the noun?

   fascinating clues   strong paper   gold tag

2. **RECOGNIZE** Look back at the online catalog entries on page 303. Find three more examples of adjective + noun phrases.
3. **APPLY** Find the adjective in the sentence below. Does it follow an action verb or a stative verb? What does it describe?

   The potholders are washable.

B. Discuss your answers with the class and read the Form charts to check them.

▶ Placement of Adjectives

ONLINE PRACTICE

BEFORE NOUNS				
	ARTICLE	ADJECTIVE	NOUN	
I saw	an	**entertaining**	play	last night.
	The	**angry**	man	shouted at me.
He explained	the	**main**	point.	
We went to	the	**same**	school.	

AFTER CERTAIN NOUNS		
	NOUN	ADJECTIVE
He is six	feet	**tall**.
I'm fifty	years	**old**.
It's	nothing	**important**.
Did you meet	anyone	**famous**?

AFTER STATIVE VERBS		
	STATIVE VERB	ADJECTIVE
The play	was	**entertaining**.
The man	looked	**angry**.
The sky	became	**cloudy**.
The child	seemed	**afraid**.

Before Nouns

- Adjectives modify (or describe) nouns.
- Adjectives usually come after an article and before a noun. Be sure to use the form of *a* or *an* that agrees with the beginning sound of the adjective (*a unique experience, an entertaining play, an honest man*).

After Certain Nouns

- Adjectives come after nouns in most expressions of measurement such as height and age.
- Adjectives also come after pronouns such as *nothing, anyone,* and *someone.*

After Stative Verbs

- Adjectives can occur alone (without a noun) following stative verbs such as *be, become, feel, seem, look,* and *appear.*
- Some adjectives cannot come before a noun. These include *glad, pleased,* and certain adjectives beginning with the letter *a*, such as *awake, asleep, afraid, alone,* and *alike.*

  The boy is **asleep** on the couch. x The asleep boy is on the couch. (INCORRECT)
- Some adjectives can only come before a noun. (These include *main, chief, principal, same, only, future, former,* and *previous.*)

  Hamlet is the **main** character. x The character of Hamlet is main. (INCORRECT)
- Use *and* to separate two adjectives that follow a verb. If more than two adjectives follow the verb, separate them with commas and the word *and.*

  His nurse was **kind and thoughtful**. We were **wet, tired, and hungry**.

▶ Formation of Adjectives

	ARTICLE	ADJECTIVE	NOUN
The bus driver saw	a	**speeding**	car.
The mother held	the	**excited**	child.
The house had	a	**broken**	window.

	ARTICLE	ADJECTIVE	NOUN
She wears		**fashionable**	clothes.
Bears are		**furry**	animals.
My father is	a	**successful**	doctor.

- Many adjectives are formed by adding *-ing* to verbs.

  speed → speed**ing** (a **speeding** car) bore → bor**ing** (a **boring** book)
- Many adjectives have the same form as past participles.

  excite → excit**ed** (an **excited** child) break → **broken** (a **broken** window)
- Many adjectives are formed by adding endings such as *-able, -ish, -ic, -y, -ful,* and *-less* to nouns.

  fashion → fashion**able** (a **fashionable** tie) success → success**ful** (a **successful** play)
- Many nouns function as adjectives when they are used to modify other nouns.

  window seat **music** box

B1 Listening for Form

CD2 T26 **Listen to each conversation. Listen carefully for the adjectives in the chart. Which noun does each describe? Check (✓) the correct column.**

Conversation 1

		MOVIE	STARS	MAN
1.	entertaining	✓		
2.	same			
3.	famous			
4.	boring			
5.	asleep			

Conversation 2

		KIDS	RIDES	ADULTS
1.	excited			
2.	frightening			
3.	fine			
4.	tired			
5.	hungry			

B2 Identifying Adjectives

Circle the adjectives in each sentence. Then draw arrows to the nouns described.

1. Matt loves that (comfortable) (old) (leather) chair.
2. My new dress is fancy, so I can't wear it to an informal occasion.
3. The tall dark man was the main character in the play.
4. When she returned my favorite silk dress, it had a huge coffee stain on it.
5. The salesman told us the rusty old car was a real bargain.
6. The theater tickets were cheap, but our balcony seats were awful.
7. The lost little boy has blond hair and blue eyes.
8. The tired old man was asleep under the shady tree.

B3 Forming Adjectives from Nouns

A. **Work with a partner. Look at these adjectives. Do you see a noun form in each one? Circle it. Then underline the ending that makes each noun an adjective.**

1. childless	**4.** friendless	**7.** heroic	**10.** hairy
2. childish	**5.** careless	**8.** successful	**11.** curly
3. helpful	**6.** dirty	**9.** athletic	**12.** useless

B. **Study the meaning of the adjective endings below. Then rewrite these sentences in a way that explains the meaning of the underlined words. Discuss your answers with your partner.**

-ish = like a

-ic = like a

-y = full of; having the quality of; having a lot of

-ful = full of; having the quality of; having a lot of

-less = without, do/does not have

1. Our neighbors are childless, but they have a lot of friends.

Our neighbors don't have children, but they have a lot of friends.

2. His behavior is childish.

3. This computer manual is helpful.

4. He was friendless when he arrived in this city.

5. The students were so surprised, they were speechless.

6. The kitchen floor is dirty.

7. Everyone thought the policeman was heroic.

8. My parents are lawyers, and they are both successful.

9. There are a lot of historic buildings in the old part of the city.

10. He always wears shirts with long sleeves because he has hairy arms.

11. She has beautiful curly hair.

12. That guidebook is useless. It's over twenty years old.

B4 Forming Sentences with Adjectives

Form sentences from these words. Punctuate your sentences correctly. Compare your sentences with a partner's.

1. and/job/challenging/her/is/rewarding

   Her job is challenging and rewarding. OR Her job is rewarding and challenging.

2. somewhere/go/want/exotic/we/expensive/to/and

   ______

3. car/bought/old/they/an

   ______

4. see/I/interesting/didn't/anything

   ______

5. feet/was/wide/room/ten/the

   ______

6. beach/sandy/the/looked/beautiful

   ______

7. do/never/I/right/anything

   ______

8. Amy/house/to/a/brick/moved

   ______

9. brother/asleep/my/is

   ______

10. a/dinner/that/delicious/was

    ______

C MEANING AND USE

Describing with Adjectives

Think Critically About Meaning and Use

A. Read the sentences and complete the tasks below.

a. Italian leather shoes are on sale today.
b. He was wearing a large blue riding helmet.
c. He bought an expensive European racing bike.
d. I can't find my favorite cotton sweatshirt.

ANALYZE Underline the adjectives in the sentences above. Then think about the meaning of the adjectives and place them in the categories below.

quality/opinion: ____________________ origin: ____________________

size: ____________________ material: ____________________

color: ____________________ kind/purpose: ____________________

B. Discuss your answers with the class and read the Meaning and Use Notes to check them.

Meaning and Use Notes

ONLINE PRACTICE

Order of Adjectives

▶ 1A Adjectives can describe many different features of a noun.

Quality/Opinion: comfortable, colorful
Size: large, small
Age: old, antique, young
Shape: round, square
Color: blue, gray
Origin: Chinese, Russian
Material: wooden, cotton
Kind/Purpose: racing, rocking

▶ 1B If two or more adjectives come before a noun, they usually follow this order: quality/opinion, size, age, shape, color, origin, material, and kind/purpose.

Quality/ Opinion	Size	Age	Shape	Color	Origin	Material	Kind/ Purpose
beautiful	tall	old	round	blue	Greek	cotton	racing
expensive	small	new	square	green	Italian	wooden	rocking

That's an **Italian racing** bike.
He wore a **blue cotton** shirt.
They have a **beautiful new rocking** chair.
He sat at an **expensive wooden** desk.

(Continued on page 310)

▶ **1C** We do not usually use more than three adjectives before a noun. It is more common to use two or three adjectives and then add other descriptive phrases to the end of the sentence.

I bought **expensive black leather** boots from Italy.

Adjectives Ending in *-ing* and *-ed*

▶ **2** Adjectives ending in *-ing* and *-ed* refer to emotions or feelings. The *-ing* adjective describes a noun that causes an emotion or feeling. The *-ed* adjective describes a noun (usually a person) that feels or experiences an emotion or feeling.

Adjective ending in *-ing*	**Adjective ending in *-ed***
It's an **exciting** match. (= The match causes excitement.)	The **excited** fans cheered wildly. (= The fans felt excitement.)
We heard a **frightening** scream. (= The scream caused fear.)	The **frightened** child cried all night. (= The child felt fear.)

C1 Listening for Meaning and Use

▶ Note 2

CD2 T27 **Listen to each sentence. Does the adjective you hear describe a noun that causes an emotion, or does it describe a noun that feels an emotion? Check (✓) the correct column.**

	CAUSES AN EMOTION	FEELS AN EMOTION
1.	✓	
2.		
3.		
4.		
5.		
6.		
7.		
8.		
9.		

C2 Classifying and Ordering Adjectives

▶ Notes 1A–1C

A. Put the adjectives below in the correct columns of the chart. (The completed chart will have four blank boxes.)

lovely	French	leather	metal	fashionable
medical	tan	round	enormous	soft
brown	glass	long	plastic	small
toy	middle-aged	handmade	triangular	circular
Greek	unusual	yellow	purple	modern
honest	huge	beautiful	Japanese	hardworking
wooden	Indian	elegant	short	white
evening	suede	antique	tiny	wool
old	rectangular	decorative	square	cylindrical
European	racing	new	elderly	green
silk	large	wedding	computer	oval
pink	young	miniature	gray	pear-shaped

QUALITY/ OPINION	SIZE	AGE	SHAPE	COLOR	ORIGIN	MATERIAL	KIND/ PURPOSE
lovely							*medical*

B. Work with a partner. Use the adjectives in the chart in part A or others of your own to describe the things below. Use at least three adjectives from different categories in each description.

1. your favorite piece of clothing

   I have a yellow silk dress from India. It's very elegant.

2. a piece of furniture
3. a person you know very well
4. a book or movie that you enjoyed
5. a car you would like to own
6. a favorite childhood toy

C3 Choosing *-ed* or *-ing* Adjectives

▶ Notes 1A, 2

Read these conversations and choose the correct adjective.

Conversation 1

A: Did you see the program *Life of a Bug* on TV last night? It was (fascinating /[1] fascinated).

B: I started to watch it, but I turned it off. I felt (disgusting /[2] disgusted) by all those insects.

A: Do you think insects are (disgusting /[3] disgusted)? To me they are really (interesting /[4] interested) creatures.

Conversation 2

A: That's an (exciting /[1] excited) idea.

B: I'm glad you like it. Unfortunately, my boss didn't seem (exciting /[2] excited) when I told her about it. I felt really (disappointing /[3] disappointed).

Conversation 3

A: I've never heard such a (boring /[1] bored) speaker.

B: I know. I felt (boring /[2] bored), too. It was (surprising /[3] surprised), though, because she's quite famous.

C4 Describing People, Places, and Things

▶ Notes 1A–1C, 2

Work with a partner. Talk about these people, places, and things.

your best friend	your favorite piece of art	your job
your boss/teacher	your hometown	your neighbors

A: *What's your best friend like?* OR *Describe your best friend.*

B: *He's short, and his hair is thick and curly. He has a big moustache and green eyes.*

C5 Writing Catalog Descriptions

▶ Notes 1A–1C, 2

Look at these pictures from a catalog, and write a description of each item. Use the adjectives from the list in exercise C2 or others of your own. Use at least three adjectives from different categories in each description.

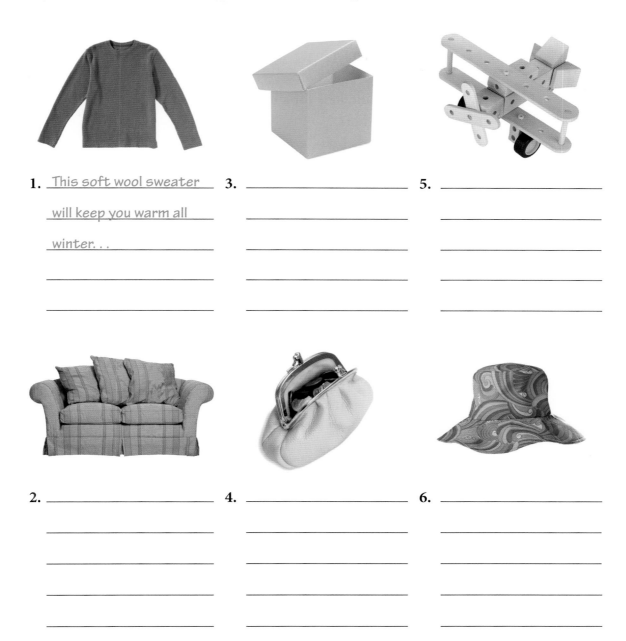

1. This soft wool sweater will keep you warm all winter. . .

3. ____________________

5. ____________________

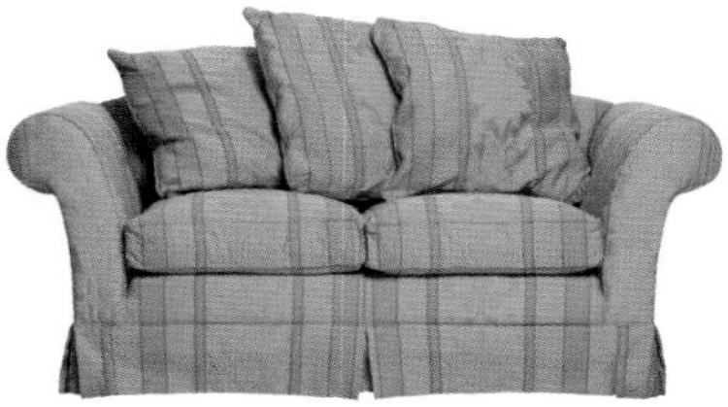

2. ____________________

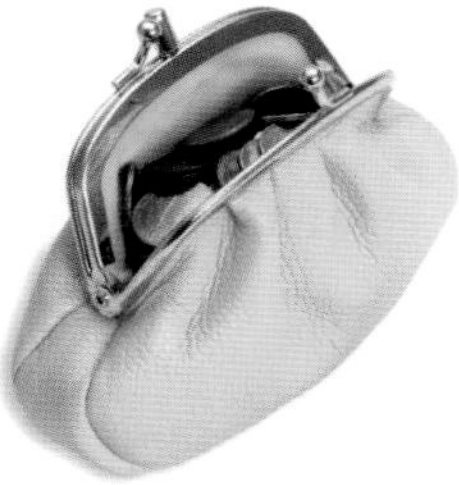

4. ____________________

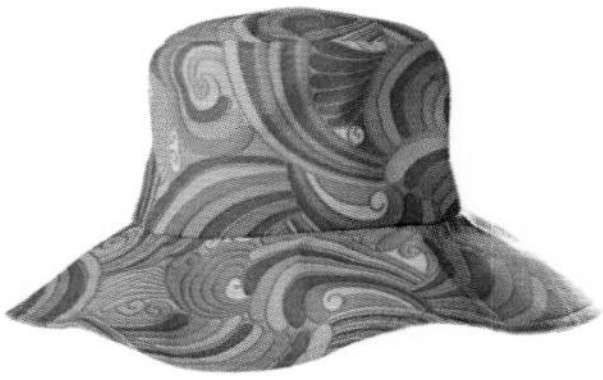

6. ____________________

WRITING Write an Advertisement

Think Critically About Meaning and Use

A. Choose the best answer to complete each conversation.

1. A: My boss is very frightening.
B: ___________
a. Maybe you should look for a new job.
b. What's he afraid of?

2. A: Was the speaker boring?
B: Yes. ___________
a. He fell asleep while he was talking!
b. I fell asleep during the speech.

3. A: We have a great German teacher this semester.
B: I know. His class is really _____.
a. exciting
b. excited

4. A: Did you like that new online game?
B: ___________
a. No, I thought he was pretty bored.
b. Yes, it certainly is an amazing game.

5. A: She's really excited!
B: ___________
a. I did, too.
b. I am, too.

6. A: Would you like to hear about some of our new products?
B: ___________
a. Thanks, but I'm not interested.
b. Thanks, but I'm not interesting.

B. Discuss these questions in small groups.

1. **ANALYZE** In 1, 2, and 5, does the person that speaker A mentions cause or experience the feeling of the adjective?
2. **GENERATE** Create a sentence with an *-ing* adjective and a sentence with an *-ed* adjective.

C. Read these pairs of sentences. Write *S* if the meaning of each pair of sentences is the same, or *D* if the meaning is different.

__S__ **1.** There are a lot of window seats on this flight.
There are a lot of seats by the window on this flight.

_____ **2.** I drove a Japanese car.
I drove a car in Japan.

_____ **3.** Sheryl was wearing a leather jacket.
Sheryl was wearing a jacket made of leather.

_____ **4.** The rocking chair is old.
The old chair is rocking.

_____ **5.** The musical instruments in this shop are made by hand.
The musical instruments in this shop are handmade.

Edit

Some of these sentences have errors. Find the errors and correct them.

I feel very ~~frustrating~~ frustrated because I never know what to buy for my brother. Last year I bought him a Swiss watch expensive for his birthday. He returned it and bought several pairs of socks wool and snow new tires for his car. This year I bought him a silk long beautiful robe. He returned that, too. He got a cordless new lawnmower instead. I've solved the problem for his graduation. I'm going to give him perfect something—I'm going to take him shopping with me! I'm sure he'll be pleasing with that.

Write

Write an advertisement for a product or something you want to sell. Follow the steps below. Use adjectives with nouns.

1. **BRAINSTORM** Think about a product to advertise, and about what you can say to convince people to buy it. Use these categories to help you.
   - appearance (size, shape, color, material)
   - uses
   - who it is for
   - special features (anything extra or surprising)
   - reasons for buying (price, quality, convenience, advantages over similar products…)
   - good things that people have to say about it

2. **WRITE A FIRST DRAFT** Before you write your draft, read the checklist below. Write your draft using adjectives with nouns.

3. **EDIT** Read your work and check it against the checklist below. Circle grammar, spelling, and punctuation errors.

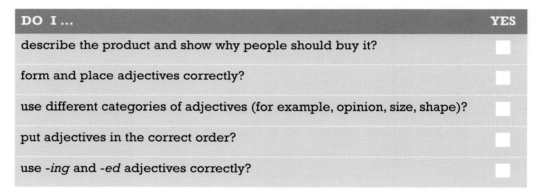

DO I …	YES
describe the product and show why people should buy it?	☐
form and place adjectives correctly?	☐
use different categories of adjectives (for example, opinion, size, shape)?	☐
put adjectives in the correct order?	☐
use *-ing* and *-ed* adjectives correctly?	☐

4. **PEER REVIEW** Work with a partner to help you decide how to fix your errors and improve the content.

5. **REWRITE YOUR DRAFT** Using the comments from your partner, write a final draft.

FOR SALE

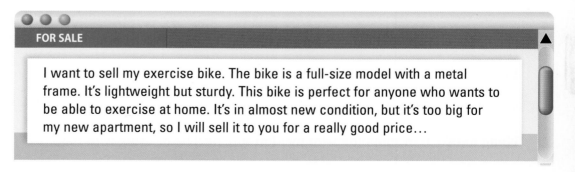

I want to sell my exercise bike. The bike is a full-size model with a metal frame. It's lightweight but sturdy. This bike is perfect for anyone who wants to be able to exercise at home. It's in almost new condition, but it's too big for my new apartment, so I will sell it to you for a really good price…

– 한 챕터 20p 3시간 걸림 –

CHAPTER 17

Adverbs

A. **GRAMMAR IN DISCOURSE: The Personality Compass** 318

B. **FORM 1: Adverbs of Manner, Possibility, Time, and Opinion** 320

She quit **unexpectedly**. **Yesterday** I found a new job.

She **probably** failed the test. **Unfortunately**, I failed the test.

C. **MEANING AND USE 1: Adverbs of Manner, Possibility, Time, and Opinion** 325

Adverbs of Manner

Adverbs of Possibility

Adverbs of Time

Adverbs of Opinion

Adverbs with Two Forms

D. **FORM 2: Adverbs of Degree** 328

The music is **really** loud. He was **such a fast runner**

He was **so fast (that)** he won the race. **(that)** he won the race.

E. **MEANING AND USE 2: Adverbs of Degree** 331

Making Adjectives and Adverbs Weaker or Stronger

Reasons and Results with *So/Such* ... + *That* Clauses

F. **FORM 3: *Too* and *Enough*** 335

It's **too** hot to eat outside. You aren't strong **enough** to pick this up.

G. **MEANING AND USE 3: Contrasting *Too* and *Enough*** 337

Too

Enough

WRITING: Write About a Sporting Event 340

PART 7 TEST: Adjectives and Adverbs 343

A GRAMMAR IN DISCOURSE

The Personality Compass

A1 Before You Read

Discuss these questions.

What kind of person are you? Are you easygoing or are you very serious? Give examples to explain the kind of person you are.

A2 Read

CD2 T28 **Read this article to find out about personality types at work. Which personality type are you?**

The Personality Compass

When some companies hire new workers, they look for people with certain kinds of personalities for certain jobs. Fortunately, there is a test that helps these companies do this. It is called the Personality Compass. The Personality Compass divides people into four basic types: Norths, Souths, Easts, and Wests.

Norths are leaders. They work very hard to reach their goals. They often have strong opinions. They are so confident and independent that they can make decisions quickly. Their motto is "Get the job done fast."

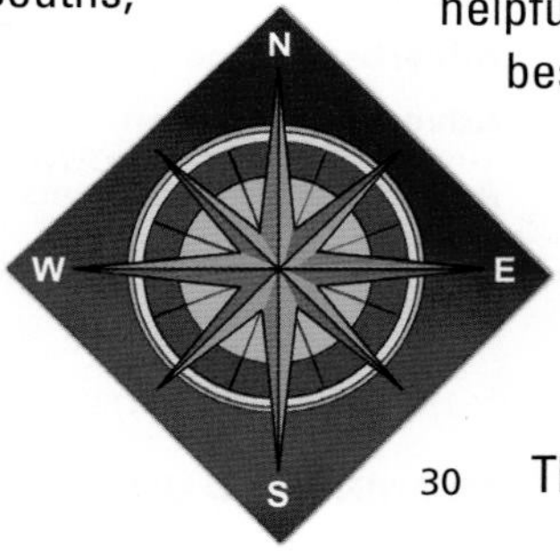

Souths work best when they work with others. They are good team players because they understand the needs of others. They are also good listeners, and they are almost always patient and helpful. Their motto is "Build the best teams."

Easts are such perfectionists that they always want to do everything right. They always plan very carefully. They are very organized and logical, and they work extremely hard. They prefer to work in a structured environment because they are good rule-followers. Their motto is "Do it right the first time."

Wests are natural risk-takers; they are not afraid to take chances. Wests are often very creative. They are also flexible, so they don't mind changing a plan after they have begun to work. They work very enthusiastically, especially on new projects. Their motto is "Don't be afraid to try something new today."

Everyone has some characteristics from all four types, but one type is usually stronger than the others. It is also very common for some people to have both a primary personality type and a secondary one. In other words, they are not "true" Norths or Souths, for example, but are instead "Northwests" or "Southeasts." However, since North-South and East-West are opposites, it is impossible for one person to have those combinations. Reread the descriptions. Which personality type are you?

---

compass: a device that shows directions (i.e., N, S, E, W)
enthusiastically: with great energy
motto: a short sentence that expresses the beliefs of a person or group
primary: main or most important
secondary: less important than something else
structured: very organized, with strict rules

A3 After You Read

Look at the jobs below. Which two do you think best match each personality type? Discuss your answers with a partner. Did you both choose the same jobs?

artist	**project manager**	**accountant**	**architect**
pilot	**construction worker**	**lawyer**	**football player**

1. Norths (confident, independent leaders): ____________________
2. Souths (good team players): ____________________
3. Easts (perfectionists, rule-followers): ____________________
4. Wests (creative risk-takers): ____________________

B FORM 1

Adverbs of Manner, Possibility, Time, and Opinion

Think Critically About Form

A. Look back at the online article on page 318 and complete the tasks below.

1. **IDENTIFY** Underline seven words that end in *-ly*. These are adverbs.
2. **ANALYZE** Which three underlined adverbs answer the question *How*? about the verb in the clause? These are adverbs of manner.
3. **RECOGNIZE** Where do the adverbs of manner occur in each clause? Do they come before or after the main verb?

B. Discuss your answers with the class and read the Form charts to check them.

ONLINE PRACTICE

ADVERBS OF MANNER

SUBJECT	(AUXILIARY +) VERB	ADVERB	
She	quit	**unexpectedly**. 뜻밖에, 예상밖에	
	has quit		

SUBJECT	(AUXILIARY +) VERB	DIRECT OBJECT	ADVERB
She	quit	her job	**unexpectedly**.
	has quit		

SUBJECT	AUXILIARY	ADVERB	VERB	
She	has	**unexpectedly**	quit	(her job).

ADVERBS OF POSSIBILITY

	ADVERB	(AUXILIARY +) VERB	
She	**probably**	failed	the test.
		has failed	

	ADVERB	*BE*	
He	**definitely**	is	at home.

	BE	ADVERB	
He	is	**definitely**	at home.

	AUXILIARY	ADVERB	VERB
He	has	**definitely**	left.

MAYBE/PERHAPS	
Maybe	I'll get a raise.
Perhaps	

ADVERBS OF TIME	
Yesterday	I found a new job.
I found a new job	**yesterday**.

ADVERBS OF OPINION		
Unfortunately,		I failed the test.
I failed the test,		**unfortunately**.
I	**unfortunately**	failed the test.

Overview

- Adverbs modify or change the meaning of verbs.
- Many adverbs are formed by adding *-ly* to an adjective. See Appendix 10 for the spelling of adverbs ending in *-ly*.

  quick → quick**ly**   definite → definite**ly**   unfortunate → unfortunate**ly**

- Adverbs can occur in different positions in a sentence. However, they never occur between a verb and its object.

  ✔ She quit her job **unexpectedly**.   ✘ She quit unexpectedly her job. (INCORRECT)

Adverbs of Manner

- Adverbs of manner usually come after the verb. In sentences with any auxiliary except *do* (that is, *be, have*, or a modal), *-ly* adverbs of manner can also be placed between the auxiliary and the verb.

  She has **unexpectedly** quit her job. You should **carefully** consider your options.

  They are **quietly** waiting for news. The temperature will **slowly** rise this week.

Adverbs of Possiblity

- Adverbs of possibility include words such as *certainly, definitely, probably, maybe,* and *perhaps.*
- When there is no auxiliary in a sentence, *-ly* adverbs of possibility come directly before the verb. In sentences with the main verb *be* or an auxiliary, *-ly* adverbs of possibility can be placed before or after *be* or the auxiliary.
- *Maybe* and *perhaps* come at the beginning of a sentence.

Adverbs of Time

- Adverbs of time can come at the beginning or end of a sentence. They include words such as *yesterday, today, tomorrow, now, recently,* and *soon.*
- *Recently* can also occur before the verb or between the auxilliary and the verb.

  I **recently** found a new job.   I have **recently** found a new job.

Adverbs of Opinion

- Most adverbs of opinion can occur at the beginning or end of a sentence or before the verb. They include words such as *fortunately, happily, incredibly, luckily, obviously, strangely,* and *surprisingly.*

(Continued on page 322)

ADVERBS VS. ADJECTIVES							
	VERB	**ADVERB**		**ARTICLE**	**ADJECTIVE**	**NOUN**
He	runs	**fast**.	He's	a	**fast**	runner.
They don't	work	**hard**.	They aren't		**hard**	workers.
She	gets up	**early**.	She has	an	**early**	class.
I	exercise	**daily**.	I do		**daily**	exercises.
He	sang	**well**.	He was	a	**good**	singer.

Adverbs vs. Adjectives

- Some adverbs don't end in *-ly*. They look like adjectives because they have the same form. They always follow the verb.

  He runs **fast**.

- Some adjectives end in *-ly*. They look like adverbs because they have the same form.

  She has an **early** class. (*Early* is an adjective in the sentence.)

- *Well* is the irregular adverb form of the adjective *good*. *Good* modifies nouns and stative verbs only. *Well* modifies action verbs. However, *well* can be used as an adjective when it refers to health.

  He played **well**. (*Well* is an adverb in this sentence.)

  I don't feel **well**. (*Well* is an adjective in the sentence.)

- Not all verbs are modified by adverbs. We modify certain stative verbs (such as *be, become, feel, seem, look,* and *appear*) with adjectives.

  It tastes **good**. I feel **terrible**. She looks **beautiful**.

> **!** Some words that end in *-ly* are never adverbs. They are adjectives that modify nouns, not verbs.
>
> **friendly** women an **ugly** sweater a **lonely** child **lovely** flowers

B1 Listening for Form

CD2 T29 **Listen to each sentence. Choose the adjective or adverb you hear.**

1. recent / recently
2. careful / carefully
3. careless / carelessly
4. unexpected / unexpectedly
5. slow / slowly
6. angry / angrily
7. lucky / luckily
8. certain / certainly

B2 Forming Adverbs of Manner

Change these adjectives to adverbs of manner. If there is no adverb form, leave the space blank. If necessary, see Appendix 10.

1. curious curiously
2. heavy
3. light
4. natural
5. realistic
6. smooth
7. lovely
8. simple

B3 Placing Adverbs in Sentences

Rewrite these sentences. Put the adverbs in parentheses in the correct places. More than one answer is possible in most of the sentences.

Adverbs of possibility

1. He is coming to the meeting. (definitely) He is definitely coming to the meeting. OR He definitely is coming to the meeting.
2. We'll see you at the soccer game. (perhaps)
3. We have met before. (probably)

Adverbs of manner

4. They greeted their guest. (enthusiastically)
5. He explained his ideas. (carefully)
6. He has left the country. (unexpectedly)

Adverbs of time

7. I'm going to finish this project. (tomorrow)
8. We're going to leave. (soon)
9. She hasn't been around. (lately)

Adverbs of opinion

10. No one was hurt in the accident. (luckily)
11. We'll need to change our plans. (obviously)
12. She gave the right answer. (surprisingly)

B4 Identifying Adverbs and Adjectives

A. Read each sentence. Is the underlined word an adverb or adjective? Check (✓) the correct column.

		ADVERB	ADJECTIVE
1.	This is a hard book; I don't really understand it.		✓
2.	The train ride seemed very fast.		
3.	When my sister went to college, I felt lonely.		
4.	I have to work really hard in my new job.		
5.	We left the lecture early because we were tired.		
6.	The bus to Denver leaves at 5:00 P.M. daily.		
7.	I'm eating fast because I need to get back to work.		
8.	He's catching an early flight to New York tomorrow.		

B. Circle the adjective or adverb that best completes each sentence.

1. Ben plays the violin (beautiful / beautifully).
2. The children are playing (quiet / quietly) in their room.
3. What's the matter with Lee? He looks (angry / angrily).
4. Carl sounded (terrible / terribly) when we spoke on the phone. Is he sick?
5. Rosa smiled (happy / happily) when she opened the door.
6. Your children are very friendly and (polite / politely).
7. I felt (bad / badly) after our fight.
8. You seemed (happy / happily) on the phone last night.

C. Work with a partner. Write sentences with these adverbs and adjectives.

1. ugly That painting is ugly.
2. recently ______
3. maybe ______
4. fast (adj.) ______
5. hard (adv.) ______

C MEANING AND USE 1

Adverbs of Manner, Possibility, Time, and Opinion

Think Critically About Meaning and Use

A. Read the sentences and complete the tasks below.

1a. It rained hard while we were sleeping.
2b. Unfortunately, it rained while we were sleeping.

2a. We have made our plans. We'll definitely leave at 7 A.M.
2b. We haven't made our plans. Maybe we'll leave at 7 A.M.

1. **EVALUATE** Look at 1a and 1b. Underline the adverb in each sentence. Which adverb describes how the action happened? Which adverb gives an opinion?
2. **INTERPRET** Look at 2a and 2b. Underline the adverb in each sentence. In which sentence is the speaker more certain about future plans?

B. Discuss your answers with the class and read the Meaning and Use Notes to check them.

Meaning and Use Notes

ONLINE PRACTICE

Adverbs of Manner

▶ **1** Adverbs of manner answer the question *How*? They describe the way someone does something or the way something happens.

He works **carefully**.

It snows **heavily** in Alaska.

Adverbs of Possibility

▶ **2** Adverbs of possibility show how sure or unsure we are about something.

More Sure ↑	• definitely, certainly	We're **definitely** going to win this game.
	• probably	If I can find a ride, I'll **probably** go.
Less Sure ↓	• maybe, perhaps	**Perhaps** you should stay home.

Adverbs of Time

▶ 3 Adverbs of time, such as *yesterday, today, now, recently,* and *soon*, answer the question *When*? They can refer to a specific time or a more indefinite time.

Specific Time	**Indefinite Time**
She saw him **yesterday**.	I saw him **recently**.

Adverbs of Opinion

▶ 4 Adverbs of opinion, such as *fortunately, happily, incredibly, luckily, obviously, strangely*, and *surprisingly*, give an opinion about an entire sentence or idea.

It **obviously** rained last night. The ground is still wet.

The plane had to make an emergency landing. **Surprisingly**, no one was hurt.

Adverbs with Two Forms

▶ 5 Some adverbs, such as *hard*, *high*, and *late*, have two forms with two meanings.

I want to pass this course. I'm studying **hard**. (*hard* = with a lot of effort)

I don't care about passing this course. I **hardly** study. (*hardly* = almost not at all)

After the storm the snow was piled **high**. (*high* = to a great height)

He is a **highly** respected writer. (*highly* = to a great degree)

He arrived at the meeting **late**. (*late* = not on time)

He hasn't gone to any meetings **lately**. (*lately* = recently)

C1 Listening for Meaning and Use

▶ Notes 2–5

CD2 T30 **Listen to each sentence. Does it have the same meaning as the sentence in the chart or a different meaning? Check (✓) the correct column.**

		SAME	DIFFERENT
1.	I saw her a short time ago.	✓	
2.	It snowed a lot last night.		
3.	He's been late for our meetings recently.		
4.	It's likely we'll go to Mexico this summer.		
5.	I'm not studying very much this year.		
6.	Some buses are not arriving on time.		

C2 Using Adverbs

▶ Notes 1–4

In your notebook, rewrite each paragraph using all of the adverbs given. Use an adverb in every sentence.

1. Adverbs of time: *recently, soon, tomorrow, yesterday*

I joined a gym. I worked out in the weight room. My muscles are sore, but I'm going to go back to the gym. I'll be strong and healthy.

I joined a gym recently... OR *Recently I joined a gym...*

2. Adverbs of manner and possibility: *hard, well, maybe, definitely*

When Lee started taking my class, she didn't know English. But she really studies. She'll pass the class. She'll be ready for an advanced class next year—if she studies a lot.

3. Adverbs of opinion: *luckily, obviously, surprisingly, unfortunately*

Children need to eat vegetables. Few children like them. My children like vegetables. They almost always ask for carrots instead of cookies.

C3 Identifying Adverbs with Different Forms

▶ Note 5

A. Choose the adverb that best completes each sentence.

1. I think very (high / highly) of Koji. He's a wonderful person.

2. The door is stuck, so you have to push it (hard / hardly).

3. I haven't seen Rita much (late / lately).

4. The children's kites were flying (high / highly) in the sky.

5. I'm really tired because I (hard / hardly) slept last night.

6. The store usually opens early, but on Mondays it opens (late / lately).

B. Now write four sentences about yourself. Use these adverbs: *late, lately, hard, hardly*.

I don't like to arrive late to class.

D FORM 2

Adverbs of Degree

Think Critically About Form

A. Read the sentences and complete the tasks below.

1a. My car runs pretty smoothly.
1b. They're very good neighbors.

2a. He was so smart that he got a scholarship.
2b. He was such a smart student that he got a scholarship.

1. **IDENTIFY** Look at 1a and 1b. Is the underlined word in each sentence an adverb or an adjective? Circle the word that modifies each underlined word.
2. **RECOGNIZE** Look at 2a and 2b. Which of the underlined words is followed by an adjective? Which is followed by an article + adjective + noun?

B. Discuss your answers with the class and read the Form charts to check them.

ONLINE PRACTICE

ADVERBS OF DEGREE

	ADVERB	ADJECTIVE
The music is	**really**	loud.
We were	**extremely**	tired.
The soup is	**very**	hot.

	ADVERB	ADVERB
The storm ended	**fairly**	quickly.
He spoke	**somewhat**	formally.
They talk	**so**	quickly.

- Adverbs of degree, such as *really, extremely, very, fairly, pretty, quite, so,* and *somewhat* come before adjectives or other adverbs.

SO … THAT 형용사 부사 다름.

	SO	ADJECTIVE	*THAT* CLAUSE
He was	so	**fast**	**(that)** he won the race.
It was		**noisy**	**(that)** I couldn't hear.

	SO	ADVERB	*THAT* CLAUSE
He talks	so	**softly**	**(that)** I can't hear him.
I walked		**slowly**	**(that)** I was late for class.

- *So* modifies another adverb or an adjective that is used alone (without a noun).
- Sentences with *so* can be followed by a *that* clause. The word *that* can be omitted without a change in meaning.

SUCH ... THAT

	SUCH	**ARTICLE**	**ADJECTIVE**	**SINGULAR COUNT NOUN**	***THAT* CLAUSE**
He was	**such**	**a**	**fast**	**runner**	**(that)** he won the race.

	SUCH		**ADJECTIVE**	**PLURAL COUNT NOUN**	***THAT* CLAUSE**
They were	**such**		**noisy**	**children**	**(that)** I couldn't concentrate.

	SUCH		**ADJECTIVE**	**NONCOUNT NOUN**	***THAT* CLAUSE**
It was	**such**		**stormy**	**weather**	**(that)** we canceled our trip.

- *Such (a/an)* modifies an adjective that is used with a noun.
- Use *such a/an* before an adjective + a singular count noun.
- Use *such* before an adjective + a plural count noun or a noncount noun.
- Sentences with *such (a/an)* can be followed by a *that* clause. The word *that* can be omitted without a change in meaning.

D1 Listening for Form

CD2 T31 **Listen to each sentence. Write the words you hear.**

1. She cooks ____so well____ that everyone wants to eat at her house.
2. He's ________________ right now.
3. We're ________________ that I can tell her anything.
4. The kids were having ________________ that they didn't want to leave.
5. They were ________________ that they fell asleep during the movie.
6. The test was ________________ that I don't think anyone passed.
7. She spoke ________________ that I couldn't hear her.
8. We arrived ________________ for the concert.

D2 Forming Sentences with Adverbs of Degree

Form sentences from these words. Punctuate your sentences correctly.

1. music/extremely/is/that/loud

   That music is extremely loud.

2. they/English/fluently/quite/speak
3. instructions/these/somewhat/are/confusing
4. he/quickly/types/really
5. those/smell/so/flowers/nice
6. the/Jenny/well/plays/very/piano
7. the/we/news/closely/follow/fairly
8. book/it's/interesting/a/not/very

D3 Completing Conversations

Complete these conversations with *so* or *such (a/an)*. Then practice them with a partner.

1. **A:** What's wrong?

   B: Traffic moved __________ slowly that it took three hours to get home.

2. **A:** Where are my jeans?

   B: They were __________ dirty that I put them in the wash.

3. **A:** Would you like to go to that Italian restaurant for dinner?

   B: I'd love to. They make __________ excellent pizzas that I could eat a whole pie by myself!

4. **A:** How was your test?

   B: Great! It went __________ well that I finished early. And I got __________ good grade that I don't have to take the final exam.

5. **A:** How did you like the movie?

   B: I thought it was __________ exciting movie that I'm going to see it again!

E MEANING AND USE 2

Adverbs of Degree

Think Critically About Meaning and Use

A. Read the sentences and complete the tasks below.

1a. Sheryl is an extremely good tennis player. She'll definitely win the match.
1b. Ana is a fairly good tennis player. She might win the match.

2a. It was so cold that the river froze.
2b. It was such a cold day that I couldn't start my car.

1. **EVALUATE** Look at the underlined adverbs in 1a and 1b. Who plays tennis better?
2. **IDENTIFY** Look at 2a and 2b. Underline the part of each sentence that shows the result of the cold weather.

B. Discuss your answers and read the Meaning and Use Notes to check them.

Meaning and Use Notes

ONLINE PRACTICE

Making Adjectives and Adverbs Weaker or Stronger

▶ 1 Use adverbs of degree before adjectives and other adverbs to make them stronger or weaker. The adverbs *extremely*, *quite*, *really*, and *very* make adjectives and other adverbs stronger. The adverbs *fairly*, *pretty*, and *somewhat* usually make adjectives and other adverbs weaker.

I did **very** well on the test. I got an A.

I didn't get an A on the test, but I still did **fairly** well. I got a B.

He was **extremely** upset about the situation. I've never heard him yell before.

She was **somewhat** upset at first. Later she calmed down.

Reasons and Results with *So/Such* ... + *That* Clauses

▶ 2 *So* and *such* are used to strengthen adjectives, adverbs, and nouns that are modified by adjectives. *So* and *such* can express the reason why something happens. The *that* clause expresses the result.

Reason	Result
The necklace was **so beautiful**	**(that)** I had to buy it.
It was **such a beautiful necklace**	**(that)** I had to buy it.

E1 Listening for Meaning and Use

▶ Notes 1, 2

CD2 T32 **Listen to these sentences and choose the best response.**

1. **a.** I like loud music, too.
   b. Maybe you should talk to him.
2. **a.** Maybe she should take lessons.
   b. Can she teach me?
3. **a.** Sorry, there was a lot of traffic.
   b. Yes, there were no cars on the roads!
4. **a.** Maybe she needs extra help.
   b. That's great.
5. **a.** They're always like that on Saturdays.
   b. So long. See you later.

E2 Using Adverbs of Degree

▶ Note 1

Read each situation. Then complete the comment with the appropriate adverb in parentheses.

1. Your friend made some soup for you. It tastes delicious. What do you say when she asks you how you like it?

   It's (somewhat / very) good. Can you give me the recipe?

2. Your math teacher just returned your final exam. You expected an A, but you got a B instead. What do you say when your brother asks you about the exam?

   I did (fairly / quite) well, but I wanted to do better.

3. You are a football coach. You are talking to one of your players who has just played a great game. What do you tell him?

   You were (really / fairly) great tonight, Tony.

4. You were going to visit friends tonight, but you are tired. You decide to call them and cancel. What do you say?

   Hi, there. Listen, I had a long day and I'm (really / somewhat) tired. Can we get together tomorrow night instead?

5. Your co-worker is enthusiastic about a new idea. You don't think it's a good idea. What do you say to her?

   I don't know. It's (somewhat / very) interesting. Let me think about it some more.

E3 Complaining

▶ Note 2

A. You and a friend are discussing recent events in your life. Answer each question with a complaint. Use *so ... (that)* in your answers.

1. You went to a restaurant last night.

   Friend: Was it expensive?

   You: It was so expensive that we had to share a main course.

   Friend: How was the food?

   You: ______________________________

2. You just started a new job.

   Friend: What's the office like?

   You: ______________________________

   Friend: How is the salary?

   You: ______________________________

3. You recently moved into a new apartment.

   Friend: How expensive is it?

   You: ______________________________

   Friend: What's your roommate like?

   You: ______________________________

4. You just started taking classes at a local university.

   Friend: What are the professors like?

   You: ______________________________

   Friend: What is the campus like?

   You: ______________________________

(Continued on page 334)

B. **Exchange books with a partner. Answer the questions again. Use your partner's answers from part A, but change *so ... (that)* to *such (a/an) ... (that)*. Make any other necessary changes.**

1. You went to a restaurant last night.

Friend: Was it expensive?

You: It was such an expensive restaurant that we had to share a main course.

Friend: How was the food?

You: ______________________________

2. You just started a new job.

Friend: What's the office like?

You: ______________________________

Friend: How is the salary?

You: ______________________________

3. You recently moved into a new apartment.

Friend: How expensive is it?

You: ______________________________

Friend: What's your roommate like?

You: ______________________________

4. You just started taking classes at a local university.

Friend: What are the professors like?

You: ______________________________

Friend: What is the campus like?

You: ______________________________

C. **Think of two more situations. In your notebook, write two questions for each. Then exchange notebooks with your partner. For each situation, write one answer with *so ... (that)* and another with *such (a/an) ... (that)*.**

F **FORM 3**

Too and *Enough*

Think Critically About Form

A. Read the sentences and answer the questions below.

a. I type too slowly to work as an administrative assistant.
b. He's good enough to be on the team.
c. We're too tired to go out tonight.
d. I read quickly enough to finish a book in a day.

1. IDENTIFY Look at the underlined words. Which are adverbs and which are adjectives? How do you know?

2. RECOGNIZE What is the position of *too* and *enough*? Do they come before or after the underlined words?

B. Discuss your answers with the class and read the Form charts to check them.

ONLINE PRACTICE

TOO

	TOO	ADJECTIVE	INFINITIVE PHRASE
It's	**too**	hot.	
It's	**too**	hot	to eat outside.

ENOUGH

	ADJECTIVE	*ENOUGH*	INFINITIVE PHRASE
You aren't	strong	**enough.**	
You aren't	strong	**enough**	to pick this up.

	TOO	ADVERB	INFINITIVE PHRASE
He works	**too**	slowly.	
He works	**too**	slowly	to finish on time.

	ADVERB	*ENOUGH*	INFINITIVE PHRASE
I jog	often	**enough.**	
I jog	often	**enough**	to stay fit.

- *Too* comes before an adjective or adverb.
- An infinitive phrase (a phrase that begins with *to* + base form of the verb) can follow the adverb or adjective.
- *Enough* follows an adjective or adverb.
- An infinitive phrase can follow *enough.*
- See Chapter 21 for more information on infinitives.

F1 Listening for Form

CD2 T33 **Listen to these statements. Write the phrases you hear with *too* and *enough*.**

1. You're too young to drive.
2. This cake is too sweet for me.
3. They don't work hard enough at school.
4. He drives too fast, and it makes me nervous.
5. Don't buy those sweaters. They're too expensive.
6. He's not tall enough to play basketball.

F2 Forming Sentences with *Too* and *Enough*

Form sentences from these words and phrases. Punctuate your sentences correctly. Compare your sentences with a partner's.

1. enough/work/Pedro/carefully/doesn't
   Pedro doesn't work carefully enough.
2. is/too/to/that dress/wear/big
   That dress is too big to weare.
3. not/enough/slowly/you're/driving
   You're not ~~enough~~ driving slowly enough
4. be/to/young/too/he looked/her father
   He looked too young to be her father
5. hard/Mark/worked/enough/get/to/a raise
   Mark morked hard enough to get a raise .
6. too/to/Dan/to school/walk/lives/far away
   Dan lives too far away to walk to school.

G MEANING AND USE 3

Contrasting *Too* and *Enough*

Think Critically About Meaning and Use

A. Read the sentences and complete the task below.

a. He worked fast enough. He finished on time.
b. He worked too fast. He made a lot of mistakes.

IDENTIFY Look at the underlined adverbs. Which one has a positive meaning? Which one has a negative meaning?

B. Discuss your answers and read the Meaning and Use Notes to check them.

Meaning and Use Notes

ONLINE PRACTICE

Too

▶ **1A** *Too* means "to an undesirable degree." It is used before adjectives and adverbs to express a negative meaning. *Not too* expresses a positive meaning when it is used with adjectives and adverbs that are negative qualities.

It's **too** crowded in here. Let's leave.

It's **not too** humid here in the summer. In fact, it's very pleasant.

▶ **1B** Do not confuse *too* and *very*.

***Too* (To an Undesirable Degree)**	***Very* (To a Great Degree)**
This town is **too** small. Everyone knows each other. There's no privacy.	This town is **very** small. Everyone knows each other. It's a friendly place.

Enough

▶ **2** *Enough* means "to an acceptable or sufficient degree." It expresses a positive meaning. *Not … enough* means "to an unacceptable or insufficient degree." It expresses a negative meaning.

He explained the problem clearly **enough**. Now I understand it.

This time I studied hard **enough** for the exam. I think I'll do well.

This jacket doesn't fit. It's **not big enough**.

She did**n't play well enough** to make the team. She was disappointed.

G1 Listening for Meaning and Use

▶ Notes 1A–2

CD2 T34 **Listen to each sentence. Choose the picture that matches it.**

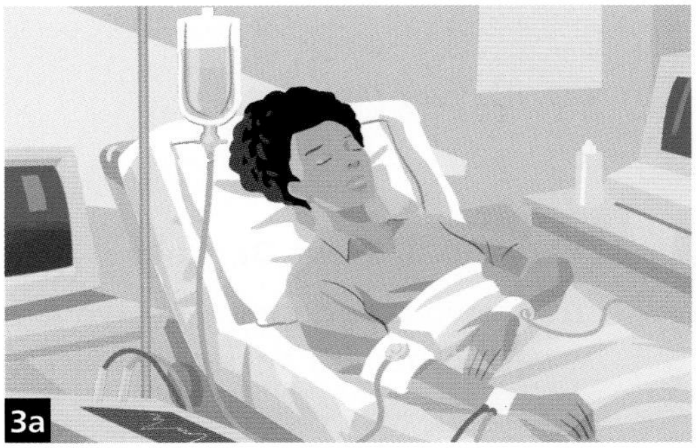

G2 Using *Too, Very,* and *So*

▶ Notes 1A–1B

Choose the word that best completes each sentence.

1. That restaurant is (too / very) crowded, so the food there is probably good. Let's try it.
2. He works (very / too) fast, so he never misses deadlines.
3. I finished my homework (so / very) quickly that I had time to watch a movie before bed.
4. This pudding is delicious. It's (too / very) sweet, and it has a nice chocolate flavor.
5. He drove (so / too) slowly that we missed the beginning of the lecture. 강의
6. Her son is (too / very) young to see that movie.

G3 Giving Reasons and Making Excuses

▶ Notes 1A, 2

Read each situation. Use the words in parentheses and an infinitive phrase to give a reason or make an excuse.

1. You didn't do your homework because you were sick last night. (too)
   I was too sick to do my homework.
2. You can't go to the movies with your friend because you're very busy. (too)
   I'm too busy to go to the movies.
3. You didn't catch the train because you were late. (not . . . enough)
   I wasn't early enough to catch the train.
4. You couldn't finish painting the kitchen because you were very tired. (too)
   I was too tired to finish painting the kitchen
5. You failed the course because you didn't study very hard. (not . . . enough)
   I didn't study hard enough to pass the final exam.
6. You didn't win the race because you couldn't swim very fast. (not . . . enough)
   I couldn't swim fast enough to win the race.

Think Critically About Meaning and Use

A. Choose the best answer to complete each conversation.

1. A: It's too late to go to the meeting.
B: __________
a. Then we should hurry.
b. That's OK. We'll just stay home.

2. A: It's such a large class that I have to go early to get a good seat.
B: __________
a. Is the classroom crowded?
b. I hate crowded classes.

3. A: I wonder how Mark is doing. I haven't seen him lately.
B: __________
a. He's fine. I spoke with him last week.
b. I know. He's always late.

4. A: My daughter's a fairly good student.
B: __________
a. Mine isn't. She's failing everything.
b. That's too bad. 걱정

5. A: It was so cold that we decided not to go to the game.
B: __________
a. Why did you stay home?
b. We didn't go, either.

6. A: He doesn't play piano very well.
B: __________
a. Well, he's only had four lessons.
b. You should be very proud of him.

7. A: You did fairly well on the test.
B: __________
a. I know, but not well enough to get an A in the class.
b. I know. I'm so disappointed.

B. Discuss these questions in small groups.

1. **COMPARE AND CONTRAST** Look at A's sentences in 4 and 7. If we delete *fairly* from each sentence, how does the meaning change?
2. **GENERATE** In 5, how can we rephrase A's statement using *such* instead of *so*? With *too*?

Edit

Some of these sentences have errors. Find the errors and correct them.

1. He's not enough strong to carry that box by himself.
2. Andrea looks beautifully in that dress.
3. He has been recently in the hospital.
4. You are such kind woman.
5. He always works hardly.
6. She's enough shy to be a teacher.
7. You aren't tall enough to wear my clothes.
8. This ice cream tastes deliciously.
9. He's such good a player that they made him captain of the team.
10. The child smiled sweetly at the photographer.

Write

Write an online news article about a sporting event. Follow the steps below to write the article. Use various kinds of adverbs.

1. **Brainstorm** Think about a sporting event to write about (a soccer or basketball game, an ice-skating competition, or any other event). It can be an event you saw or an imaginary event. Take notes about what you will say. Use these categories to help you.
   - the event—what, when, and where
   - who competed
   - how they played
   - what happened—first, next, and then
   - the crowd, the feeling
   - the result

2. **Write a First Draft** Before you write your draft, read the checklist below. Write your draft using various kinds of adverbs.

3. **Edit** Read your work and check it against the checklist below. Circle grammar, spelling, and punctuation errors.

DO I ...	YES
clearly describe the sporting event?	☐
use adverbs of manner, possibility, time, and opinion?	☐
use adverbs of degree, including *too* or *enough*, to strengthen or weaken an adjective or adverb?	☐
use *so/such (a/an) ... (that)* at least once?	☐
place the adverbs correctly in the sentence?	☐
use the correct form for adverbs?	☐

4. **Peer Review** Work with a partner to help you decide how to fix your errors and improve the content.

5. **Rewrite Your Draft** Using the comments from your partner, write a final draft.

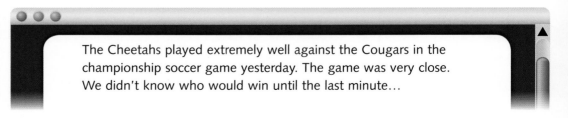

> The Cheetahs played extremely well against the Cougars in the championship soccer game yesterday. The game was very close. We didn't know who would win until the last minute...

PART 7 TEST | Adjectives and Adverbs

Choose the correct word or words to complete each sentence.

1. Larry is __________ impatient to be a good manager.
   a. so **b.** enough **c.** too **d.** such
2. Have you seen any good movies __________?
   a. too late **b.** late **c.** lately **d.** late enough
3. Robin always wears very __________ clothes.
   a. fashion **b.** fashioned **c.** fashionable **d.** fashioning
4. Yuki should win because she's a __________ runner.
   a. quickly **b.** fast **c.** well **d.** so quick

Choose the correct response to complete each conversation.

5. **A:** Do you need another table lamp?
   B: No, I have enough (lamps / tables).
6. **A:** Koji failed physics.
   B: I'm not surprised. He (studied hard / hardly studied).
7. **A:** Do you want to work with us on this project?
   B: Yes, I'm very (interested / interesting) in it.
8. **A:** I saw a (fascinated / fascinating) show on TV last night.
   B: What was it about?

Complete each sentence with the adverb form of the adjective in parentheses.

9. The children laughed __________ (excited).
10. He sang his solo __________ (beautiful) last night.
11. Ken always speaks __________ (careful).

Complete each sentence with an adjective. Use the noun in parentheses and an ending below to make an adjective.

-ful -less -y -able -ic

12. Read the instructions with care. Be __________ (care) to follow them.
13. You won't feel any pain. The doctor uses a __________ (pain) procedure.
14. She doesn't get a lot of sleep at night. That's why she's always so __________ (sleep) in class.

Reorder each set of words to make a sentence with *too* or *enough*. Remember to use a capital letter at the beginning of the sentence and a period at the end.

15. hasn't/enough/studied/hard/she

She hasn't studied hard enough.

16. is/too/that/rock/lift/heavy/to

rock is too heavy to lift Is that rock too heavy to lift?

17. isn't/to/enough/well/travel/she

She isn't well enough to travel.

Match the correct response to the question.

b **18.** What movie did you see?

c **19.** What does the museum look like?

d **20.** How do you like your teacher?

a. He's bored. 지루하게 느낀다.

b. A funny Italian comedy.

c. It's a huge glass building.

d. He's boring. 지루한 사람이다, 지루한 것이다.

e. Some cold mineral water, please.

f. The tan shoulder bag.

PART

8

Comparatives and Superlatives

CHAPTER

18

Comparatives

A. GRAMMAR IN DISCOURSE: Early to Rise Makes Teens ... Less Attentive? **346**

B. FORM 1: Comparatives **348**

Comparative Forms of Adjectives, Adverbs, and Nouns

tall — tall**er**
expensive — **more** expensive
hard — hard**er**
quickly — **more** quickly
good — well — **better**
homework — **more** homework

The Comparative in Sentences

Lisa is **taller than I (am)**.
Lisa is **taller than me**.

C. MEANING AND USE 1: Making Comparisons **352**

Talking About Differences

Expressing Greater and Lesser Degrees

Pronouns and Formality

Changing Situations

D. FORM 2: *As ... As* with Adjectives, Adverbs, and Nouns **356**

She is **as tall as Dan (is)**.

E. MEANING AND USE 2: *As ... As* with Adjectives, Adverbs, and Nouns **358**

***As ... As* to Talk About Things That Are Equal or Similar**

Negative Statements with *As ... As* to Talk About Differences

Vocabulary Notes: Using Descriptive Phrases with *As ... As*

WRITING: Write a Paragraph Comparing Teenagers in Two Countries **362**

A GRAMMAR IN DISCOURSE

Early to Rise Makes Teens … Less Attentive?

A1 Before You Read

Discuss these questions.

There is a proverb in English that says "Early to bed and early to rise, makes a man healthy, wealthy, and wise." What do you think this means? Do you agree with it?

A2 Read

CD2 T35 **Read this online newspaper article about high school students. Is sleeping later a good idea?**

http://www.worldnews.us

Home | News | Business | Sports | Entertainment | Health | Blog | A&E/Living

Early to Rise Makes Teens… Less Attentive?

PHILADELPHIA—Crystal Irwin would like to pay closer attention in her first-period class, but she's simply too tired. She can barely keep her eyes open. Can schools do anything to help students like Crystal? One solution is to change school starting times and let teens sleep longer.

In the United States many high school students get less sleep than younger students. This is because American high schools generally start earlier than elementary schools, and, of course, teenagers stay up later. Doctors say that teenagers need more sleep. According to a number of studies, too little sleep can make students less attentive in class and more difficult to deal with. "When people don't have enough sleep, they get upset more easily," a researcher says.

The first high school to change its starting time was in Edina, Minnesota. In 1996 it moved its daily starting time from 7:25 A.M.

to 8:30 A.M., and its finishing time from 2:05 P.M. to 3:10 P.M. When schools have moved to a later starting time, the results have been positive. According to teachers, especially first-period teachers, students are more awake in class. The students participate more enthusiastically, and classes seem to go more smoothly. Counselors say that students seem happier and that they are nicer to one another. There is a better climate in the school.

Despite the positive results, some parents and teachers do not want schedule changes. They think that people who sleep late are lazier than people who get up early. Researchers believe that this way of thinking comes from the time when most people lived on farms and had to get up early to work. At that time people believed late risers weren't as hardworking or successful as early risers. This clearly isn't true of high school students today. Indeed, one student says when his school changed its starting time, he immediately noticed that "everyone was more alert."

---

alert: awake and paying attention
attentive: watching or listening carefully
climate: the general attitude or feeling in a place
counselors: school employees who give students advice
smoothly: easily and without problems

A3 After You Read

Write *T* for true or *F* for false for each statement.

__T__ **1.** Some students are very tired and cannot pay attention in class.

____ **2.** American high schools usually start later than elementary schools.

____ **3.** Doctors believe that teenagers need more sleep.

____ **4.** The first high school to change its schedule was in Iowa.

____ **5.** Teachers say the results have been negative.

____ **6.** Some parents and teachers do not like the schedule change.

B FORM 1

Comparatives

Think Critically About Form

A. Look back at the online article on page 346 and complete the tasks below.

1. **IDENTIFY** Four examples of comparative adjectives and adverbs are underlined. Which are adjectives? Which are adverbs? There are two ways to form the comparative of adjectives and adverbs. What are they?
2. **RECOGNIZE** Find two more examples of each underlined form.

B. Discuss your answers with the class and read the Form charts to check them.

▶ Comparative Forms of Adjectives, Adverbs, and Nouns

ONLINE PRACTICE

ADJECTIVES		
ONE SYLLABLE	**TWO SYLLABLES**	**THREE OR MORE SYLLABLES**
tall—tall**er**	simple—simple**r**	beautiful—**more** beautiful
cold—cold**er**	happy—happ**ier**	expensive—**more** expensive
cute—cute**r**	famous—**more** famous	creative—**more** creative
big—big**ger**	polite—polite**r**/**more** polite	intelligent—**more** intelligent

ADVERBS	
ONE SYLLABLE	**TWO OR MORE SYLLABLES**
hard—hard**er**	quickly—**more** quickly
late—late**r**	clearly—**more** clearly

IRREGULAR FORMS		
ADJECTIVE	**ADVERB**	**COMPARATIVE**
good	well	**better**
bad	badly	**worse**

NOUNS			
COUNT NOUN	**COMPARATIVE**	**NONCOUNT NOUN**	**COMPARATIVE**
a book	**more** books	homework	**more** homework

Adjectives with One Syllable

- Add *-er* to form the comparative of most one-syllable adjectives. If the adjective ends in *e*, add *-r*. If it ends with a single vowel and a consonant, double the final consonant and add *-er*.

Adjectives with Two Syllables

- If the adjective ends in *le*, add *-r*. If it ends in a consonant + *y*, change *y* to *i* and add *-er*. For most other two-syllable adjectives, use *more*.
- Some two-syllable adjectives can use either *-er* or *more*. See Appendix 11.

Adjectives with Three or More Syllables

- Use *more* with adjectives of three or more syllables.

Adverbs with One Syllable

- Add *-er* to form the comparative of most one-syllable adverbs. If the adverb ends in *e*, add *-r*.

Adverbs with Two or More Syllables

- Use *more* instead of *-er* with most adverbs of two or more syllables ending in *ly*.

Irregular Forms

- Some adjectives and adverbs have irregular comparative forms. See Appendix 12.

  She sings **better** than I do. He is a **worse** student than I am.

Nouns

- To form the comparative, use *more* with count and noncount nouns.

▶ The Comparative in Sentences

	COMPARATIVE	*THAN*	SUBJECT (+ VERB OR AUXILIARY)
Lisa is	**taller**	**than**	**her brother (is).** **he is.**
Tony works	**harder**		**you (work).** **you (do).**
We read	**more books**		**our friends (read).** **they (do).**

	COMPARATIVE	*THAN*	OBJECT PRONOUN
Lisa is	**taller**	**than**	**him.**
Tony works	**harder**		**you.**
Lisa reads	**more** books		**them.**

(Continued on page 350)

- *Than* often follows comparative forms. If *than* is not used, it is still implied.

  I'm **older than** my sister. I'm also **taller** (than my sister).

- *Than* can be followed by a noun or by a subject pronoun + an optional verb or auxiliary.

  We read **more** books **than our friends (read).** We read **more** books **than they (do)**.

- *Than* can also be followed by an object pronoun. An object pronoun is always used alone without a verb after it.

  Lisa is **taller than him**.

> **!** Do not use both *-er* and *more* in a comparative.
>
> Lisa is **taller than he is**. X Lisa is more taller than he is. (INCORRECT)

B1 Listening for Form

CD2 T36 **Listen to each conversation. Which comparative form do you hear? Check (✓) the correct column.**

	-ER	*MORE*
1.		✓
2.		
3.		
4.		
5.		
6.		

B2 Working on Comparative Adjectives and Adverbs

Write the correct comparative form. Use *-er* or *more*.

1. fast *faster*
2. messy ______
3. handsome ______
4. happily ______
5. hot ______
6. expensive ______
7. loudly ______
8. large ______
9. dangerously ______
10. complicated ______
11. late ______
12. polite ______

B3 Working on Comparatives in Sentences

Complete each conversation with the comparative forms of the adjectives, adverbs, or nouns in parentheses.

Conversation 1

Amy: What do you think? Should I buy the book or the e-book?

Betty: Well, the book is ___cheaper___ (1) (cheap) than the e-book, but the e-book will last ________ (2) (long).

Conversation 2

Stefan: Your newspaper is ________ (1) (thick) than my newspaper.

Josh: It probably just has ________ (2) (advertisements).

Conversation 3

Carlos: Is André a ________ (1) (good) tennis player than I am?

Miguel: I'm not sure. He hits the ball ________ (2) (hard) than you, but you move ________ (3) (quickly) than he does.

Conversation 4

Mr. Orr: So how is college compared to high school?

Yuji: It's definitely ________ (1) (difficult) and the professors give ________ (2) (homework) than my teachers did in high school. But it's getting easier. My grades were ________ (3) (bad) last semester than they are this semester.

Conversation 5

Emma: You look like your sister.

Luisa: I know. But actually, we're very different. She's ________ (1) (tall) and ________ (2) (thin) than me. Her hair is ________ (3) (curly) than mine, and she has ________ (4) (freckles).

C MEANING AND USE 1

Making Comparisons

Think Critically About Meaning and Use

A. Read the sentences and answer the questions below.

a. Jake likes his new job. He's making more money.
b. Jake's new apartment is less expensive than his old one.

EVALUATE Which comparison talks about a larger amount? Which comparison talks about a smaller amount?

B. Discuss your answers with the class and read the Meaning and Use Notes to check them.

Meaning and Use Notes

ONLINE PRACTICE

Talking About Differences

▶ 1A Use comparatives with adjectives, adverbs, and nouns to talk about differences between two things (people, objects, ideas, places, or actions).

My father is **older than** my mother.

The new computer runs **more smoothly than** the old one.

There are **more cars than** buses on the highways.

▶ 1B You can use the comparative without *than* when the meaning is clear from context.

She's a good student, but I think he's **smarter**. (= smarter than she is)

We sang well, but they sang **better**. (= better than we did)

Expressing Greater and Lesser Degrees

▶ 2A Use *more* or *-er* with adjectives and adverbs to show that something is a larger quantity, degree, or size than something else. Use *less* with adjectives and adverbs to show that something is a smaller quantity, degree, or size than something else.

More/-er ... Than	***Less ... Than***
Diamonds are **more expensive than** rubies.	Rubies are **less expensive than** diamonds.
He works **more quickly than** she does.	She works **less quickly than** he does.

Less can sound awkward with adjectives and adverbs that have one syllable. To avoid this, use the comparative form of an adjective or adverb with the opposite meaning.

I'm **shorter than** my brother. X I'm less tall than my brother. (NOT USUAL)

▶ **2B** Use *more* with count or noncount nouns to talk about larger quantities. Use *fewer* with count nouns and *less* with noncount nouns to talk about smaller quantities.

Count Nouns

Mexico City has **more people than** Seattle.

Seattle has **fewer people than** Mexico City.

Noncount Nouns

The Smiths have **more money than** the Johnsons.

The Johnsons have **less money than** the Smiths.

Pronouns and Formality

▶ **3** When *than* is followed by a subject pronoun alone, the sentence has a more formal tone. When it is followed by a subject pronoun + verb or auxiliary, it is neutral in tone (neither formal nor informal). When it is followed by an object pronoun, it has a more informal tone.

More Formal

He is **older than** I.

Neutral

He is **older than** I am.

More Informal

He is **older than** me.

Changing Situations

▶ **4** A comparative form can be repeated and joined with *and* to show that a situation is changing. This use of the comparative is common with verbs of change such as *get*, *become*, and *grow*, especially in the present continuous.

He looks **older and older** every day.

I have **less and less time** to study.

Taxes are getting **higher and higher**.

Car engines are becoming **more and more efficient**.

C1 Listening for Meaning and Use

▶ Notes 1A, 1B, 2A

CD2 T37 **Listen to each situation and the question that follows. Choose the correct answer.**

1. **a.** Dan is.
   (b.) Mike is.
2. **a.** Ana's coat was.
   b. Rick's coat was.
3. **a.** Our team did.
   b. Their team did.
4. **a.** Betty did.
   b. Her classmates did.
5. **a.** Maria does.
   b. Frank does.
6. **a.** The B4 bus is.
   b. The D2 bus is.

C2 Expressing Differences

▶ Notes 1A, 2A, 2B

Read the two sentences. Then write a comparative sentence with the adjective, adverb, or noun in parentheses.

1. Texas has an area of 267,277 square miles.
   California has an area of 158,869 square miles.

   (larger) *Texas has a larger area than California (has/does).*

2. Cheetahs can run up to 70 miles per hour.
   Greyhounds can run up to 40 miles per hour.

   (quickly) ____________________

3. There are exactly 36 inches in a yard.
   There are a little more than 39 inches in a meter.

   (long) ____________________

4. Earth travels around the Sun in 365 days.
   Mercury travels around the Sun in 88 days.

   (slowly) ____________________

5. A kilogram has 1,000 grams.
   A pound has 454 grams.

   (heavy) ____________________

6. China's population is more than 1.3 billion.
   India's population is more than 1.2 billion.

   (people) ____________________

C3 Rephrasing Comparatives

▶ Note 3

Make each sentence more formal, more informal, or more neutral in tone.

1. My son is taller than me.
   (more neutral) My son is taller than I am.
2. I take more classes than he does.
   (more informal) ______
3. I've been waiting longer than them.
   (more neutral) ______
4. Jack has more experience than I.
   (more informal) ______
5. He worked harder than she did.
   (more formal) ______
6. He got more presents than me.
   (more neutral) ______
7. They've lived here for more years than we have.
   (more informal) ______
8. She's more friendly than he is.
   (more formal) ______

C4 Talking About Changing Situations

▶ Note 4

Think about the place where you live. Choose six of the topics below to make sentences about how things are changing. Use the present continuous with *get*, *become*, or *grow* and the comparative form of an adjective with *and*.

the air	**the economy**	**my neighborhood**	**the prices**	**the stores**
the buses	**the houses**	**the people**	**the schools**	**the traffic**

The air is getting more and more polluted.

D FORM 2

As ... *As* with Adjectives, Adverbs, and Nouns

Think Critically About Form

A. Read the sentences and complete the tasks below.

a. My car isn't as new as your car.
b. Sheryl looks as young as he looks.
c. We walked as fast as them.
d. Dan doesn't talk as loudly as Mark does.

1. IDENTIFY Underline the adjectives and circle the adverbs.

2. RECOGNIZE Which sentences end with an auxiliary or a verb? Which ends with a noun? Which ends with an object pronoun?

B. Discuss your answers with the class and read the Form Notes to check them.

ONLINE PRACTICE

ADJECTIVES

	AS + ADJECTIVE + *AS*	SUBJECT (+ VERB OR AUXILIARY)
She is	as tall as	Dan (is).

	AS + ADJECTIVE + *AS*	OBJECT PRONOUN
She is	as tall as	him.

ADVERBS

	AS + ADVERB + *AS*	SUBJECT (+ VERB OR AUXILIARY)
He works	as hard as	Eve (works). she (does).

	AS + ADVERB + *AS*	OBJECT PRONOUN
He works	as hard as	her.

PLURAL COUNT NOUNS

	AS MANY + NOUN + *AS*	SUBJECT (+ VERB OR AUXILIARY)
I have	as many MP3s as	they (have). they (do).

	AS MANY + NOUN + *AS*	OBJECT PRONOUN
I have	as many MP3s as	him.

NONCOUNT NOUNS

	AS MUCH + NOUN + *AS*	SUBJECT (+ VERB OR AUXILIARY)
He has	as much money as	Carla (has). she (does).

	AS MUCH + NOUN + *AS*	OBJECT PRONOUN
He has	as much money as	her.

- Use *as* ... *as* with adjectives and adverbs.
- Use *as many* ... *as* with plural count nouns. Use *as much* ... *as* with noncount nouns.
- The second *as* can be followed by a noun or a subject pronoun + an optional verb or auxiliary.
- The second *as* can also be followed by an object pronoun. An object pronoun is always used alone.
- To form a negative statement with *as* ... *as*, use the negative form of the verb + *as (much/many)* ... *as*.

  She is not **as tall as he is**. He doesn't have **as much money as I do**.

D1 Listening for Form

CD2 T38 **Listen to each conversation. What form of *as* ... *as* does the second speaker use? Write the *as* ... *as* phrase you hear.**

1. My college isn't small. It's ___as big as___ your college.
2. Yes, but it's going to take me a while to finish it. I don't read ______________ you do.
3. I'm ______________ you are.
4. Not great. It seems to have ______________ my old car.
5. It's hard. The other kids already did this stuff. I can't work ______________ they can.

D2 Rephrasing Sentences with *As ... As*

In your notebook, rewrite each sentence in three different ways.

1. Lee works as hard as his sister.

   Lee works as hard as she. Lee works as hard as she does. Lee works as hard as her.

2. We've spent as much money as the Swansons.
3. Rita's son isn't as old as Sheryl's son.
4. Rick didn't take as many classes as his brother.
5. He doesn't have as many stamps as I do.
6. They played better than Mike and I.

E

MEANING AND USE 2

As … As with Adjectives, Adverbs, and Nouns

Think Critically About Meaning and Use

A. Read the sentences and answer the questions below.

a. Ben is as tall as Matt.
b. Dan isn't as tall as Ben.

1. **COMPARE AND CONTRAST** In which sentence are the boys the same height?
2. **COMPARE AND CONTRAST** In which sentence are the boys different heights?

B. Discuss your answers with the class and read the Meaning and Use Notes to check them.

Meaning and Use Notes

ONLINE PRACTICE

As … As to Talk About Things That Are Equal or Similar

▶ 1A Use *as … as* with adjectives, adverbs, and nouns to say that two things (people, objects, actions, etc.) are equal or similar.

My office is **as big as** his office.

The student explained the problem **as simply as** the teacher.

We saved **as much money as** Gina did.

They have **as many friends as** us.

▶ 1B Use *about, almost,* and *nearly* before *as … as* to say that two things are close but not quite equal.

My office is almost **as big as** his office. (His office is bigger than my office by a small amount.)

Elena is nearly **as tall as** Eva. (Eva is taller than Elena by a small amount.)

▶ 1C You can omit the second part of an *as … as* phrase when the meaning is clear from context.

Yes, she's a good student, but he's **as good**. (= as good as she is.)

Negative Statements with *As* ... *As* to Talk About Differences

▶ 2 Use negative statements with *as* ... *as* to talk about differences between two things. A negative statement with *as* ... *as* has the same meaning as a comparative sentence with *less* or *fewer*.

Ken is not **as athletic as** Tom. (= Ken is less athletic than Tom.)

He didn't finish **as quickly as** us. (= He finished less quickly than us.)

I don't have **as much energy as** they do. (= I have less energy than they do.)

He doesn't know **as many students as** I do. (= He knows fewer students than I do.)

> ! *Less* can sound awkward with adjectives and adverbs that have one syllable. Use a negative statement with *as . . . as* instead.
>
> **I'm not as tall as my brother.** X **I'm less tall than my brother.** (NOT USUAL)

E1 Listening for Meaning and Use

▶ Notes 1A, 2

CD2 T39 **Listen to each statement and the question that follows. Choose the correct answer to the questions. Choose c if neither a nor b is correct.**

1. **a.** Atlanta Braves
b. New York Yankees
c. neither

2. **a.** Russian
b. Chinese
c. neither

3. **a.** Carlene
b. Janet
c. neither

4. **a.** Techno computers
b. Quantum computers
c. neither

5. **a.** teachers
b. nurses
c. neither

6. **a.** Paul's children
b. Bob's children
c. neither

7. **a.** rattlesnakes
b. king cobras
c. neither

E2 Expressing Similarities and Differences

▶ Notes 1–2

A. Look at the pictures of Derek's and Koji's apartments. In your notebook, write sentences about the two men. Use the words below and *as ... as, nearly/almost as ...* , and *not as ... as.*

Derek's apartment

Koji's apartment

1. Derek's apartment/messy

   Derek's apartment isn't as messy as Koji's.

2. Koji/clean/frequently
3. Koji/books/bookcase
4. Derek/dress/casually
5. Derek/interested/sports

B. Work with a partner. Look at the pictures again. Make at least four more comparisons with *as ... as* phrases.

Koji's furniture isn't as nice as Derek's.

Vocabulary Notes

Using Descriptive Phrases with *As* ... *As*

There are many common descriptive phrases with *as* ... *as* in English. These phrases are used to compare a subject to something (such as an animal or object) that people associate with a certain quality or feeling.

An example of one of these phrases is *as free as a bird*. We use this phrase to express the idea that someone or something is or feels very free: for example, *I have finished my exams, and now I'm as free as a bird.*

We sometimes use these phrases in speech and writing to make a description more lively and colorful. Here is a list of some of these phrases:

as free as a bird	as cold as ice	as tough as nails
as strong as an ox	as gentle as a lamb	as hungry as a bear
as old as the hills	as quiet as a mouse	as light as a feather

E3 Using Descriptive Phrases with *As* ... *As*

Complete the sentences with one of the descriptive phrases from the Vocabulary Notes above.

1. Can we turn up the heat? It's freezing in here. My hands are ___as cold as ice___ .
2. Don't be afraid of the boss. He can sound mean, but he's really ________ .
3. Wow! I can lift this bicycle with one hand. It's ________ .
4. No one heard me come in. I didn't make any noise. I was ________ .
5. Don't try to move that big TV by yourself. It's really heavy. Ask Mike to help you. He's ________ .
6. My kids are all in college now. I don't have to cook meals or spend hours cleaning. These days I feel ________ .
7. I haven't had anything to eat all day. I'm ________ .
8. His great-grandfather is 97 years old. He's ________ .
9. That old, retired gym teacher insists on ordering everyone around. He's ________ .

WRITING Write a Paragraph Comparing Teenagers in Two Countries

Think Critically About Meaning and Use

A. Read each sentence and choose the best response.

1. A: I don't run as fast as Greg.
B: __________
a. Good, then you should win the race easily.
b. That's OK. You could still get second place.

2. A: The red dress is more expensive than the blue one.
B: __________
a. Well, if you want to save money, get the blue one.
b. I like the red one better and it's cheaper, too.

3. A: You're as smart as I am.
B: __________
a. Then why are my grades worse?
b. You're always criticizing me.

4. A: My grades are getting better and better.
B: __________
a. Maybe you're trying too hard.
b. That's because you've been studying.

5. A: He's not arriving as early as we thought.
B: __________
a. That's good. I haven't finished cleaning the house yet.
b. Oh, dear! Will we be ready in time?

6. A: I don't have as much money as you do.
B: __________
a. OK. Then I'll pay for dinner.
b. OK. Then you pay for dinner.

7. A: Ana doesn't work as quickly as Sheryl.
B: __________
a. That's why Sheryl stays later.
b. That's why Ana stays later.

B. Discuss these questions in small groups.

1. **GENERATE** What are two other ways of stating the comparisons in 6 and in 7?
2. **GENERATE** What are three other ways of stating the comparison in 2?

Edit

Find the errors in this paragraph and correct them.

My new job is ~~more good~~ better than my old one. I am more happyer here. There are several reasons why. For one thing, we have flextime. That means that we can arrive at work anytime between 7:00 and 10:00 and leave eight hours later. In general, this company doesn't have as much rules as my old company does. Also, the building is nicer of the old building, and my office is biger than my old office. There are more windows in this building than in my old building. The work is more hard than the work at my old job, but I like the challenge of hard work. I like my new boss more than my old boss. She's less bad tempered than he was, and she's helpfuler. Finally, I really like my co-workers. They are so much more nice that the people I used to work with. We have a lot of fun together. The day goes by more quicker. I'm glad I came here.

Write

Write a paragraph comparing and contrasting teenagers in two different countries. Follow the steps below. Use comparative adjectives, adverbs, and nouns.

1. **BRAINSTORM** Think about two countries and about ways ways teenagers in the two countries are similar and ways they are different. Use these categories to help you.
   - school and study habits
   - clothing
   - relationships with friends
   - free-time activities and interests
   - attitude
   - relationships with brothers and sisters

2. **WRITE A FIRST DRAFT** Before you write your draft, read the checklist below. Write your draft using sentences with comparative adjectives, adverbs, and nouns.

3. **EDIT** Read your work and check it against the checklist below. Circle grammar, spelling, and punctuation errors.

DO I ...	YES
show similarities and differences between teenagers in the two countries?	☐
make comparisons with adjectives, adverbs, and nouns?	☐
use comparisons with *than* to show differences?	☐
use comparisons with *(not) as ... as* to show differences and similarities?	☐
use the correct comparative forms of adjectives and adverbs?	☐
use the correct sentence form in comparatives?	☐

4. **PEER REVIEW** Work with a partner to help you decide how to fix your errors and improve the content.

5. **REWRITE YOUR DRAFT** Using the comments from your partner, write a final draft.

There are many differences between the young people in the United States and the young people in Japan. In general, the young people in Japan are more serious about life...

PART

8

Comparatives and Superlatives

CHAPTER

19

Superlatives

A. GRAMMAR IN DISCOURSE: **Strange but True** 366

B. FORM: **Superlatives** 368

Superlative Forms of Adjectives, Adverbs, and Nouns

tall — **the** tall**est**

quickly — **the most** quickly

expensive — **the most** expensive

good — **the best**

hard — **the** hard**est**

money — **the most** money

Prepositional Phrases After Superlatives

My sister is **the tallest in the family.**

C. MEANING AND USE: **Superlatives** 372

Comparing Members of a Group

Emphasizing or Weakening Superlatives

Using *The Most, The Least,* and *The Fewest*

WRITING: **Write a Thank-you Email** 377

PART 8 TEST: **Comparatives and Superlatives** 379

A GRAMMAR IN DISCOURSE

Strange but True

A1 Before You Read

Discuss these questions.

What is the tallest building in the world? What is the longest river? Which country has the most people? If you need information like this, where can you look?

A2 Read

CD2 T40 **Read this magazine article to find out the story behind the first *Guinness* record book.**

Strange but True !?

How big was the world's biggest lollipop? (6,514 pounds) Who has walked backward in iron shoes the fastest? (Zhang Zhegui and Kan Yong; 10 meters in 34 seconds) How small is the smallest horse? (17.5 inches) If you would like to know the answers to thousands of questions like these, you can find them in *Guinness World Records*™. For over 50 years *Guinness* has recorded the world's superlatives: the strongest person, the most valuable stamp, the fastest talker, the most expensive meal, the most dangerous ant, the worst pollution, and the world's tallest building.

The smallest horse in the world

The History of a Best-Seller

On a hunt in 1951 in Ireland, Sir Hugh Beaver had a question. He couldn't shoot a certain kind of bird, the golden plover. Was the golden plover the fastest of all birds in Europe? He looked everywhere, but he couldn't find the answer to his question.

He thought that other people must have similar questions, so he got the idea for a book that could answer them. On August 27, 1955, the first *Guinness* record book was printed. By the end of that year it was a bestseller.

Two years later the first U.S. version of *Guinness* appeared. By 1989 sales around the world had risen to over 60 million. That equals 163 piles of books, each as high as Mount Everest. The book has now sold more than 120 million copies in 37 languages.

Getting into Guinness

It's not easy to be a world-record holder. For example, do you think you can collect the most bus tickets? You'll have to collect more than 200,000 of them! Or what about dribbling a basketball for the longest time without stopping? You'll have to dribble for more than 55½ hours!

You can try to set a record, though, and be successful. In 1979, Ashrita Furman decided to set a *Guinness* record. He did, and he now has set more than 200 of them, including the world's biggest lollipop. This is the most *Guinness* records that one person has set.

---

best-seller: a new book that has sold more copies than other books

dribbling: bouncing a basketball up and down with short repeated bounces

lollipop: a piece of hard candy on a stick

set a record: do something better than anyone has done before

A3 After You Read

Match each number with what it represents.

___c___ **1.** 6,514 pounds

______ **2.** 1955

______ **3.** over 200

______ **4.** over 120 million

______ **5.** 55½

______ **6.** over 200,000

a. the number of hours someone dribbled a basketball

b. the number of bus tickets someone has collected

c. the weight of the biggest lollipop

d. the number of *Guinness* books sold so far

e. the most *Guinness* records one person has set

f. the year the first *Guinness* record book was published

B FORM

Superlatives

Think Critically About Form

A. Look back at the article on page 366 and complete the tasks below.

1. **IDENTIFY** Find the superlative form of these adjectives: *big*, *strong*, *valuable*, and *expensive*.
2. **SUMMARIZE** There are two ways to form the superlative of adjectives. What are they?
3. **RECOGNIZE** Find one more example of each form.

B. Discuss your answers with the class and read the Form charts to check them.

▶ Superlative Forms of Adjectives, Adverbs, and Nouns

ONLINE PRACTICE

ADJECTIVES

ADJECTIVE	COMPARATIVE	SUPERLATIVE
tall	taller	**the** tall**est**
cute	cuter	**the** cute**st**
big	bigger	**the** big**gest**
simple	simpler	**the** simple**st**
happy	happier	**the** happ**iest**

ADJECTIVE	COMPARATIVE	SUPERLATIVE
famous	more famous	**the most** famous
polite	politer more polite	**the** polite**st** **the most** polite
beautiful	more beautiful	**the most** beautiful
expensive	more expensive	**the most** expensive
intelligent	more intelligent	**the most** intelligent

ADVERBS

ADVERB	COMPARATIVE	SUPERLATIVE
hard	harder	**the** hard**est**
late	later	**the** late**st**
quickly	more quickly	**the most** quickly
clearly	more clearly	**the most** clearly

IRREGULAR FORMS

ADJECTIVE	COMPARATIVE	SUPERLATIVE
good	better	**the best**
bad	worse	**the worst**

ADVERB	COMPARATIVE	SUPERLATIVE
well	better	**the best**
badly	worse	**the worst**

NOUNS					
COUNT NOUN	COMPARATIVE	SUPERLATIVE	NONCOUNT NOUN	COMPARATIVE	SUPERLATIVE
a book	more books	**the most** books	money	more money	**the most** money

Adjectives with One Syllable

- Use *the* + adjective + *-est* to form the superlative of most one-syllable adjectives. If the adjective ends in *e,* add *-st.* If it ends with a single vowel and a consonant, double the consonant and add *-est.*

Adjectives with Two Syllables

- If the adjective ends in *le,* add *-st.* If it ends in a consonant + *y,* change *y* to *i* and add *-est.* For most other two-syllable adjectives, use *the most* + adjective.
- Some two-syllable adjectives can use either *-est* or *the most.* See Appendix 11.

Adjectives with Three or More Syllables

- Use *the most* + adjective with adjectives of three or more syllables.

Adverbs with One Syllable

- Use *the* + adverb + *-est* to form the superlative of most one-syllable adverbs. If the adverb ends in *e,* add *-st.*

Adverbs with Two or More Syllables

- For most adverbs with two or more syllables ending in *ly,* use *the most* + adverb.
- Use *the most* + adverb with adverbs of three or more syllables.

Irregular Adjectives and Adverbs

- Some adjectives and adverbs have irregular superlative forms. See Appendix 12.

Nouns

- To form the superlative, use *the most* with count and noncount nouns.

▶ Prepositional Phrases After Superlatives

	SUPERLATIVE	PREPOSITIONAL PHRASE
My sister is	**the tallest**	**in the family**.
He works	**the hardest**	**of all the employees**.
They have	**the most children**	**on the block**.

Do not use *than* after a superlative.

He works **the hardest** of all the employees.

✗ He works the hardest than all the employees. (INCORRECT)

B1 Listening for Form

CD2 T41 Listen to each sentence. Which form of the adjective or adverb do you hear? Check (✓) the correct column.

	COMPARATIVE	SUPERLATIVE
1.		✓
2.		
3.		
4.		
5.		
6.		

B2 Forming Adjectives and Adverbs

Complete this chart with the missing forms of each adjective or adverb.

	BASE FORM	COMPARATIVE FORM	SUPERLATIVE FORM
1.	*beautifully*	*more beautifully*	the most beautifully
2.		higher	
3.	badly		
4.		more rapidly	
5.			the sleepiest
6.		more famous	
7.	early		
8.	good		
9.			the happiest
10.		more softly	
11.	wet		
12.	lovely		

B3 Working with Superlatives

Complete this webpage article with the superlative form of the words in parentheses.

http://www.planets.us

Today's planetarium show begins with a guided tour of the planets in our solar system. Mercury is ___the closest___ (1) (close) planet to the Sun, and it therefore has ______________ (2) (short) orbiting time (just 88 Earth days to go around the Sun). Mercury is also ______________ (3) (tiny) planet, now that scientists no longer consider Pluto a planet. From Earth, Venus is ______________ (4) (bright) planet; Venus is also the planet with ______________ (5) (hot) surface temperature. Earth is ______________ (6) (dense) planet. Leaving Earth, we come to Mars, ______________ (7) (red) of all the planets, and then to Saturn and Jupiter. Many people say that Saturn is ______________ (8) (beautiful) planet in the solar system because of its amazing ring system. Jupiter is ______________ (9) (massive) planet, with a mass 318 times Earth's, and it has ______________ (10) (great) diameter, 11.2 times Earth's. Jupiter also has ______________ (11) (intense) magnetic field. Finally, we reach Uranus and Neptune, ______________ (12) (blue) of all the planets. Neptune is also ______________ (13) (windy) planet, with storms that are five times more powerful than ______________ (14) (strong) tornadoes on Earth.

C MEANING AND USE

Superlatives

Think Critically About Meaning and Use

A. Read the sentences and answer the questions below.

a. August was warmer than July.
b. August was the warmest month of the year.

1. **EVALUATE** Which sentence compares things in a group of three or more things?
2. **EVALUATE** Which sentence compares only two things?

B. Discuss your answers with the class and read the Meaning and Use Notes to check them.

Meaning and Use Notes

ONLINE PRACTICE

Comparing Members of a Group	
▶ **1A**	Use the superlative of adjectives, adverbs, and nouns to compare things in a group—three or more people, objects, ideas, places, or actions. The superlative shows that one member has more (or less) of something than all other members. Paris was **the most interesting** city that we visited. (Paris was more interesting than all of the other cities.) I'm **the youngest** of four children. (I am younger than any of the other children.)
▶ **1B**	Superlative adjectives are often followed by a noun. The noun indicates the thing you are comparing. Superlative adjectives can also be used without a noun if the context indicates the missing noun. All the teachers here are good. Ms. Jordan is probably **the best**. (= the best teacher)
▶ **1C**	Superlatives are often followed by a prepositional phrase. The prepositional phrase indicates the group in the comparison. Who is **the richest man** <u>in the world</u>? (all men in the world = the group) She's **the most popular student** <u>in the class</u>. (all students in the class = the group) He's **the best actor** <u>on TV</u>. (all actors on TV = the group)
▶ **1D**	Superlatives are also often followed by clauses. These, too, indicate the group. Often the clauses are in the present perfect with *ever*. *The Pink Panther* is **the funniest movie** <u>that I've ever seen</u>.

Emphasizing or Weakening Superlatives

▶ **2A** The prepositional phrase *of all* gives the superlative more emphasis. It means "of all the people, places, or other things in the group." It doesn't change the meaning of the superlative.

I think mountain climbing is **the most dangerous sport** <u>of all</u>.

Everyone made an effort, but John tried **the hardest** <u>of all</u>.

▶ **2B** You can use *one of* before the superlative of an adjective. *One of* weakens the superlative because it means that the thing you are talking about is not unique by itself, but is part of a group of things that are unique.

New York is <u>one of</u> **the most famous cities** in the world. (New York and some other cities are more famous than the rest of the cities in the world.)

Using *The Most, The Least,* and *The Fewest*

▶ **3A** Use the *most* or *-est* with adjectives and adverbs to show that something is a higher degree, quantity, or size than all the other members of a group. Use *the least* to show that something is a lower degree, quantity, or size than all the other members of a group.

Diamonds are **the most expensive gems** in this shop.

He's **the richest man** in the world.

He's **the least talkative** of our friends.

> **!** *The least* sometimes sounds awkward with one-syllable adjectives and adverbs. To avoid this, use the superlative form of an adjective or adverb with the opposite meaning.
>
> I'm **the shortest** in my family. **X** I'm the least tall in my family. (INCORRECT)

▶ **3B** Use *the most* with count or noncount nouns to talk about the largest quantities. Use *the fewest* with count nouns and *the least* with noncount nouns to talk about the smallest quantities.

Count Nouns	Noncount Nouns
He made **the most mistakes**.	I had **the most trouble** with the test.
You made **the fewest mistakes**.	She had **the least trouble** with the test.

C1 Listening for Meaning and Use

▶ Notes 1A–1D, 2A, 3A, 3B

CD2 T42 **Read the situations and questions below. Then listen to the conversations and answer the questions.**

Situation 1

A woman has three daughters: Alison, Caitlin, and Megan. One of them is five years old, one is seven, and one is eleven.

1. Who is five years old? Caitlin
2. Who is eleven years old? ____________

Situation 2

There are three restaurants: Isabelle's, Sun Palace, and Seaview. One of them is a block away, one is two miles away, and one is five miles away.

1. Which restaurant is a block away? ____________
2. Which restaurant is five miles away? ____________

Situation 3

Three boys played in a practice basketball game: Ed, Pete, and Tom. One of them made two baskets, one made ten, and one made fifteen.

1. Who made two baskets? ____________
2. Who made fifteen baskets? ____________

C2 Asking for Opinions and Preferences

▶ Notes 1A, 1B, 1D

A. Use each set of words and phrases to write a question with *what* or *who*. Use a superlative and a clause with *ever* and the present perfect.

1. easy subject/study What is the easiest subject that you've ever studied?
2. interesting book/read ____________
3. unusual person/know ____________
4. pretty place/visit ____________
5. bad movie/see ____________

B. Work with a partner. Take turns asking and answering the questions in part A.

A: *What is the easiest subject that you have ever studied?*

B: *The easiest subject that I've ever studied is geography.*

C3 Weakening Superlatives

▶ Note 2B

Read the situations. Write sentences with *one of . . .* + superlative.

1. You have just moved to New York. When you call your family, your sister asks if the New York subway system is larger than any other subway system in the United States. You know that Boston and Chicago have large subway systems, too. You say:

   New York has one of the largest subway systems in the U.S.

2. You're talking about sports with your friend. You say that basketball is more popular than any other sport in the world. Your friend knows that basketball is very popular, but he thinks that soccer may be more popular. He says:

   Basketball is ______

3. You wonder whether diamonds are more valuable than other gems. You research the subject and find out that diamonds are valuable, but other gems are sometimes more valuable. What have you learned?

   Diamonds are ______

4. You and your friend are driving through Death Valley in California. It is very hot! Your friend asks if Death Valley is hotter than any other place on Earth. You're not really sure. You say:

   Death Valley is ______

C4 Making Recommendations

▶ Notes 1A–1C

Work with a partner. Imagine that you have a new neighbor. Use the words in parentheses to make recommendations with superlatives.

1. (beautiful/place) The most beautiful place in town is Memorial Park.
2. (good/restaurant) ______
3. (near/supermarket) ______
4. (nice/hotel) ______
5. (popular/neighborhood) ______
6. (big/mall) ______
7. (cheap/movie theater) ______
8. (interesting/store) ______

C5 Expressing Thanks

▶ Notes 1A–D, 2A, 2B, 3A

Complete this email with the superlative of the words in parentheses.

From: Rita Smith
To: Carol Jones
Subject: Thanks!

Hi Carol,

Thank you so much for the birthday gift! I received many fabulous presents this year, but yours was *the most wonderful* (1) (wonderful) of all! You can imagine my smile when I tore off the wrapping and saw ______ (2) (late) edition of *Guinness World Records®*! Only you could have chosen something so appropriate for the one who was voted "girl with ______ (3) (weird) sense of humor" in high school!

It may not be ______ (4) (serious) reference in the world, but it's certainly one of ______ (5) (enjoyable). I love reading about ______ (6) (long) surviving headless chicken, ______ (7) (smelly) flower in the world, and the man with ______ (8) (wide) waist! But you know us library science majors!

The book appeals to my serious side as well. Did you know that Switzerland has ______ (9) (high) use of solar energy in the world and that World War II ______ (10) (bloody) war in the history?

Again, many thanks for the wonderful surprise. You really are ______ (11) (great)! This was one of ______ (12) (nice) birthdays I've ever had.

Your friend,

Rita

WRITING Write a Thank-you Email

Think Critically About Meaning and Use

A. Complete each conversation.

1. A: John got an A, and the rest of us got B's and C's.

B: ___________

a. So John did the best of all.

b. So John got one of the highest grades.

2. A: Their youngest son is 12 years old.

B: ___________

a. How old are their other sons?

b. How old is their other son?

3. A: Jan is one of the fastest runners on the team.

B: ___________

a. Who else is fast?

b. Is anyone else fast?

4. A: She's the best dancer I know.

B: ___________

a. Who is better?

b. She must be great!

B. Discuss these questions in small groups.

1. **DRAW A CONCLUSION** In 2, what can we conclude about the family?

2. **APPLY** Consider the incorrect choice in 2. What could A say to make it correct?

Edit

Find the errors in this paragraph and correct them.

I think that Paris is ^the most wonderful~~est~~ city in the world. It certainly is the more fascinating. It has some of the most good art museums in the world. It also has some of the interestingest architecture, such as the Eiffel Tower. Then there is French food. I've been to many cities, and Paris has the best restaurants than all. Of course, Paris is not the most cheap place to visit. In fact, it is one of the most expensive place in the world, especially for hotels. But there are a few cheap hotels. Youth hostels cost the less of all, so I stay in youth hostels.

Write

Imagine that it's your birthday and your friends have arranged a wonderful day for you as a surprise. Follow the steps below to write them a thank-you email telling them how much you enjoyed the day. Use superlative for adjectives, adverbs, and nouns.

1. **BRAINSTORM** Think about all things that made this the best birthday you ever had. Use these categories to help you.
   - what you liked about the day
   - where you went
   - what you did
   - presents you got
   - how you feel now

2. **WRITE A FIRST DRAFT** Before you write your draft, read the checklist below and look at the example email on page 376. Write your draft using superlatives.

3. **EDIT** Read your work and check it against the checklist below. Circle grammar, spelling, and punctuation errors.

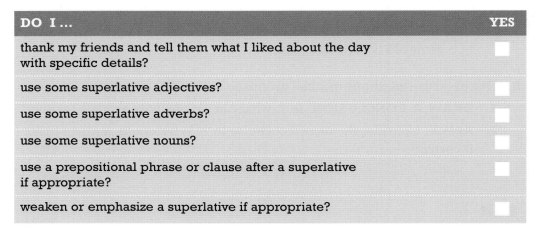

DO I …	YES
thank my friends and tell them what I liked about the day with specific details?	☐
use some superlative adjectives?	☐
use some superlative adverbs?	☐
use some superlative nouns?	☐
use a prepositional phrase or clause after a superlative if appropriate?	☐
weaken or emphasize a superlative if appropriate?	☐

4. **PEER REVIEW** Work with a partner to help you decide how to fix your errors and improve the content.

5. **REWRITE YOUR DRAFT** Using the comments from your partner, write a final draft.

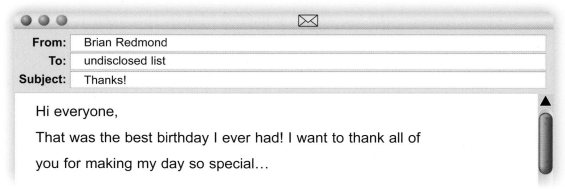

From: Brian Redmond
To: undisclosed list
Subject: Thanks!

Hi everyone,

That was the best birthday I ever had! I want to thank all of you for making my day so special…

PART 8 TEST | Comparatives and Superlatives

Choose the correct word or words to complete each sentence.

1. Chinese is a __________ language to learn than French.

a. more harder **b.** more hard **c.** harder **d.** most hard

2. California has the most inhabitants in the United States. Wyoming and Alaska have __________.

a. the fewest **b.** least **c.** the least **d.** lesser

3. Tokyo has __________ Kyoto.

a. more inhabitants than **b.** more inhabitants **c.** inhabitants than **d.** greater inhabitants

4. Carbon is one of __________ elements in the world.

a. more common **b.** most common **c.** the most common **d.** most common of

Choose the correct response to complete each conversation.

5. **A:** My best friend from college is in New York now.

B: ______________

a. Where do your other college friends live?

b. Where does your other college friend live?

c. Where your friend live?

d. Where is your friend live?

6. **A:** ______________

B: That's a tough question, but I think Bob is the best.

a. Who are some of the best students in your class?

b. Who is the best student in your class?

c. Who is the best students in your class?

d. Who does the best student in your class?

7. **A:** ______________

B: I guess the new car wasn't a good investment.

a. My new car is more efficient than my old one.

b. My new car is less efficient than my old one.

c. My new car is efficient than my old one.

d. My new car is the efficient car than my old one.

8. **A:** Dan is one of the best musicians in the class.

B: ______________

a. Who are the other talented musicians?

b. Are there any other talented musicians?

c. Who is the other talented musicians?

d. Is there any other talented musicians?

9. **A:** I'm nearly as old as Tina.

   B: I know. ________________

   a. She's only a few months younger.
   b. You're only a little younger than Tina is.
   c. She is younger from Tina.
   d. She is a bit younger from Tina.

10. **A:** I think Liberty Gardens is the most beautiful place in the city.

    B: ________________

    a. Oh, yes, by far. I totally agree.
    b. Yes, there are many beautiful places.
    c. Oh no, by far.
    d. Yes that's right, it is not beautiful.

11. **A:** Donna is the best computer programmer in our company.

    B: ________________

    a. Who is better?
    b. Yes, she is.
    c. Who are better?
    d. No, she is good.

Complete each sentence with the comparative form of the word in parentheses.

12. Your suitcase is ______________________ (heavy) than mine.
13. Bob's handwriting is ______________________ (bad) than my handwriting!
14. Martina cooks ______________________ (good) than Louisa does.

Complete each sentence with *as … as* and the correct form of the words in parentheses.

15. His car is ______________________ (not/fast/mine/be).
16. She has ______________________ (much/work/he/have).
17. I can't type ______________________ (quickly/Sheryl).

Match the sentence parts.

____ **18.** Colorado has some of
____ **19.** Soccer is probably
____ **20.** The ostrich is

a. the strongest of all storms.
b. the largest birds in the world.
c. the best places for skiing.
d. the rarest gems on Earth.
e. the most famous gem.
f. the biggest bird on Earth.
g. the most popular sport of all.
h. the largest state in the U.S.

PART

9

Gerunds, Infinitives, and Phrasal Verbs

CHAPTER

20

Gerunds

A. GRAMMAR IN DISCOURSE: **10 Easy Ways to Start Saving Money** **382**

B. FORM 1: **Gerunds as Subjects and Objects** **384**

Overview

Gerunds as Subjects and Objects

Exercising isn't fun.

I enjoy **shopping**.

C. FORM 2: **Gerunds After Prepositions** **387**

We walked **instead of driving**.

D. MEANING AND USE: **Gerunds** **389**

Referring to Activities and States

Do You Mind ... ?, I Don't Mind ... , **and** ***Would You Mind ... ?***

Other Common Uses

WRITING: **Write an Application Essay About Your Plans** **393**

A GRAMMAR IN DISCOURSE

10 Easy Ways to Start Saving Money

A1 Before You Read

Discuss these questions.

Do you try to save money? How do you do it? Is it easy or difficult?

A2 Read

CD2 T43

Read these tips to learn ten things that you can do to save money.

10 Easy Ways to Start Saving MONEY

Saving money is very difficult for many people. Here are some ways to make it easier.

1

Before starting, write down your expenses. For one week, every time you spend money, write down how much money you spent and what you spent it on. This will help you save by showing you where your money goes.

2

Divide your expenses into two groups—the things that you need and the things that you want. Think about cutting some of your "wants." These cuts will help you save money.

3

Make a monthly budget. A budget is a plan for spending the money you have. Include in your budget all your needs and some of your wants. Each month stay within your budget. This is very important. Many people love making budgets but hate staying within them. Saving is a need, so include it in your budget. Save some money each month, and put this money in the bank; even small amounts of money add up.

4

Start taking your lunch to work or to school. How much do you save by not buying lunch? Each day put this money in a large jar.

5

Save all of your change. Instead of spending your coins, put them in the jar, too. You won't notice the difference, and by the end of the year you could have several hundred dollars. Each time your jar is full, put the money in the bank.

6

Make it difficult to spend money. Before going out, check your wallet. Don't take much money with you and leave your credit cards at home.

7

Don't go shopping when you don't need to buy anything. Do you find it hard to be in stores without buying things? If so, stay away from stores.

8

Wait a while before making a large purchase. Give yourself time to change your mind. If you wait 24 hours, you may decide not to make the purchase.

9

If you get unexpected money, don't spend it. Put any gifts of money in the bank. You didn't expect this money, so you won't miss it.

10

When you do have to buy something, use the Internet. Shopping on the Internet not only saves money, it saves time.

If you are tired of not having any money in the bank, try these ten easy ways to start saving money. You will be surprised at how quickly your situation will change.

Adapted from *"Ten Easy Ways to Start Saving Money"*

---

expenses: money spent for specific purposes

purchase: something bought

A3 After You Read

Write *T* for true and *F* for false for each statement.

__T__ **1.** Writing down your expenses will help you save money.

_____ **2.** Your wants are more important than your needs.

_____ **3.** A budget is a plan for earning money.

_____ **4.** You don't have to stay within your budget every month.

_____ **5.** Saving works only with large amounts of money.

_____ **6.** Taking your lunch to work is cheaper than buying lunch.

_____ **7.** Always carry a lot of money so that you will be ready for an emergency.

_____ **8.** Waiting to make large purchases is a good idea.

B FORM 1

Gerunds as Subjects and Objects

Think Critically About Form

A. Read the sentences and complete the tasks below.

1a. Saving is difficult for many people.
1b. She is saving a lot of money.

2a. I started taking my lunch to work.
2b. Taking my lunch to work saves money.

1. **IDENTIFY** Look at the underlined forms in 1a and 1b. Which one is in the present continuous? Which one is a gerund? How do you know?
2. **RECOGNIZE** Look at the underlined gerund phrases in 2a and 2b. In which sentence is the underlined phrase the subject? In which sentence is the underlined phrase the object of the main verb?
3. **EXPLAIN** Are gerunds singular or plural? How do you know?

B. Discuss your answers with the class and read the Form charts to check them.

▶ Overview

ONLINE PRACTICE

AFFIRMATIVE GERUNDS	
GERUND	
Exercising	is important.
Budgeting carefully	is difficult.
Budgeting your money	

NEGATIVE GERUNDS	
***NOT* + GERUND**	
Not exercising	is bad for you.
Not budgeting carefully	is a mistake.
Not budgeting your money	

▶ Gerunds as Subjects and Objects

GERUNDS AS SUBJECTS		
GERUND (SUBJECT)	**THIRD-PERSON SINGULAR VERB**	
Learning math	is	difficult.
Exercising	isn't	fun.

GERUNDS AS OBJECTS		
SUBJECT	**VERB**	**GERUND (OBJECT)**
I	enjoy	**shopping**.
We	discussed	**moving to Ohio**.

Overview

- A gerund is the base form of a verb + *-ing.* It can be one word (*exercising*), or it can be part of a longer phrase with an adverb (*budgeting carefully*), a noun (*budgeting your money*), or a prepositional phrase (*moving to Ohio*).
- A gerund functions as a singular noun.
- All verbs except modal auxiliaries have gerund forms.
- See Appendix 3 for the spelling of verbs ending in *-ing.*

Gerunds as Subjects

- A gerund can function as the subject of a sentence. A subject gerund takes a third-person singular verb.

Listening is an important skill. **Learning math** takes time.

Gerunds as Objects

- A gerund can be the object of certain verbs. These verbs include:

avoid	discuss	finish	like	prefer
begin	dislike	go	love	quit
continue	enjoy	hate	miss	start

- See Appendix 13 for a list of verbs that can be followed by gerunds.

B1 Listening for Form

CD2 T44 Listen to each statement. Listen carefully for the *-ing* form in the chart. Do you hear a gerund or the present continuous? Check (✓) the correct column.

		GERUND	PRESENT CONTINUOUS
1.	shopping	✓	
2.	saving		
3.	working		
4.	eating		
5.	buying		
6.	taking		
7.	having		
8.	spending		

B2 Working on Gerunds as Subjects

Complete these sentences with gerunds. Use the words in parentheses.

1. Finding a job (find/a job) isn't easy.
2. Taking classes (take/classes) can help improve job skills.
3. Not having money (not/have/money) isn't much fun.
4. Staying within a budget (stay/within a budget) can be difficult.
5. Not carrying credit cards (not/carry/credit cards) is a way to spend less.
6. Shopping on the Internet (shop/on the Internet) saves time and money.
7. Travelling (travel) costs less with student discounts.
8. Saving a lot of money (save/a lot of money) takes time.

B3 Working on Gerunds as Objects

Complete each conversation with a verb + gerund. Use the words in parentheses.

1. **A:** You lost a lot of weight. How did you do it?

   B: It was easy. I quit eating (quit/eat) sweets.

2. **A:** I thought you and Jim were moving to Portugal.

   B: We often discuss moving (discuss/move), but I don't think we'll ever leave London.

3. **A:** That dinner was expensive. What happened to our new budget?

   B: It's OK. We can starting budget / start budgeting (start/budget) tomorrow.

4. **A:** We don't have much money in the bank right now.

   B: Maybe we should consider not going (consider/not/go) on vacation.

5. **A:** Do you like college?

   B: I'm not sure yet. I miss being (miss/be) with my family.

6. **A:** I couldn't get tickets for the basketball game.

   B: That's OK. It will be on TV. I like watching (like/watch) basketball on TV.

C FORM 2

Gerunds After Prepositions

Think Critically About Form

A. Look at the sentences and complete the tasks below.

a. He won a prize for swimming the fastest.
b. She wasn't accustomed to getting bad grades.
c. I don't approve of lying.
d. Do you worry about making enough money?

IDENTIFY Underline the gerund in each sentence. Circle the word that comes directly before each gerund. What kind of word is it?

B. Discuss your answers with the class and read the Form charts to check them.

ONLINE PRACTICE

PREPOSITION + GERUND		
	PREPOSITION	**GERUND**
I'll call	**before**	**leaving town.**
We walked	**instead of**	**driving.**

VERB + PREPOSITION + GERUND		
	VERB + PREPOSITION	**GERUND**
We	worried **about**	**losing.**
I	believe **in**	**telling the truth.**

***BE* + ADJECTIVE + PREPOSITION + GERUND**		
	***BE* + ADJECTIVE + PREPOSITION**	**GERUND**
We	were tired **of**	**studying hard.**
He	was afraid **of**	**losing his job.**

Preposition + Gerund

- Gerunds can follow prepositions such as *about, for, in, instead of, of,* and *to.*

Verb + Preposition + Gerund

- Many verb + preposition combinations can be followed by gerunds. These include *approve of, believe in, disapprove of, plan on, think about,* and *worry about.*
- See Appendix 13 for a list of verb + preposition combinations that can be followed by gerunds.

(Continued on page 388)

Be + Adjective + Preposition + Gerund

- Many *be* + adjective + preposition combinations can be followed by a gerund. These include *be accustomed to/be used to, be afraid of, be fond of, be good at, be interested in, be surprised at,* and *be tired of.* See Appendix 13 for a list of more *be* + adjective + preposition phrases that are followed by gerunds.

C1 Listening for Form

CD2 T45 **Listen and complete these sentences with the words you hear.**

1. Are you <u>interested in going</u> to a movie tonight?
2. You should drink tea ____________ coffee.
3. John is talking ____________ his job.
4. I'm looking ____________ Mr. Johnson's class.
5. I'm ____________ TV.

C2 Working on Gerunds After Verb + Preposition

Match each sentence beginning on the left to its correct sentence ending on the right.

d	1. Jorge is talking	a. of being in school.
c	2. I believe	b. at explaining things.
f	3. We're looking forward	c. in treating people fairly.
e	4. We're planning	d. about buying an apartment.
a	5. He's tired	e. on leaving early today.
b	6. She's good	f. to traveling to Europe next summer.

C3 Working on Gerunds After Adjective + Preposition

Work in pairs. Take turns asking and answering these questions. Answer with adjective + preposition combinations and gerunds.

1. What are you afraid of doing?

   A: *What are you afraid of doing?*

   B: *I'm afraid of flying.*

2. What are you good at doing?

   I'm good at making new friends

3. What are you interested in doing?

   I'm interested in making money

4. What are you tired of doing?

   I'm tried of studying all the time.

5. What are you fond of doing?

   I'm found of watching old movies.

D MEANING AND USE

Gerunds

Think Critically About Meaning and Use

A. Read the sentences and answer the questions below.

a. I don't like playing tennis, but I love watching it.
b. Would you mind opening the door, please? My hands are full.
c. You can stop the elevator by pressing this button.

1. **EVALUATE** In which sentence is the speaker expressing a like or dislike?
2. **EVALUATE** In which sentence is the speaker making a polite request?
3. **EVALUATE** In which sentence is the speaker explaining how to do something?

B. Discuss your answers with the class and read the Meaning and Use Notes to check them.

Meaning and Use Notes

ONLINE PRACTICE

	Referring to Activities and States
▶ **1A**	Use a gerund to refer to an activity or state. **Activity** **Learning a foreign language** is hard work. **State** I don't like **being hungry.**
▶ **1B**	Use *go* + gerund to refer to common activities. *Go* can be used in any tense. I went **sightseeing** when I was in Paris. When you visit a national park, you can go **hiking**, **camping**, and **fishing**.
▶ **1C**	Use verbs such as *like, dislike, hate,* and *enjoy* + gerund to talk about liking or disliking activities and states. I hate **eating alone**. In his spare time, John enjoys **fixing old cars**.

(Continued on page 390)

Do You Mind ... ?, *I Don't Mind ...* , and *Would You Mind ... ?*

▶ **2A** The verb *mind* means "dislike, feel bothered." *Mind* + gerund is usually used in questions and negative statements to express likes and dislikes.

Expressing Likes and Dislikes

A: Do you mind **getting up early for work**? (= Does getting up early bother you?)

B: No, I don't mind. I'm used to it. (= No, it doesn't bother me.)

I don't mind **driving at night.** (= Driving at night doesn't bother me.)

▶ **2B** Use the phrase *would you mind* + gerund to make polite requests. An answer of *no* means that the listener agrees to the request.

Making Polite Requests

A: Sorry to bother you, but would you mind **closing that window?**

B: No, not at all. (= OK. I'll close it.)

Other Common Uses

▶ **3A** Use *by* + gerund to explain how to do something.

Explaining How to Do Something

You can make better cookies by **adding extra butter**.

▶ **3B** Gerunds are often used in signs that permit or forbid an activity.

Signs

Taking photos is not allowed. **Talking during the exam** is strictly forbidden.

D1 Listening for Meaning and Use

▶ Notes 1A, 1C, 2A, 2B, 3A

CD2 T46 **Listen to each sentence. Is the speaker expressing a like or dislike, making a polite request, or explaining how to do something? Check (✓) the correct column.**

	LIKE OR DISLIKE	POLITE REQUEST	HOW TO DO SOMETHING
1.	✓		
2.			
3.			
4.			
5.			

D2 Making Polite Requests

▶ Note 2B

Look at the pictures. Take turns making and responding to a polite request for each situation. Use *would you mind* and a gerund in your requests.

A: Would you mind passing the salt?
B: No, not at all.

D3 Talking About How to Do Things

▶ Note 3A

Work with a partner. Take turns asking and answering these questions. Use *by* + gerund. Compare answers with two other students.

1. How do you find a job?
   By going to an employment service.
2. How do you keep your money safe? By putting ~~it~~ in ~~the~~ a bank
3. How do you decide what to eat? By looking in the refrigerator
4. How do you get a raise? By working hard
5. How do you find out the meaning of unknown words? By looking in a dictionary
6. How do you choose a roommate? By interviewing several people.

D4 Making Lists of Activities

▶ Notes 1A, 1B

Complete these lists with gerunds.

Relaxing Activities

1. Reading a novel
2. ______
3. ______
4. ______

Stressful Activities

1. Taking an exam
2. ______
3. ______
4. ______

Healthy Activities

1. Swimming
2. ______
3. ______
4. ______

Not Allowed in Class

1. Texting
2. ______
3. ______
4. ______

Think Critically About Meaning and Use

A. Choose the best answer to complete each conversation.

1. A: Would you mind opening the window?
   B: ___________
   a. No, not at all.
   b. Sure, go ahead and open it.

2. A: What do you like doing at night?
   B: ___________
   a. Watching television.
   b. By watching television.

3. A: These days I have to get up early for work.
   B: ___________
   a. Do you mind getting up early?
   b. Would you mind getting up early?

4. A: I need to save money, but keeping to a budget won't be easy.
   B: ___________
   a. Yes, they will. Don't worry.
   b. Yes, it will. Don't worry.

B. Discuss these questions in small groups.

1. **PREDICT** In 1, what do you think is going to happen next? Why?
2. **GENERATE** Consider B's incorrect response in 2. What could A say to make it correct?

Edit

Some of these sentences have errors. Find the errors and correct them.

1. We avoid to drive at night.
2. Save money can be difficult.
3. Walking are good exercise.
4. He got sick by stand out in the rain.
5. Shopping and eating are my two favorite activities.
6. No buying everything you want is a good way to save money.

Write

Write about your plans for the future as part of an application for college, graduate school or a job. Follow the steps below. Use gerunds.

1. **BRAINSTORM** Think about some plans for yourself that are related to your future studies or profession. Take notes about what you will say. Use these categories to help you.
   - activities you want to continue doing
   - activities you want to begin doing
   - changes you want to make in your life
   - things you look forward to doing
   - subjects you plan on studying
   - work you hope to be doing after completing your studies or when you start the job

2. **WRITE A FIRST DRAFT** Before you write your draft, read the checklist below. Write your draft using gerunds.

3. **EDIT** Read your work and check it against the checklist below. Circle grammar, spelling, and punctuation errors.

DO I ...	YES
explain my plans for the near future and show how they are relevant to my studies or profession?	☐
use affirmative and negative gerunds?	☐
use gerunds as subjects?	☐
use gerunds as objects?	☐
use gerunds after prepositions?	☐

4. **PEER REVIEW** Work with a partner to help you decide how to fix your errors and improve the content.

5. **REWRITE YOUR DRAFT** Using the comments from your partner, write a final draft.

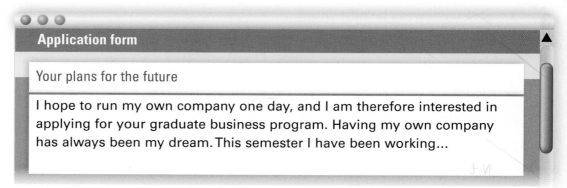

Application form

Your plans for the future

I hope to run my own company one day, and I am therefore interested in applying for your graduate business program. Having my own company has always been my dream. This semester I have been working...

CHAPTER

21

Infinitives

A. **GRAMMAR IN DISCOURSE: The *Twenty-One* Game Show Scandal** 396

B. **FORM: Infinitives** 398

He agreed **to speak slowly.**

He taught me **to cook.**

(In order) to win, he cheated.

It took two years **to learn the truth.**

C. **MEANING AND USE 1: Infinitives** 402

Referring to Activities and States

Giving Reasons with *In Order* + Infinitive

Sentences with *It* Subject ... + Infinitive

D. **MEANING AND USE 2: Contrasting Gerunds and Infinitives** 405

Verbs Taking Only Gerunds

Verbs Taking Only Infinitives

Verbs Taking Gerunds or Infinitives with No Difference in Meaning

Verbs Taking Gerunds or Infinitives with a Difference in Meaning

WRITING: Write Your Online Profile 409

A

GRAMMAR IN DISCOURSE

The *Twenty-One* Game Show Scandal

A1 Before You Read

Discuss these questions.

What are television game shows? Do you ever watch them? Do you enjoy them? Why or why not?

A2 Read

CD2 T47 **Read this online encyclopedia article to find out about a famous scandal involving a game show.**

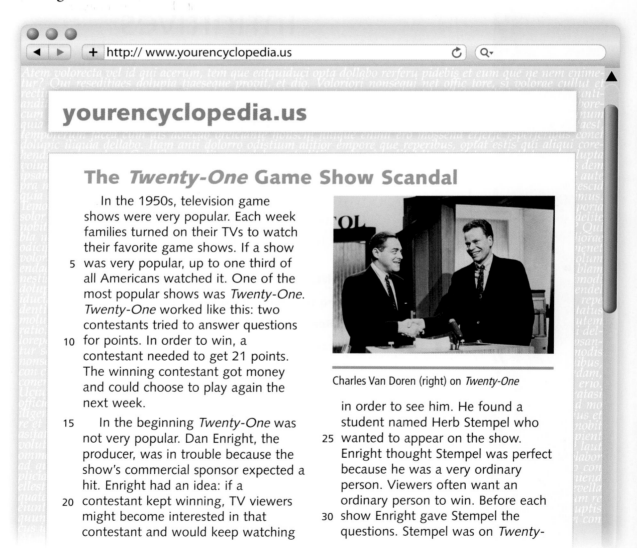

http:// www.yourencyclopedia.us

yourencyclopedia.us

The *Twenty-One* Game Show Scandal

In the 1950s, television game shows were very popular. Each week families turned on their TVs to watch their favorite game shows. If a show was very popular, up to one third of all Americans watched it. One of the most popular shows was *Twenty-One*. *Twenty-One* worked like this: two contestants tried to answer questions for points. In order to win, a contestant needed to get 21 points. The winning contestant got money and could choose to play again the next week.

Charles Van Doren (right) on *Twenty-One*

In the beginning *Twenty-One* was not very popular. Dan Enright, the producer, was in trouble because the show's commercial sponsor expected a hit. Enright had an idea: if a contestant kept winning, TV viewers might become interested in that contestant and would keep watching in order to see him. He found a student named Herb Stempel who wanted to appear on the show. Enright thought Stempel was perfect because he was a very ordinary person. Viewers often want an ordinary person to win. Before each show Enright gave Stempel the questions. Stempel was on *Twenty-*

One for eight weeks. He pretended not to know the questions, and the viewers believed this. Stempel won more than $69,000 and became famous. *Twenty-One* became a hit.

Soon, however, people started to get tired of Stempel. Enright decided not to keep Stempel on the show anymore. This time he looked for someone who was not ordinary. He found Charles Van Doren—a handsome English professor from a famous family. Enright convinced Van Doren to cheat. He then told Stempel to give the wrong answer on the next show. Stempel was unhappy, but he agreed to lose by not answering correctly.

Van Doren became the new champion of *Twenty-One*. He stayed on the show for 15 weeks and won almost $130,000. Each week millions of people watched Van Doren win more money.

The show's ratings were high, and everyone was happy—except Herb Stempel. He told newspaper reporters his story, but no one believed him. Finally, the government began to investigate. It took two years to learn the whole story. In the end, Charles Van Doren admitted cheating and apologized.

The TV station cancelled *Twenty-One*. Enright lost his job and left the United States. Van Doren lost his job, too, and he refused to say anything more about the show. The TV viewers were surprised and angry. The show seemed so real. Van Doren seemed so wonderful. It was hard to accept the truth.

For many years Stempel and Enright were forgotten. Then, in 1994, the famous actor Robert Redford turned this strange story into a movie entitled *Quiz Show*. To find out more about the scandal, as well as Stempel and Enright, watch Redford's award-winning movie.

contestant: a person who participates in a game show

hit: a very popular TV show

ratings: a measure of how popular a TV show is

scandal: a situation that shocks people

sponsor: a company that pays for a TV show in return for being able to advertise on the show

A3 After You Read

Write *T* for true or *F* for false for each statement.

__F__ **1.** In the 1950s few Americans watched game shows on TV.

____ **2.** *Twenty-One* was not popular before Herb Stempel appeared on it.

____ **3.** Herb Stempel was happy when Charles Van Doren won on the show.

____ **4.** When Herb Stempel told everyone how he won on *Twenty-One*, they immediately believed him.

____ **5.** Charles Van Doren was sorry that he cheated.

____ **6.** *Twenty-One* was canceled.

B FORM

Infinitives

Think Critically About Form

A. Read the sentences and complete the tasks below.

1a. They <u>speak</u> to the producer before the show.
1b. The producer told them <u>to speak</u> clearly.

2a. He wanted to be on the show.
2b. The producer wanted him to cheat.

1. **IDENTIFY** Look at the underlined forms in 1a and 1b. Which is in the simple present? Which is an infinitive?
2. **RECOGNIZE** Look at 2a and 2b. In which does the infinitive directly follow the verb? In which does the infinitive follow the object of the verb? Look back at lines 37–49 of the online article on page 397. Find a verb + infinitive and a verb + object + infinitive.

B. Discuss your answers with the class and read the Form charts to check them.

▶ Overview

ONLINE PRACTICE

AFFIRMATIVE INFINITIVES		
SUBJECT	VERB	INFINITIVE
He	agreed	**to leave.** **to speak slowly.** **to help me.**

NEGATIVE INFINITIVES		
SUBJECT	VERB	*NOT* + INFINITIVE
He	agreed	**not to leave.** **not to speak quickly.** **not to bother me.**

▶ Infinitives

INFINITIVES AFTER VERBS			
SUBJECT	VERB	INFINITIVE	
I	learned	**to cook.**	

SUBJECT	VERB	OBJECT	INFINITIVE
He	taught	me	**to cook.**

SUBJECT	VERB	(OBJECT)	INFINITIVE
I	wanted	him	**to cook.**

(*IN ORDER* +) INFINITIVE		
SUBJECT	**VERB**	**(*IN ORDER* +) INFINITIVE**
He	cheated	**(in order) to win.**

(*IN ORDER* +) INFINITIVE	SUBJECT	VERB
(In order) to win,	he	cheated.

IT SUBJECT ... + INFINITIVE			
SUBJECT	**VERB**	**ADJECTIVE**	**INFINITIVE**
It	was	difficult	**to lie.**

SUBJECT	VERB	NOUN PHRASE	INFINITIVE
It	took	two years	**to learn the truth.**

Overview

- An infinitive is *to* + the base form of the verb. It can be two words (*to leave*), or it can be part of a longer phrase with an adverb (*to speak slowly*) or an object (*to help me*).
- All verbs except modal auxiliaries have infinitive forms.

Infinitives After Verbs

- Infinitives follow verbs in three main patterns:

VERB + INFINITIVE

agree	continue	hate	learn	wait
begin	decide	hope	plan	

VERB + OBJECT + INFINITIVE

advise	cause	order	teach
allow	invite	remind	tell

VERB + (OBJECT) + INFINITIVE

ask	expect	need	promise	prefer
choose	help	pay	want	

- See Appendix 14 for a list of verbs that can be followed by infinitives.

In Order + Infinitive

- Infinitives can follow the expression *in order*.
- With affirmative infinitives, we often leave out *in order* and use the infinitive alone.

It Subject ... + Infinitive

- An infinitive can function as the subject of a sentence: *To lie is wrong*. However, this form is not common. It is more usual to start the sentence with *It* and use the infinitive at the end of the sentence. *It* refers to the infinitive.

  It is wrong **to lie**. (*It* = to lie)
- *It* is followed by a limited group of verbs, including *be, cost, seem,* and *take*.

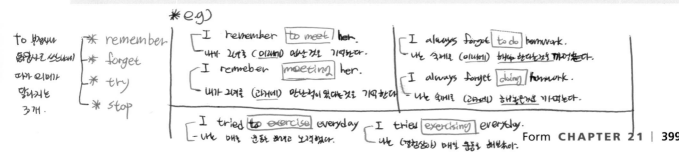

B1 Listening for Form

CD2 T48 Listen to each sentence. Does it have an infinitive? Check (✓) the correct column.

	INFINITIVE	NO INFINITIVE
1.	✓	
2.		
3.		
4.		
5.		
6.		
7.		
8.		

B2 Working on Infinitives

Complete these sentences by choosing the correct answers. In some of the sentences, both answers are correct.

1. I agreed ___________.
  a. not to tell
  b. him not to tell

2. I asked ___________.
  a. to leave
  b. him to leave

3. I allowed ___________.
  a. to go
  b. him to go

4. They decided ___________.
  a. to study
  b. him to study

5. We want ___________.
  a. to look at it
  b. him to look at it

6. We told ___________.
  a. not to ask
  b. him not to ask

7. I expect ___________.
  a. to finish soon
  b. him to finish soon

8. We plan ___________.
  a. to help
  b. him to help

9. They invited ___________.
  a. to come
  b. him to come

10. I need ___________.
  a. to stay
  b. him to stay

B3 Working on *In Order* + Infinitive

In your notebook, write each sentence in two different ways.

1. I need to sit in front of the class in order to see.

   In order to see, I need to sit in front of the class. *I need to sit in front of the class to see.*

2. In order to get good seats, we left early. We left early to get good seats.
3. I drink coffee to stay awake. In order to stay awake, I drink coffee.
4. To get a scholarship, you need to do well in school. In order to get a scholarship, you need to do well.
5. In order to get a better job, she's going to study English. She's going to study English to get a better job.
6. I didn't tell her about losing the money in order to avoid an argument.

B4 Working on *It* Subject ... + Infinitive

Use these words to write sentences with *It* subject ... + infinitive.

1. be/useful/know/foreign languages

   It is useful to know foreign languages.

2. take/time/learn/a language well

   It takes time to learn a language well

3. be/expensive/eat/in restaurants

   It is expensive to eat in restaurants.

4. cost/a lot/fly/first class

   It costs a lot to fly first class.

5. be/important/not/tell/lies

   It is important not to tell lies.

6. seem/better/talk/about your problems

   It seems better to talk about your problems.

7. be/dangerous/drive/on icy roads

   It is dangerous to drive on icy roads.

8. be/wise/not/argue with friends

   It is wise not to argue with friends.

C MEANING AND USE 1

Infinitives

Think Critically About Meaning and Use

A. Read the sentences and complete the tasks below.

a. I left the house early in order to arrive on time.
b. She hated to eat alone.
c. It isn't easy to leave your family.

1. IDENTIFY Underline the infinitive in each sentence.

2. EVALUATE Which sentences express a feeling about an activity? In which sentence does the infinitive express a reason for doing something?

B. Discuss your answers with the class and read the Meaning and Use Notes to check them.

Meaning and Use Notes

ONLINE PRACTICE

Referring to Activities and States

▶ **1** An infinitive usually follows a verb and refers to an activity or state. Use verbs such as *like, love, hate, prefer,* and *want* + infinitive to express likes, dislikes, and other feelings toward these activities and states.

I hate **to go to the mall alone**.

He wants **to own his own home**.

Giving Reasons with *In Order* + Infinitive

▶ **2A** Use *in order* + infinitive to express a reason for doing something. This is called the purpose infinitive. It can answer the question *Why?*

A: Why did you go to your son's school?
B: I went **in order to meet his teacher**.

In order to finish the cooking early, I started first thing in the morning.

▶ **2B** *In order* is often left out, especially in conversations or in instructions.

A: Why did you leave work early?
B: **To go to the doctor**. I had a 3:00 appointment.

Call the number below **to get more information**.

Sentences with *It* Subject ... + Infinitive	
▶ **3A**	In sentences with *It* subject ... + infinitive, *it* refers to the infinitive at the end of the sentence. **It** takes a long time **to learn another language**. (*It* = to learn another language) **It** wasn't easy **to find an apartment**. (*It* = to find an apartment) **It** is better **not to say anything**. (*It* = not to say anything)
▶ **3B**	*It* subject ... + infinitive sentences can have the same meaning as sentences with subject gerunds. **It** was difficult **to lie**. = Lying was difficult. **It** took two years **to learn the truth**. = Learning the truth took two years.

C1 Listening for Meaning and Use

▶ Notes 1, 2A, 2B

CD2 T49 **Listen to each sentence. How is the infinitive used? Check (✓) the correct column.**

	TO EXPRESS A LIKE, DISLIKE, OR WANT	TO GIVE A REASON FOR DOING SOMETHING
1.	✓	
2.		
3.		
4.		
5.		
6.		
7.		
8.		

C2 Expressing Likes and Dislikes

▶ Note 1

Complete these sentences with infinitives. Share your answers with another student. Do you agree with each other?

1. Most children hate *to go to bed on time.*
2. Athletes often prefer ________________
3. Some adults don't like ________________
4. Many Americans like ________________
5. Most of my friends like ________________
6. Few people hate ________________

C3 Giving Reasons

▶ Notes 2A, 2B

Answer these questions with at least one reason. Use (*in order* +) infinitive.

1. Why do stores raise their prices?
   In order to make more money. OR *To pay for their expenses.*
2. Why do people climb mountains?
3. Why do people take vacations?
4. Why are you taking this class?
5. Why do people go to libraries?
6. Why do people work?

C4 Rephrasing Gerunds and Infinitives

▶ Notes 3A, 3B

A. **Rewrite these sentences. Change sentences with *It* subject … + infinitive to sentences beginning with gerunds. Change sentences beginning with gerunds to sentences with *It* subject … + infinitive.**

1. It's fun to learn a language.
   Learning a language is fun.
2. Learning to type is not easy.
3. It will take several days to drive across the country.
4. Going camping will be fun.
5. Ignoring people isn't nice.
6. It doesn't have to cost a lot to take a vacation.

B. **Work with a partner. Write two more sentences beginning with a gerund or *It* subject … + infinitive. Ask your partner to rephrase them as in part A.**

D MEANING AND USE 2

Contrasting Gerunds and Infinitives

Think Critically About Meaning and Use

A. Read the sentences and answer the questions below.

1a. When I stopped eating ice cream every day, I lost five pounds.
1b. When I stopped to eat ice cream every day, I gained five pounds.

2a. It started raining a few minutes ago. Take an umbrella.
2b. It started to rain a few minutes ago. Take an umbrella.

COMPARE AND CONTRAST Compare the underlined phrases in each pair of sentences. Which pair has the same meaning? Which pair has different meanings?

B. Discuss your answers with the class and read the Meaning and Use Notes to check them.

Meaning and Use Notes

ONLINE PRACTICE

Verbs Taking Only Gerunds

▶ 1 Some verbs take only gerunds. These verbs include *avoid, dislike, enjoy, finish, miss, prohibit,* and *resist.* See Appendix 13 for a list of more verbs.

Paul enjoys **swimming**.

I finished **reading the book**.

Verbs Taking Only Infinitives

▶ 2 Some verbs take only infinitives. These verbs include *agree, expect, need, offer, plan, promise* and *want.* See Appendix 14 for a list of more verbs.

Joe wants **to leave**.

I expect **to receive her email** today.

Verbs Taking Gerunds or Infinitives with No Difference in Meaning

▶ 3 Some verbs can take either gerunds or infinitives with no difference in meaning. These verbs include *begin, continue, hate, like, love, prefer,* and *start.* See Appendix 15 for a list of more verbs.

Gerund		Infinitive
I began **feeling sick** after dinner.	=	I began **to feel sick** after dinner.
It starts **snowing** in December.	=	It starts **to snow** in December.

(Continued on page 406)

After continuous forms of *begin* or *start*, use an infinitive, not a gerund.

Infinitive	Gerund
I <u>was beginning</u> **to feel** sick.	X I was beginning feeling sick. (INCORRECT)
He <u>was starting</u> **to get** better.	X He was starting feeling better. (INCORRECT)

Verbs Taking Gerunds or Infinitives with a Difference in Meaning

▶ 4A Some verbs can take either gerunds or infinitives, but with a difference in meaning. After *stop*, *forget*, and *remember*, the gerund refers to something that happened <u>before</u> the action of the main verb. The infinitive refers to something that happened <u>after</u> the action of the main verb.

Gerund

I <u>stopped</u> **drinking coffee**.
(I was a coffee drinker.
Then I stopped.)

He <u>remembered</u> **mailing the package**.
(He mailed the package. Then
he remembered doing it.)

Infinitive

I <u>stopped</u> **to drink some coffee**.
(I stopped what I was doing.
Then I drank some coffee.)

He <u>remembered</u> **to mail the package**.
(He remembered the package.
Then he mailed it.)

▶ 4B The verb *forget* is usually used with an infinitive. With a gerund, *forget* is most common in sentences with *will never*.

Infinitive

I <u>forgot</u> **to go to her lecture.**
She was mad at me.
(First = I forgot.
Second = I didn't go.)

Gerund

<u>I'll never forget</u> **going to her lecture**.
It was so much fun!
(First = I went to the lecture.
Second = I won't forget it.)

D1 Listening for Meaning and Use

▶ Notes 3, 4A, 4B

CD2 T50 **Listen to these pairs of sentences. Do they have the same meaning or different meanings? Choose the correct answer.**

1. same different
2. same different
3. same different
4. same different
5. same different
6. same different

D2 Contrasting Gerunds and Infinitives

▶ Notes 1, 2

Complete each sentence with a gerund or infinitive.

1. I finished ___reading___ (read) the book you lent me. It was really good.
2. She expects us ___to finish___ (finish) our essays by Friday.
3. Do you miss ___seeing___ (see) your family and friends?
4. They dislike ___getting___ (get) phone calls late at night.
5. He promised ___to make___ (make) less noise after I complained.
6. Jim says he wants ___to quit___ (quit) his job.

D3 Rephrasing Gerunds and Infinitives

▶ Notes 1–4

A. Replace the underlined words with a verb + gerund without changing the meaning of the sentence. If this is not possible, write *no change possible*.

Conversation 1

A: I'll start to load (1) the car. ___start loading___

Did you remember to turn off (2) the light? ___no change possible___

B: Yes, but I forgot to lock the front door. ___forgot locking___

Conversation 2

A: Do you like to cook (1)? ___like cooking?___

B: Yes, but I prefer to eat out (2). ___prefer eating out___

B. Replace the underlined words with an infinitive without changing the meaning of the sentence. If this is not possible, write *no change possible*.

Conversation 1

A: Do you like working (1) at home? ___like to work___

B: Yes. I've been much happier since I stopped working (2) in an office. ___stopped to work___

Conversation 2

A: I finished writing (1) my paper this morning. ___finished to writing.___

B: That's great! I just began writing (2) mine. ___began to write.___

D4 Making Suggestions

▶ Notes 1–4

A. **Work in small groups. Choose one of the topics below. Make suggestions by completing each sentence with either a gerund or an infinitive.**

Starting an Exercise Program

Organizing Your Time

Choosing a Career

Learning a Language

Studying for Final Exams

Choosing a University

Suggestions for Starting an Exercise Program

1. Start thinking about different exercises.
2. Plan to join a gym.
3. Remember ______
4. Avoid Studying Final Exams.
5. Try to Learn a Language.
6. Consider Choosing a University.
7. Don't stop ______
8. Finally, don't forget ______

B. **Work with a partner from a different group. Share your suggestions. Can you add any ideas to your partner's list?**

WRITING Write Your Online Profile

Think Critically About Meaning and Use

A. Choose the best answer to complete each conversation.

1. A: She stopped _____ when she saw the accident.
B: How brave!
a. to help
b. helping

2. A: We stopped _____ you, but there was no answer.
B: I went out for a while.
a. to call
b. calling

3. A: _____ cheap tickets, come back an hour before the show.
B: Thanks for the advice!
a. To get
b. Getting

4. A: Do you remember _____ to me about your boss?
B: Yes, last week in the lunch room. Why?
a. to talk
b. talking

B. Discuss these questions in small groups.

1. COMPARE AND CONTRAST In 1, how does the meaning of A's comment change when the incorrect answer is put into the sentence?

2. ANALYZE In which conversations does A use an infinitive to express a reason or purpose for doing something?

Edit

Some of these sentences have errors. Find the errors and correct them.

1. We avoid to drive at night.
2. It is useful have an extra key for your house.
3. I was starting saying something when he interrupted.
4. He continued to ask questions.
5. In order get your driver's license, you have to take a test.
6. I'm looking forward to finish this report.

Write

Imagine that you are writing your profile on a social networking site. Write a description of your likes and dislikes. Follow the steps below. Use verbs with gerunds and infinitives.

1. **Brainstorm** Think of different categories and the things you like and dislike in each. Use these categories to help you.
   - school and work activities
   - sports (playing and watching)
   - music
   - TV programs, movies, books
   - activities with friends and other leisure activities
   - places you go (in your hometown, on vacation)

2. **Write a First Draft** Before you write your draft, read the checklist below. Write your draft using verbs such as *dislike*, *enjoy*, *hate*, *like*, *prefer*, and *want* with infinitives and gerunds.

3. **Edit** Read your work and check it against the checklist above. Circle grammar, spelling, and punctuation errors.

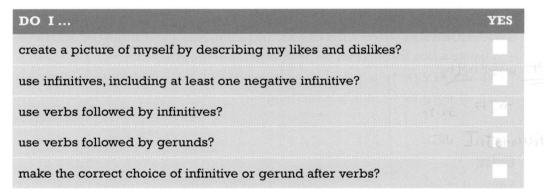

DO I ...	YES
create a picture of myself by describing my likes and dislikes?	☐
use infinitives, including at least one negative infinitive?	☐
use verbs followed by infinitives?	☐
use verbs followed by gerunds?	☐
make the correct choice of infinitive or gerund after verbs?	☐

4. **Peer Review** Work with a partner to help you decide how to fix your errors and improve the content.

5. **Rewrite Your Draft** Using the comments from your partner, Write a final draft.

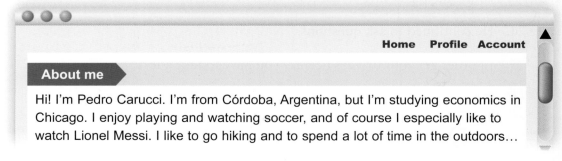

Home **Profile** **Account**

About me

Hi! I'm Pedro Carucci. I'm from Córdoba, Argentina, but I'm studying economics in Chicago. I enjoy playing and watching soccer, and of course I especially like to watch Lionel Messi. I like to go hiking and to spend a lot of time in the outdoors...

CHAPTER

22

Phrasal Verbs

A. **GRAMMAR IN DISCOURSE: "Eggstraordinary" Breakfasts Are Easy!** 412

B. **FORM: Phrasal Verbs** 414

Transitive Phrasal Verbs

I **left out** the sugar.

I **left** the sugar **out**.

I **left** it **out**.

She **looked after** the children.

Intransitive Phrasal Verbs

We **grew up** overseas.

C. **MEANING AND USE: Phrasal Verbs** 418

Idiomatic Meanings

Predictable Meanings

WRITING: Write Instructions on How to Do Something 421

PART 9 TEST: Gerunds, Infinitives, and Phrasal Verbs 423

A GRAMMAR IN DISCOURSE

"Eggstraordinary" Breakfasts Are Easy!

A1 Before You Read

Discuss these questions.

What's your favorite breakfast? Do you like to eat eggs? If you do, how do you cook them?

A2 Read

CD2 T51 **Read the directions from a cooking website on the following page to find out the best way to fry an egg.**

A3 After You Read

Look at the information again and number these steps for frying an egg.

_____ Take the egg out of the pan.

_____ Turn the heat down to low.

_____ Wait until the white is slightly hard.

_____ Wait about 15 seconds.

_____ Put oil or butter in the pan.

__1__ Turn on the stove to medium heat.

_____ Turn the egg over.

_____ Break the egg into the pan.

http://www.allabouteggs.us

Nutrition | Egg Facts | Recipes | Home

all about eggs

"Eggstraordinary" Breakfasts Are Easy!

Do you start each day with a boring bowl of cereal? Do you try to get by without breakfast? Why put up with an ordinary breakfast—or no breakfast at all—when you can eat eggs? Eggs are one of the most popular breakfast foods in the United States. There are many different ways to prepare them. Most of these ways are easy. Consider, for example, fried (over easy) eggs. Follow these simple steps (remember to start out with fresh eggs) and you can count on delicious fried eggs every time.

Heat up the pan

Put a frying pan on the stove, and turn the stove on to medium. Figure out the amount of butter or oil you will need. (Use about two teaspoons of butter or one teaspoon of oil per egg. To cut down on fat, use less butter or oil and a non-stick pan.) Put the butter or oil in the pan, and heat up the pan for a couple of minutes.

Cook the eggs

To crack an egg, gently hit it against the side of the pan. Then break it open and let the white and yolk fall out. Turn the heat down to low, so the eggs will cook slowly. This is very important. If the heat is too high, your eggs won't turn out well. When the whites are slightly hard, use a spatula to turn the eggs over. Wait about 15 seconds and your eggs will be ready. If you prefer a harder yolk, wait up to one minute.

Take the eggs out and season them

Once the eggs are ready, take them out with a spatula and put them on a warm plate. Season them with salt and pepper. Now sit down, pick up a fork, and enjoy your "eggstraordinary" breakfast!

Adapted from *Learn2.com*

"eggstraordinary": a made-up word that sounds like extraordinary (special, not ordinary)

nonstick pan: a pan with a special surface that food does not stick to

season: to add flavor to something

spatula: a cooking tool for lifting and turning food

yolk: the yellow part of the egg

B FORM

Phrasal Verbs

Think Critically About Form

A. Read the sentences and complete the tasks below.

1a. He turned off the stove.
1b. The eggs turned out well.
2a. Turn on the stove.
2b. Turn the stove on.

1. **IDENTIFY** Look at the underlined phrasal verbs in 1a and 1b. In which sentence does the phrasal verb have an object? Circle it. In which sentence does the phrasal verb not have an object?

2. **RECOGNIZE** Look at 2a and 2b. Circle the objects in these sentences. In which sentence does the object come after the phrasal verb? In which sentence does the object separate the phrasal verb?

B. Discuss your answers with the class and read the Form charts to check them.

▶ Transitive Phrasal Verbs

ONLINE PRACTICE

SEPARABLE TRANSITIVE PHRASAL VERBS

SUBJECT	VERB + PARTICLE	OBJECT NOUN
I	**left out**	the sugar.

SUBJECT	VERB	OBJECT NOUN	PARTICLE
I	**left**	the sugar	**out**.

SUBJECT	VERB	OBJECT PRONOUN	PARTICLE
I	**left**	it	**out**.

INSEPARABLE TRANSITIVE PHRASAL VERBS

SUBJECT	VERB + PARTICLE	OBJECT NOUN OR PRONOUN
She	**looked after**	the children.
He	**counts on**	you.
We	**cut down on**	fat.
They	**dropped out of**	school.

▶ Intransitive Phrasal Verbs

INSEPARABLE INTRANSITIVE PHRASAL VERBS		
SUBJECT	VERB + PARTICLE	
We	**grew up**	overseas.
He	**dropped by**	yesterday.

Overview

- A phrasal verb consists of a verb and a particle. *Up, down, on, off, after, by, in,* and *out* are examples of particles.
- Particles look like prepositions, but they often have different meanings. Unlike prepositions, particles often change the meaning of the verb they combine with.

VERB + PREPOSITION	PHRASAL VERB
I **ran out** the door. (I left quickly.)	Can I borrow some paper? **I ran out.** (I used all of my paper. I have no more.)

- See Appendix 17 for a list of phrasal verbs and their meanings.

Transitive Phrasal Verbs

- Transitive phrasal verbs take objects.
- Most transitive phrasal verbs are separable; that is, we can put an object noun after the phrasal verb or between the verb and the particle.

VERB + PARTICLE + NOUN	VERB + NOUN + PARTICLE
She **turned on** the stove.	She **turned** the stove **on**.

- If the object of a separable transitive phrasal verb is a pronoun, it must separate the verb and the particle. It cannot follow the phrasal verb.

  She **turned** it **on**. ✗ She turned on it. (INCORRECT)

- Separable transitive phrasal verbs include *call up, figure out, fill out, leave out, pick up, put down, try on,* and *turn down.*
- Some transitive phrasal verbs are inseparable; that is, you cannot place the object between the verb and the particle. Inseparable phrasal verbs include *call for, come across, count on, go over,* and *look after.*

  She **looked after** the children.
  ✗ She looked the children after. (INCORRECT)

  She **looked after** them.
  ✗ She looked them after. (INCORRECT)

- Some inseparable transitive phrasal verbs consist of three words. The verb + particle is followed by a preposition. The object always follows the preposition. These verbs include *cut down on, drop out of, go along with, look up to, put up with, run out of,* and *stick up for.*

  We **cut down on** fat. They **dropped out of** school.

Intransitive Phrasal Verbs

- Phrasal verbs that do not take objects are called intransitive phrasal verbs. These verbs include *break down, come out, drop by, grow up, run out, show up,* and *watch out.*

  We **grew up** overseas. He **dropped by** yesterday.

B1 Listening for Form

CD2 T52 **Listen to these sentences with phrasal verbs. Write the particle you hear.**

1. take *out*
2. grows ______
3. ran ______ of
4. look ______
5. give ______
6. made ______
7. turn ______
8. get ______ with

B2 Working on Separable Phrasal Verbs

In your notebook, rewrite these sentences in two different ways. First, place the object between the verb and the particle. Then, replace the object with a pronoun.

1. We picked up the children from school.
   We picked the children up from school.
   We picked them up from school.
2. Fill out the application.
3. He tried on his new suit.
4. You should call up Bill after lunch.
5. She dropped off her daughter.
6. I put on my warm coat.
7. Please take out the garbage.
8. I can't figure out this problem.

B3 Working on Inseparable Phrasal Verbs

Complete each conversation with the correct form of the phrasal verb in parentheses and an appropriate object pronoun.

다시 봐야

1. **A:** Did I leave my gloves here?
   B: Yes. I *came across them* (come across) when I cleaned.
   ~을 우연히 발견하다
2. **A:** I'm going away for the weekend, and I can't take my cat.
   B: Why don't you leave it with me? I ~~looked up~~ will look after it. (look after).
3. **A:** How are you getting to the airport?
   B: A car from my company is coming by for me (come by for) in about an hour.
   ~을 위해 들르다
4. **A:** Your children seem to get along well.
   잘 지내다.
   B: They do. Rachel is five years older than Alexis, and she really looks up to ~~her~~ him (look up to).
   ~을 존경하다

5. **A:** Did you finish your report?

   B: Yes, but I want ______________________ (go over) once more.

6. **A:** Do you drink coffee in the morning?

   B: Yes. I can't ______________________ (do without).

7. **A:** Do you have any of those new stamps?

   B: I'm sorry, but we ______________________ (run out of) earlier today.

8. **A:** Our hotel room is really cold!

   B: I know! We shouldn't ______________________ (put up with)!

B4 Working on Transitive and Intransitive Phrasal Verbs

A. Underline the phrasal verb in each sentence and identify it as transitive or intransitive.

1. Look up the phone number online. transitive
2. I came across your watch while I was cleaning. ______________
3. My friend Chris is going to drop by this afternoon. ______________
4. We have to be there at 11, so I'll pick up the boys at 10. ______________
5. The weather was terrible, so they called off the race. ______________
6. Next week we'll go over phrasal verbs again. ______________
7. You might have left out a word here. ______________
8. His plane took off on time. ______________

B. Look at the sentences with transitive phrasal verbs again. Where possible, change each sentence so that the object is between the verb and particle. Why is it not possible to change some of the sentences?

Look the phone number up online.

C MEANING AND USE

Phrasal Verbs

Think Critically About Meaning and Use

A. Read the sentences and complete the task below.

a. Please pick up the chair and move it over there.
b. I pick up the children at 3:00 every day.
c. He'll pick up French easily because he's a good language learner.

1. **EVALUATE** The phrasal verb *pick up* has more than one meaning. In which sentence does it mean "learn"?
2. **EVALUATE** In which sentence does it mean "lift"?
3. **EVALUATE** In which sentence does it mean "go somewhere and get somebody"?

B. Discuss your answers with the class and read the Meaning and Use Notes to check them.

Meaning and Use Notes

ONLINE PRACTICE

Idiomatic Meanings

▶ 1A Many phrasal verbs are like idiomatic expressions. Their meaning is different from the meaning of the individual words combined. See Appendix 17 for a list of phrasal verbs and their meanings.

Keep up the good work. (*keep up* = continue)
The plane **took off** late. (*took off* = left)

▶ 1B Some phrasal verbs have more than one meaning. Some meanings may be transitive, and others may be intransitive.

Transitive	Intransitive
It was warm, so I **took off** my coat. (*took off* = removed)	The plane **took off** at 10:00. (*took off* = left)
He's not telling the truth. He **made up** that story. (*made up* = created, invented)	Last night they had a big fight. This morning they **made up**. (*made up* = became friends again)

▶ 1C Many phrasal verbs have the same meaning as an equivalent one-word verb. Phrasal verbs are more common in conversation. Their one-word equivalents sometimes sound more formal.

Phrasal Verbs		**One-Word Verbs**
I **took off** my coat because I was hot.	=	I removed my coat because I was hot.
The dress didn't fit so she **took it back**.	=	The dress didn't fit so she returned it.

Predictable Meanings

▶ 3B With certain particles, you can use the meaning of the particle to guess the meaning of the phrasal verb. Some examples are *through* (from beginning to end), *over* (again), and *up/down* (completely). *Up* and *down* can also mean a change in amount (increase or decrease).

Don't make a quick decision. You need to **think** the problem **through** first.

My speech is finished, but I wish I could **do** it **over**. It was a disaster.

He **tore up** the letter. Then he threw all the little pieces in the garbage.

Their house **burned down**. They lost everything.

Turn down the music. It's too loud.

C1 Listening for Meaning and Use

▶ Notes 1A, 1B

CD2 T53 **Listen to each sentence. Choose the meaning of the phrasal verb you hear.**

1. take off
   a. leave
   (b.) remove
2. take off
   a. leave
   b. remove
3. let out
   a. finish
   b. make bigger
4. let out
   a. finish
   b. make bigger
5. turn down
   a. refuse
   b. make lower
6. turn down
   a. refuse
   b. make lower
7. work out
   a. be OK
   b. exercise
8. work out
   a. be OK
   b. exercise
9. make up
   a. invent
   b. end a fight
10. make up
    a. invent
    b. end a fight
11. pick up
    a. lift
    b. learn
12. pick up
    a. lift
    b. learn

C2 Rephrasing Phrasal Verbs

▶ Note 1C

Replace the phrasal verb in each sentence with one of the verbs below.

choose   delay   postpone   remove   return   review

1. If you need to go, I don't want to hold you up.

   If you need to go, I don't want to delay you.

2. Before you give me your test, you should go over your work very carefully.

   ____

3. If you've finished your dinner, I'll take away your plates.

   ____

4. If some people can't come today, maybe we should put off the meeting.

   ____

5. I need the dictionary for a minute; I'll give it back to you right away.

   ____

6. Can you help me pick out a dress for tonight?

   ____

C3 Understanding Phrasal Verbs

▶ Notes 1A, 2

Complete this paragraph by choosing the correct phrasal verbs.

I (ran into / ran over)[1] an old friend by accident the other day. I was going to (pick up / pick out)[2] my son from school, when suddenly my car (broke up / broke down)[3]. I (called up / called in)[4] my husband on my cell phone. While I was waiting for him to (turn down / turn up)[5], another car crashed into my car. The driver (got into / got out)[6] of the car to (check in / check out)[7] the damage. It was my friend Alicia. I hadn't seen her since college. Fortunately, nobody was hurt. It was nice to (catch up / catch on)[8] while we were waiting for my husband and the tow truck.

Think Critically About Meaning and Use

A. Choose the best answer to complete each conversation.

1. A: Did anyone else see that note?
   B: No, I ____ after I read it.
   a. tore it
   b. tore it up

2. A: Hey, Bob! Great to see you.
   B: Great to see you, too! Come on in! ____ your jacket.
   a. Take off
   b. Remove

3. A: What happened? Why were you so late?
   B: Our flight didn't take ____ until 11:30.
   a. up
   b. off

4. A: What is the homework for tomorrow?
   B: Read the story ____, but this time read only the important parts.
   a. over
   b. up

B. Discuss these questions in small groups.

1. **EXPLAIN** In 1, consider the incorrect choice. Why is it inappropriate here?
2. **EXPLAIN** In 2, consider the incorrect choice. Why is it inappropriate here?

Edit

Some of these sentences have errors. Find the errors and correct them.

1. I can look your children after tomorrow if you want.
2. Tom is always on time; you can count out him.
3. I haven't seen your laptop, but I'll tell you if I come across.
4. The doctor told me to cut salt down on.
5. I'm not going to put up with that noise any longer.
6. It's not a very good paper; I might do over it.

Write

Imagine that you are giving your blog readers some advice on how to do something. Write a list of step-by-step instructions for them to follow. Follow the steps below. Use phrasal verbs.

1. **BRAINSTORM** Think about a useful process you know and about how to do it. Take notes about what you will write. Use these categories to help you.
   - the things you need
   - steps from first to last
   - the end result
   - helpful hints (for making the process better or faster)

2. **WRITE A FIRST DRAFT** Before you write your draft, read the checklist below. Write your draft using phrasal verbs. (See Appendix 17 for a list of phrasal verbs and their meanings.)

3. **EDIT** Read your work and check it against the checklist below. Circle grammar, spelling, and punctuation errors.

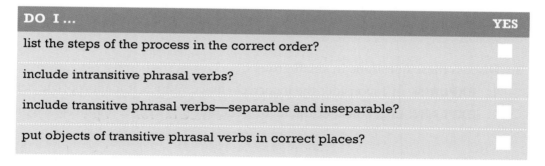

DO I ...	YES
list the steps of the process in the correct order?	☐
include intransitive phrasal verbs?	☐
include transitive phrasal verbs—separable and inseparable?	☐
put objects of transitive phrasal verbs in correct places?	☐

4. **PEER REVIEW** Work with a partner to help you decide how to fix your errors and improve the content.

5. **REWRITE YOUR DRAFT** Using the comments from your partner, write a final draft.

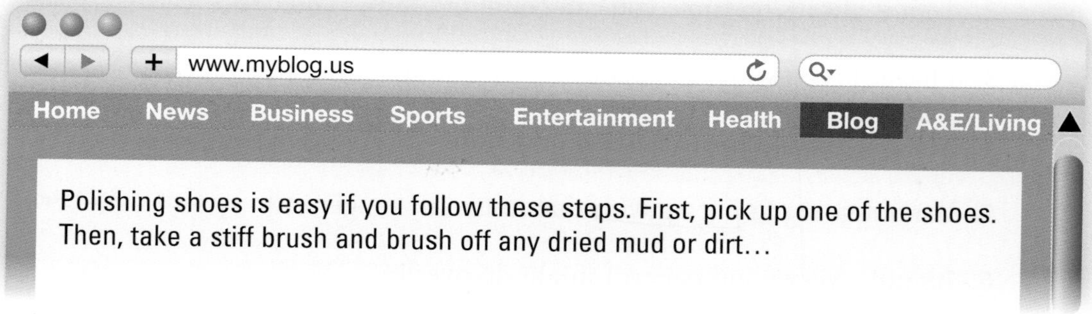
www.myblog.us
Home
News
Business
Sports
Entertainment
Health
Blog
A&E/Living
Polishing shoes is easy if you follow these steps. First, pick up one of the shoes. Then, take a stiff brush and brush off any dried mud or dirt...

PART 9 TEST | Gerunds, Infinitives, and Phrasal Verbs

Choose the correct word or words to complete each conversation.

1. **A:** Why is Jack late?
B: He stopped (to buy / buying) chocolates.

2. **A:** I'll never forget (visiting / to visit) my grandmother.
B: That's good. She was angry the last time you forgot.

3. **A:** (How do you get / Would you mind getting) the new bus schedules?
B: By calling the bus company or checking on the Internet.

Choose a phrasal verb that has the same meaning as the word in bold in each sentence.

4. Can you see what's **delaying** traffic?

a. holding up **c.** holding in
b. holding on **d.** holding out

5. Remind me to **return** these CDs to Janet.

a. give away **c.** give in
b. give back **d.** give up

Complete each sentence with the gerund form of the word or words in parentheses.

6. ____________________ (not/have) a car isn't a problem in a big city.

7. ____________________ (prepare) your own meals can save you money.

8. ____________________ (fix) appliances was my grandfather's hobby.

Choose a particle or particle + preposition below to complete each phrasal verb.

out down on by out of up on

~을 싫어하는 ~의 밖으로, ~로 떨어져서

9. Can you figure ____out____ this text message? figure out : ~을 생각해내다. 이해하다

10. Would you pick ____up____ my dry cleaning?

11. I'll drop ____by____ to visit you this week. drop by : 잠깐들르다.

Match the sentence parts.

f **12.** Brian is talking

d **13.** Sue is planning

b **14.** He's ashamed

a. on going to Morocco.

b. of not passing his finals.

c. for causing the crash.

d. to living here.

e. in saving the environment.

f. about buying a car.

g. at keeping a secret.

Reorder each set of words to make a sentence. Remember to use a capital letter at the beginning of the sentence and a period at the end.

15. me/to/expects/English/speak/my teacher

My teacher expects to me speak English.

16. expensive/go/to college/it's/to

It's expensive to go to college.

17. want/lunch/to/at/restaurant/eat/I/new/that

That I want to eat lunch ~~that~~ at new restaurant.

Rewrite each sentence by putting the underlined words in a different position.

18. You <u>left</u> <u>the subject</u> <u>out</u> in that sentence.

You left out the subject in that sentence.

19. Dad tried on <u>the wrong size</u>.

20. Look <u>the number</u> up in my address book.

I look up the number in my address book.

Appendices

1 **Spelling of Verbs and Nouns Ending in -*s* and -*es*** A-2

2 **Pronunciation of Verbs and Nouns Ending in -*s* and -*es*** A-3

3 **Spelling of Verbs Ending in -*ing*** A-3

4 **Spelling of Verbs Ending in -*ed*** A-4

5 **Pronunciation of Verbs Ending in -*ed*** A-4

6 **Irregular Verbs** A-5

7 **Common Stative Verbs** A-6

8 **Common Irregular Plural Nouns** A-7

9 **Common Adjectives Ending in -*ed* and -*ing*** A-7

10 **Spelling Rules for Adverbs Ending in -*ly*** A-7

11 **Adjectives with Two Comparative and Superlative Forms** A-8

12 **Irregular Comparative and Superlative Forms** A-8

13 **Gerunds** A-9

14 **Infinitives** A-10

15 **Verb + Infinitive or Gerund** A-10

16 **Contractions with Verb and Modal Forms** A-11

17 **Phrasal Verbs** A-12

18 **Phonetic Symbols** A-15

1 Spelling of Verbs and Nouns Ending in *-s* and *-es*

1. For most third-person singular verbs and plural nouns, add *-s* to the base form.

Verbs	**Nouns**
swim — swims	lake — lakes

2. If the base form ends with the letter *s*, *z*, *sh*, *ch*, or *x*, add *-es*.

Verbs	**Nouns**
miss — misses	box — boxes

3. If the base form ends with a consonant + *y*, change *y* to *i* and add *-es*. (Compare vowel + *y*: obey — obeys; toy — toys.)

Verbs	**Nouns**
try — tries	baby — babies

4. If the base form ends with a consonant + *o*, add *-s* or *-es*. Some words take *-s*, some words take *-es*, some take both *-s* and *-es*. (Compare vowel + *o*: radio — radios; zoo — zoos.)

-*s*

auto — autos

photo — photos

piano — pianos

solo — solos

-*es*

do — does

echo — echoes

go — goes

hero — heroes

potato — potatoes

tomato — tomatoes

Both -*s* and -*es*

tornado — tornados/tornadoes

volcano — volcanos/volcanoes

zero — zeros/zeroes

5. If the base form of certain nouns ends with a single *f* or *fe*, change the *f* or *fe* to *v* and add *-es*.

calf — calves

shelf — shelves

knife — knives

Exceptions

belief — beliefs

chief — chiefs

roof — roofs

scarf — scarfs/scarves

2 Pronunciation of Verbs and Nouns Ending in *-s* and *-es*

1. If the base form of the verb or noun ends with the sound /s/, /z/, /ʃ/, /ʒ/, /tʃ/, /dʒ/, or /ks/, then pronounce *-es* as an extra syllable /ɪz/.

Verbs		**Nouns**	
slice — slices	watch — watches	price — prices	inch — inches
lose — loses	judge — judges	size — sizes	language — languages
wash — washes	relax — relaxes	dish — dishes	tax — taxes
		garage — garages	

2. If the base form ends with the voiceless sound /p/, /t/, /k/, /f/, or /θ/, then pronounce *-s* and *-es* as /s/.

Verbs		**Nouns**	
sleep — sleeps	work — works	grape — grapes	cuff — cuffs
hit — hits	laugh — laughs	cat — cats	fifth — fifths
		book — books	

3. If the base form ends with any other consonant or with a vowel sound, then pronounce *-s* and *-es* as /z/.

Verbs	**Nouns**
learn — learns	name — names
go — goes	boy — boys

3 Spelling of Verbs Ending in *-ing*

1. For most verbs, add *-ing* to the base form of the verb.

   sleep — sleeping   talk — talking

2. If the base form ends in a single *e*, drop the *e* and add *-ing* (exception: be — being).

   live — living   write — writing

3. If the base form ends in *ie*, change *ie* to *y* and add *-ing*.

   die — dying   lie — lying

4. If the base form of a one-syllable verb ends with a single vowel + consonant, double the final consonant and add *-ing*. (Compare two vowels + consonant: eat — eating.)

   hit — hitting   stop — stopping

5. If the base form of a verb with two or more syllables ends in a single vowel + consonant, double the final consonant only if the stress is on the final syllable. Do not double the final consonant if the stress is not on the final syllable.

   admit — admitting   begin — beginning   develop — developing   listen — listening

6. Do not double the final consonants *x*, *w*, and *y*.

   fix — fixing   plow — plowing   obey — obeying

4 Spelling of Verbs Ending in *-ed*

1. To form the simple past and past participle of most regular verbs, add *-ed* to the base form.

brush — brushed	play — played

2. If the base form ends with *e,* just add *-d.*

close — closed	live — lived

3. If the base form ends with a consonant + *y*, change the y to *i* and add *-ed*. (Compare vowel + *y*: play — played; enjoy — enjoyed.)

study — studied	dry — dried

4. If the base form of a one-syllable verb ends with a single vowel + consonant, double the final consonant and add *-ed*.

plan — planned	shop — shopped

5. If the base form of a verb with two or more syllables ends with a single vowel + consonant, double the final consonant and add *-ed* only when the stress is on the final syllable. Do not double the final consonant if the stress is not on the final syllable.

prefer — preferred	enter — entered

6. Do not double the final consonants *x*, *w*, and *y*.

coax — coaxed	snow — snowed	stay — stayed

5 Pronunciation of Verbs Ending in *-ed*

1. If the base form of the verb ends with the sounds /t/ or /d/, then pronounce *-ed* as an extra syllable /ɪd/.

/t/	/d/
start — started	need — needed
wait — waited	decide — decided

2. If the base form ends with the voiceless sounds /f/, /k/, /p/, /s/, /ʃ/, /tʃ/, or /ks/, then pronounce *-ed* as /t/.

laugh — laughed	jump — jumped	wish — wished	fax — faxed
look — looked	slice — sliced	watch — watched	

3. If the base form ends with the voiced sounds /b/, /g/, /dʒ/, /m/, /n/, /ŋ/, /l/, /r/, /ð/, /v/, /z/, or with a vowel, then pronounce *-ed* as /d/.

rob — robbed	hum — hummed	call — called	wave — waved
brag — bragged	rain — rained	order — ordered	close — closed
judge — judged	bang — banged	bathe — bathed	play — played

6 Irregular Verbs

Base Form	Simple Past	Past Participle
arise	arose	arisen
be	was/were	been
beat	beat	beaten
become	became	become
begin	began	begun
bend	bent	bent
bet	bet	bet
bind	bound	bound
bite	bit	bitten
bleed	bled	bled
blow	blew	blown
break	broke	broken
bring	brought	brought
build	built	built
buy	bought	bought
catch	caught	caught
choose	chose	chosen
come	came	come
cost	cost	cost
creep	crept	crept
cut	cut	cut
deal	dealt	dealt
dig	dug	dug
dive	dove/dived	dived
do	did	done
draw	drew	drawn
drink	drank	drunk
drive	drove	driven
eat	ate	eaten
fall	fell	fallen
feed	fed	fed
feel	felt	felt
fight	fought	fought
find	found	found
fit	fit	fit
flee	fled	fled
fly	flew	flown
forget	forgot	forgotten
forgive	forgave	forgiven
freeze	froze	frozen
get	got	gotten
give	gave	given
go	went	gone

Base Form	Simple Past	Past Participle
grow	grew	grown
hang	hung	hung
have	had	had
hear	heard	heard
hide	hid	hidden
hit	hit	hit
hold	held	held
hurt	hurt	hurt
keep	kept	kept
know	knew	known
lay (= put)	laid	laid
lead	led	led
leave	left	left
lend	lent	lent
let	let	let
lie (= recline)	lay	lain
light	lit	lit
lose	lost	lost
make	made	made
mean	meant	meant
meet	met	met
pay	paid	paid
prove	proved	proven/proved
put	put	put
quit	quit	quit
read	read	read
ride	rode	ridden
ring	rang	rung
rise	rose	risen
run	ran	run
say	said	said
see	saw	seen
sell	sold	sold
send	sent	sent
set	set	set
sew	sewed	sewn
shake	shook	shaken
shine	shone	shone
shoot	shot	shot
show	showed	shown
shrink	shrank	shrunk
shut	shut	shut
sing	sang	sung

Base Form	Simple Past	Past Participle
sink	sank	sunk
sit	sit	sit
sleep	slept	slept
slide	slid	slid
speak	spoke	spoken
speed	sped	sped
spend	spent	spent
spin	spun	spun
split	split	split
spread	spread	spread
spring	sprang	sprung
stand	stood	stood
steal	stole	stolen
stick	stuck	stuck
stink	stank	stunk
strike	struck	struck
string	strung	strung
swear	swore	sworn

Base Form	Simple Past	Past Participle
sweep	swept	swept
swim	swam	swum
swing	swung	swung
take	took	taken
teach	taught	taught
tear	tore	torn
tell	told	told
think	thought	thought
throw	threw	thrown
understand	understood	understood
undertake	undertook	undertaken
upset	upset	upset
wake	woke	woken
wear	wore	worn
weep	wept	wept
wet	wet	wet
win	won	won
write	wrote	written

7 Common Stative Verbs

Emotions and Attitudes

admire
appreciate
care
desire
despise
dislike
doubt
envy
fear
hate
like
love
mind
need
prefer
regret
respect
want

Senses and Sensations

ache
burn
feel
hear
hurt
itch
notice
see
smell
sound
sting
taste

Knowledge and Beliefs

agree
believe
consider
disagree
expect
feel (= think)
find
forget
guess
hope
imagine
know
mean
notice
realize
recognize
remember
suppose
think
understand

Descriptions and Measurements

appear
be
cost
equal
look (like)
measure
resemble
seem
sound (like)
taste
weigh

Possession and Relationships

belong
consist of
contain
depend on
have
include
own
possess

8 Common Irregular Plural Nouns

Singular	Plural
child	children
fish	fish
foot	feet
man	men
mouse	mice
person	people
tooth	teeth
woman	women

9 Common Adjectives Ending in *-ed* and *-ing*

-ed	*-ing*	*-ed*	*-ing*
amazed	amazing	relaxed	relaxing
amused	amusing	satisfied	satisfying
annoyed	annoying	shocked	shocking
bored	boring	surprised	surprising
confused	confusing	terrified	terrifying
depressed	depressing	tired	tiring
disappointed	disappointing		
embarrassed	embarrassing		
excited	exciting		
fascinated	fascinating		
frightened	frightening		
interested	interesting		

10 Spelling Rules for Adverbs Ending in *-ly*

1. Many adverbs of manner are formed by adding *-ly* to an adjective.
   careful — carefully   quick — quickly
2. If the adjective ends with a consonant + *y*, change the *y* to *i* and add *-ly*.
   easy — easily   happy — happily
3. If the adjective ends in *le*, drop the *e* and add *-y*.
   gentle — gently   suitable — suitably
4. If the adjective ends in *ic*, add *-ally*.
   fantastic — fantastically   terrific — terrifically

11 Adjectives with Two Comparative and Superlative Forms

Adjective	Comparative	Superlative
common	commoner more common	the commonest the most common
friendly	friendlier more friendly	the friendliest the most friendly
handsome	handsomer more handsome	the handsomest the most handsome
happy	happier more happy	the happiest the most happy
lively	livelier more lively	the liveliest the most lively
lovely	lovelier more lovely	the loveliest the most lovely
narrow	narrower more narrow	the narrowest the most narrow
polite	politer more polite	the politest the most polite
quiet	quieter more quiet	the quietest the most quiet

12 Irregular Comparative and Superlative Forms

Adjective	Adverb	Comparative	Superlative
bad	badly	worse	the worst
far	far	farther/further	the farthest/furthest
good	well	better	the best
(a) little	(a) little	less	the least
much/many	much/many	more	the most

13 Gerunds

Verb + Gerund

These verbs may be followed by gerunds, but not by infinitives:

acknowledge	detest	keep (= continue)	recall
admit	discuss	loathe	recollect
anticipate	dislike	mean (= involve)	recommend
appreciate	endure	mention	regret
avoid	enjoy	mind (= object to)	report
can't help	escape	miss	resent
celebrate	excuse	omit	resist
consider	feel like	postpone	resume
defend	finish	practice	risk
defer	go	prevent	suggest
delay	imagine	prohibit	tolerate
deny	involve	quit	understand

Verb with Preposition + Gerund

These verbs or verb phrases with prepositions may be followed by gerunds, but not by infinitives:

adapt to	believe in	depend on
adjust to	blame for	disapprove of
agree (with someone) on	care about	discourage (someone) from
apologize (to someone) for	complain (to someone) about	engage in
approve of	concentrate on	forgive (someone) for
argue (with someone) about	consist of	help (someone) with
ask about	decide on	

Be + Adjective + Preposition + Gerund

Adjectives with prepositions typically occur in *be* + adjective phrases. These phrases may be followed by gerunds, but not by infinitives:

be accustomed to	be familiar with	be nervous about
be afraid of	be famous for	be perfect for
be angry (at someone) about	be fond of	be proud of
be ashamed of	be glad about	be responsible for
be capable of	be good at	be sad about
be certain of/about	be happy about	be successful in
be concerned with	be incapable of	be suitable for
be critical of	be interested in	be tired of
be discouraged from	be jealous of	be tolerant of
be enthusiastic about	be known for	be upset about

14 Infinitives

These verbs may be followed by infinitives, but not by gerunds:

Verb + Infinitive

agree	decide	offer	struggle
aim	decline	plan	swear
appear	demand	pledge	tend
arrange	fail	pretend	volunteer
care	hope	refuse	wait
claim	intend	resolve	
consent	manage	seem	

Verb + Object + Infinitive

advise	get	persuade	tell
command	hire	remind	trust
convince	invite	require	urge
force	order	teach	warn

Verb + (Object) + Infinitive

ask	desire	need	want
beg	expect	pay	wish
choose	help	prepare	would like
dare	know	promise	

15 Verb + Infinitive or Gerund

These verbs may be followed by infinitives or gerunds:

attempt	continue	neglect	start
begin	forget	prefer	stop
can't bear	hate	propose	try
can't stand	like	regret	
cease	love	remember	

16 Contractions with Verb and Modal Forms

Contractions with *Be*

I am	=	I'm
you are	=	you're
he is	=	he's
she is	=	she's
it is	=	it's
we are	=	we're
you are	=	you're
they are	=	they're
I am not	=	I'm not
you are not	=	you're not / you aren't
he is not	=	he's not / he isn't
she is not	=	she's not / she isn't
it is not	=	it's not / it isn't
we are not	=	we're not / we aren't
you are not	=	you're not / you aren't
they are not	=	they're not / they aren't

Contractions with *Be Going To*

I am going to	=	I'm going to
you are going to	=	you're going to
he is going to	=	he's going to
she is going to	=	she's going to
it is going to	=	it's going to
we are going to	=	we're going to
you are going to	=	you're going to
they are going to	=	they're going to
you are not going to	=	you're not going to / you aren't going to

Contractions with *Will*

I will	=	I'll
you will	=	you'll
he will	=	he'll
she will	=	she'll
it will	=	it'll
we will	=	we'll
you will	=	you'll
they will	=	they'll
will not	=	won't

Contractions with *Would*

I would	=	I'd
you would	=	you'd
he would	=	he'd
she would	=	she'd
we would	=	we'd
you would	=	you'd
they would	=	they'd
would not	=	wouldn't

Contractions with *Was* and *Were*

was not	=	wasn't
were not	=	weren't

Contractions with *Have*

I have	=	I've
you have	=	you've
he has	=	he's
she has	=	she's
it has	=	it's
we have	=	we've
you have	=	you've
they have	=	they've
have not	=	haven't
has not	=	hasn't

Contractions with *Had*

I had	=	I'd
you had	=	you'd
he had	=	he'd
she had	=	she'd
we had	=	we'd
you had	=	you'd
they had	=	they'd
had not	=	hadn't

Contractions with *Do* and *Did*

do not	=	don't
does not	=	doesn't
did not	=	didn't

Contractions with Modals and Phrasal Modals

cannot	=	can't
could not	=	couldn't
should not	=	shouldn't
have got to	=	've got to
has got to	=	's got to

17 Phrasal Verbs

Separable Transitive Phrasal Verbs

Many two-word transitive phrasal verbs are separable. This means that a noun object can separate the two words of the phrasal verb or follow the phrasal verb. If the object is a pronoun (*me*, *you*, *him*, *her*, *us*, *it*, or *them*), the pronoun must separate the two words of the phrasal verb. Pronoun objects cannot follow the phrasal verb.

Noun Object	Pronoun Object
She **turned** the offer **down**.	She **turned** it **down**.
She **turned down** the offer.	x She **turned down** it. (INCORRECT)

These are some common separable transitive phrasal verbs and their meanings:

Phrasal Verb	Meaning
bring (someone) up	raise someone (a child)
bring (something) up	introduce a topic
brush (something) off	remove something by brushing
call (something) off	cancel something
call (someone) up	telephone someone
clean (something) up	clean something completely
do (something) over	do something again
dry (something) off	dry something with a towel
fill (something) out	complete a form with information
get (someone) up	awaken someone
give (something) back	return something
hand (something) in	give something to a person in authority
hold (something) up	delay something
leave (something) out	omit something
let (something) out	alter clothes to make them larger
look (something) over	examine something carefully or review it
look (something) up	look for information in a book or on the Internet
make (something) up	invent something
mark (something) down/up	decrease/increase the price of something
pick (something) out	choose something
pick (something/someone) up	lift something or someone; stop to get something or someone
put (something) away	put something in its usual place
put (something) off	postpone something
put (something) together	assemble something
take (something) away	remove something
take (something) back	return something
take (something) off	remove an article of clothing
talk (something) over	discuss something
tear (something) up	destroy something by ripping
think (something) through	consider something thoroughly

Phrasal Verb	Meaning
throw (something) away	get rid of something
try (something) on	put on clothing to see how it looks
turn (something) down	refuse a request; lower the heat or volume
turn (something) in	give something to a person in authority
turn (something) off	stop a machine or a light
turn (something) on	start a machine or a light
turn (something) over	turn something so that its top is facing down
use (something) up	use something until no more is left

Nonseparable Transitive Phrasal Verbs

Some two-word and most three-word transitive phrasal verbs cannot be separated. This means that a noun object or pronoun object cannot separate the parts of the phrasal verb.

Noun Object	Pronoun Object
The teacher **called on** Sally.	The teacher **called on** her.
x The teacher **called** Sally **on**. (INCORRECT)	x The teacher **called** her **on**. (INCORRECT)

These are some common nonseparable transitive phrasal verbs and their meanings:

Phrasal Verb	Meaning
break into (something)	enter something illegally, such as a car or house
call on (someone)	ask someone to speak, especially in a class or meeting
come across (something)	find something unexpectedly
come by for (someone)	pick someone up, especially in a car
count on (someone)	depend on someone
cut down on (something)	use less of something
do without (something)	manage without having something
drop out of (something)	quit something, especially school
end up with (something)	have or get something in the end
find out (something)	discover something
get around (something)	avoid something
get on with (something)	continue something
go along with (someone/something)	agree with someone/something
get over (something)	recover from something, such as an illness
go over (something)	review something, such as a report
look after (someone)	take care of someone
look into (something)	research a subject
look up to (someone)	admire someone
put up with (something/someone)	tolerate something or someone
run into (someone)	meet someone unexpectedly
take after (someone)	resemble someone; act like someone

Intransitive Phrasal Verbs

Intransitive phrasal verbs do not take objects.

My car **broke down** yesterday. What time do you usually **get up**?

These are some common intransitive phrasal verbs and their meanings:

Phrasal Verb	Meaning
blow up	explode
break down	stop working properly
burn down	burn completely
catch up	find out the latest news
come back	return
come over	visit
drop by	visit, especially unexpectedly
eat out	eat in a restaurant
fall down	suddenly stop standing
get up	get out of bed
give up	stop trying, lose hope
go down	(of computers) stop functioning; (of prices or temperature) become lower; (of ships) sink; (of the sun or moon) set
go off	(of lights or machines) stop functioning; (of alarms) start functioning; explode or make a loud noise
grow up	become an adult
hold on	wait on the telephone
look out	be careful
make out	manage or progress
move out	stop living somewhere, especially by removing all of your possessions
pass out	lose consciousness
show up	appear
start out	begin
take off	leave (usually by plane)
talk back	answer in a rude way
turn up	appear or arrive
wake up	stop sleeping
work out	exercise

18 Phonetic Symbols

Vowels

i	**see** /si/	u	**too** /tu/	oʊ	**go** /goʊ/
ɪ	**sit** /sɪt/	ʌ	**cup** /kʌp/	ər	**bird** /bərd/
ɛ	**ten** /tɛn/	ə	**about** /əˈbaʊt/	ɪr	**near** /nɪr/
æ	**cat** /kæt/	eɪ	**say** /seɪ/	ɛr	**hair** /hɛr/
ɑ	**hot** /hɑt/	aɪ	**five** /faɪv/	ɑr	**car** /kɑr/
ɔ	**saw** /sɔ/	ɔɪ	**boy** /bɔɪ/	ɔr	**north** /nɔrθ/
ʊ	**put** /pʊt/	aʊ	**now** /naʊ/	ʊr	**tour** /tʊr/

Consonants

p	**pen** /pɛn/	f	**fall** /fɔl/	m	**man** /mæn/
b	**bad** /bæd/	v	**voice** /vɔɪs/	n	**no** /noʊ/
t	**tea** /ti/	θ	**thin** /θɪn/	ŋ	**sing** /sɪŋ/
t̬	**butter** /ˈbʌt̬ər/	ð	**then** /ðɛn/	l	**leg** /lɛg/
d	**did** /dɪd/	s	**so** /soʊ/	r	**red** /rɛd/
k	**cat** /kæt/	z	**zoo** /zu/	j	**yes** /jɛs/
g	**got** /gɑt/	ʃ	**she** /ʃi/	w	**wet** /wɛt/
tʃ	**chin** /tʃɪn/	ʒ	**vision** /ˈvɪʒn/		
dʒ	**June** /dʒun/	h	**how** /haʊ/		

Glossary of Grammar Terms

ability modal *See* **modal of ability**.

action verb A verb that describes a thing that someone or something does. An action verb does not describe a state or condition.

Sam **rang** the bell.
I **eat** soup for lunch.
It **rains** a lot here.

active sentence In active sentences, the agent (the noun that is performing the action) is in subject position and the receiver (the noun that receives or is a result of the action) is in object position. In the following sentence, the subject **Alex** performed the action, and the object **letter** received the action.

Alex mailed the letter.

adjective A word that describes or modifies the meaning of a noun.

the **orange** car
a **strange** noise

adverb A word that describes or modifies the meaning of a verb, another adverb, an adjective, or a sentence. Many adverbs answer such questions as *How? When? Where?* or *How often?* They often end in -**ly**.

She ran **quickly**. She ran **very** quickly.
a **really** hot day **Maybe** she'll leave.

adverb of degree An adverb that makes adjectives or other adverbs stronger or weaker.

She is **extremely** busy this week.
He performed **very** well during the exam.
He was **somewhat** surprised by her response.

adverb of frequency An adverb that tells how often a situation occurs. Adverbs of frequency range in meaning from *all of the time* to *none of the time.*

She **always** eats breakfast.
He **never** eats meat.

adverb of manner An adverb that answers the question *How?* and describes the way someone does something or the way something happens. Adverbs of manner usually end in -**ly**.

He walked **slowly**.
It rained **heavily** all night.

adverb of opinion An adverb that expresses an opinion about an entire sentence or idea.

Luckily, we missed the traffic.
We couldn't find a seat on the train, **unfortunately**.

adverb of possibility An adverb that shows different degrees of how possible we think something is. Adverbs of possibility range in meaning from expressing a high degree of possibility to expressing a low degree of possibility.

He'll **certainly** pass the test.
Maybe he'll pass the test.
He **definitely** won't pass the test.

adverb of time An adverb that answers the question *When?* and refers to either a specific time or a more indefinite time.

Let's leave **tonight** instead of **tomorrow**.
They **recently** opened a new store.

adverbial phrase A phrase that functions as an adverb.

Amy spoke **very softly**.

affirmative statement A sentence that does not have a negative verb.

Linda went to the movies.

agreement The subject and verb of a clause must agree in number. If the subject is singular, the verb form is also singular. If the subject is plural, the verb form is also plural.

He comes home early.
They come home early.

article The words **a**, **an**, and **the** in English. Articles are used to introduce and identify nouns.

a potato **an** onion **the** supermarket

auxiliary verb A verb that is used before main verbs (or other auxiliary verbs) in a sentence. Auxiliary verbs are usually used in questions and negative sentences. **Do**, **have**, and **be** can act as auxiliary verbs. Modals (**may**, **can**, **will**, and so on) are also auxiliary verbs.

Do you have the time?
I **have** never been to Italy.
The car **was** speeding.
I **may** be late.

base form The form of a verb without any verb endings; the infinitive form without *to*. Also called *simple form*.

sleep be stop

clause A group of words that has a subject and a verb. *See also* **dependent clause** and **main clause**.

If I leave, . . .
The rain stopped.
. . . when he speaks.
. . . that I saw.

common noun A noun that refers to any of a class of people, animals, places, things, or ideas. Common nouns are not capitalized.

man cat city pencil grammar

comparative A form of an adjective, adverb, or noun that is used to express differences between two items or situations.

This book is **heavier than** that one.
He runs **more quickly than** his brother.
A CD costs **more money than** a cassette.

complex sentence A sentence that has a main clause and one or more dependent clauses.

When the bell rang, we were finishing dinner.

conditional sentence A sentence that expresses a real or unreal situation in the *if* clause, and the (real or unreal) expected result in the main clause.

If I have time, I will travel to Africa.
If I had time, I would travel to Africa.

consonant A speech sound that is made by partly or completely stopping the air as it comes out of the mouth. For example, with the sounds /p/, /d/, and /g/, the air is completely stopped. With the sounds /s/, /f/, and /l/, the air is partly stopped.

contraction The combination of two words into one by omitting certain letters and replacing them with an apostrophe.

I will = **I'll** we are = **we're**
are not = **aren't**

count noun A common noun that you can count as an individual thing. It usually has both a singular and a plural form.

orange — oranges woman — women

definite article The word the in English. It is used to identify nouns based on information the speaker and listener share about the noun. The definite article is also used for making general statements about a whole class or group of nouns.

Please give me **the** key.
The scorpion is dangerous.

dependent clause A clause that cannot stand alone as a sentence because it depends on the main clause to complete the meaning of the sentence. Also called *subordinate clause*.

I'm going home **after he calls**.

determiner A word such as **a**, **an**, **the**, **this**, **that**, **these**, **those**, **my**, **some**, **a few**, and **three** that is used before a noun to limit its meaning in some way.

those videos

direct object A noun or pronoun that refers to a person or thing that is directly affected by the action of a verb.

John wrote **a letter**.
Please buy **some milk**.

first person One of the three classes of personal pronouns. First person refers to the person *(I)* or people *(we)* who are actually speaking or writing.

future A time that is to come. The future is expressed in English with **will**, **be going to**, the simple present, or the present continuous. These different forms of the future often have different meanings and uses.

I **will** help you later.
David **is going to** call later.
The train **leaves** at 6:05 this evening.
I'm driving to Toronto tomorrow.

general quantity expression A quantity expression that indicates whether a quantity or an amount is large or small. It does not give an exact amount.

a lot of cookies　　**a little** flour
a few people　　**some** milk

general statement A generalization about a whole class or group of nouns.

Whales are mammals.
A daffodil is a flower that grows from a bulb.

generic noun A noun that refers to a whole class or group of nouns.

I like **rice**.
A bird can fly.
The laser is an important tool.

gerund An -ing form of a verb that is used in place of a noun or pronoun to name an activity or a state.

Skiing is fun.　　He doesn't like **being sick**.

***if* clause** A dependent clause that begins with **if** and expresses a real or unreal situation.

If I have the time, I'll paint the kitchen.
If I had the time, I'd paint the kitchen.

imperative A type of sentence, usually without a subject, that tells someone to do something. The verb is in the base form.

Open your books to page 36.
Be ready at eight.

impersonal *you* The use of the pronoun **you** to refer to people in general rather than a particular person or group of people.

Nowadays **you** can buy anything on the Internet.

indefinite article The words **a** and **an** in English. Indefinite articles introduce a noun as a member of a class of nouns or make generalizations about a whole class or group of nouns.

Please hand me **a** pencil.
An ocean is **a** large body of water.

independent clause *See* **main clause.**

indirect object A noun or pronoun used after some verbs that refers to the person who receives the direct object of a sentence.

John wrote a letter **to Mary**.
Please buy some milk **for us**.

infinitive A verb form that includes **to** + the base form of a verb. An infinitive is used in place of a noun or pronoun to name an activity or state expressed by a verb.

Do you like **to swim**?

information question A question that begins with a **wh**- word.

Where does she live?
Who lives here?

intonation The change in pitch, loudness, syllable length, and rhythm in spoken language.

intransitive verb A verb that cannot be followed by an object.

We finally **arrived**.

irregular verb A verb that does not form the simple past by adding *-d* or *-ed* endings.

put — put — put
buy — bought — bought

main clause A clause that can be used by itself as a sentence. Also called *independent clause.*

I'm going home.

main verb A verb that can be used alone in a sentence. A main verb can also occur with an auxiliary verb.

I **ate** lunch at 11:30.
Kate can't **eat** lunch today.

mental activity verb A verb such as **decide**, **know**, and **understand** that expresses an opinion, thought, or feeling.

I don't **know** why she left.

modal The auxiliary verbs **can, could, may, might, must, should, will,** and **would**. They modify the meaning of a main verb by expressing ability, authority, formality, politeness, or various degrees of certainty. Also called *modal auxiliary*.

You **should** take something for your headache.

Applicants **must** have a high school diploma.

modal of ability **Can** and **could** are called modals of ability when they express the ability to do something.

He **can** speak Arabic and English.
Can you play the piano?
Yesterday we **couldn't** leave during the storm.
Seat belts **can** save lives.

modal of necessity **Should** and **must** are called modals of necessity along with the phrasal modals **ought to, have to,** and **have got to**. They express various degrees of necessity in opinions, obligations, rules, laws, and other requirements.

Students **must** take two upper-level courses in order to graduate.
Employees **should** wear identification tags at all times.
We**'ve got to** arrive before the ceremony starts.

modal of possibility **Could, might, may, should, must,** and **will** are called modals of possibility when they express various degrees of certainty ranging from slight possibility to strong certainty.

It **could / might / may / will** rain later.

modal of prohibition **Must not** is called a modal of prohibition when it means that something is not allowed (prohibited).

Drivers **must not** change lanes without signaling.

modal of request **Can, could, will,** and **would** are called modals of request when they are used for asking someone to do something. They express various degrees of politeness and formality.

Can you **pass** the sugar, please?
Would you **tell** me the time?

modify To add to or change the meaning of a word. Adjectives modify nouns (expensive cars). Adverbs modify verbs (very fast).

negative statement A sentence with a negative verb.

I **didn't see** that movie.

He **isn't** happy.

noncount noun A common noun that cannot be counted. A noncount noun has no plural form and cannot occur with **a, an,** or **a** number.

information mathematics weather

nonseparable Refers to two- or three-word verbs that don't allow a noun or pronoun object to separate the two or three words in the verb phrase. Certain two-word verbs and almost all three-word verbs are nonseparable.

Amy **got off** the bus.
We **cut down on** fat in our diet.

noun A word that typically refers to a person, animal, place, thing, or idea.

Tom rabbit store computer mathematics

noun clause A dependent clause that can occur in the same place as a noun, pronoun, or noun phrase in a sentence. Noun clauses begin with **wh-** words, **if, whether,** or **that**.

I don't know **where he is**.
I wonder **if he's coming**.
I don't know **whether it's true**.
I think **that it's a lie**.

noun phrase A phrase formed by a noun and its modifiers. A noun phrase can substitute for a noun in a sentence.

She drank **milk**.
She drank **chocolate milk**.
She drank **the milk**.

object A noun, pronoun, or noun phrase that follows a transitive verb or a preposition.

He likes **pizza**.
She likes **him**.
Go with **her**.
Steve threw **the ball**.

particle Words such as **up**, **out**, and **down** that are linked to certain verbs to form phrasal verbs. Particles look like prepositions but don't express the same meanings.

He got **up** late.
Tom works **out** three times a week.
They turned **down** the offer.

passive sentence Passive sentences emphasize the receiver of an action by changing the usual order of the subject and object in a sentence. In the sentence below, the subject (T**he letter**) does not perform the action; it receives the action or is the result of an action. The passive is formed with a form of **be** + the past participle of a transitive verb.

The letter was mailed yesterday.

past continuous A verb form that expresses an activity in progress at a specific time in the past. The past continuous is formed with **was** or **were** + verb + -**ing**. Also called *past progressive.*

A: What **were** you **doing** last night at eight o'clock?
B: I **was studying**.

past participle A past verb form that may differ from the simple past form of some irregular verbs. It is used to form the present perfect, for example.

I have never **seen** that movie.

past progressive *See* **past continuous**.

phrasal modal A verb that is not a true modal, but has the same meaning as a modal verb. Examples of phrasal modals are **ought to**, **have to**, and **have got to**.

phrasal verb A two- or three-word verb such as **turn down** or **run out of**. The meaning of a phrasal verb is usually different from the meanings of its individual words.

She **turned down** the job offer.
Don't **run out of** gas on the freeway.

phrase A group of words that can form a grammatical unit. A phrase can take the form of a noun phrase, verb phrase, adjective phrase, adverbial phrase, or prepositional phrase. This means it can act as a noun, verb, adjective, adverb, or preposition.

The **tall man** left.
Lee **hit the ball**.
The child was **very quiet**.
She spoke **too fast**.
They ran **down the stairs**.

plural The form of a word that refers to more than one person or thing. For example, **cats** and **children** are the plural forms of **cat** and **child**.

possibility modal *See* **modal of possibility**.

preposition A word such as **at**, **in**, **on**, or **to**, that links nouns, pronouns, and gerunds to other words.

prepositional phrase A phrase that consists of a preposition followed by a noun or noun phrase.

on Sunday
under the table

present continuous A verb form that indicates that an activity is in progress, temporary, or changing. It is formed with **be** + verb + -**ing**.
Also called *present progressive.*

I'm watering the garden.
Ruth **is working** for her uncle.
He**'s getting** better.

present perfect A verb form that expresses a connection between the past and the present. It indicates indefinite past time, recent past time, or continuing past time. The present perfect is formed with **have** + the past participle of the main verb.

I've seen that movie.
The manager **has** just **resigned**.
We**'ve been** here for three hours.

present progressive *See* **present continuous**.

pronoun A word that can replace a noun or noun phrase. **I**, **you**, **he**, **she**, **it**, **mine**, and **yours** are some examples of pronouns.

proper noun A noun that is the name of a particular person, animal, place, thing, or idea. Proper nouns begin with capital letters and are usually not preceded by **the**.

Peter Rover India Apollo 13 Buddhism

purpose infinitive An infinitive that expresses the reason or purpose for doing something.

In order to operate this machine, press the green button.

quantity expression A word or words that occur before a noun to express a quantity or amount of that noun.

a lot of rain
few books
four trucks

real conditional sentence A sentence that expresses a real or possible situation in the **if** clause and the expected result in the main clause. It has an **if** clause in the simple present, and the **will** future in the main clause.

If I get a raise, I won't look for a new job.

regular verb A verb that forms the simple past by adding **-ed**, **-d**, or changing **y** to **i** and then adding **-ed** to the simple form.

hunt — hunted
love — loved
cry — cried

rejoinder A short response used in conversation.

A: I like sushi.
B: **So do I.**
C: **Me too.**

response An answer to a question, or a reply to other types of spoken or written language.

A: Are you hungry?
B: **Yes, in fact I am. Let's eat.**

A: I'm tired of this long winter.
B: **So am I.**

second person One of the three classes of personal pronouns. Second person refers to the person (**you**, singular) or people (**you**, plural) who are the listeners or readers.

separable Refers to certain two-word verbs that allow a noun or pronoun object to separate the two words in the verb phrase.

She **gave** her job **up**.

short answer An answer to a **Yes/No** question that has **yes** or **no** plus the subject and an auxiliary verb.

A: Do you speak Chinese?
B: **Yes, I do. / No, I don't.**

simple past A verb tense that expresses actions and situations that were completed at a definite time in the past.

Carol **ate** lunch.
She **was** hungry.

simple present A verb tense that expresses general statements, especially about habitual or repeated activities and permanent situations.

Every morning I **catch** the 8:00 bus.
The earth **is** round.

singular The form of a word that refers to only one person or thing. For example, **cat** and **child** are the singular forms of **cats** and **children**.

stative verb A type of verb that is not usually used in the continuous form because it expresses a condition or state that is not changing. **Know**, **love**, **resemble**, **see**, and **smell** are some examples.

subject A noun, pronoun, or noun phrase that precedes the verb phrase in a sentence. The subject is closely related to the verb as the doer or experiencer of the action or state, or closely related to the noun that is being described in a sentence with *be*.

Erica kicked the ball.
He feels dizzy.
The park is huge.

subordinate clause *See* **dependent clause**.

superlative A form of an adjective, adverb, or noun used to compare a group of three or more people, things, or actions. The superlative shows that one member of the group has more (or less) than all of the others.

This perfume has **the strongest** scent.
He speaks **the fastest** of all.
That machine makes **the most noise** of the three.

tag question A type of question that is added to the end of a statement in order to express doubt, surprise, and certainty. Certain rising or falling intonation patterns accompany these different meanings.

You're feeling sick, **aren't you**?
He didn't leave, **did he**?

tense The form of a verb that shows past, present, and future time.

He **lives** in New York now.
He **lived** in Washington two years ago.
He**'ll live** in Toronto next year.

third person One of the three classes of personal pronouns. Third person refers to some person (**he**, **she**), people (**they**), or thing (**it**) other than the speaker/writer or listener/reader.

three-word verb A phrasal verb such as **break up with**, **cut down on**, and **look out for**. The meaning of a three-word verb is usually different from the individual meanings of the three words.

time clause A dependent clause that begins with a word such as **while**, **when**, before, or after. It expresses the relationship in time between two different events in the same sentence.

Before Sandy left, she fixed the copy machine.

time expression A phrase that functions as an adverb of time.

She graduated **three years ago**.
I'll see them **the day after tomorrow**.

transitive verb A verb that is followed by an object.

I **read** the book.

two-word verb A phrasal verb such as **blow up**, **cross out**, and **hand in**. The meaning of a two-word verb is usually different from the individual meanings of the two words.

used to A special past tense verb. It expresses habitual past situations that no longer exist.

We used to go skiing a lot. Now we go snowboarding.

verb A word that refers to an action or a state.

Gina **closed** the window.
Tim **loves** classical music.

verb phrase A phrase that has a main verb and any objects, adverbs, or dependent clauses that complete the meaning of the verb in the sentence.

Who **called you**?
He **walked slowly**.
I **know what his name is**.

voiced Refers to speech sounds that are made by vibrating the vocal cords. Examples of voiced sounds are /b/, /d/, and /g/.

bat **d**ot **g**et

voiceless Refers to speech sounds that are made without vibrating the vocal cords. Examples of voiceless sounds are /p/, /t/, and /f/.

u**p** i**t** i**f**

vowel A speech sound that is made with the lips and teeth open. The air from the lungs is not blocked at all. For example, the sounds /a/, /o/, and /i/ are vowels.

***wh-* word** **Who**, **whom**, **what**, **where**, **when**, **why**, **how**, and **which** are **wh**- words. They are used to ask questions and to connect clauses.

***Yes/No* question** A question that can be answered with the words **yes** or **no**.

Can you drive a car?
Does he live here?

Index

A

a/an, see Indefinite articles
Ability, *see* Modals of ability
-able, adjectives formed with, 305
about, with *as … as,* 358
Accepting and refusing offers, 194
ache, in present continuous, 37
Actions, *see also* Conditions; Events; Repeated actions; Situations; States
  and gerunds, 389
  and infinitives, 402
  and present perfect, 100–101
Action verbs, in statements about ability, 163
Activities, *see also* Actions; Events; Situations
Activities in progress
  and past continuous, 76
  and present continuous, 36–37, 40
Additions, see *and, and … either, and … too, and … neither, and so, but,* and Tag questions
Adjectives, 301–316
  vs. adverbs, 322
  and adverbs of degree, 331
  in *be* + adjective + preposition + gerund, 387, 388
  comparative forms of, 348–350, 352–353, 356–359
  ending in *-ing* and *-ed,* 310
  formation of, 305
  order of, 309–310
  placement of, 304–305
  and *so … that* clauses, 328–329
  and *such … that* clauses, 328–329
  superlative forms of, 368–369, 373
  with *too* and *enough,* 335, 337
Adverbs, 317–342
  vs. adjectives, 322
  adverbs of degree, 328–329, 331
  adverbs of frequency
    and simple present, 12
    and tag questions, 232
    and *used to,* 65
  adverbs of manner, possibility, time, and opinion, 320–322
  comparative forms of, 348–350, 352–353, 356–359
  with gerunds, 385
  and present continuous, 40
  and present perfect, 104
  and *so … that* clauses, 328–329
  superlative forms of, 368–369, 372–373
  too and *enough,* 335, 337
  with two forms, 326
  with *will* and *be going to,* 130
Advice
  and *if* clauses, 147
  and imperatives, 22
  with modals and phrasal modals, 202–204, 208–210
    a few, in quantity expressions, 265, 266, 270–272
Affirmative imperatives, 20
Affirmative short answers, *see* Short answers
Affirmative statements, *see* Statements
afraid, placement of, 305
after
  in future time clauses, 141, 144
  in past time clauses, 84
a great deal of, in quantity expressions, 265, 266, 270
agree, with infinitives, 405
Agreeing to and refusing requests, 186–187
Agreement, in clauses with *too, so, not … either,* and *neither,* 250
alike, placement of, 305
a little, in quantity expressions, 265, 266, 270–272
almost, with *as … as,* 358
alone, placement of, 305
a lot of, in quantity expressions, 265, 266, 270, 271
already, with present perfect, 104
am, see *be*
Amounts
  and general quantity expressions, 270–272
  and specific quantity expressions, 276–277
and, see also *and … either; and … too*
  with adjectives, 305
  with comparatives, 353
and … either, 243
  meaning and use of, for combining ideas, 255
and … neither, 246–247
  meaning and use of, for similarities, 250
and … too, 242, 243
  meaning and use of,

and … too (continued)
for combining ideas, 255
for similarities, 250
and neither, 248
meaning and use of,
for combining ideas, 255
for similarities, 250
and so, 247, 248
meaning and use of,
for combining ideas, 255
for similarities, 250
any, in general quantity expressions, 265, 266
anyone, and adjectives, 305
a piece of, in specific quantity expressions, 277
appear, and adjectives, 305
are/aren't, see *be*
aren't I?, 227
Articles, 281–298, *see also* Definite articles; Indefinite articles; No article
and adjectives, 305
forms of, 264–265, 284–285
meaning and use of, 287–289
with nouns in general statements, 293–294
with prepositional phrases, 292
as … as, 356–359, 361
asleep, placement of, 305
Auxiliary verbs, see also *be; do; have;* and Modals
and adverbs, 321
avoid, with gerunds, 405
awake, placement of, 305

B

Background information, and past continuous, 79
bad, 349
Base form of verb, in infinitives, 399
be, see also *be able to; be going to; is/isn't; was/wasn't; were/weren't*
and adjectives, 305
and adverbs of frequency, 12
with *and … too, and … either,* and *but,* 242–243
with *and so* and *and neither,* 246–247
in *be* + adjective + preposition + gerund, 387, 388
with *it* subject … + infinitive, 399
in present continuous, 32–33
in short answers to questions with *be* about future possibility, 168
in simple past, 51
in simple present, 7
in tag questions, 226, 227, 230
be able to
forms of, 160
meaning and use of, 162–163, 170
become
and adjectives, 305
and comparisons, 353
before
in future time clauses, 141, 144
in past time clauses, 84
begin, with gerunds or infinitives, 405–406
be going to
forms of, 114–115
with future time clauses and *if* clauses, 140–142
meaning and use of, 119–120, 130–131
as modal of future possibility, 168
reduced forms of, 118
with time expressions, 122
break down, 415
but, 243
meaning and use of,
for combining ideas, 255
for differences, 251
by, with gerunds, 390

C

call for, 415
call up, 415
can
as modal of permission, forms of, 181
as modal of present and future ability
forms of, 158–159
meaning and use of, 162, 166
as modal of request
forms of, 180
meaning and use of, 186–187
cannot/can't
in agreeing to and refusing requests, 186, 187
as modal of ability, 158, 159
Cause and effect
and *if* clauses, 146
and *so/such … that* clauses, 331
certainly
as adverb of possibility, 321
in agreeing to requests, 187
Certainty/uncertainty
and *if* clauses, 147
and tag questions, 231–232
with *will* and *be going to,* 130, 171
Changing situations, and comparatives, 353
chief, placement of, 305
Classification, with general statements, 294
Clauses, 81, 141
dependent clauses, 81, 141
if clauses, for future, 141–142, 146–147
main clauses, 141
future time clauses, 140
if clauses, 141
past time clauses, 80–81, 83–84
so … that clauses, 328–329, 331

such … that clauses, 329, 331
after superlatives, 372
Collective nouns, specific quantity expressions for, 277
Combining ideas, with *and … too, and … either, and so, and neither,* and *but,* 255
come, with present continuous as future, 119
come across, 415
come out, 415
Comma
with future time clauses, 141
with *if* clauses, 142
with imperatives, 23
with past time clauses, 81
Commands, and imperatives, 22
Comparatives, 345–364
forms of, 348–350, 356–357
vs. superlatives, 368–369
meaning and use of, 352–353, 358–359, 361
Comparisons, *see also* Comparatives; Superlatives
with *would like, would prefer,* and *would rather,* 194
Completed actions, and simple past, 57, 76, 100
Conditions, *see also* Situations; States
and simple present, 12
Conjunctions, 239–258, see also *and; and … either; and … too; and neither; and so;* and *but*
Containers, specific quantity expressions for, 277
continue, with gerunds or infinitives, 405
Continuing time up to now, and present perfect, 97
Continuous tenses, *see* Past continuous; Present continuous
Contractions
with affirmative short answers, 115
with modals of future possibility, 167, 168
with phrasal modals of advice and necessity, 204, 205
in present continuous, 32, 33
in present perfect, 93
with *will,* 125, 126, 129
with *would like, would prefer,* and *would rather,* 182
Conversation
with *not … many* and *not … any,* 270
and tag questions, 236
and *too, so, not … either,* and *neither,* 250
cost, with *it* subject + infinitive, 399
could/couldn't
as modal of advice, necessity, and prohibition
forms of, 202, 203
meaning and use of, 208, 209
as modal of future possibility
forms of, 167, 168
meaning and use of, 170
as modal of past ability
forms of, 159–160
meaning and use of, 163
as modal of permission, forms of, 181
as modal of request
forms of, 180
meaning and use of, 186–187
Count nouns, 264–266
with articles, 284–285, 287, 293–294
with comparatives, 353, 356, 357
with specific quantity expressions, 276–277
and *such … that* clauses, 329
with superlatives, 373
count on, 415
cut down on, 415

D

-d/-ed (for simple past and past participles), 50, 51, 93
pronunciation of verbs ending in, 53
Definite articles
forms of, 264–265, 284–285
meaning and use of, 288–289
in general statements, 293–294
with superlatives, 368–369, 372–373
definitely, 320, 321, 325
Definitions
general statements as, 294
and simple present, 11
Degree, adverbs of, 328–329, 331, 337
Dependent clauses, 81, 141
Descriptions, with *as … as,* 361
Desires, with *would like,* 193
did/didn't, see also *do*
and simple past, 50–51
and *used to,* 62–63
did you, pronunciation of, 56
Differences
and *but,* 251
and comparatives, 352, 359
Directions, and imperatives, 22
Discourse, *see also* Background information; Conversation
with *and … too, and … either, and so, and neither,* and *but,* 255
dislike, with gerunds, 389, 405
do, see also *did/didn't; does/doesn't; don't*
in clauses with *and … too, and … either,* and *but,* 242–243
in clauses with *and so* and *and neither,* 246–247
in simple present, 6–7
in tag questions, 227–228
with imperatives, 12

do (continued)
with phrasal modals of advice and necessity, 204, 205
with present continuous as future, 119
does/doesn't, see also *do*
in negative statements, 183
in simple present, 6–7
don't
in imperatives, 20
in negative statements, 183
Doubt, and tag questions, 232
down, as particle, 415, 419
do you mind ... ?, 390
drop by, 415
drop out of, 415

E

early, 322
-ed (for simple past and past participle), see *–d/–ed*
-ed, adjectives formed with, 310
either, see also *and ... either*
in short responses, 252
Emphasis, and superlatives, 373
enjoy, with gerunds, 389, 405
enough, 335, 337
Equal things, and *as ... as,* 358
-er (for comparatives), 349, 350, 352
-est (for superlatives), 368–369, 372–373
Events, *see* Actions; Events in sequence; Simultaneous events; Situations
Events in sequence
and future time clauses, 144
and past time clauses, 84
ever
with indefinite past time, 101
with superlatives, 372
expect, with infinitives, 405
Explanations, with gerunds, 390
extremely, 328, 331

F

Facts, *see also* Definitions; Descriptions; Scientific facts
and simple present, 11
fairly, 328, 331
fast, 322
feel
and adjectives, 305
in present continuous, 37
in statements about ability, 163
few, in quantity expressions, 270, 271
fewer, 353, 359
fewest, 373
figure out, 415
fill out, 415
finish, with gerunds, 405
for, and present perfect, 97
forget, with gerunds or infinitives, 406
Formality/informality, *see also* Reduced forms
and *be going to,* 118
and comparatives, 353
and *did you,* 56
and *have* and *has,* 95
and imperatives, 23
negative imperatives, 20
and modals and phrasal modals of advice, necessity, and prohibition, 207, 214
and offers, 193, 194
and phrasal verbs, 419
and pronouns in short responses, 252
and *of* in quantity expressions, 269
and requests, 186, 187, 193
and tag questions, 230
and *will,* 129
and *would you mind* + gerund, 390
former, placement of, 305
fortunately, 321, 326
-ful, adjectives formed with, 305
Future, 109–152, see also *be going to; will*
future time clauses
forms of, 140–141
meaning and use of, 144
modals of future ability
forms of, 158–159, 160
meaning and use of, 162–163
modals of future possibility
forms of, 167–168
meaning and use of, 170–171
future, placement of, 305
Future possibility, *see* Modals of future possibility
Future time clauses
forms of, 140–141
meaning and use of, 144

G

General quantity expressions
forms of, 265–266
meaning and use of, 270–272
vs. specific quantity expressions, 276
General statements
nouns in, 293–294
as opinions, 209, 293–294
General truths, and simple present, 11
Gerunds, 381–394
forms of, 384–385, 387–388
meaning and use of, 389–390
vs. infinitives, 403, 405–406
get, in comparisons, 353
glad, placement of, 305
go
with gerunds, 389
with present continuous as future, 119
go along with, 415
good, 322, 349, 369
go over, 415

grow, in comparisons, 353
grow up, 415

H

Habits
  and simple present, 11
  and *used to,* 65
had better
  forms of, 203–204
  meaning and use of, 208, 209
happily, 321, 326
hard, 326
hardly, 326
has/hasn't, see also *have*
  in present perfect, 92–93
  reduced forms of, 95
hate
  with gerunds or infinitives, 389, 402, 405
have, see also *has/hasn't; have got to; have to*
  in clauses with *and … too, and … either,* and *but,* 242–243
  in clauses with *and so* and *and neither,* 246–247
  in past continuous, 77
  in present continuous, 37
  in present perfect, 92–93
  in simple present, 7
  in tag questions, 226, 227
    reduced forms of, 95
    with present continuous as future, 119
have got to
  forms of, 203–204, 207
  meaning and use of, 208, 210, 214
have to
  forms of, 203–204, 207
  meaning and use of, 208, 210, 214, 215
hear, in statements about ability, 163
high, 326
highly, 326
how many, 265, 266
how much, 265, 266
hurt, in present continuous, 37

I

I, vs. *me,* in short responses, 252
-ic, adjectives formed with, 305
Identifying nouns, with articles, 288–289
Idioms, phrasal verbs as, 418
I don't mind … , 390
if clauses, for future
  forms of, 141–142
  meaning and use of, 146–147
Imperatives, 17–28
  forms of, 20
  meaning and use of, 22–23
Impossibility, *see* Possibility/impossibility
I'm sorry, in refusing requests, 187
in, in future time expressions, 122
incredibly, 321, 326
Indefinite articles, *see also* No article
  and adjectives, 305
  forms of, 284–285
    with nouns, 264–265
  meaning and use of, 287
    in general statements, 293–294
Indefinite nouns, 287
  in general statements, 294
Indefinite past time, and present perfect, 100–101
Infinitives, 395–410
  forms of, 398–399
    with *too* and *enough,* 335, 337
    with *would like* and *would prefer,* 183
  meaning and use of, 402–403, 405–406
Informality, *see* Formality/informality
Information, *see also* Background information; Certainty/uncertainty; Classification; Definitions; Facts; General truths; Introducing topics; Plans; Predictions; Reasons
Information questions
  in future
    with *be going to,* 115
    with *will,* 126
  with *how many* and *how much,* 265, 266
  with modals of ability
    with *can* for present and future ability, 159
    with *could* for past ability, 160
  with modals of advice, necessity, and prohibition, 202, 203
  with modals of future possibility, 168
  with modals of permission, 181
  in past continuous, 73
  with phrasal modals of advice and necessity, 205
  in present continuous, 33, 40
  in present perfect, 93
    with adverbs, 104
  in simple past, 51
  in simple present, 7
  with *used to,* 63
  with *would like, would prefer,* and *would rather,* 182–183
-ing, see also Gerunds; Past continuous; Present continuous
  adjectives formed with, 305, 310
in order, with infinitives, 399, 402

Inseparable phrasal verbs, 414, 415
Instructions, and imperatives, 22
Intentions, and *be going to* and present continuous, 119
Interrupted events, 83
Intonation, with tag questions, 231–232
Intransitive verbs, phrasal verbs as, 414–415, 418
Introducing topics, with indefinite articles, 287
Irregular comparatives, 348, 349
Irregular superlatives, 368
Irregular verbs
past participles of, 92–93
in simple past, 40–51
-ish, adjectives formed with, 305
is/isn't, 81, see also *be*
vs. present perfect, 93
it
as subject, with infinitives, 399, 403
and tag questions, 228
I think, with advice and opinions, 209

K

know, 37, 77
know how to, vs. *can,* 166

L

Lack of necessity, with modals and phrasal modals, 202–204, 214–215
late, 326
lately, 326
Laws, 214
least, 373
leave out, 415
less, with comparatives, 352–353, 359
-less, adjectives formed with, 305
like, see also *would like*
with gerunds or infinitives, 389, 402, 405
vs. *would like,* 193
little, in quantity expressions, 265, 266, 270–272
look
and adjectives, 305
in present continuous, 37
look after, 415
look up to, 415
lots of, in quantity expressions, 270
love, with gerunds or infinitives, 402, 405
luckily, 321, 326
-ly
adverbs formed with, 321
as adjective ending, 322
as adverb ending, 322

M

main, placement of, 305
Main clauses, 141
and future time clauses, 140
and *if* clauses, 141
and past time clauses, 80–81, 83–84
Manner, adverbs of, 320–321, 325
many
with comparatives, 356, 357
in quantity expressions, 265, 266, 270–272
may
as modal of future possibility
forms of, 167, 168
meaning and use of, 170, 171
as modal of permission, forms of, 181
may be
vs. *maybe,* 170
maybe
as adverb of possibility, 320, 321, 325
with advice and opinions, 209
vs. *may be,* 170
me, vs. *I,* in short responses, 252
mean
in past continuous, 77
in present continuous, 37
Measurements
and adjectives, 305
specific quantity expressions for, 277
might
as modal of advice
forms of, 202, 203
meaning and use of, 208, 209, 214
as modal of future possibility
forms of, 167, 168
meaning and use of, 170, 171
mind, with gerunds, 390
miss, with gerunds, 405
Modals, 154–220, *see also* Modals and phrases of request, permission, desire, and preference; Modals of ability; Modals of advice, necessity, and prohibition; Modals of future possibility; Phrasal modals of advice and necessity
with *and . . . too, and . . . either,* and *but,* 242–243
with *and so* and *and neither,* 246–247
and tag questions, 226, 227, 232
Modals and phrases of request, permission, desire, and preference, 177–198
forms of, 180–183
meaning and use of, 186–187, 190–191, 193–194
Modals of ability, see also *be able to; can; could*
forms of, 158–160
meaning and use of, 162–163

Modals of advice, necessity, and prohibition
forms of, 202–203
meaning and use of, 208–210, 214–215
Modals of future possibility
forms of, 167–168
meaning and use of, 170–171
Modals of possibility, *see* Modals of future possibility
more, in comparatives, 349, 350, 352–353, 368–369
most, in superlatives, 368–369, 372–373
much
in comparatives, 356, 357
in quantity expressions, 265, 266, 270–272
Musical instruments, with *the,* 294
must
forms of, 202, 203
meaning and use of, 210, 214, 215

N

Names, *see* Personal names
Narrative, *see also* Background information
and past continuous vs. simple past, 79
nearly, with *as . . . as,* 358
Necessity/lack of necessity, with modals and phrasal modals, 202–204, 214–215
need, with infinitives, 405
Negative imperatives, 20
Negatives, *see also* Negative short answers; Negative statements
and *as . . . as,* 359
and tag questions, 232, 235
with gerunds, 384
with infinitives, 398
with *too* and *enough,* 337
Negative short answers
in past continuous, 72
in present continuous, 33
in present perfect, 93
in simple past, 51
in simple present, 7
with *used to,* 62
Negative statements
with *and . . . either* and *but,* 242–243
with *and so* and *and neither,* 247
with *be able to,* 160
with comparatives, 357
in future
with *be going to,* 114
with *will,* 125
with modals of ability, 163
with *can* for present and future ability, 158
with *could* for past ability, 159
with modals of advice, necessity, and prohibition, 202, 203
with modals of future possibility, 167, 168
with modals of permission, 181
in past continuous, 72
with phrasal modals of advice and necessity, 204, 205
in present continuous, 32, 40
in present perfect, 92
with adverbs, 104
with quantity expressions, 271, 272
in simple past, 50
in simple present, 6, 7
with tag questions, 226–228, 230
with *used to,* 62
with *would like, would prefer,* and *would rather,* 182–183
neither, see also *and neither*
in short responses, 252
for similarities, 250
never, with present perfect, 104
next, in future time expressions, 122
no, in quantity expressions, 265, 266, 271
No article (Ø), 264–265, 284, 285, 287, 293
Noncount nouns
with articles, 284–285, 287, 293
forms of, 264–266
meaning and use of, 270-272
with comparatives, 353, 356, 357
with specific quantity expressions, 276–277
with superlatives, 373
and *such … that* clauses, 329
not, see also Negatives; Negative short answers; Negative statements
and *neither,* 247
not … any, 270
not … either,
for similarities, 250
not … many, 270
nothing, and adjectives, 305
Nouns, *see also* Articles; Count nouns; Noncount nouns
with adjectives, 304–305
comparative forms of, 348–350, 352–353, 356–359
in general statements, 293–294
with gerunds, 385
and quantity expressions, 261–280
and *such … that* clauses, 329
superlative forms of, 368–369, 373–373
now, 321, 326

O

Object
gerunds as, 384, 385
Object *(continued)*
with infinitives, 399
with phrasal verbs, 415
Object pronouns
in comparisons, 350
in short responses with *too, either,* and *neither,* 252
obviously, 321, 326
of, in quantity expressions, 266, 269, 276–277
of all, with superlatives, 373
offer, with infinitives, 405
Offers
and imperatives, 22
with *would like,* 193
OK, in agreeing to requests, 187
on, as particle, 415
one of, with superlatives, 373
only
placement of, 305
in quantity expressions, 272
Opinions
adverbs of opinion, 321, 325
and general statements, 209, 294
Order of adjectives, 309–310
ought to
forms of, 203–204, 207
meaning and use of, 208, 209, 214
out, as particle, 415
over, as particle, 419
own, and present continuous, 37

P

Particles, *see* Phrasal verbs
Past, 45–88, *see also* Continuing time up to now; Indefinite past time; Past continuous; Past participles; Past time clauses; Present perfect; Simple past
modals of past ability
forms of, 159–160
meaning and use of, 163
Past continuous, 73–79
forms of, 72–73
meaning and use of, 76–77, 79
and simultaneous events and interrupted events, 83
Past participles
and adjectives, 305
in present perfect, 92–93
Past time clauses, 80–85
forms of, 80–81
meaning and use of, 83–84
with *since,* 97
Perfect modals, *see* Past modals
perhaps
as adverb of possibility, 320, 321, 325
with advice and opinions, 209
Permission, with modals, 181, 190–191
Personal names, with imperatives, 23
Phrasal modals of advice and necessity
forms of, 203–204
meaning and use of, 208–210, 214–215
Phrasal verbs, 411–422
forms of, 414–415
meaning and use of, 418–419
Physical sensations, and stative verbs, 37
pick up, 415
plan, with infinitives, 405
Plans, and *be going to* and present continuous, 119–120, 131
please
with imperatives, 23
with requests, 186, 193
pleased, placement of, 305
plenty of, in quantity expressions, 270
Politeness, *see* Formality/informality
Portions, specific quantity expressions for, 277
Possibility/impossibility, *see also* Modals of future possibility
adverbs of, 320–321, 325
and *if* clauses, 147
Predictions
and *be going to,* 120, 130
and *if* clauses, 147
and *will,* 130
prefer, see also *would prefer*
with gerunds or infinitives, 402, 405
Preferences, with *would like, would prefer,* and *would rather,* 194
Prepositional phrases, after superlatives, 369, 372–373
Prepositions, *see also* Prepositional phrases
gerunds after, 387–388
vs. particles, 415
Present, 1–44, *see also* Modals of present possibility; Present continuous; Simple present
modals of present ability
forms of, 158–159, 160
meaning and use of, 162
Present continuous, 29–44
with comparatives, 353
forms of, 32–33
as future, 115, 168
meaning and use of, 36–37, 40
as future, 119–120, 122
Present perfect, 89–108
forms of, 92–93, 95
meaning and use of, 97, 100–101, 104
with superlatives, 372
pretty, 328, 331
previous, placement of, 305

principal, placement of, 305
probably
as adverb of possibility, 320, 321, 325
with *will* and *be going to,* 130
prohibit, with gerunds, 405
Prohibition, with modals, 202–203, 215
promise, with infinitives, 405
Promises
and *if* clauses, 147
with *will,* 131
Pronouns
and adjectives, 305
with comparatives, 353
in information questions, 33, 93
object pronouns
with comparatives, 350
in short responses with *too, either,* and *neither,* 252
in short responses with *too, either,* and *neither,* 252
subject pronouns
in short responses with *too, either,* and *neither,* 252
in tag questions, 228, 230
Pronunciation, *see also* Reduced Forms
of *can* vs. *can't,* 159
of *have* and *has,* 95
of *used to,* 63
of verbs
ending in *-d/-ed,* 53
ending in *-s/-es,* 9
Proper nouns, and tag questions, 228
put down, 415
put up with, 415

Q

Quantity expressions, 261–280
general quantity expressions
forms of, 265–266
meaning and use of, 270–272, 276
specific quantity expressions
forms of, 266
meaning and use of, 276–277
Questions, *see* Information questions; Tag questions; *Yes/No* questions
Quick decisions, with *will,* 131
quite
as adverb of degree, 328, 331
in quantity expressions, 272

R

rather, see *would rather*
really, 328, 331
Reasons
in accepting and refusing offers, 194
and *in order* + infinitive, 402
in refusing requests, 187
recently, 321, 326
Reduced forms
of *be going to,* 118
of *did you,* 56
of *has/hasn't,* 95
of *have,* 95
of tag questions, 230
of *will,* 129
Refusing offers, 194
Refusing requests, 186–187
Rejoinders, with *too, so, not . . . either,* and *neither,* 250
remember
with gerunds or infinitives, 406
in statements about ability, 163
Repeated actions
and present perfect, 100
and simple past, 57
and simple present, 11
and *used to,* 65
Requests
and imperatives, 22
with modals
forms of, 180
meaning and use of, 186–187, 193
with *would like,* 193
with *would you mind* + gerund, 390
Requirements, 214
resist, with gerunds, 405
Responses, with *too, so, not . . . either,* and *neither,* 250
Routines, and simple present, 11
Rules, laws, and requirements, 14
run out of, 415

S

same, placement of, 305
Scheduled events, and simple present, 11
Scientific facts, and simple present, 11
see
in simple present and present continuous, 37
in statements about ability, 163
seem, 37, 77
and adjectives, 305
with *it* subject + infinitive, 399
Separable transitive phrasal verbs, 414, 415
Sequential events, *see* Events in sequence
-s/-es (for simple present), 6, 7
pronunciation of verbs ending in, 9
several, in quantity expressions, 265, 266, 270
Shapes, specific quantity expressions for, 277
Short answers
contractions with, 115, 126
in future
with *be going to,* 114
with *will,* 125
with modals of ability

Short answers *(continued)*
with *can* for present and future ability, 158
with *could* for past ability, 159
with modals of advice, necessity, and prohibition, 202
with modals of future possibility, 167, 168
with modals of permission, 181
in past continuous, 72
with phrasal modals of advice and necessity, 205
in present continuous, 33
in present perfect, 93
in simple past, 51
in simple present, 7
for tag questions, 226–228
with *used to,* 62
with *would like, would prefer,* and *would rather,* 182–183
to *Yes/No* questions with modals of request, 180
Short responses
with *too, either,* and *neither,* 252
should/shouldn't
forms of, 202, 203
meaning and use of, 208, 209, 214
show up, 415
Signs, with gerunds, 390
Similarities
with *and ... too, and ... either, and so, and neither, too, so, not ... either,* and *neither,* 250
and *as ... as,* 358
Simple past, 47–68
forms of, 50–51, 53, 56, 62–63
meaning and use of, 57, 60, 61, 63
for completed actions, 76, 100
for events in sequence, 84
for interrupted events, 83
in narratives, 79
with *since,* 97
and tag questions, 227, 228
Simple present, 3–16
forms of, 6–7, 9
in future time clauses, 141
with *if* clauses, 142
meaning and use of, 11–12
and stative verbs with, 37
and time expressions, 61, 65
and tag questions, 227, 228
Simultaneous events, and past time clauses, 83
since, and present perfect, 97
Situations, *see also* Actions; Conditions; Events; States
changing situations, and comparatives, 353
and *used to,* 65
so, 328, see also *and so*
in quantity expressions, 272
for similarities, 250
so ... that clauses, 328–329, 331
so far, with present perfect, 104
some
as indefinite article, 284, 285, 287
in quantity expressions, 265, 266, 270
someone, and adjectives, 305
somewhat, 328, 331
soon, 321, 326
Specific quantity expressions
forms of, 266
meaning and use of, 276–277
Speech, *see* Conversation; Discourse; Formality/informality; Intonation
start, with gerunds or infinitives, 405–406
Statements, *see also* General statements; Negative statements
with *and ... too, and ... either,* and *but,* 242–243
with *and so* and *and neither,* 246–247
with *be able to,* 160
in future
with *be going to,* 114
with *will,* 125
with modals of ability, 163
with *can* for present and future ability, 158
with *could* for past ability, 159
with modals of advice, necessity, and prohibition, 202, 203
with modals of future possibility, 167, 168
with modals of permission, 181
in past continuous, 72
with phrasal modals of advice and necessity, 204, 205
in present continuous, 32, 40
in present perfect, 92
with adverbs, 104
with *ever,* 101
with quantity expressions, 271, 272
in simple past, 50
in simple present, 6, 7
and tag questions, 226–228, 230, 236
with *used to,* 62
with *would like, would prefer,* and *would rather,* 182–183
States, *see also* Conditions; Situations
and gerunds, 389
and infinitives, 402
and present perfect, 100

and simple past, 57
and simple present, 12
and *used to,* 65
Stative verbs
and adjectives, 304–305
and adjectives vs. adverbs, 322
and past continuous, 77
and present continuous, 37
and simple present, 12, 37
in statements about ability, 163
stick up for, 415
still
and present continuous, 40
and present perfect, 104
stop, with gerunds or infinitives, 406
Stories, *see* Narrative
strangely, 321
Subject
gerunds as, 384, 385, 403
of imperatives, 20, 22
infinitives as, 399
it subject, with infinitives, 399, 403
and simple present, 7
Subject pronouns
in short responses with *too, either,* and *neither,* 252
in tag questions, 228, 230
such . . . that clauses, 329, 331
Suggestions, with modals and phrasal modals, 209
Superlatives, 365–378
forms of, 368–369
meaning and use of, 372–373
sure, in agreeing to requests, 187
Surprise, and tag questions, 232
surprisingly, 321, 326

T

Tag questions, 223–238
answers to, 235
forms of, 226–228
meaning and use of, 231–232
reduced forms of, 230
take, with *it* subject + infinitive, 399
taste
in past continuous, 77
in present continuous, 37
in statements about ability, 163
Tense, *see also* Future; Past; Present
changes in, and time expressions, 61
than
and comparatives, 349–350, 352–353
and superlatives, 369
with *would rather,* 194
thank you, in accepting and refusing offers, 194
that, and tag questions, 228
that clauses, see *so … that* clauses; *such … that* clauses
the, see Definite articles
the … after next
in future time expressions, 122
the fewest, 373
the least, 373
the most, 373
then, with *if* clauses, 141, 142
there is/there are
with specific quantity expressions, 266
and tag questions, 228
these, and tag questions, 228
they, and tag questions, 228
think
in past continuous, 77
in present continuous, 37
this
in future time expressions, 122
and tag questions, 228
those, and tag questions, 228
through, as particle, 419
Time, *see* Continuing time up to now; Future time clauses; Indefinite past time; Past time clauses; Time expressions
adverbs of, 321, 326
Time clauses, *see* Future time clauses; Past time clauses
Time expressions
for future, 122
in past time clauses, 81
and present continuous, 36, 40
with present continuous, 119
and present perfect, 97, 100
and simple past, 57, 60, 61
and simple present, 61
and *used to,* 65
Time words, *see* Time expressions
to, see Infinitives
today
as adverb of time, 321, 326
in future time expressions, 122
tomorrow
as adverb of time, 321
in future time expressions, 122
tonight, in future time expressions, 122
too, 335, 337, see also *and … too*
in quantity expressions, 272
in short responses, 252
for similarities, 250
Transitive verbs, phrasal verbs as, 414–415, 418
try on, 415
turn down, 415
turn out, 415

U

Uncertainty, *see* Certainty/uncertainty
understand, 37, 77
in statements about ability, 163
unexpectedly, 320, 321
up, as particle, 415, 419

used to
forms of, 62–63
meaning and use of, 65

V

Verb phrases
with *and ... too, and ... either,* and *but,* 242–243
with *and so* and *and neither,* 246–247
Verbs, *see also* Action verbs; *be; do;* Future; *have;* Past; Present; Stative verbs; Verb phrases; other specific verbs
action verbs, in statements about ability, 163
and adverbs, 321
auxiliary verbs, and adverbs, 321
with gerunds, 387, 405–406
with infinitives, 398–399, 405–406
in past time clauses, 81
phrasal verbs, 411–422
forms of, 414–415
meaning and use of, 418–419
pronunciation of
ending in *-d/-ed,* 53
ending in *-s/-es,* 9
very
as adverb of degree, 328, 331
vs. *too,* 337

W

want
with infinitives, 402, 405
and *would like,* 193
Warnings
and *if* clauses, 147
and imperatives, 22
with modals and phrasal modals, 209
was/wasn't, see also *be; was/were*
in past continuous, 72
was/were, see also *be*
in negative statements or questions, 51
in past continuous, 72
watch out, 415
weigh, 37, 77
well, 322, 349, 369
were/weren't, see also *be; was/were*
in past continuous, 72
what, as subject in information questions, 7, 33, 51, 63, 73
when
in future time clauses, 141, 144
in past time clauses, 83, 84
while
in future time clauses, 141
in past time clauses, 83
who, as subject in information questions, 7, 33, 51, 63, 73
Wh- questions, *see* Information questions
will (for future), *see also* Future continuous
forms of, 125–126
with *be able to,* 160
with future time clauses and *if* clauses, 140–142
meaning and use of, 130–131, 170–171
as modal of future possibility, 167, 168
reduced forms of, 129
with *be able to,* 162–163
will, as modal of request, see also *will* (for future); *won't*
forms of, 180
meaning and use of, 186–187
will never, 406
won't
in agreeing to and refusing requests, 186, 187
in negative short answers to *Yes/No* questions with modals of request, 180
would like
forms of, 182–183
meaning and use of, 193–194
would prefer
forms of, 182–183
meaning and use of, 194
would rather
forms of, 182–183
meaning and use of, 194
would/wouldn't, as modal of request, see also *would like; would prefer; would rather; would you mind ... ?*
forms of, 180
meaning and use of, 186
would you mind ... ?, 390

Y

-y, adjectives formed with, 305
Yes/No questions
in future
with *be going to,* 114
with *will,* 125
with modals of ability
with *can* for present and future ability, 158
with *could* for past ability, 159
with modals of advice, necessity, and prohibition, 202, 203
with modals of future possibility, 167, 168
with modals of permission, 181
with modals of request, 180
in past continuous, 72
with phrasal modals of advice and necessity, 205
in present continuous, 33, 40
in present perfect, 93
with adverbs, 104
with *ever,* 101

in simple past, 51
in simple present, 7
and tag questions, 227, 231
with *used to,* 62
with *would like, would prefer,* and *would rather,* 182–183
yesterday, 321, 326
yet, 104
you
as subject of imperatives, 20, 22, 23
in *Yes/No* questions with modals of request, 180

Z

Zero article (Ø), 264–265, 284, 285, 287, 293

Grammar Sense
ONLINE PRACTICE

How to Register for Grammar Sense Online Practice

Follow the steps to register for *Grammar Sense Online Practice.*

1. Go to www.grammarsensepractice.com and click on **Register**
2. Read and agree to the terms of use. **I Agree.**
3. Enter the Access Code that came with your Student Book. Your code is written on the inside back cover of your book.

   [ ] [ ] [ ] [ ] **Enter**

4. Enter your personal information (first and last name, email address, and password).
5. Click on the Student Book that you are using for your class.

It is very important to select your book. You are using Grammar Sense 2. Please click the **BLUE** Grammar Sense 2 cover.

If you don't know which book to select, **STOP**. Continue when you know your book.

6. Enter your class ID to join your class, and click NEXT. Your class ID is on the line below, or your teacher will give it to you on a different piece of paper.

   ______________________________ **Next**

   You don't need a class ID code. If you do not have a class ID code, click Skip. To enter this code later, choose Join a Class from your Home page.

7. Once you're done, click on Enter Online Practice to begin using ***Grammar Sense Online Practice.***

Enter Online Practice

Next time you want to use ***Grammar Sense Online Practice***, just go to www.grammarsensepractice.com and log in with your email address and password.